PANDEMIC EXPOSURES
ECONOMY AND SOCIETY IN THE TIME OF CORONAVIRUS

Hau
Books

Director
Anne-Christine Taylor

Editorial Collective
Deborah Durham
Catherine V. Howard
Vita Peacock
Nora Scott
Hylton White

Managing Editor
Nanette Norris

Editorial Officer
Jane Sabherwal

Hau Books are published by the
Society for Ethnographic Theory (SET)

www.haubooks.org

PANDEMIC EXPOSURES

ECONOMY AND SOCIETY IN THE TIME OF CORONAVIRUS

*Edited by Didier Fassin
and Marion Fourcade*

Hau Books
Chicago

© 2021 Hau Books

Pandemic Exposures: Economy and Society in the Time of Coronavirus, edited by Didier Fassin and Marion Fourcade, is licensed under CC BY-NC-ND 4.0
https://creativecommons.org/licenses/by-nc-nd/4.0/legalcode

Cover design: Ania Zayco
Layout design: Deepak Sharma, Prepress Plus
Typesetting: Prepress Plus (www.prepressplus.in)

ISBN: 978-1-912808-80-9 [Paperback]
ISBN: 978-1-912808-82-3 [PDF]
ISBN: 978-1-912808-84-7 [eBook]
LCCN: 2021931410

Hau Books
Chicago Distribution Center
11030 S. Langley Ave.
Chicago, Il 60628
www.haubooks.org

Hau Books publications are printed, marketed, and distributed by The University of Chicago Press.
www.press.uchicago.edu

Printed in the United States of America on acid-free paper.

Contents

List of Figures ix

Acknowledgements xi

INTRODUCTION

Exposing and Being Exposed 1
   Didier Fassin and Marion Fourcade

Part I. Political Economies 19

CHAPTER 1

Meet the New Normal, Same as the Old Normal:
The State-Market Balance and Economic Policy Debates
After the Pandemic 21
   Ravi Kanbur

CHAPTER 2

No Epistemological Standstill on Sovereign Debt:
The Preservation of the Market Order in Pandemic Times 37
   Benjamin Lemoine

CHAPTER 3

Ad Hoc Generosity in Times of COVID: A Chronicle of Plights, Hopes, and Deadlocks   59
Lena Lavinas

CHAPTER 4

Gifts, Grifts, and Gambles: The Social Logics of the Small Business Administration Relief Loan Programs   83
Sarah Quinn

CHAPTER 5

Central Bank Planning for Public Purpose   105
Benjamin Braun

CHAPTER 6

Authoritarianism and Pandemics: China, Turkey, and Hungary   123
Latif Tas

CHAPTER 7

Stretching Time: COVID and Sudan's Current Transitions   139
Rebecca Glade and Alden Young

Part II. Moral Economies   153

CHAPTER 8

The Moral Economy of Life in the Pandemic   155
Didier Fassin

CHAPTER 9

To Kill or Let Die: How Americans Argue about Life, Economy, and Social Agency   177
Webb Keane

CHAPTER 10

Protecting the Elderly or Saving the Economy? Turkey's Ageist
Lockdown Policy during the COVID Pandemic 193
Başak Can and Ergin Bulut

CHAPTER 11

Reflections on Mutual Aid 209
Z. Fareen Parvez

CHAPTER 12

Carceral Contagion: Prisons and Disease 227
Wendy Warren

Part III. Everyday Economies 245

CHAPTER 13

Agricultural Day Labor in Spain: The Logics of (Pandemic)
Capitalism 247
Susana Narotzky

CHAPTER 14

Making a Living, Resisting Collapse, Building the Future:
Livelihood in Times of Pandemic and Lockdown 275
Isabelle Guérin, Nithya Joseph, and G. Venkatasubramanian

CHAPTER 15

Crisis as Preexisting Condition: Yemen Between Cholera,
Coronavirus, and Starvation 295
Nathalie Peutz

CHAPTER 16

Searching for Life in Times of Pandemic 321
Federico Neiburg and Handerson Joseph

Part IV. Knowledge Economies — 343

CHAPTER 17

The Great Online Migration: COVID and the Platformization of American Public Schools — 345
Marion Fourcade

CHAPTER 18

"CBDCs Mean Evolution, not Revolution": Central Bank Digital Currencies in the Time of COVID — 369
Horacio Ortiz

CHAPTER 19

Modeling Pandemic — 385
Fleur Johns

CHAPTER 20

The Pandemic Economy of Face Masks: From Critical Shortage to Fashion Accessory and Political Statement — 405
Virág Molnár

CHAPTER 21

COVID and the Death Drive of Toxic Individualism — 433
Ed Cohen

Index — 447

List of Figures

Figure 1: Three ways of organizing the cohabitation of capitalism, democracy, and technocracy.

Figure 2: Image of an elderly man who wishes to go out but cannot because an excavator is digging a hole right in front of his apartment building. (Source: Üsküdar Belediyesi, "Sizleri çok seviyoruz ama bize bunu yaptırmayın," Twitter, March 21, 2020.)

Figure 3: Estimated percentage of US K-12 public school students attending school in virtual-only, in-person, or hybrid mode. (Source: Burbio's K-12 School Opening Tracker (https://cai.burbio.com/school-opening-tracker/). Reproduced by permission from Dennis Roche, Burbio.com.)

Figure 4: Flyer on a lamppost advertising professional grade PPE, Greenwich Village, New York. (Source: Photograph by Virág Molnár.)

Figure 5: Signs asking for mask wearing on entrance door of Thai restaurant in Cobble Hill, Brooklyn. (Source: Photograph by Virág Molnár.)

Figure 6: Local fashion boutique on Atlantic Avenue, Brooklyn, selling its masks on Etsy. (Source: Photograph by Virág Molnár.)

Figure 7: Local fashion boutique donating income from masks to charity, Cobble Hill, Brooklyn. (Source: Photograph by Virág Molnár.)

Figure 8: Cleaner in the West Village selling face masks, New York. (Source: Photograph by Virág Molnár.)

Figure 9: Street vendor's stand at Borough Hall, downtown Brooklyn, selling Black Lives Matter-themed masks. (Source: Photograph by Virág Molnár.)

Figure 10: Luxury lingerie brand selling a "care mask" in its flagship SoHo store. (Source: Photograph by Virág Molnár.)

Figure 11: PPE vending machine at the Barclays Center subway stop, Brooklyn. (Source: Photograph by Virág Molnár.)

Figure 12: Public service announcement of the obligation to wear a mask at the Canal Street subway station in New York City. (Source: Photograph by Virág Molnár.)

Figure 13: Street art in Gowanus, Brooklyn, of Black Lives Matter protestor wearing a Covid mask. (Source: Photograph by Virág Molnár.)

Figure 14: "No mask, no pizza" sign at a pizzeria in Brooklyn. (Source: Photograph by Virág Molnár.)

Figure 15: Sign on entrance door to a coffee shop in SoHo requesting patrons to wear masks. (Source: Photograph by Virág Molnár.)

Acknowledgements

This collective volume was made possible by the yearlong exchanges between its authors, brought together for the theme "Economy and Society" we jointly coordinated in the School of Social Science at the Institute for Advanced Study, in 2019–20. Although they were not able to contribute to our book in the end, we thank Jeremiah Arowosegbe, Anne-Claire Defossez, Herbert Docena, Alondra Nelson, Julia Ott, and Chloe Thurston for their insightful participation in our discussions as we were preparing this volume. The critical but generous remarks of our three anonymous reviewers have been extraordinarily useful in helping us consolidate the introduction and improve each chapter. We express our gratitude to the editorial committee of HAU Books for having immediately supported our project and to Hylton White whose constant engagement has permitted an expeditious publication. Finally, we are greatly indebted to Timothy Anh, Munirah Bishop and Caroline Jeannerat for their gentle and efficient editorial assistance in preparing the final version of the manuscript.

INTRODUCTION

Exposing and Being Exposed

Didier Fassin and Marion Fourcade

Being Exposed to the Pandemic

In the early months of the COVID-19 pandemic, societies around the world struggled to come to terms with what many saw as a series of simple, urgent, and perhaps misleading alternatives: protecting lives or saving businesses; tolerating a high mortality or causing a deep recession; keeping national borders open or sealing them; sacrificing some liberties and rights or defending them. We struggled with these questions, too. As a group of faculty and members from the Institute for Advanced Study in Princeton, United States, we were in the middle of a yearlong collective reflection on the theme "Economy and Society" — a theme that had long been central to our own personal research agendas — when we found ourselves confronted with the rapid expansion of the novel coronavirus. As we were writing our chapters, the pandemic blew past its one-year anniversary. It is indeed important to situate chronologically our collective effort to apprehend a permanently evolving configuration whose analysis may at every moment be contradicted by new facts and eventually be proven wrong. Albeit tragic, the spread of COVID-19 (henceforth COVID, for simplicity's sake) to every part of the world with various levels of intensity offered a valuable opportunity to observe up close how dramatic but variable government responses, latent structural issues, and moral or techno-political struggles around the disease have begun to transform (or not) the socioeconomic fabric of twenty-first-century societies. The project born from these observations generated exchanges, workshops, and, eventually, the current volume.

The social and economic upheavals that occurred in the wake of the pandemic seem unprecedented in modern times, not because of the spread or severity of the infection but because of the responses it generated and the questions it posed. In many countries, economic production, social relations, and political norms were upended in a scramble for virus containment. As borders closed and travel ground to a halt, the physical world shrank, while the virtual world expanded endlessly. New fault lines emerged between individuals, occupations, and organizational forms that could thrive under social distancing and those that could not; and between countries, many in East Asia and the South Pacific, that quickly brought the contagion under control and those where it has wreaked havoc, such as the US, and much of Europe and Latin America, while the epidemiological situations of entire regions, such as sub-Saharan Africa and parts of the Middle East, remained unclear.

Everywhere, biopolitics — or interventions oriented to the preservation of life — has redefined the present moment. By an extraordinary inversion, the economy was relegated to second place in the preoccupation of governments, behind public health. The new guides for public action were not fiscal rules nor stock market movements anymore, but the number of cases, occupied hospital beds, and dead bodies (Boyer 2020). Economic experts unexpectedly bowed to public health ones, who urged an immediate stop to the economic machine in a desperate bid to reduce viral transmission as seriously ill patients overwhelmed under-resourced hospitals. In wealthy countries, the national budget — that most guarded and conservative of public functions — became the profligate vehicle to maintain a comatose economy and a population locked down in a suspensive state, unproductive but not impoverished. This exceptional intervention was to last only a short while, but the pandemic dragged on, progressing through deadly waves and genetic mutations. Even though their distribution was hampered by uneven access and distrust, the providential arrival of vaccines in spring 2021 defined a new economic horizon. As various sectors of the economy regained momentum, government supports dwindled. The socialization of income and corporate costs moved from being seen as a necessary buffer to an obstacle to people returning to work.

The deployment of pandemic relief, like the path of disease, had been uneven and unequal, laying bare stark disparities in life conditions. People, groups, and nations never had equal life chances to begin with, but the pandemic and the turmoil it caused exposed these social inequities much more crudely and produced new ones, although along similar hierarchies as the old ones. Within nations, the old, the sick, the poor, and the vulnerable — prisoners, migrants, ethno-racial minorities — as well as so-called "frontline" and "essential" workers died at much higher rates. Across the world, wealthy countries, notably the US, or regions such as the European Union, started borrowing heavily against the future to support their populations, while poorer ones were unable to do so, or struggled to pay back existing debts. Many of the latter are tottering on the verge of default today, desperate to renegotiate these contracts. The disease took its toll, but so did and will do the immediate and long-term consequences of lockdowns and economic collapse — including hunger, unemployment, poverty, isolation, social stigma, organized disinformation, and massive population displacements.

While the crisis was framed as exogenous, a struggle against an alien agent, countries' inability to deal with the surge in hospitalized patients, which motivated radical actions to "flatten the pandemic curve," had endogenous roots. These stemmed from a decades-long erosion of health-care commitments, from the decline in public hospital beds to the delocalization of masks and medicine production, from the evisceration of public health surveillance to insufficient capacities for testing. The crisis was also about the antecedent neoliberal drive to cut both government spending and global production costs. Several heads of state promised that from thereon out, health should be considered a common good and protected as such. But inadequate resources, lack of preparedness, slow reactivity, and, in the worst cases, deliberate skepticism resulted in countless unnecessary deaths. In Donald Trump's US and Jair Bolsonaro's Brazil, the recommendations of experts spurred a new cultural struggle, denying the severity and somber prognosis of the epidemic in these countries, pitching a false opposition between life and economy, and transforming face masks, store warnings, and protective behaviors into vicious political markers. Compelled by the American president's will, hazardous decisions by the Centers for Disease Control and Prevention and the Food and Drug Administration ruined these institutions' reputations in a matter of weeks. Elsewhere, the temptation to forge numbers, to muzzle critique, to carry emergency powers too far proved difficult to resist. China obfuscated investigations of the virus' origins and clamped down on those who challenged the government's narrative or the official death toll. Protected by the fog of the pandemic, Hungary completed its autocratic conversion and Israeli Prime Minister Benjamin Netanyahu announced his intention to go forward with a plan to annex the West Bank. The French government passed controversial laws extending police prerogatives and overseeing nonprofit organizations, while states in East Asia used the opportunity to normalize digital surveillance.

At the same time, the pandemic has offered an opportunity to contemplate new political possibilities and social utopias. With elites left and right fixated on the necessity to sustain bare life through unprecedented economic and biopolitical interventions, aspirations about basic income, debt relief, revamped public infrastructures, and environmental action suddenly found an echo among newly emboldened politicians and social movements. The time seemed ripe to rediscover the transformative power of government, question everything that is wrong with major institutions, and avoid a likely post-pandemic return to business as usual. Against the notion that the pandemic ought to be treated as a manageable parenthesis in an otherwise preordained history, social movements sought to frame it as a revelatory tipping point, exemplifying the many unaddressed, man-made calamities faced by humanity.

Most specifically, COVID offered a stark demonstration that the unequal ravages of a novel virus are the natural extension of old patterns of subjection whose cruelest consequences, from growing inequalities to accelerating climate change, have always fallen selectively on some populations rather than others (Mbembe 2021). That long history erupted publicly in the early summer of 2020, when cities throughout the world filled up with densely packed crowds chanting "Black Lives Matter." Sparked by the murder of George Floyd by a Minneapolis policeman and the endless string of similar events that preceded and followed it in many countries, the global protests and associated solidarity élan openly defied COVID restrictions and official bans on public gatherings to force a broader social reckoning that reached deep into the psyche of Western racism and colonialism. Much less visible and much less mourned were the deaths in the Mediterranean Sea or the Sonoran Desert of thousands of migrants and refugees fleeing violence, persecution, and impoverishment endured in countries like Afghanistan, Somalia, and Libya, still suffering from the legacies of Western imperialist policies and military interventions. In fact, the new reasons of state deployed during COVID may have supercharged the indifference and hostility of host countries to the needs and plight of these exiles, much to the alarm of the activists and charities that worked tirelessly to support them. The development and repercussions of all these movements, and of the injustices so forcefully exposed, are still playing themselves out — not only in the world of politics but also in our respective disciplines. That, too, made the COVID moment a particularly significant one for our group. It did not simply give us a new object; it rocked our analytical foundations.

Pandemic Exposures

Pandemic Exposures: Economy and Society in the Time of Coronavirus addresses these multiple, and sometimes contradictory, dimensions of the pandemic through social and economic lenses.

Our first analytical imperative, however, is to properly construct our object, and therefore it begins with a critique of its very premise. We must remember that notwithstanding the virus's global reach, the pandemic seemed to barely register in places plagued by ongoing cataclysms — such as Haiti, Yemen, and Sudan, which are taken up in this volume, but also in the Middle East and Central Africa. We must remind ourselves that a focus on the virus produces its own blind spots, by obscuring the much graver, and much more ordinary, plights faced by the poor everywhere. For them, COVID changed nothing, or so very little. In 2020, the more than 800,000 acute respiratory infection mortality and the 400,000 malaria deaths in Africa dwarfed the 83,000 who officially succumbed to COVID-19, although in each case underreporting is highly probable. Conflicts, famine, exodus, political chaos, endemic disease, and the never-ending struggle for survival did not disappear. They just disappeared from view, eclipsed by the headline-grabbing tragedies closer to home. In that regard, one of the major characteristics of the pandemic, especially in the first months, has been the narrowing of the economy of attention. Narrowing must be understood in two ways. First, the pandemic, the response to it, the number of cases and deaths became the quasi-exclusive topic in the news and in conversations. Second, interest in the pandemic and its consequences turned inward, for both individuals and nations.

Our second imperative, then, is to contextualize the pandemic as an object that is good to think *with*, rather than an object that must be thought *about*. We use it opportunistically, to sharpen our analysis of social relations in the economy. Hence our title, *Pandemic Exposures*, an acknowledgement of the bright light that the coronavirus outbreak shone on aspects of our own research, guiding late-stage realizations, reorientations, and revisits. Each author, therefore, is attentive to the empirical specificities of their case and questions how COVID simultaneously transforms their object of study and uncovers less perceptible trends. The pandemic is certainly foregrounded, but also contextualized and situated, fusing the general and the particular, disruptions and continuities. The pandemic exposes — it makes bodies vulnerable again, so many of them at once. Overwhelmed morgues, refrigerated trucks, and mass graves in Tehran, Manaus, Bergamo, and New York City seemed unthinkable — except, perhaps, to the veteran physicians who witnessed the ravages of AIDS on the African continent. The pandemic exposes — it makes the mundane strange and the familiar dangerous, upending the normal unfolding of everyday life. Experts are already pondering the long-term consequences of isolation and deficient socialization: an epidemic (another one!) of solitude and mental illness; children's cognitive and emotional development stunted; older people dying without seeing their loved ones for one last time. The pandemic exposes — it conjures up new imaginaries out of latent forces, provokes ruptures and brutal realignments. The world becomes suddenly aware of a new normal in the relationship between man and nature, the power of new technologies to reorganize social activities, and the true capacities of government. In an effort to rein in a reality that has become uncontrollable, graphs, maps, statistics circulate like gossip, while false rumors and conspiracy theories circulate by the numbers. The pandemic exposes — it renders more visible, and perhaps consolidates, the veiled social divisions that never go away: the forces of inequality, exclusion, marginality. The question is not so much how many have or will die, but who dies, who loses or must give up their jobs, who struggles to survive, who stops sending or receiving remittances, who is shut out of the social safety net, who has no right to have rights. The pandemic exposes — it overwhelms culture and politics. The silent crowd wears its quiet submission on its face, but the fight against the virus also elicits talk of heroism and sacrifice, disbelief and insurgency, resilience and resistance. Meanwhile, profiteers of all types play on people's needs, expectations, hopes, and fears. In 2020, the British charity Oxfam published a report titled *Pandemic Profiteers Exposed*, pointing the finger at the big pharmaceutical and tech companies.

Our third imperative was to place this cacophony of topics and analyses in conversation. Time, we realized, is at the center of the world's engagement with the pandemic. On the most immediate level were the critical, urgent questions on everyone's minds: Would there be a second wave? A third? What is the time span between infection and death? When will a vaccine be available? When will it end — or will it *ever* end? The uncertainty has yielded a flourish of speculations, concerns, and predictions, informed by both lay and expert knowledge. An industry of mathematical projections has coalesced, with dozens of research centers producing extraordinarily different results. The Trump administration put its faith in the optimistic curves peddled by a Gates Foundation-supported institute at the University of Washington. At the other end of the spectrum, the French government trusted the alarmist data produced by a team of statisticians at Imperial College, London.

At a more meta level, events surrounding the pandemic are also marked by their relationship to time — some suggest historical continuities, others point to temporary changes in course or pattern, and yet others announce major shifts under way. Altogether, we identify three temporalities of COVID, each with its own set of modalities. On the longer end of the spectrum is the temporality of historical time. It is the temporality of continuity, the path dependency of institutions and the silent work of social structures. It is both reassuring and infuriating: on the one hand, the social order did not collapse, supply chains were disrupted but continued to function, as did organizations; on the other hand, why did it take so long for some of them to adapt to the new environment? Precious time was lost. Habits, cultures, and rules stood in the way.

The temporality of historical time comes under several modalities, but the chapters in this volume focus on one of them especially, which we call *revelations*: everywhere the pandemic acted as a striking revelator, or an eye-opener, of durable, underlying social realities. Perhaps most relevant in that category is the revelation of class and social status inequalities in the exposure to disease, in the deployment of care and vaccines, and in the distribution of government supports. None of it was new. Although the conditions were unprecedented and the virus was unknown, history inexorably repeated itself, adding new injuries to past ones. Other revelations of the pandemic include the heightened relevance of mutual aid structures for the poor, or the insalubrity of institutions of confinement such as prisons, detention centers, and nursing homes, suddenly brought to the public eye for propagating contagion.

On the shorter end is the temporality associated with the emergency proper, what we could call emergency time. Its most obvious dimension is the declaration of states of emergency constantly reinstated in many countries — including half those of the European Union — with temporary restrictions of civil liberties and fundamental rights as well as the expansion of executive power at the expense of the legislative and of the police at the expense of the justice system. This is the time toward which most of this volume's contributions orient themselves. There, the modalities of pandemic exposures appear under three main forms: *suspensions*, *accelerations*, and *reversals* of existing tendencies. The most noticeable experience associated with the pandemic, perhaps, was as a bracketing, or a dramatic slowing down, of normal life: work, school, socializing, and more. In the modality of *suspension*, the pandemic is about waiting. Waiting to return to work, for schools to reopen, for one's turn to get a vaccine, to finally take off that face mask. There is also a spatial dimension to suspension, marked by immobility, stretched out physical distances, and inactive social networks: unexpected solidarities might emerge, but those habituated to "make do" and "get by" through social connections also find that their usual supports have withdrawn.

Other aspects of life under COVID are marked by dramatic *accelerations*. The time demands nimbleness, adaptation, adjustments. A lot of hope is placed in technological mediations, which take center stage: work, funerals, religious services, court activities, doctor's appointments, and global summits all moved online. For those fortunate enough to be connected to a digital device, space has shrunk, and time has expanded indefinitely. Diasporic communities forced into stillness and inactivity have found in social media a channel through which they could care for each other. Researchers, including some in this volume, found a new way to do fieldwork and maintain a feeling of immediacy and connection. For others, the conventionally neat divide between public and private has dissolved. Anchors broadcast the news, politicians campaign, and movie stars communicate from their own living room — but so do school teachers and administrative staffers. This leap into forced digitality may be perceived as an unbearable encroachment, or as a great liberation, depending on who is thrown into it. But there is no mistaking the transformational nature of the moment.

Finally, the third modality of emergency time is that of *reversals*. During the pandemic, the seemingly unthinkable suddenly became possible: governments distributing money like there was no tomorrow, overturning neoliberal convention; international financial institutions considering a debt moratorium, in a move away from their own, usually stern, prescriptions; prisons temporarily emptied of their minor offenders, undoing long-lasting punitive trends; women dropping out of the workforce en masse, reversing decades-long progresses; mass migrations back home, whether voluntary or forced.

Both accelerations and reversals may give way to the third temporality of the pandemic, which we call *structural transformations*. Here, the pandemic does not simply reveal or provisionally alter existing tendencies and patterns, it serves as a tipping point for plunging into a different regime altogether. In some cases, COVID opened a window that may never close again: the temporary becomes permanent. Everything from the mundane to the critical may be affected. One possible structural transformation concerns the changing nature of political sovereignty. As we already suggested, the pandemic gave an opportunity for states to toughen public security and surveillance under the guise of emergency. Remarkably, both electorates and representatives have quite readily accepted efforts in that direction, precipitating a durable regression of democratic foundations in both illiberal and liberal countries.

Another structural transformation we discuss has to do with technology. Social distancing made contactless transactions and interactions a necessity, which stifled opposition to far-reaching reorganizations of work. But once penetrated by the demons of automation and virtualization, all institutions are up for tech "disruption" and reimagining — and that may include fundamental ones, such as schools, workplaces, and money, or essential forms of social organization, such as cities and transportation systems. In many domains, the conditions playing out during the pandemic have already created lock-in effects, determining the tracks along which these transformations are likely to unfold in the future. Because the revolution in practices touches public institutions as much as private ones, the shift toward digitization also contributes to a transfer of material and epistemic power toward the corporate sector. By controlling the physical infrastructures through which all social activities may be organized, large digital firms inevitably alter these activities' goals and philosophy. Eschewing traditional notions of the public good, they have already started priming well-established public functions such as education and health care for a capitalistic overhaul.

Pandemic Exposés

Pandemic Exposures is a mosaic of twenty-one chapters written by anthropologists, sociologists, historians, economists, political scientists, and legal and literary scholars. They cover a broad empirical ground, with studies situated in North and Latin America, Europe, Africa, Asia and Oceania, although we would have liked to have a more substantial representation from the Global South. The writing process has benefited from the unique collaboration of an international and interdisciplinary group of scholars gathered around the theme "Economy and Society" during a full year at the Institute for Advanced Study. Together, we built a common experience via a biweekly seminar, informal conversations, exchanges of papers, and the convening of two workshops dedicated to the preparation of the present volume. We did not develop specific projects but instead each of us tried to deepen what had been his or her topic of research to re-examine it in light of the pandemic. We do not propose a new paradigm for "economy and society." Our goal is more modest: to offer a mosaic, the pieces of which are either general interpretations calling for further empirical investigations or detailed descriptions calling for possible theoretical frameworks, the combination of the two providing a global perspective on the social and economic transformations — transient or structural — of contemporary societies in the time of the pandemic.

The book is divided into four parts, each of which emphasizes a different problematization of the pandemic to be found in the world. In keeping with our guiding theme, we use the term of "economies" (in the intentional plural) to designate the distinctive political, normative, material, and technological relationships by which people and institutions grapple with the pandemic. These relations form "economies" in the sense that they have to be produced, evaluated, and set in motion. Whether circulating as practical solutions, or ethical principles, or political creeds, or rational plans, they find themselves set against one another to define priorities and alternatives. By the choices (and non-choices, for those who can do nothing but try to survive) it implies, COVID loudly asks the question: What and, most importantly, who is it that matters — to people, groups, organizations, governments? And it leaves enough traces in its wake for social scientists to begin formulating an answer. From the coolness of expert reason to the detached brutality of statistics or the vivid feel of human experience, COVID reveals the multiple hierarchies of worth at play in each particular place, at this particular moment. The task of our mosaic is to expose their logic and their consequences. While Part I looks at economies from above, through the action of governments, Part III analyzes them from below, by studying the adjustments that people have made (or not, as it were) in their efforts to cope with a new reality. Part II offers a sort of transition between these two viewpoints, by being attentive to the norms and values that both people and institutions mobilize to justify their actions. Part IV examines the technological mediations and forms of knowledge, both lay and expert, that the pandemic conditions have nurtured or made indispensable.

The first part, "Political Economies," zeroes in on those accounts that see the pandemic as a question of public, primarily economic, management. It deals with the ongoing and imagined transformations of economic structures in the context, or as a possible outcome, of the pandemic. Pundits, politicians, and scientists have wondered what economies and societies on a global scale will look like in the aftermath of the pandemic. The volume opens with a provocative text by Ravi Kanbur, who draws on his own astute observations of more than thirty years of economic policy debates to argue that the COVID-era rebalancing of economic power toward the state will not be permanent. In his view, economic knowledge and ideology progresses through dialectical cycles rather than revolutionary paradigm shifts. He predicts that after the current hiatus we will soon be back to the "old normal" of the market. Benjamin Lemoine echoes this analysis for the international economy. While international institutions are under pressure to restructure the debt of countries facing what they frame as an exogenous shock, temporary concessions are likely to preserve the "old normal" of the laws of the market — and the hegemony of New York and London as global financial centers. And just as international financiers are discussing ad hoc measures of debt suspension, so countries have relied on ad hoc state generosity to shore up income in a time of forced economic distress. Lena Lavinas's investigation of pandemic-related income support programs in Brazil, the US, and the United Kingdom suggests that the new schemes can at best be thought of as temporary palliatives that do not fundamentally strengthen structures of social provision in the domains of care, public services, and risk protection. Furthermore, Lavinas identifies a dangerous trend of temporary wage supports serving as collateral supporting the persistent reliance of households on debt.

Scaling up from individuals to corporations, Sarah Quinn looks at the half-trillion dollars in emergency loans made available to small businesses in the US. She shows how the rollout of these emergency supports in 2020 was marred by discrimination, unfairness, and outright fraud, thus reproducing the historical promises, but also the well-known pathologies, of American credit programs. Benjamin Braun argues that this conflict between democratic equity and financial capitalism plays out on a much bigger scale in the growing willingness of central banks

— and especially the Federal Reserve in the US in the wake of the COVID recession — to backstop even the most predatory actors of the financial system. Progressives, he argues, must seize the moment to socialize central bank planning and thus mobilize the monetary power of the state in the service of economic justice and sustainability instead of that of an oversized, extractive financial system. This strategy, of course, presumes forms of democratic mobilization that are sometimes near impossible. Shifting the analytical lens toward authoritarian states, Latif Tas offers a sobering analysis of the striking ability of leaders in China, Hungary, and Turkey to obfuscate the true scale of the pandemic, muzzle dissent, information, and criticism (from doctors in particular), and demand loyalty and sacrifice from their subdued populations. Looking at a different political context, Rebecca Glade and Alden Young suggest that the health crisis has put in peril the tentative foundation of a democratic regime in Sudan, barely a year after the fall of the dictatorship. Even though the country, by most standard measures, performed quite well against the disease, the disruptions associated with COVID suspended the reconstruction of the Sudanese state and politics at the same time as it upheld the power of the military wing of the transitional government.

The second part, "Moral Economies," analyzes the moral stakes of the decisions and pronouncements made in relation to the pandemic, focusing on the circulation of values, sentiments, and emotions. As mentioned earlier, the most remarkable features of the response to the pandemic have been the confinement of entire populations, the suspension of liberties and rights, and the interruption of economic activities with major social consequences — although in different ways and with different intensity. All these policies were officially justified on the sole basis of preserving human lives. Interestingly, this valuation of life as a supreme good is a relatively recent phenomenon, as Didier Fassin shows. He asks two questions: Which life? And whose lives? To the first one, his answer is that what is to be protected is the physical life, the fact of being alive, rather than the social life, the self-realization of the person. To the second one, his answer is that, even under this limited definition of life, a moral hierarchy is implicitly established among human beings, as prisoners, migrants, ethno-racial minorities, and the poor face a heavier death toll. Moreover, the presentist approach to the pandemic leaves aside the long-term consequences in terms of lives lost, due to premature deaths, and injured ones as a result of the foretold socioeconomic crisis. Webb Keane also reflects on ethical debates spurred by the pandemic. He expounds the meanings of the choices made by those in favor of, and against, lockdowns in the US and draws a striking parallel with the famous trolley problem in moral philosophy. Indeed, the alternative seems to be between letting older people die (or risk dying) and killing the economy (or exposing it to a crash). However, this framing remains too simplistic, as many invisible choices were made before the pandemic already, through the logic of the market, the production of inequalities, the rationing of health care, which have, in the end, generated disparities in mortality.

Since the measures adopted to confront the crisis were decided in large part to prevent older people from dying, there was an alternative between restricting confinement to the elderly and confining everyone. As Başak Can and Ergin Bulut explain, contrary to most countries that chose the second option for ethical and legal reasons, Turkey decided on the first option in order to let the rest of the population go to work or to school. They describe this policy as ageist and paternalistic and consider its consequences in terms of the isolation of older people from their loved ones. Focusing on India and the US, Fareen Parvez examines a very different, almost inverse, model of social relations: that of mutual aid. She shows that spontaneous practices of solidarity try to avoid the constraining intervention of social bureaucracies and provide instead direct interactions among people to help each other. However, these initiatives are always at risk of either being co-opted by the state, through funding in particular, or being in conflict with it, as it regards them as rivals. In the end, mutual aid may both contribute to what leftist critics see as a neoliberal form of assistance *and* participate in the empowerment of communities.

This kind of empowerment is unavailable to those who remain under the strict control of the state, such as prisoners, however. Adopting a global perspective, Wendy Warren examines how severely prisons have been struck by the pandemic. On the one hand, the fear of clusters has led to the liberation of prisoners in many countries, proving empirically that alternatives to incarceration were imaginable. On the other hand, preventing the circulation of the virus also meant further restrictions of the already very limited rights of inmates. Warren's discussion of a prison reform movement born in England in reaction to deadly infections in correctional institutions bolsters her argument that this pandemic, like others that preceded it, represents a test case for the moral economy of punishment.

The third part, "Everyday Economies," explores the changes as well as the continuities already perceptible in ordinary practices and common experiences in relation to the new norms and constraints imposed in the name of virus prevention. For the vast majority, everyday life under pandemic conditions has been associated with economic struggles. One of the most vexing, yet untold, labor issues in Europe is the dire living conditions of temporary migrant workers. Susana Narotzky analyzes vegetable and fruit production in the Spanish agricultural sector, which was deemed essential during the pandemic. Studying both legal rules and social practices, she describes the implicit hierarchy of the migrants' worth in this extremely racialized and gendered context, which the pandemic rendered more visible and more tragic. The ultimate paradox of this situation is indeed that these workers appear to be both essential and worthless. Indeed, the mobile nature of migrant workers everywhere and their insalubrious living conditions made them particularly vulnerable to the suspicion that they harbor and spread the virus. In this respect, Isabelle Guérin, Nithya Joseph, and G. Venkatasubramanian's findings on the moral stigmatization of migrant laborers in India very much echo Narotzky's. However, a key difference is that, as urban-based, domestic migrants working in India's informal economy, they were not deemed essential but useless. The pandemic-related national lockdown offered the government the perfect cover to crack down on this vagrant population. The vast majority were forced to leave on short notice and head back to the rural areas where they came from, causing painful emotional, social, and economic transitions. The poorest, often Dalits or Muslims, who were already discriminated against by the nationalist government, were most affected, and the authors show how, after a phase of sideration, life resumed its course, but in a contracted way, with scarcer resources, increased debts, growing dependency, and restricted sociability, potentially announcing structural transformation of life and work in rural areas. As the authors write, "people survive, but they do not come out unscathed."

Survival also aptly describes the situation of millions of displaced Yemenis, including those studied by Nathalie Peutz in Djibouti. Their pandemic-related hardships come on top of years of war, destitution, menacing starvation, and even of another epidemic — cholera. Far from home, they survive in crowded camps, whose environments facilitate the spread of the virus and the constitution of clusters. The difference between the current and previous situations is that COVID — like war — kills quickly, while ordinary camp life, Peutz's interlocutors in Djibouti tell her, often resembles a slow death. Whereas in most of the world the pandemic is a unique phenomenon generating exceptional measures, for these populations, and many others confronted with similar afflictions, it is only an additional layer of adversity on top of others. The historical background and the social conditions are quite different in Haiti, but Federico Neiburg and Handerson Joseph offer a similar analysis. There, the accumulation of human-caused and natural disasters have made COVID one calamity among others, adding to decades of civil war, international interventions, social breakdown, food crises, catastrophic earthquakes, devastating hurricanes, and HIV and cholera epidemics. Yet the governmental response to the pandemic had dramatic consequences, they argue, since the sudden immobility of both people and monies complicated what is called there the "search for life"—the quest for a living. For most, economic worries and political concerns vastly exceed preoccupations regarding the new virus.

The fourth and final part, "Knowledge Economies," explores the mobilization of new technologies and the dialectics between expert and lay knowledge, which have framed the very understanding of the pandemic and, in return, reshaped people's relations to the world. Marion Fourcade discusses how the great migration of American public schools online reveals in stark fashion these institutions' latent dependency on an increasingly complex field of technology vendors, all eager to "disrupt" and reinvent them. Not only has the pandemic exposed the inequalities of the digital divide, but it has also given rise to new, unregulated forms of data surveillance and strengthened the economic power of large digital firms. Horacio Ortiz offers another illustration of tech acceleration, by analyzing how the pandemic has provided an opening for the world's central banks to hasten the rolling out of their digital currencies (CBDCs). In spite of the revolutionary potential of these technologies, however, he finds in the blueprints that they have produced a strong desire to preserve the continuity of the financial intermediation regime, dominated by private banks.

Turning toward the impact of expert knowledge on public culture, Fleur Johns looks at the use of epidemiological, demographic, sociological, and economic models to apprehend the pandemic and its consequences. She analyzes the production of claims to authority and demands over resources to discuss the mechanics of power embedded in these apparently neutral tools. Johns reminds us that models are, in Langdon Winner's (1980) words, "artefacts with politics": they obscure as much as they reveal, and their short-term orientation makes it impossible to conceive of the pandemic as a systemic phenomenon. And even though lay people consume them avidly, in practice models have no epistemic privilege when it comes to knowing how to act around the virus. Rather, the unleashing of tremendous government power in deference to experts has sparked vicious struggles around masks, vaccines, mobility, and social distancing. Amplified by social media, these have accelerated an already perceptible shift in the politics of knowledge (Eyal 2019), marked by a democratic resentment toward social constraint and a recentering of authority toward the individual self, who knows best what is good for them. Thus, Virág Molnár shows in her chapter how in numerous countries (with perhaps the exception of East Asia) face masks have become the most iconic exemplar of the cultural struggles associated with the pandemic: they have gone from objects of suspicion and even repression to indispensable instruments in the fight against contagion; from being implicated in elaborate scams to becoming fashion statements; and from specialized medical equipment to homemade solutions, worn by nearly everyone. Finally, Ed Cohen brings this cultural and cognitive struggle home in the last chapter, critiquing the individualistic and bellicose epistemics that suffuses both scientific and popular talk about viruses. In his view, the medical conception of immunity as (quasi-military) host defense naturalizes an understanding of disease that leads people to disregard the danger that *they* pose to others — what Cohen calls the death drive of toxic individualism.

In sum, the phrase "pandemic exposures" of our title can be understood in multiple ways. To the question, What does the pandemic expose? the answer is certainly not univocal. The expansion of the coronavirus infection on a global scale has unveiled the unpreparedness of many governments, inconsistencies and lack of coordination between institutions, the vulnerability of many health-care systems weakened by years of neoliberal reorganization, the power of experts in decision-making, the role of security issues in policy making, the unequal structures of societies, and the easily awakened specters of conspiracy, xenophobia, and racism. But it has also revealed latent forms of solidarity alongside old forms of domination, the extraordinary adaptability of technology from the swift vaccine breakthroughs to the virtualization of schools, and the thriving of certain branches and companies even while the rest of the economy was taking a nosedive. Conversely, to the question, Who did the pandemic expose? the answer is more straightforward. Those who were already the most subjected to diverse sorts of marginalization, oppression, and stigmatization, on the grounds of class, race, caste, or gender position, have been most affected by the health crisis not only in terms of incidence and mortality of the infection but also in terms of its long-term consequences, with entire populations — and possibly countries — rendered more vulnerable by income, job or learning losses, spiraling debts, and the ever-present hazard of a reorganized division of labor. This diagnosis also applies internationally, with some caveats. As of August 2021, only 2 percent of the African population had been vaccinated by the COVID-19 Vaccines Global Access (COVAX) program (an international consortium led by the World Health Organization). And despite this still notable effort, global solidarity on other matters — such as debt relief, or emergency funds — has been in short supply. With a few exceptions (such as India), the pandemic in countries of the Global South has registered in a more muted way internationally, in a classic show of indifference, and perhaps even domestically, as other endemic scourges take precedence or state capacities limit the possibilities for action.

By contrast, in the wealthiest part of the world — the Global North — the pandemic has been regarded and treated as a dramatic and exceptional event. In fact, it is precisely because wealthy countries approached COVID as a circumscribed problem, a disaster bounded in time and place, that what Roi Livne (2021) calls "substantivist" economic interventions — interventions centered on subsistence supports — could be safely envisioned. As the present volume makes clear, these actions were unprecedented in modern times, but few of us believe that they will durably persist beyond the pandemic. COVID has triggered a steep increase in the debt burden of individuals, corporations, and governments, which may come to weigh on the future. Meanwhile, capitalist platforms have never been so profitable nor so bold in their ambitions to reshape and even take over traditional public functions, already weakened by decades of retrenchment. The fact that states have taken a lot of space during the pandemic thus masks a real fragility. It is up to politics to rebuild and reinvent them.

Didier Fassin and Marion Fourcade, August 15, 2021

References

Boyer, Robert. 2020. *Les capitalismes à l'épreuve de la pandémie*. Paris: La Découverte.

Eyal, Gil. 2019. *The Crisis of Expertise*. Cambridge: Polity.

Livne, Roi. 2021. "COVID, Economized." *Sociologica* 15 (1): 21–42. https://doi.org/10.6092/issn.1971-8853/11636.

Mbembe, Achille. 2021. "The Universal Right to Breathe." *Critical Inquiry* 47 (S2): S58–S62. https://doi.org/10.1086/711437.

Winner, Langdon. 1980. "Do Artifacts Have Politics?" *Daedalus* 109 (1): 121–36.

Part I. Political Economies

CHAPTER I

Meet the New Normal, Same as the Old Normal

The State-Market Balance and Economic Policy Debates After the Pandemic

Ravi Kanbur

Introduction

The economic impact of the pandemic of 2020 has been dramatic. Estimates of the growth downturns in the gross domestic product are tentative and varied, but there is an overall consistency, and they tell a sobering story. The recovery from the decline, the shape of the "V" curve, is uncertain, depending on policies. The sharp dislocation will surely change the initial conditions for future trajectories significantly.

The focus of this chapter is not, however, on the direct economic impact but on the consequences of the pandemic for economic policy debates and thinking. Of course there are many detailed and specific aspects of policy, for example the efficacy of different types of lockdown, on which lessons are being learned. But my perspective here is that of a broader canvas, in particular the prediction and the hope that there will be significant and dramatic changes in the balance between state and market, the pandemic having demonstrated the central role of the state in bringing the virus under control. Here one cannot help but notice a certain breathlessness in claims that nothing will ever be the same again

— the new normal in the economic policy discourse will give a much higher weight to state relative to market.

I wish to argue, both from past experience and from the inherent nature of economic policy debates, that such a dramatic paradigm shift in the balance between state and market is unlikely. My prediction is that, once the immediate crisis has passed, these debates, and their resolutions, will settle back into an old pattern of cycling between emphasis on directional moves toward one end or the other of the spectrum, without a permanent significant displacement.

The argument develops over four sections. The first begins by reviewing some of the claims that the pandemic will, or should, make dramatic changes in the balance between state and market. The second section takes a historical perspective and considers the fate of similar claims made in history. It argues that those predictions of major changes did not pan out over the medium term. The third section considers why such dramatic and permanent shifts are unlikely in the realm of economic policy and the balance between state and market. The last section concludes.

New Normal Predictions and Hopes

The pandemic has led to an outburst of predictions and hopes of what the new normal in economic policy might look like in the years to come as we pass through the impacts of the crisis. No doubt the immediate shock and severity of the crisis has led to this rethinking of global futures. I here review a small selection of these contributions and pronouncements. But before doing that, let us consider for a moment the severity of the present crisis compared to previous global crises, to put in historical context the economic basis for these calls for a radical reassessment of policy.

At the time of the last global crisis, the financial crash of 2008–9, Barry Eichengreen and Kevin O'Rourke (2010) quite naturally compared what came to be called the Great Recession to the previous global economic plunge, the Great Depression of the 1930s. The basic conclusion was that the dip in global output was dramatically smaller and less prolonged in the Great Recession than in the Great Depression, thus justifying the nomenclature. In the 1930s, the index of world production fell by close to 40 percent over thirty-five months before recovery began. In 2008–9, the same index fell by less than 15 percent and the recovery began within ten months. The dominant reason for the difference was policy. Fiscal and monetary stimulus brought about a shallower trough during, and a more rapid recovery from, the second crash, the lessons of the first crash having been learned by policy makers.

It is still very early days for a full assessment of the current pandemic shock,[1] but Paul De Grauwe and Yumei Ji (2020) have conducted a similar exercise to that of Eichengreen and O'Rourke (2010) using data from the United States (US), the European Union (EU), and China. The EU had the sharpest drop in industrial production, of just over 25 percent, but the recovery began only three months after the collapse started. For the US and China the drop was less and the "V" shape recovery began after three months or less. Six months after the crisis started, output is estimated to be around 10 percent below its precrisis level for the US, and the recovery is even stronger for the EU and China.

These estimates may, of course, evolve and worsen but, despite the immediacy of the difficulties and disruption of daily life, and intense coverage in the media, actual data so far do not suggest an economic crisis of the severity of the Great Recession, and certainly nothing like that of the Great Depression. Yet there has been no shortage of forecasts of a major rupture to the economic system and of predictions, and hope, of radical realignment in economic policy. I will cite six examples to illustrate the strands in this line of thinking.

In terms of the future of the world economy, Adam Tooze (2020) writes: "The COVID-19 shock has raised globalization angst to a new pitch. The World Trade Organization (WTO) is predicting that trade may fall by a record 32 percent. The lockdowns were disruptive enough. But as the economic crisis deepens, 2020 is beginning to look like something worse: a perfect disruptive storm." Indeed, when Tooze looks ahead, he sees "the death of globalization" as the result of a number of forces, with the pandemic being the proverbial last nail in the coffin.

Pinelopi Goldberg (2020) continues the theme by stating the attacks that are being mounted on trade and openness in the wake of the crisis: "The COVID-19 crisis has emboldened advocates of protectionism and deglobalization. Familiar concerns about lost manufacturing jobs and rising inequality, or the desire in some circles to 'punish' (scapegoat) China with higher tariffs, have now been augmented by an argument against global supply chains. According to this view, widely distributed production has made economies less self-sufficient, and therefore less

---

1. This chapter was essentially completed in October 2020.

resilient. The solution is to reshore existing business operations, offshore less in the future, and reduce reliance on trade more generally." Goldberg mounts a defense against these attacks, but their presence shows the nature of debates to come post-pandemic on free trade versus state intervention in international commerce.

That global trends were already problematic before the pandemic, and that the pandemic has merely shone an unforgiving light on them, is the perspective taken by Olivier Bouin and his colleagues (2020). They start by highlighting the paradoxical state of anxiety that existed in the world even before the pandemic, paradoxical because this was despite the enormous progress in economic and social indicators in the world over the past three-quarters of a century since the end of the Second World War. The anxiety is the result of key deficits in the patterns of development, among them growing inequality. The issue of inequality would have had to be tackled even without the pandemic, but the unequal impact of the pandemic itself has thrown the issue into sharp relief.

A fourth example of big picture thinking in the wake of the crisis comes in the writings of Dani Rodrik. Rodrik (2020) echoes Tooze and Goldberg in saying that there will be a move away from what he calls "hyper-globalization" toward national autonomy, although, unlike Goldberg, Rodrik supports such a move. The main thrust of Rodrik's argument is the prediction that there will be a rebalancing between state and market, toward the state. But such a rebalancing, according to Rodrik, has been building for a while and will merely be accelerated by the pandemic: "There is nothing like a pandemic to highlight markets' inadequacy in the face of collective-action problems and the importance of state capacity to respond to crises and protect people. The COVID-19 crisis has raised the volume on calls for universal health insurance, stronger labor-market protections (including of gig workers), and protection of domestic supply chains for critical medical equipment" (Rodrik 2020).

Continuing the theme of rebalancing state and market, Daron Acemoglu (2020) leaves us in no doubt that, "given the nature and scale of the demands being placed on modern states, it is clear that 'business as usual' will no longer suffice, even if it remains the easiest option." He then considers several possibilities as alternatives. First, "China-lite," where "Western democracies would try to emulate China by worrying less about privacy and surveillance, while permitting more state control over private companies." Second, "Digital Serfdom," where technology companies would dominate in a world of rising inequality with some redistribution as a palliative. Third, "Welfare State 3.0," which would follow from the first wave of introduction of the welfare state before and after the Second World War and the retreat of the second wave in the Reagan-Thatcher-shaped 1980s. This evolution of the welfare state to version 3.0 would respond to the fact that "many advanced economies need a stronger social safety net, better coordination, smarter regulation, more effective government, a significantly improved public health system, and, in the US case, more reliable and equitable forms of health insurance." Acemoglu concedes that this could be "wishful thinking" but holds out the hope that the crisis of the pandemic will mean that this is the path that would be followed.

The above writings of academics and professional economists are, of course, echoed in general discourse. A narrative has become established that the preceding years of deregulation and weakening of the state explain the poor response to the pandemic in the United Kingdom (UK) and the US. Nordic countries, where the state has remained relatively strong, have done much better. Tom Kibasi (2020), for example, views recent experience as confirmation of this thesis: "Among advanced countries, Britain and the US have had the weakest responses to the pandemic. On both sides of the Atlantic, the state has been maligned and undermined by years of free-market ideology that has long held government to be an obstacle to progress, rather than an engine of it. We are all paying the price of this foolish ideology. Building back better needs to start with jettisoning the notion that problems are best solved individually rather than collectively. All our lives depend on it." More hope than prediction, but still a call for rebalancing state and market away from a direction that is argued to have gone out of kilter.

State and Market: Predicted New Normals in History

It should be clear even to the casual observer that the pandemic has unleashed considerable thinking and writing about the evolution of the world post-pandemic, in particular on economic policy after the crisis. We have seen six illustrative examples in the previous section. The balance between state and market has received a great deal of attention from analysts and commentators, with both prediction and hope that the state would take on a dramatically bigger role relative to the market, emerging from its central role in addressing the pandemic.

There is, of course, a long history of thinking, writing, and prediction on the balance between state and market. For example, in his magisterial account of Tudor government in sixteenth century England, Geoffrey Elton (1974: 185) puts this balance in the context of the longue *durée*:

> The doctrine of the body politic knit together demanded obedience and assistance from the governed and put upon the government the duty of looking after the welfare of its subjects. It was once thought that this represented typically medieval doctrine with which the *laissez faire* principles that dominated the state from 1660 to 1906 could be usefully contrasted; more recent development has shown that attitudes to the state which regarded it either as a natural protector or an unholy but necessary evil may alternate without regard to the categories of historical development. In fact, the Tudor revolution produced a much more effective example of the paternal state than anything the middle ages knew — something so effective that only the twentieth century has come to eclipse it. The sixteenth century called this sort of thing "commonwealth" or "common weal."

Elton characterizes laissez-faire as the dominant doctrine for a long time up to the twentieth century — the old normal. In an extraordinarily prescient piece of writing, in 1926 John Maynard Keynes predicted "The End of Laissez Faire." The essay begins with an account of the rise to prominence of the laissez-faire doctrine in the eighteenth and nineteenth centuries:

> The individualism of political philosophers pointed to laissez-faire. The divine or scientific harmony (as the case might be) between private interest and public advantage pointed to laissez-faire. But above all, the ineptitude of public administrators strongly prejudiced the practical man in favour of laissez-faire — a sentiment which has by no means disappeared. Almost everything which the state did in the eighteenth century in excess of its minimum function was, or seemed, injurious or unsuccessful. ... Thus the ground was fertile for a doctrine that, whether on divine, natural, or scientific grounds, state action should narrowly be confined and economic life left, unregulated so far as may be, to the skill and good sense of individual citizens actuated by the admirable motive of trying to get on in the world. (Keynes [1926] 1978: 275–76)

However, Keynes wrote that this state of affairs was about to rebalance: "But a change is in the air. We hear but indistinctly what were once the clearest and most distinguishable voices that have ever instructed mankind. The orchestra of diverse instruments, the chorus of articulate sound, is receding at last into the distance" (Keynes [1926] 1978: 272).

Why the predicted change? For Keynes it was that the market system could not address key emerging issues and state intervention was essential:

> Many of the greatest economic evils of our time are the fruits of risk, uncertainty, and ignorance. It is because particular individuals, fortunate in situation or in abilities, are able to take advantage of uncertainty and ignorance, and also because for the same reason big business is often a lottery, that great inequalities of wealth come about; and these same factors are also the cause of the unemployment of labour, or the disappointment of reasonable business expectations, and of the impairment of efficiency and production. ... I believe that the cure for these things is partly to be sought in the deliberate control of the currency and of credit by a central institution. ... My second example relates to savings and investment. I believe that some coordinated act of intelligent judgement is required as to the scale on which it is desirable that the community as a whole should save, the scale on which these savings should go abroad in the form of foreign investments, and whether the present organisation of the investment market distributes savings along the most nationally productive channels. I do not think that these matters should be left entirely to the chances of private judgement and private profits, as they are at present. (Keynes [1926] 1978: 291–92)

Keynes's battles with the UK treasury in the 1930s are well known, and the postwar consensus on economic policy has the appellation "Keynesian" with good reason. However, the consensus of the 1950s on a greatly expanded role for the state lasted for only so long. As Acemoglu (2020) noted above, the pendulum began to swing back again in the 1980s — the Reagan-Thatcher era. And at the end of this decade came the fall of the Berlin Wall, an event regarded at the time by observers as cataclysmic in its consequences and implications. Most famously, of course, Francis Fukuyama (1989) pronounced "the end of history," meaning by this that the big debates of the century were over. Liberal politics and market economics had triumphed. He did not use the term, but he was in effect predicting a new normal, indeed proclaiming that it had arrived.

It was not to be. Writing in 2001, only a decade after the proclamation, I noted: "The end of history lasted for such a short time" (Kanbur

2001: 1083). The disasters of transition to market economies in the previously centrally planned economies, too rapid and too ill-planned (I use the term advisedly), highlighted the institutional basis of a functioning market economy. To this was added the equally disastrous "lost decade" of austerity and marketization in Latin America in the 1980s. To cap it all, the financial crisis of 1997, the conditions for which were ripe after the deregulation of financial markets in the 1980s and 1990s, became in effect the first global economic crisis of the emerging century. Toward the end of the 2000s, less than two decades after Fukuyama's pronouncement of the end of history, the Commission on Growth and Development (2008: 4), headed by two Nobel Prize winners, Robert Solow and Michael Spence, and comprising leading lights of the economic policy making elite of developed and developing countries, concluded as follows: "In recent decades governments were advised to 'stabilize, privatize and liberalize.' There is merit in what lies behind this injunction — governments should not try to do too much, replacing markets or closing the economy off from the rest of the world. But we believe this prescription defines the role of government too narrowly. Just because governments are sometimes clumsy and sometimes errant, does not mean they should be written out of the script. On the contrary, as the economy grows and develops, active, pragmatic governments have crucial roles to play."

The publication of the commission's report coincided with the financial crisis of 2008–9, the last big global crisis with an economic impact comparable to the pandemic — in fact, as we have seen, an even bigger impact. During the crisis, we saw similar writings on the role of the state. "We are all Keynesians in a fox hole" was the adage as central banks loosened monetary policy and governments adopted expansionary fiscal policy. I was among many who wrote that the crisis should be a warning bell of crises to come and that governments should prepare for them by strengthening and expanding social protection (Kanbur 2010). Again, prediction and hope that the balance of state and market would be pushed toward state by the crisis.

However, the actual outcome was a swing back of the pendulum in the 2010s as government policy, especially in Europe, turned back to austerity and fiscal cuts in the face of worries about the consequences of high levels of public debt. An influential academic paper by Carmen Reinhart and Kenneth Rogoff (2010) argued that high levels of debt above a certain threshold had a deleterious effect on growth. This paper, whose calculations were later found to be erroneous, is among those held to have given the intellectual foundation for austerity policies. In the broader discourse, Yanis Varoufakis (2017), Greece's former finance minister and an economist in his own right, gives an insider's account of the battles of ideology and politics in those times, a battle he considers to have been won by the supporters of austerity and big bank bailouts. This brings us full circle to the pandemic and a new round of hope and prediction, as illustrated in the previous section.

Paradigm Shifts and Dialectics

We have seen that the predicted and hoped-for shift in state-market balance after the pandemic is part of a cycle of movement in thinking and policy that has been with us for a long time.[2] Rather than a permanent shift in one direction or another ("nothing will ever be the same again"), it is a pendulum that has swung back and forth. If history is any guide, after a reorientation for a few years, perhaps even a decade, we are likely to swing back to the old questions of how much state intervention there should be and to a market-oriented disposition.

But why is this the case? The question was posed in a debate in economics and the history of economic thought that took place after the 1962 publication of Thomas Kuhn's book *The Structure of Scientific Revolutions*. Kuhn famously argued that in the natural sciences there were "paradigm shifts," radical changes in thinking and frameworks as exemplified by the Copernican or Newtonian revolutions — the word revolution being used deliberately: "Probably the single most prevalent claim advanced by the proponents of a new paradigm is that they can solve the problems that have led the old one to a crisis. ... Copernicus thus claimed that he had solved the long-vexing problem of the length of the calendar year, Newton that he had reconciled terrestrial and celestial mechanics, Lavoisier that he had solved the problems of gas-identity and of weight relations, and Einstein that he had made electrodynamics compatible with a revised science of motion" (Kuhn 1962: 153).

Whether or not paradigm shifts were indeed to be seen in the natural sciences — and there has been considerable debate on this — a natural enough question was whether there had been revolutions in economic thinking. The conclusion seemed to be that political economy broadly construed did not exhibit such Kuhnian paradigm shifts that swept all

---

2. This section draws on Kanbur (2016).

before them. Martin Bronfenbrenner (1971: 2) offered three possible candidates for the label of revolution:

> The first is a laissez-faire revolution. ... A conventional date is 1776, when Adam Smith's *Wealth of Nations* was published. ... The second possible revolution is the breakup of the classical school which followed Smith, and which was led in turn by David Ricardo and John Stuart Mill. A conventional date for this second, or "utility," revolution is 1870. The third possible revolution is the breakup of the neoclassical Cambridge School which arose from the utility revolution under the aegis of Alfred Marshall and his successor A. C. Pigou. This revolution occurred during the Great Depression. A conventional date is 1936, the appearance of J. M. Keynes' *General Theory*.

Bronfenbrenner concluded that none of these had the characteristics to match revolutions in the Kuhnian sense but were more in the manner of syntheses of doctrines and their contradictions. A Hegelian thesis-antithesis-synthesis dialectic seemed to describe best the evolution of thinking in political economy.

But why, in turn, should the evolution of political economy thinking be one of dialectical process rather than paradigm shifts? Its close symbiotic relationship with economic policy may provide an answer. This symbiosis goes back a long way. In 1795, Edmund Burke wrote a long letter to Prime Minister William Pitt ("Pitt the Younger") entitled "Thoughts and Details on Scarcity," arguing against government subsidy of agricultural wages during a time of crisis caused by poor harvests. However, although it was directed to a specific policy issue, the frame of thinking that led to Burke's conclusions was broader:

> Of all things, an indiscreet tampering with the trade of provisions is the most dangerous, and it is always worst in the time when men are most disposed to it: that is, in the time of scarcity. Because there is nothing on which the passions of men are so violent, and their judgment so weak, and on which there exists such a multitude of ill-founded popular prejudices. ... But the throats of the rich ought not to be cut, nor their magazines plundered; because, in their persons they are trustees for those who labour, and their hoards are the banking-houses of these latter. Whether they mean it or not, they do, in effect, execute their trust — some with more, some with less fidelity and judgment. But on the whole, the duty is performed, and every thing returns, deducting some very trifling commission and discount,

to the place from whence it arose. When the poor rise to destroy the rich, they act as wisely for their own purposes as when they burn mills, and throw corn into the river, to make bread cheap. (Burke 1999: 195)

It should, of course, be very clear that the reasons Burke gives for not interfering with the workings of the market are the very reasons that others argued for intervention. Keynes was a follower of Burke in many respects. Indeed, he has been called a "Burkean conservative." But on this he differed from his hero, writing more than a century and a quarter later:

Let us clear from the ground the metaphysical or general principles upon which, from time to time, laissez-faire has been founded. It is not true that individuals possess a prescriptive "natural liberty" in their economic activities. There is no "compact" conferring perpetual rights on those who Have or on those who Acquire. The world is not so governed from above that private and social interest always coincide. It is not so managed here below that in practice they coincide. It is not a correct deduction from the principles of economics that enlightened self-interest always operates in the public interest. Nor is it true that self-interest generally is enlightened; more often individuals acting separately to promote their own ends are too ignorant or too weak to attain even these. Experience does not show that individuals, when they make up a social unit, are always less clear sighted than when they act separately. (Keynes [1926] 1978: 287–88)

The difference between Keynes and Burke has of course echoed in the political economy discourse and the debate has swung back and forth. But the reason for the debate, and for the cycles, was well stated by Burke (1999: 195–96):

It is one of the finest problems in legislation, and what has often engaged my thoughts whilst I followed that profession, 'What the State ought to take upon itself to direct by the public wisdom, and what it ought to leave, with as little interference as possible, to individual discretion.' Nothing, certainly, can be laid down on the subject that will not admit of exceptions, many permanent, some occasional. But the clearest line of distinction which I could draw, whilst I had my chalk to draw any line, was this: That the State ought to confine itself to what regards the State, or the creatures of the State, namely, the exterior establishment of its religion; its magistracy; its revenue; its military force by sea and land; the corporations that owe their existence to its fiat; in a word, to every thing that is *truly and properly* public, to the public peace, to the public safety, to the public order, to the public prosperity.

Keynes agreed with this characterization when he wrote in "The End of Laissez Faire": "The important thing for government is not to do things which individuals are doing already, and to do them a little better or a little worse; but to do those things which at present are not done at all." He further stated that "the chief task of economists at this hour is to distinguish afresh the *Agenda* of government from the *Non Agenda*" (Keynes [1926] 1978: 291). In this view, what mattered was what was on the *Agenda*, and if this changed dramatically, then the balance between state and market would shift. Such continuity along the spectrum of state and market does not sit well with the proclamation of "The End of Laissez Faire," but this inconsistency is not the first in Keynes in his self-proclaimed task of saving capitalism rather than ending it.

Thus, at the heart of the evolution of the political economy discourse is Burke's question of "what the State ought to take upon itself to direct by the public wisdom, and what it ought to leave, with as little interference as possible, to individual discretion," and Keynes's call "to distinguish afresh the *Agenda* of government from the *Non Agenda*." As new situations arise the *Agenda* shifts, and then shifts again, sometime involving the state more, sometimes less. Hence cycles, rather than cataclysmic paradigm shifts.

Conclusion

What will happen to economic policy debates after the pandemic? The majority view seems to be that nothing will ever be the same again. A new normal will be upon us. A combination of prediction and hope points to a major reorientation of the state-market balance toward the state. The last time we had such millennialist thinking was, of course, after the financial crisis of 2008–9, when a different sort of contagion spread through the world. Two decades before the great financial crisis, the fall of the Berlin Wall ushered in the new normal claims of that era:

the very end of history, and the final victory of liberal politics and (neo) liberal economics.

This chapter began with an account of current "new normal" statements from prominent academic sources on how economic policy will shift in favor of state and away from market. It then gave an account of past "new normal" claims and how those turned out to be reversed in due course. It presented a theory of evolution in political economy thinking, drawing on the work of Edmund Burke, John Maynard Keynes, and Thomas Kuhn, arguing that the evolution is more likely to take the form of cycles rather than a linear development in one direction or another.

Of course, the current pandemic will wreak economic havoc and reset at least some of the initial conditions for the global economy. The unsettled times and the proclamations of the new normal will surely be with us for several years. However, if past patterns are anything to go by, at the decade's end it is as good a prediction as any that the new normal will be the same as the old normal.

References

Acemoglu, Daron. 2020. "The Post COVID State." *Project Syndicate*, June 5, 2020. https://www.project-syndicate.org/onpoint/four-possible-trajectories-after-covid19-daron-acemoglu-2020-06.

Bouin, Olivier, Marie-Laure Djelic, Marc Fleurbaey, Ravi Kanbur, and Elisa Reis. 2020. "Addressing the Equity, Freedom and Sustainability Deficits to Maintain Social Progress despite COVID-19." *The Pandemic in the Age of Anxiety* (blog), *International Social Science Council*. April 21, 2020. https://council.science/current/blog/equity-freedom-sustainability/.

Bronfenbrenner, Martin. 1971. "The 'Structure of Revolutions' in Economic Thought." *History of Political Economy* 3 (1): 1–11. https://doi.org/10.1215/00182702-3-1-136.

Burke, Edmund. 1999. *The Portable Edmund Burke*, edited by Issac Kramnick. London: Penguin.

Commission on Growth and Development. 2008. *The Growth Report: Strategies for Sustained Growth and Inclusive Development*. Washington, DC: World Bank.

De Grauwe, Paul, and Yumei Ji. 2020. "A Tale of Three Depressions." VoxEU, Centre for Economic Policy Research, September 24, 2020. https://voxeu.org/article/tale-three-depressions.

Eichengreen, Barry, and Kevin O'Rourke. 2010. "What Do the New Data Tell Us?" VoxEU, Centre for Economic Policy Research, March 8, 2010. https://voxeu.org/article/tale-two-depressions-what-do-new-data-tell-us-february-2010-update.

Elton, G. R. 1974. *England under the Tudors*. London: Methuen.

Fukuyama, Francis. 1989. "The End of History?" *The National Interest*, no. 16: 3–18.

Goldberg, Pinelopi K. 2020. "The New Empty Argument against Free Trade." *Project Syndicate*, May 12, 2020. https://www.project-syndicate.org/commentary/covid19-case-for-global-supply-chains-by-pinelopi-koujianou-goldberg-2020-05.

Kanbur, Ravi. 2001. "Economic Policy, Distribution and Poverty: The Nature of Disagreements." *World Development* 29 (6): 1083–94. https://doi.org/10.1016/S0305-750X(01)00017-1.

Kanbur, Ravi. 2010. "Macro Crises and Targeting Transfers to the Poor." In *Globalization and Growth: Implications for a Post-Crisis World*, edited by Michael Spence and Danny Leipziger, 109–22. Washington, DC: Commission on Growth and Development.

Kanbur, Ravi. 2016. "The End of Laissez-Faire, the End of History, and the Structure of Scientific Revolutions." *Challenge* 59 (1): 35–46. https://doi.org/10.1080/05775132.2015.1123572.

Keynes, John Maynard. (1926) 1978. "The End of Laissez-Faire." In *The Collected Writings of John Maynard Keynes, Volume IX: Essays in Persuasion*, edited by E. Johnson and D. Moggridge, 272–94. Cambridge: Royal Economic Society.

Kibasi, Tom. 2020. "The Pandemic Has Exposed How Weak the State Is After 10 Years of Tory Misrule." *Guardian*, September 29, 2020. https://www.theguardian.com/commentisfree/2020/sep/29/pandemic-weak-state-10-years-tory-misrule.

Kuhn, Thomas S. (1962) 1970. *The Structure of Scientific Revolutions*. 2nd edition. Chicago: University of Chicago Press.

Reinhart, Carmen M., and Kenneth S. Rogoff. 2010. "Growth in a Time of Debt." *American Economic Review* 100 (2): 573–78. https://doi.org/10.1257/aer.100.2.573.

Rodrik, Dani. 2020. "Making the Best of a Post Pandemic World." *Project Syndicate*, May 12, 2020. https://www.project-syndicate.org/commentary/three-trends-shaping-post-pandemic-global-economy-by-dani-rodrik-2020-05.

Tooze, Adam. 2020. "The Death of Globalisation has been Announced Many Times: But This Is a Perfect Storm." *Guardian*, June 2, 2020. https://www.theguardian.com/commentisfree/2020/jun/02/end-globalisation-covid-19-made-it-real.

Varoufakis, Yanis. 2017. *Adults in the Room: My Battle with the European and American Deep Establishment*. New York: Farrer, Straus, and Giroux.

CHAPTER 2

No Epistemological Standstill on Sovereign Debt

The Preservation of the Market Order in Pandemic Times

Benjamin Lemoine

The pandemic has caused a general collapse. Lockdown policies designed to ease pressure on hospitals, fully mobilized to treat COVID-19 patients, have caused growth rates to plummet. States face exorbitant health costs, collapsing tax revenues, and rising sovereign debt levels. Fragile states have experienced a decrease in export revenues (linked to the global recession) as well as extreme risk aversion among investors. Capital flight to safety (re-invested into high-income countries' financing needs)[1] has led to a sudden halt in flows to emerging countries. Bond markets have frozen, leaving some governments unable to refinance maturing debt and limiting their capacity to manage the economic and social effects of the pandemic. Low and middle-income countries of the Global South are plunged into unknown territories of insolvency, and budget pressures have been accompanied by a new wave

---

1. Nonresident capital outflows in emerging markets are estimated by the Institute of International Finance to be close to USD 100 billion over a forty-five-day period starting in late February 2020. This compares to less than USD 20 billion in the three months following the 2008 financial crisis (Gelpern, Hagan, and Mazarei 2020).

of sovereign debt downgrades by credit rating agencies, surpassing peaks during prior crises (Bulow et al. 2020). Since the first outbreak of the COVID-19 pandemic, the question of debt relief (or at least suspension of debt service and interest payments) has become a prominent matter of public debate. High precrisis debt vulnerabilities may develop into unsustainable burdens that will require relief, assistance, moratorium, or cancellation.

In April 2020, during the first peak of the pandemic, the International Monetary Fund (IMF) prompted governments to do "whatever it takes ... to save lives and protect people" while immediately adding that "they must make sure to keep the receipts" (cited in Gaspar, Lam, and Raissi 2020, and IMF 2020b). This ambiguous directive summarizes the macro design of the Fund's treatment of public finance during the pandemic: if everything is collapsing due to an uncontrollable crisis, it is essential first and foremost to preserve the pillars of the financial order and ensure the continuity of market fundamentals — the accountability of expenditures, the targeted and temporary character of emergency excessive spending, a moratorium on debt interests avoiding the (still unthinkable) default on payment of principal, and no return to administrated and planned economies. By reviewing different types of sovereign debt policies, this chapter explores how, within the crisis, the apparatuses of power "regress towards the habitus" (Dobry 2009)[2] and maintain the categories of understanding debt that were governing societies before the pandemic.

Collapse and Resilience of Debt Problematization

A "shock," a "black swan," an "original" phenomenon, "not previously seen," "truly unique," "unprecedented in its magnitude," and a trigger for "extraordinary levels of uncertainty": economists and political experts have used countless figures of speech to describe the pandemic and its economic, political, and social effects. Analyses, produced in

---

2. By virtue of the hypothesis of "regression towards habitus," and contrary to the idea that crises are "liberating" and give actors "a wider space of choice" than that "available to them in routinized or stable contexts," it is necessary to grasp how social structures are actualized in a particular way during the specific situational logic of this health crisis (Dobry 2009). All translations from French are by the author.

the heat of the battle, have resulted in a dominant vision: the virus is *exogenous*. It is framed as a "phenomenon totally independent of the way in which financial globalization and neomercantilism have shaped the various spheres of social life and our relationship to nature in present-day societies" (Théret 2021: 72). The metaphor of the shock precisely conveys a notion of the pandemic as unpredictable and non-reproducible as such — a "one-shot" that has come to strike from outside our political-economic regimes.[3] Such a presentation is questionable. First, as Michel Aglietta and Sabrina Khanniche (2020: 1) point out, "the current crisis is a warning for the future. It is not an exogenous shock because it is not unrelated to the degradation of biodiversity for which our capitalist societies are responsible. It has hit a global economy where financial vulnerabilities inherited from the previous crisis have accumulated." Second, many explanations clarify how such long-lasting health crises are consubstantial with our globalized economy and society.[4] The abusive commodification of nature that puts pressure on ecosystems and encourages zoonotic diseases (Wallace et al. 2020), "the absolute irrationality of globalized supply-chain values for essential goods (masks, tests, medicines, small equipment) in time of epidemic recurrence"(Théret 2021: 72), and the organized failure of public health systems over the last twenty-five years — caused by drastic austerity measures, under-investment, and creeping privatization — are among the numerous structural candidates for endogenous problematization and may explain why governments' (mis)management of the pandemic was reduced to crude last-resort measures such as lockdowns.

Beyond competing narratives, or a floating intellectual *zeitgeist*, the endogenous or exogenous character of the crisis associated with the pandemic is an object of policy struggle. In this chapter, I consider the exogenous construction of the pandemic — a phenomenon that has impacted, from the outside, our political and economic systems — as materially inscribed in crisis management devices (Mitchell 2002). I use

---

3. Durand (2021) thus comments on regulation school economist Robert Boyer's (2020) analysis of the pandemic crisis in terms of exogenous or endogenous.
4. "The crisis is not caused by the virus alone, it is the virus that resonates with society. … The crisis feeds on all the social, political, economic and territorial dysfunctions that were already there" (Levy-Mozziconacci, Mesclier, and Metzger 2020).

the concept of problematization to emphasize that such constructions of the COVID-19 crisis refer not only to rhetorical or lexical activity but also to material processes — accounting, legal, and financial techniques — conveying an order of causalities as well as a set of solutions.[5] I focus on debt-restructuring workouts, laws, and procedures to show how the dominant exogenous framing of the pandemic leads to partial, short-term remedies whose purpose is precisely not to upset the fundamentals of the global financial order. Such problematizations function as technologies of continuation for the pre-COVID order, rendering invisible any structural implications and policy lessons for the future and preventing the emergence of the naively branded "world-after" (or the "new-normal").

Temporary Fixes and Incomplete Suspension of Austerity Routines

On April 15, 2020, the Group of Twenty (G20), an international forum that brings together governments, central bank governors, and international organizations, endorsed a suspension of debt service for the world's seventy-six poorest countries. The outcome was not a cancellation but a postponement of payment granted on a case-by-case basis: the Debt Service Suspension Initiative (DSSI), supported by the World Bank and the IMF, would only apply to bilateral debt and, therefore, exclude debts owed to the private sector. Such a mode of treatment contrasts with other more radical proposals calling for "extensive debt forgiveness" or for the cancellation of the external debts that most poor countries have contracted with rich states, multilateral institutions, and private creditors. The DSSI program was extended by the G20 until mid-2021. China, Africa's major creditor but still only an "observer" member of the Paris Club (which convenes bilateral official creditors under the auspices of the French treasury), is willing to join this "common framework." Private sector participation takes place on a voluntary

---

5. Brice Laurent (2017: 19) understands problematization as the "conditions of possibility of certain qualifications of questions, the way through which they can be transformed into problems for which solutions could be proposed. [This] ... collective production ... [a] 'specific work of thought' ... cannot be separated from the practices and technologies through which it is enacted."

basis.[6] While many debtor countries did not make use of it,[7] fearing that their sovereign credit ratings would be downgraded, Chad — slightly indebted (42 percent of its GDP) but approaching a liquidity crisis — was the first country during the COVID-19 era to ask for debt restructuring under this framework.[8] Chad will benefit from IMF support (its Extended Credit Facility and Extended Fund Facility, amounting to USD 560 million) based on a four-year economic reform program. Although the IMF strategy during the pandemic appears to delay or suspend its routines of imposing structural reforms and conditionality on borrowing countries, many suspicions arise while reading between the lines of the institution's official documents — the IMF is still calling on governments to implement "appropriate policies to address the crisis" (Rivié 2020). The European Network on Debt and Development (Eurodad), a Brussels-based nongovernmental organization specializing in sovereign debt, reviewed IMF staff reports for eighty countries and reported that "72 countries that have received IMF financing are projected to begin a process of fiscal consolidation as early as 2021." In other words, these countries will be locked "in a decade-long crisis of debt and austerity" (Munevar 2020: 3).

DSSI measures focus on liquidity — maintaining countries' access to finance, both from official and market sources. However, attempts to regulate the crisis through minor technocratic fixes (instead of structural transformations) are also influencing decisions related to treatment of debt stocks, when insolvency looms and countries are unable to repay. The main concern of a restructuring is the collective action and coordination of debt holders (be they official or commercial). The London Club universe, where large commercial banks sharing a "common fate" with the indebted state met to discuss their claims around a table and reach a consensus, disappeared in the 1990s. Emerging

---

6. According to informal sources, the Paris Club and the G20 have agreed that henceforth no restructuring action will be taken without the equal participation of both private and public creditors.
7. Within the DSSI framework, about fifty countries — the vast majority of which are African states — have obtained a moratorium on their public debt.
8. In the case of Chad, this is the result of a high debt burden (amassed with the Swiss-based trader Glencore-backed by oil sales) and low oil revenue. Zambia and Ethiopia and other countries may apply for debt rescheduling in the coming months (Rouaud 2021).

market countries' debt now circulates on a secondary market where it is bought and sold (Potts 2017), which can expose countries to purchases by distressed-debt investors who do not base their business model on cooperation but rather on legal opportunism by asserting their rights as creditors in courts most favorable to private finance, such as New York or London. In 2001, when Argentina defaulted on its debt, paving the way for a long-lasting saga involving vulture funds, the IMF's then-deputy managing director Anne Krueger proposed a statutory reform: the sovereign debt restructuring mechanism. This proposal sparked significant opposition from the United States (US) Department of the Treasury and the global private finance community. Historically, the case-by-case, ad hoc, and discretionary approaches defended by creditor countries, banks, and private investors have conflicted with the structural, rules-based, and supra-sovereign mechanisms demanded by debtor countries from the Global South (Deforge and Lemoine 2021; Helleiner 2008).

While Kristalina Georgieva, the IMF's current managing director, recognizes that "reform of the international debt architecture is urgently needed" (Georgieva, Pazarbasioglu, and Weeks-Brown 2020), the foremost priority seems to be to implement a "temporary by design" initiative and to strengthen the existing contractual and market-based framework. The introduction of a statutory mechanism — a supra-sovereign court, which would impose on all creditors a way out of debt renegotiations, including those creditors who make their living from litigation — is not part of the discussion. Rather, an IMF interdepartmental working group developed different routes to reform "aspects of the current debt architecture that require fixing" (IMF 2020a)[9] and to "make it harder for holdouts to paralyze a majority of creditors willing to restructure" (*Financial Times* 2020a). The note lays out reform options to "augment on the margins" the current market-based and contractual approach, such as the collective action clauses included in certain bond contracts. Statutory mechanisms are treated as "last resort" solutions. The same is true of the provisions that allow the use of domestic law ("anti-vulture fund" legislation) to thwart creditors' attempts at recovery through asset seizures. The recourse to domestic legal measures in order to curb the actions of these procedural funds that are recalcitrant to restructuring agreements could

---

9. This working group of experts brings together several IMF departments: legal; monetary and capital markets; and strategy, policy, and review.

eventually be considered but in a strictly "targeted" and "time-bound" manner.

Paradoxically, it seems there is an urgent need to strengthen the framework within which debt is usually monitored. Thus the president of the International Public Sector Accounting Standards Board, a transnational organization that has been lobbying for years to align public sector accounting methods to the standards of private finance (to better inform creditors investing in sovereign debt), sees the crisis as an opportunity. Aligning public power practices to the canons of financial investment would allow countries to be better prepared (Angeli-Aguiton, Cabane, and Cornilleau 2019) for the painful political arbitrations that will certainly take place between social publics competing over the diminishing pie of public finance: taxes and income redistribution that go through public power. Governments should arm themselves and the population with these methods, which "provide a complete picture of the state of a government's finances" (Carruthers 2020), quantifying implicit and contingent liabilities.

Criticized for their refusal to abide by the "common framework," private creditors, mainly represented by the Institute for International Finance (IIF), argue that "they are committed not to provide threats, not to give ultimatums, not to make pronouncements, but to understand and work with [borrower] countries on addressing their primary concerns": "If our message was truly to 'buck up or pay up,' why would we collectively spend thousands of hours, and untold resources, tailoring a solution that would assuage the borrower's number one concern?"[10] The IIF has thus proposed its own "terms of reference" (IIF 2020), a "flexible template" for organizing restructurings while refusing "a top-down, or one-size-fits-all, approach": "put simply, Zambia isn't Kenya, Kenya isn't Mongolia, and Mongolia isn't Pakistan. Each country enters this crisis in a unique fiscal situation, and has a unique debt repayment profile." Once again, the treatment on a case-by-case basis is retained as an essential condition, which leaves countries much more vulnerable since they have less weight individually. But it also gives the private sector the opportunity to accept or reject the debt workouts: "It's imperative that

---

10. The IFF tried to debunk the critique raised in Bolton et al. (2020) and answered to what it considered as "myths" through a public email entitled "Setting the Record Straight — Private Sector Involvement in the DSSI." Quotes from the IIF below are extracted from this email. The IIF also launched a public campaign (IIF 2020).

creditors are able to coordinate with each country individually and tailor the solution that works best for all stakeholders."

Legal Assertion of the "Exogenous" and Exceptional Character of the Crisis

At the forefront of the international scene, but critical of the private sector's strategic sidebar behavior, some solutions to low-income countries' overindebtedness have consisted in asserting the exceptional character of the COVID crisis in order to set up specific resolutions. The instruments combine particular concepts of international law and direct it toward the suspension of the rules of law as usual. Sovereign borrowers would be able to invoke the defense of necessity, the "State of Necessity" (SoN),[11] in order to justify a standstill on debt service payment and a stay on litigation or enforcement actions initiated by creditors. The concept is narrow, well-framed from a legal point of view, restricted and limited in time, guaranteeing a return to normalcy afterwards: "A state can invoke necessity to excuse its non-performance of an 'international obligation' if non-performance is the only way to address 'a grave and imminent peril' …; non-performance is excused only while the threat persists. The state must resume performance when the crisis ends, and it may have to pay compensation for any loss caused by its non-compliance" (Weidemaier 2020).

The purpose is to ensure the orderly progress and conclusion of insolvency proceedings, whether through the restructuring of debt or the liquidation of the debtor, and to secure the equality of creditors in that process by prohibiting unjustified payments to some of the creditors, thereby also preventing them from rushing to the courts. Standstill makes it possible to preserve a balance of interests between debtors and creditors. This technique requires all parties to concede real sacrifices and losses. The idea is to have creditors partially subsidize the cost of the crisis. Law professors and practitioners Mark Weidemaier and Mitu Gulati (2020a: 283) insist that this loss refers to the shared burden and balanced approach to sacrifices: "[Investors] would be subsidizing the crisis response, although this does not make them unique. So is every

---

11. The State of Necessity is a rule of customary international law expressed in Article 25 of the International Law Commission's draft Articles on Responsibility of States for Internationally Wrongful Acts.

other person with a claim on the sovereign's resources, including the citizens and residents for whose welfare the state is responsible."

A famous precedent is that of the US in 1933.[12] Citing "public policy grounds," the government imposed a massive haircut on its lenders by abrogating the gold clauses in its debt contracts via congressional action.[13] It was justified by the magnitude of the crisis, "arguably the worst it had ever seen," requiring "extreme steps (such as the abrogation of a contract term) needed to be taken to improve general welfare" (Gulati 2020). Another, albeit failed, precedent is that of Argentina in 2001 (Waibel 2007). That year, Argentina faced a near-total economic collapse, marked by "a fall in GDP per capita of 50 percent, an unemployment rate of over 20 percent, a poverty rate of 50 percent, strikes, demonstrations, violent clashes with police, dozens of civilian casualties and a succession of 5 presidents in 10 days" (Bernasconi-Osterwalder, Brewin, and Maina 2020). The government took "emergency" measures — freezing utility rates, nationalizing assets, devaluing the currency, and restructuring sovereign bonds — that negatively affected foreign investors with whom the country had protection agreements. This resulted in Argentina being respondent to over fifty investor-state dispute settlements and taken to the International Centre for Settlement of Investment Disputes by the companies that had participated before in the privatization of certain public services sectors such as energy (Thjoernelund 2009).

Among the conditions of possibility for the invocation of a SoN is the idea that a government that makes use of the concept should not be held responsible for the situation of overindebtedness to which it is reduced and which is precisely that which leads it to activate this suspensive rule of international law. Argentina was defeated in the courts

---

12. There are numerous debates about the recognition and acceptance by US and New York municipal law of the doctrine of necessity as defined under international law (Weidemaier 2020).
13. Before their abrogation under the Roosevelt administration for all types of debts (public and private), gold clauses established that debts were to be paid in "gold coin." With the abrogation, all existing contracts denominated in gold were annulled, creditors could not demand payment in gold or gold equivalents anymore, and Congress stated that no such contracts could be written in the future. This episode is considered as one of the "first step(s) in what would become one of the largest transfers of wealth (from creditors to debtors) in the history of the world" (Edwards, Longstaff, and Garcia-Marin 2015).

because the government was considered the architect of its own misfortune. Such a requirement functions as an auto-limitation for states to invoke a SoN since "a sovereign default is typically the result of multiple causes, including the economic policies of the defaulting government" (Goldmann 2020: 8). However, it is a difficult task to clear a state from the situation in which it currently finds itself. At the very least, it would imply dissociating one particular government decision from the state apparatus in the long run. This condition of *exogeneity* also contributes to problematizing the pandemic itself as an exceptional phenomenon, relatively detached from the authorities in power, which has hit countries, indeed the world, from the outside.[14] It implies that sovereign states — present and past governments' track records — are not held responsible. With hindsight, the SoN doctrine may naturalize a partial understanding of the pandemic and obscure the fact that financialized capitalism, the unpreparedness of public health systems, and the abusive commodification of nature are all tightly entangled. The imposition of lockdowns by governments is itself the result of deficiencies caused by the neoliberal software that has dominated public policy for several decades now. Thus, it seems difficult not to blame austerity and the constant search for health policies at the lowest cost, which have silently revolutionized services in welfare states — known as "bankruptcy politics" or "politics of public services fallibility" — and made them vulnerable to and unprepared for a pandemic (Juven and Lemoine 2018). Similarly, chronic under-investment in developing countries decided by elites in power or due to an unequal global financing system, that is, geopolitical factors, could also be blamed. Yet it is undoubtedly true that certain states, particularly those under debt-restructuring scrutiny, would benefit from a specific treatment: avoiding laying the blame on domestic public policies might loosen the IMF's hard-conditionality lending policies. Therefore, mobilizing the SoN defense incorporates and conveys ambiguous statements on COVID causalities: while it allows debt relief for certain states, it also reconstructs the pandemic as an event that is limited in time, unpredictable, and impossible to anticipate. For governments (beyond creditors), invoking a SoN in this precise pandemic situation enables the non-discussion of their political responsibility in this disaster. Indeed, lawyers (and the financial community at large) are

---

14. From this point of view, Bolsonaro's Brazil, or Trump's US, which are considered to have badly mismanaged the pandemic, could be given a pass in the name of SoN and benefit from it.

taking for granted the fact that "it is implausible to suggest that any particular state contributed to its own misfortune when the dire economic costs of the pandemic are being felt in 'every' state" (Weidemaier and Gulati 2020a: 279). But what, precisely, the genealogy of financialized sovereign debt reveals is how sovereign states, in order to construct a competitive bond market, reorganized the meaning of sovereignty and aligned their policy priorities in order to stabilize a credible commitment to investors. To issue durable "safe assets," that is, bonds without any financial or political risks for investors, governments had to offer financiers many guarantees (such as low inflation, competitive labor, an attractive tax regime, the disqualification of direct public intervention in the matter of credit and money) at the expense of another fraction of the population: the social creditors benefiting from the welfare state (Lemoine 2016).

The SoN also constructs COVID as an exogenous virus, *disembedded* from politics and from governments' ideological choices. It also prevents state apparatuses from taking any long-term responsibility. Proposals for mobilizing the rule of the SoN make it possible to re-hierarchize the social claims (and publics) served by the state, but exclusively on a temporary basis (Bolton et al. 2020a, 2020b, 2020c).[15] Unlike the rule of force majeure, which is absolute (supervening events prevent an obligor from performing their obligations at all), the rule of "necessity" is relative: the question becomes that of the threshold of social or health-related suffering that is no longer acceptable and would trigger the rule of necessity, legally releasing a state from its financial obligations to creditors because those bonds have become subordinated to other state commitments considered of greater interest. By striking what is considered an appropriate balance between the concerns of creditors and the state's need to protect its residents, this rule, designed as acceptable to market forces, guarantees the exceptional and provisional nature of this propensity to re-hierarchize between the financial creditors (formal creditors) and social or informal creditors (citizens) of sovereign debt.

---

15. That is to say, "in the narrow set of circumstances where nations — through no fault of their own — need to compromise certain legal obligations in order to divert resources to meet the urgent needs of their population" (Bolton et al. 2020c).

The Political as a Contract-Consolidator

The solution of the SoN and the standstill aims not at destabilizing the markets, but, on the contrary, at improving and completing them. Its champions are keen to reassure that this recourse would not fundamentally challenge the order of the international debt market (Bolton et al. 2020a, 2020b, 2020c). The main market pillar that would be preserved is the safeguard against the risk of moral hazard on the sovereign side. Contrary to the idea that embracing the necessity defense would, according to some reluctant lawyers, or creditors, "open the floodgates, allowing sovereigns to invoke necessity in all sorts of dubious circumstances" and be tantamount to opening a Pandora's box, "recognizing the necessity defense in the context of COVID is consistent with investors' reasonable expectations" (Weidemaier and Gulati 2020b). The SoN defense would be inseparable from the specific context of the pandemic. The advocates of the standstill solution also explicitly assert that "such interventions do not automatically undermine credit markets or undermine freedom of contracting; in some instances, they have had the opposite effect, resurrecting debt markets following the intervention" (Bolton et al. 2020c). While preventing default, these devices aim to strengthen "incomplete" contracts by inserting clauses that refer to "exceptions for contingencies such as a global pandemic like COVID-19" (Bolton et al. 2020c). As for natural disasters, the idea is to transform unexpected and devastating events into manageable situations for equipped and augmented contracts and markets. Such "baby steps" and market experiments "should be as replicable, scalable, and generalizable as possible"(Gelpern 2020). Multilateral institutions, such as the G20, considered a neutral body of expertise, would play a "certifying role" by validating "the extreme and urgent nature of the present crisis … confirming [its] severity … and providing clear guideposts for when the crisis ends" (Weidemaier and Gulati 2020a: 279). Political institutions would be reduced to the role of reinforcing the debt market by displaying its credibility in deciding on the situation, triggering (or not) certain contractual clauses: "The political intervention in debt contracts in these events serves the role of completing incomplete debt contracts. By certifying the event and by modifying the terms of the debt contract in ways that the contracting parties themselves would have wanted had they been able to, the intervention, far from undermining credit markets, helps support these markets" (Bolton et al. 2020c; Bolton et al. 2020b: 8).

Assigning this type of script to politics is typical of neoliberalism: political institutions (supranational and multilateral) or specific bodies (administrators or trustees) would have to be deployed in order to "manage or oversee the insolvent debtor during the restructuring" (Goldmann 2020: 2) and verify that there is no abuse of the exceptional procedure (Weidemaier and Gulati 2020a).[16] These solutions are fundamentally linked to a pre-COVID order in which it is normal and legitimate that states are the *equals* of market players and remain at arm's length from private investors. Standstill and SoN present many advantages for the financial community: by being temporary, by asserting and enacting the *exogenous* and *disembedded* nature of COVID from politics and the financialized economic order, and, finally, by reproducing auto-regulated debt markets, these legal devices function as tactics of "ancient-world" continuation. Sovereign powers affected by overindebtedness, in times of crisis, are limited to claiming (or asserting) the official statement of a circumscribed SoN, limited in time and capable of suspending contract law in order to respect it more fully later on. Better still, these "pause" and standstill mechanisms — "giving countries breathing space" (Hagan 2020) — are specifically designed not to "destroy the sovereign debt market" but rather to "augment" it by incorporating clauses in contracts that materialize a new source of uncertainty to be managed: the pandemic and the systemic risk it conveys. These solutions can be thought of in analogy with the way in which financial technologies aim to respond to climate change and environmental challenges by making them a quantifiable risk, and therefore controllable in an unchanged economic system — for instance, by introducing new financial compensation tools (such as carbon credits or catastrophe bonds) (Aguiton 2018). These market-driven techniques are in line with instruments such as collective action clauses[17] in that they deal with the issues of creditors' coordination and holdouts that are prompt to litigate in debt restructurings. In each case it is a question of responding with instruments embedded in a market paradigm with its relevant fundamentals, and the way in which politics

---

16. "Whether this is a serious risk depends on whether a tribunal can accurately verify that a state of necessity has really occurred. If not — if the defense is not easily verifiable — then the risk of opportunism is enhanced" (Weidemaier and Gulati 2020).
17. A collective action clause allows a supermajority of bondholders to agree to a debt restructuring that is legally binding on all holders of the bond, including those who vote against the restructuring.

and democratic institutions (with a delimited scope of action) must respect this perimeter of market instruments' self-regulation.

But the SoN would also, paradoxically, make it possible to suspend bilateral treaties that bind states — a large network of treaties providing international legal protections to foreign investors (Shearman & Sterlin 2020) — and could embroil them in investor-state dispute settlement procedures. Unprecedented measures to tackle the COVID pandemic crisis, to keep economies afloat, and, more generally, to conform with the duty of states to protect public health could be considered harmful to the interests and claims of foreign investors. As such, these measures could potentially be deemed to be noncompliant with international investment law and thus challenged in the courts.[18]

However, as Anna Gelpern (2020), a legal scholar specializing in sovereign debt and financial regulation, has asked: "If you have sovereignty, who needs necessity?" The need to invoke the SoN goes hand in hand with a specific configuration of relations in which political forces and considerations are striving not to "percolate into otherwise strictly legal/contractual debates between arm's length counterparties" (RP 2020), that is to say, between states and private investors. The transformation of the very concept of sovereignty, gradually embedded in the financial sphere, is political per se. Since the 1970s, and particularly following the outbreak of the Latin American crisis, the restriction of sovereign immunity inscribed in bond commitments has enabled creditors to enforce their contractual terms (Gaillard 2014). The history of disputes between creditors and debtors in the field of sovereign debt can be described as the growing capacity of private creditors to enforce sanctions and assert their rights as holders of securities and bonds. As Matthias Goldmann (2020: 7) reminds us, "In principle, sovereign immunities could serve the same purpose as a standstill rule. However, sovereign debt instruments are nowadays regularly considered *acta iure gestionis*. Under public international law, states may therefore not invoke jurisdictional immunity in order to stop holdout litigation. Domestic courts usually interpret the legal provisions on sovereign immunities applicable in their jurisdiction in the same way, and do not grant immunity as a defense against such

---

18. For instance, states may issue compulsory licenses for patented drugs and devices, or, to support their overburdened public health-care systems, they may opt to temporarily nationalize private hospitals or order the temporary or permanent requisition of medical devices and other movable assets.

suits. On top of that, the standard terms of sovereign debt instruments routinely contain waivers of immunity."

State sovereignty and the very conception of general interest have been reshaped at a global scale by financial reason and, in the case of emerging countries — unable to issue debt in their own currency and to attract capital using their domestic law — this has also resulted in the incorporation of creditor-oriented legal devices. It is only after sovereignty has been embedded in global finance that sovereignty needs to have recourse to the SoN. The ability to define extraordinary circumstances brings to mind Schmitt's famous *decisionist* definition of the essence of sovereignty from his *Political Theology* — "Sovereign is he who decides on the exception" (Schmitt [1922] 2005: 5). But it seems that identifying the exception when dealing with the pandemic within the current debt market configuration consists of circumscribing the perimeter of a defined pathology, a parenthesis, while refusing to profoundly question the regular rule of operation between states and between public, social, and private creditors. The quest for democracy must challenge such a confinement inside market infrastructure, in order to open the financial toolkit — beyond technical fixes of the debt regime — and implement the necessary policies to respond to "new-world" challenges.

Sovereign Debt Routines

This chapter has described how tension over the endogenous or exogenous problematization of the COVID crisis has played out on the particular terrain of sovereign debt, states' legitimate modes of financing, and the state-investor relationship. Debt problematization is at a crossroads. Spiraling public deficits spur governments to subvert many taboos — the temptation of direct financing from governments, financial repression, and the return of financial sovereignty are all on the rise. Yet the debt *habitus* and routines of problematization have shown themselves strongly resilient, distributed across different constituencies and organizations such as the IMF, private investors, economists, and lawyers: domestic and fiscal blame as a causality, (delayed) austerity as a solution, and market-driven case-by-case treatments when restructuring is unavoidable. While they may appear heterodox at first glance, COVID-crisis policies are technologies of market-order conservation that eliminate from the discussion any structural, sustainable, or subversive solutions to market order. Measures consistent with the awareness of an economic and social situation not seen since the Second World War have remained buried: a public (international) bankruptcy court, nonmarket financing of sovereign states, cooperation/solidarity between countries of the Global South in international commercial and financial transactions, economic planning, capital controls, a structural break with the deep-rooted causes of the pandemic's lengthy duration, and, more specifically, the inability of the state and public health systems to deal with it without resorting to crude and coarse measures.

Although a consensus regarding sovereign debt standstill has gained ground — among international public and private organizations such as the IMF, the World Bank, and the IIF — the various relaxations of the debt constraint imposed in the name of "emergency," "exception," and "necessity" are only being conceded on a temporary basis and in order to preserve the essential: that in "normal" times, it is the market's laws, calculations, and truths that decide the value of things, individuals, companies, or states. This chapter has focused on states considered as peripheral in the international finance architecture. But in countries considered as central in the global financial system, despite singular features reinforced by the pandemic — such as low interest rates, the implicit (and indirect) monetization of debt (through the "new normal" of the secondary market repurchase in the case of the European Central Bank), the vulnerability of the private sector and its inability to live without the safety net of public financial assistance, especially during lockdown episodes — no *epistemological standstill* on sovereign debt categories of understanding seems to be emerging.

Acknowledgements

I would like to thank the Institute for Advanced Study and the 2019–20 members of the School of Social Sciences. I especially thank Didier Fassin and Marion Fourcade.

References

Aglietta, Michel, and Sabrina Khanniche. 2020. "La vulnérabilité du capitalisme financiarisé face au coronavirus." *La lettre du Cepii*, no. 407: 1–4.

Aguiton, Sara A. 2018. "Fortune de l'infortune: Financiarisation des catastrophes naturelles par l'assurance." *Zilsel* 2 (4): 21–57. https://doi.org/10.3917/zil.004.0021.

Angeli-Aguiton, Sara, Lydie Cabane, and Lise Cornilleau. 2019. "Politiques de la 'mise en crise.'" *Critique internationale* 4 (85): 9–21. https://doi.org/10.3917/crii.085.0009.

Bernasconi-Osterwalder, Nathalie, Sarah Brewin, and Nyaguthii Maina. 2020. "Protecting against Investor-State Claims amidst COVID-19: A Call to Action for Governments." International Institute for Sustainable Development, April 14, 2020. https://www.iisd.org/articles/protecting-against-investor-state-claims-amidst-covid-19-call-action-governments.

Bolton, Patrick, Lee Buchheit, Pierre-Olivier Gourinchas, Mitu Gulati, Chang-Tai Hsieh, and Ugo Panizza. 2020a. "How to Prevent a Sovereign Debt Disaster: A Relief Plan for Emerging Markets." *Foreign Affairs*, June 4, 2020.

Bolton, Patrick, Lee C. Buchheit, Pierre-Olivier Gourinchas, Mitu Gulati, Chang-Tai Hsieh, Ugo Panizza, and Beatric Weder di Mauro. 2020b. "Born Out of Necessity: A Debt Standstill for COVID-19." Policy Insight no. 103, Center for Economic Policy Research, Duke Law School Public Law and Legal Theory Series no. 2020–23. https://ssrn.com/abstract=3586785.

Bolton, Patrick, Lee C. Buchheit, Pierre-Olivier Gourinchas, Mitu Gulati, Chang-Tai Hsieh, Ugo Panizza, and Beatric Weder di Mauro. 2020c. "Necessity Is the Mother of Invention: How to Implement a Comprehensive Debt Standstill for COVID-19 in Low- and Middle-Income Countries." VoxEU, Centre for Economic Policy Research, April 21, 2020. https://voxeu.org/article/debt-standstill-covid-19-low-and-middle-income-countries.

Boyer, Robert. 2020. *Les capitalismes à l'épreuve de la pandémie*. Paris: La Découverte.

Bulow, Jeremy, Carmen Reinhart, Kenneth Rogoff, and Christoph Trebesch. 2020. "The Debt Pandemic." *Finance and Development* (Fall), 12–16.

Carruthers, Ian. 2020. "How Accounting Transparency Can Help with the Tough Decisions ahead after Covid-19." Public Finance Focus, April 23, 2020. https://www.publicfinancefocus.org/viewpoints/2020/04/how-accounting-transparency-can-help-tough-decisions-ahead-after-covid-19.

Deforge, Quentin, and Benjamin Lemoine. 2021. "The Global South Debt Revolution That Wasn't: UNCTAD from Technocratic Activism to Technical Assistance." In *Sovereign Debt Diplomacies: Rethinking Sovereign Debt from Colonial Empires to Hegemony*, edited by Pierre Pénet and Juan F. Zendejas, 232–58. Oxford: Oxford University Press.

Dobry, Michel. 2009. *Sociologie des crises politiques: La dynamique des mobilisations multisectorielles*, Paris: Presses de Sciences Po.

Durand, Cédric. 2021. "Quand l'histoire économique nous mord la nuque: À propos de l'ouvrage de Robert Boyer, Les capitalismes à l'épreuve de la pandémie." *Revue de la Régulation: Capitalismes, Institutions, Pouvoirs* 30 (1). https://doi.org/10.4000/regulation.19363.

Edwards, Sebastian, Francis Longstaff, and Alvaro Garcia-Marin. 2015. "The U.S. Debt Restructuring of 1933: Consequences and Lessons." Working Paper no. 21694, National Bureau of Economic Research.

Financial Times. 2020. "Time is Right for a New International Debt Architecture." October 5, 2020. https://www.ft.com/content/ee211af6-5e8a-4ca9-87a4-75bdbed35cf5.

Gaillard, Norbert. 2014. *When Sovereigns Go Bankrupt. A Study on Sovereign Risk*. Cham: Springer.

Gaspar, Vitor, W. Raphael Lam, and Mehdi Raissi. 2020. "Fiscal Policies to Contain the Damage from COVID-19." IMF Blog, April 15, 2020. https://blogs.imf.org/2020/04/15/fiscal-policies-to-contain-the-damage-from-covid-19/.

Gelpern, Anna. 2020. "Methinks necessity is a stretch." Comment on Credit Slips (blog), February 4, 2020, 10:28 p.m. https://www.creditslips.org/creditslips/2020/01/the-necessity-defense-in-sovereign-debt-cases.html.

Gelpern, Anna, Sean Hagan, and Adnan Mazarei. 2020. "Debt Standstills can Help Vulnerable Governments Manage the COVID-19 Crisis." *Peterson Institute for International Economics*, April 7, 2020.

Georgieva, Kristalina, Ceyla Pazarbasioglu, and Rhoda Weeks-Brown. 2020. "Reform of the International Debt Architecture is Urgently Needed." IMF (blog), October 1, 2020. https://blogs.imf.org/2020/10/01/reform-of-the-international-debt-architecture-is-urgently-needed/.

Goldmann, Matthias. 2020. "Necessity and Feasibility of a Standstill Rule for Sovereign Debt Workouts." Paper prepared for the First Session of the Debt Workout Mechanism Working Group, January 23, 2020. https://unctad.org/en/PublicationsLibrary/gdsddf2014misc4_en.pdf?user=4818.

Gulati, Mitu. 2020. "Necessity in the Time of Covid-19." *Credit Slips*, February 6. https://www.creditslips.org/creditslips/GulatiAuthor.html/page/2/.

Hagan, Sean. 2020. "Sovereign Debt Restructuring: The Centrality of the IMF's Role." Working Paper 20-13, Peterson Institute for International Economics. https://www.piie.com/publications/working-papers/sovereign-debt-restructuring-centrality-imfs-role.

Helleiner, Eric. 2008. "The Mystery of the Missing Sovereign Debt Restructuring Mechanism." *Contributions to Political Economy* 27 (1): 91–113. https://doi.org/10.1093/cpe/bzn003.

IIF (Institute of International Finance). 2020. "IIF Letter to G20, IMF, World Bank and Paris Club on the Private Sector Terms of Reference for the G20/Paris Club DSSI." Institute for International Finance, May 28, 2020. https://www.iif.com/Publications/ID/3919/IIF-Letter-To-G20-IMF-World-Bank-and-Paris-Club-On-the-Private-Sector-Terms-of-Reference-for-the-G20Paris-Club-DSSI.

IMF (International Monetary Fund). 2020a. "The International Architecture for Resolving Sovereign Debt Involving Private-Sector Creditors — Recent Developments, Challenges, and Reform Options." IMF Policy Paper no. 2020/043, October 1, 2020.

IMF. 2020b. "Keeping the Receipts: Transparency, Accountability, and Legitimacy in Emergency Responses." Fiscal Affairs, Special Series on Fiscal Policies to Respond to COVID-19, October 13, 2020. https://oc-hub.org/community/resources/keeping-the-receipts-transparency-accountability-and-legitimacy-in-emergency-responses/.

Juven, Pierre-André, and Benjamin Lemoine. 2018. "Bankruptcy Politics: Public Services and the Law of Survival." *Actes de la recherche en sciences sociales* 1–2 (221–22): 4–19. https://doi.org/10.3917/arss.221.0004.

Laurent, Brice. 2017. *Democratic Experiments: Problematizing Nanotechnology and Democracy in Europe and the United States*. Cambridge, MA: MIT Press.

Lemoine, Benjamin. 2016. "The Politics of Public Debt Structures: How Uneven Claims on the State Colonize the Future." *Near Futures Online*, 1 (March). http://nearfuturesonline.org/the-politics-of-public-debt-structures-how-uneven-claims-on-the-state-colonize-the-future/.

Levy-Mozziconacci, Annie, Évelyne Mesclier, and Pascale Metzger. 2020. "Les sciences sociales à l'écart de la gestion de crise sanitaire." *Libération*, October 14, 2020. https://www.liberation.fr/debats/2020/10/14/les-sciences-sociales-a-l-ecart-de-la-gestion-de-crise-sanitaire_1802237/.

Mitchell, Timothy. 2002. *The Rule of Experts: Egypt, Techno-Politics, Modernity*. Berkeley: University of California Press.

Munevar Daniel. 2020. "Arrested Development: International Monetary Fund Lending and Austerity post COVID-19." Eurodad, Briefing paper, October 2020. https://www.eurodad.org/arrested_development.

Potts, Shaiana. 2017. "Deep Finance: Sovereign Debt Crises and the Secondary Market 'Fix.'" *Economy and Society* 46 (3-4): 452–75. https://doi.org/10.1080/03085147.2017.1408215.

Rivié, Milan. 2020. "6 Months after the Official Announcements of Debt Cancellation for the Countries of the South: Where do we Stand?" Committee for the Abolition of Illegitimate Debt, September 18, 2020. https://www.cadtm.org/spip.php?page=imprimer&id_article=18948.

Rouaud, Pierre-Olivier. 2021. "Chad: 1st Country in COVID Era to Ask for Restructuring of its Debt." *Africa Report*, February 3, 2021. https://www.theafricareport.com/62933/chad-1st-country-in-covid-era-to-ask-for-restructuring-of-its-debt/.

RP. 2020. "Comment on 'The "Necessity" Defense in Sovereign Debt Cases' by Mitu Gulati." Credit Slips, January 29, 2020. https://www.creditslips.org/creditslips/2020/01/the-necessity-defense-in-sovereign-debt-cases.html.

Schmitt, Carl. (1922) 2005. *Political Theology: Four Chapters on the Concept of Sovereignty*. Translated and with an introduction by Georg Schwaab. Foreword by Tracy B. Strong. Chicago: University of Chicago Press.

Shearman & Sterlin. 2020. "COVID & International Investment Protection," *Perspectives*, April 14, 2020. https://www.shearman.com/perspectives/2020/04/covid-19-international-investment-protection.

Théret, Bruno. 2021. "De la crise financière à la crise sanitaire: un aller-retour?" In *COVID-19: Regards croisés sur la crise*, edited by Bruno Bouchard and Djalil Chafai, 71–73. Parisé Université Paris Dauphine–PSL.

Thjoernelund, Marie Christine Hoelck. 2009. "State of Necessity as an Exemption from State Responsibility for Investments." *Max Planck Yearbook of United Nations Law Online* 13 (1): 421–79. https://doi.org/10.1163/18757413-90000045.

Waibel, Michael. 2007. "Two Worlds of Necessity in ICSID Arbitration: CMS and LG&E." *Leiden Journal of International Law* 20 (3): 637–48.

Wallace, Rob, Alex Leibman, Luis Fernando Chaves, and Rodrick Wallace. 2020. "COVID-19 and Circuits of Capital." *Monthly Review* 72 (1).

Weidemaier, Mark. 2020. "Further Thoughts on Necessity as a Reason to Defer Sovereign Debt Obligations." *Credit Slips* (blog), April 23, 2020. https://www.creditslips.org/creditslips/2020/04/further-thoughts-on-necessity-as-a-reason-to-defer-sovereign-debt-obligations.html.

Weidemaier, W. Mark C., and Mitu Gulati. 2020a. "Necessity and the COVID-19 Pandemic." *Capital Markets Law Journal* 15 (3): 277–83. https://doi.org/10.1093/cmlj/kmaa013.

Weidemaier, Mark, and Mitu Gulati. 2020b. "Necessity in the Time of COVID-19." Credit Slips, April 21, 2020. https://www.creditslips.org/creditslips/2020/04/necessity-in-the-time-of-covid-19.html.

CHAPTER 3

Ad Hoc Generosity in Times of COVID

A Chronicle of Plights, Hopes, and Deadlocks

Lena Lavinas

January 2020: Year I of the Pandemic. Policy responses to address the COVID outbreak have mostly been ad hoc measures and have generally worked at the margins of social protection systems. A first glance indicates that multibillion-dollar emergency relief packages have privileged transitory budgets and programs rather than reinforcing welfare institutions that have faced decades of defunding and discrediting. Might these ad hoc measures be a way of preventing postcrisis trajectories from reinforcing social and economic rights and reversing the current social order so steeped in market fundamentalism and the cult of individual agency? If so, the strategies that have been used might make it easier to impose new rounds of austerity once the worst of the COVID crisis has passed, diminishing the chances of strengthening public systems of provision (Bayliss and Fine 2020) and putting redistribution at the top of the agenda.

The actions of states during the pandemic have largely been oriented toward preserving employment and earnings through direct payments. Furlough schemes and short-lived stipends were "fast-tracked" to prevent acute poverty and guarantee a minimum income to those forced out of their jobs. As these were not customary measures, not only did the monetary value of the benefits often greatly exceed that paid by regular anti-poverty schemes or unemployment insurance, but the number of recipients, earlier compressed by means-testing rules and other eligibility criteria, also increased sharply. Voices who had pushed for austerity and conditionality at all times in the past changed their tune and called for universal basic income schemes everywhere — if not forever, then at least temporarily (*Financial Times* 2020b). All at once, generous emergency stimulus payments turned into the blueprint for fighting the economic fallout of the pandemic.

Consequently, fiscal and monetary orthodoxy that previously constrained public spending, greatly reducing the power of social policies, started being relaxed, while mounting public deficits became accepted, breaking a venerable norm. Worldwide central banks stepped in to provide liquidity, slashing interest rates even further and supporting immense credit flows as stock markets plummeted drastically amid the turmoil. After four decades of neoliberalism, it has become clear that austerity policies have ravaged public service provision through severe budget cuts and waves of privatization. Financial markets have taken over, providing private health insurance, fully funded pension schemes, student loans, and consumer credit to offset low and stagnating earnings and cutbacks in welfare benefits. If COVID provoked a grand rupture, it also seemed to offer a glimmer of hope about the possibility of reckoning with clearly broken social provisions. Seeking better to understand what has unfolded in this space of possibility, I systematically compiled media and academic reports of government crisis responses in the realm of social protection. Together, they allow an account to emerge — of facts, hopes, and frustrations at this critical moment, nurturing visions of a neoliberal dusk. The aim of this chapter is to challenge the sufficiency of the ad hoc rescue and recovery policies that have prevailed in the fight against the coronavirus pandemic from January 2020 to January 2021, when the vaccination rollout finally began. I argue that, although strikingly generous at first sight and often novel in scope and scale, policy responses to the pandemic, and the profound disruptions it provoked, unveiled more than addressed the entrenched cracks in welfare regimes that have exacerbated social vulnerability and the discrediting of the common good over the last few decades. To envision the potential legacy of the corona crash (Blakeley 2020) in transforming social welfare policies, I here examine what has been the essence and extent of emergency programs in providing immediate relief, if they have cohered with existing social protection edifices, and what new social schemes or progressive policies have sprung up in the wake of COVID.

Nations worldwide have put forward a wide variety of initiatives, in distinct fields, which are impossible to fully track. In this chapter, I focus on a handful of countries, among them the United States (US), Brazil, and the United Kingdom (UK), and follow up on what state interventions have featured from year I to year II of the pandemic. These countries reflect a diversity of welfare regimes that range from more universal to more residual systems of provision. However, taken together they speak to the global convergence in patterned social policy responses to the COVID pandemic around the guarantee of liquidity to preserve the integrity of financialized markets. In this sense, it expands upon the policy arsenal first rehearsed after the 2007–8 global financial crisis, only here so as to include social policy in addition to dovish monetary policy to respond to the specter of systemic market failures. In short, I am interested in whether lavish "ad hoc" measures, in the midst of a structural crisis, indicate a transition to sturdier and more dignified social policies, and in what direction they might promote change.

This introduction briefly contextualizes the economic blow of the coronavirus and positions the objectives of the chapter. The second section depicts relief and emergency programs that were enacted to mitigate the consequences of the economic fallout, exploring their reach. Following this, section three analyzes whether governments are reframing their interventions to open the possibility for more far-reaching reforms in the post-pandemic period, or whether they are just planning a return to normalcy, that is, back to preexisting norms and practices that already failed to respond to the needs and expectations of people. The conclusion offers some insights into the significance of these all-encompassing measures drafted to address old and new challenges in social policy.

Unfolding "Ad Hoc" Programs

In her last book, Wendy Brown (2019: 27) defined the social as "where citizens of vastly unequal backgrounds and resources are potentially brought together and thought together. It is where we are politically enfranchised and gathered (not merely cared for) through provision of goods." However, as soon as it struck, the pandemic seemed to contradict the possibility of such a social realm defined by the common good. Quickly, it became clear that individual strategies taking shape according to income-linked opportunities would prevail and deepen the social divide.

In the US, the better-off created huge traffic jams in their rush to escape from big cities devastated by the virus, heading to their country homes or to newly rented accommodations where they would confine themselves safely. Meanwhile, millions more were queuing in their "still-paying-off-the-loan" cars to obtain supplies at food banks on the outskirts of cities. The same scene was repeated at the doors of food aid charities in the UK, overwhelmed by growing numbers of families facing food shortage. One of the immediate consequences of shutting down economies and the constraints of social isolation was an uncontrolled surge in food insecurity.

The pandemic immediately exposed the vulnerability of low-wage and front-line workers, many of whom were forced to resort to food banks given the weakening of food supply chains and the impossibility of their continuing to live paycheck to paycheck. At the food banks, they joined welfare recipients and those who usually do not qualify for social assistance: the typical beneficiaries of food charities. In a short time, however, middle-class families came to thicken the rows of those struggling to feed themselves — dubbed "the newly hungry" (Butler 2020). Having lost jobs and income, and being highly indebted with mortgages, loans, rents, medical bills, and the like, the easy and often unique way to squeeze the family budget was to slash food expenditures and rely on donations. As Matthew Desmond (2020) puts it, "the rent eats first, even during a pandemic." In the US, millions of children who depend on school-provided meals saw their already precarious nutritional situation aggravated due to school shutdowns.

In the UK, where the number of people earning below the minimum wage has risen more than fivefold due to reduced pay (Partington 2020), public authorities had to revise their tight budgets to provide a greater number of free school meals and expand holiday hunger schemes to ensure children would be spared severe food insecurity. To fight food hardship, the US enacted the Pandemic Electronic Benefit Transfer (Dean et al. 2020) from March 2020, an emergency federal program aimed at guaranteeing lump-sum payments to thirty million children previously eligible for free or reduced-price meals at school, encompassing those living in households that fell into poverty. The program was optional for states, which would be required to assume half of the costs. The monthly amount ranged from USD 250–450 per child in grocery benefits, reaching a total of USD 10 billion.

In Brazil, the federal government deliberately ignored the latent food crisis prior to the pandemic (a reversal of its own food security policies): in 2017 and 2018, only 63.3 percent of all Brazilian households had adequate food security (IBGE 2017–18), as compared to 77.4 percent in 2013 (IBGE 2013). During the pandemic, food security indicators deteriorated further: at least 10.3 million people — 5 percent of Brazilians — are suffering from severe food insecurity. Private donations to local food banks doubled but were nevertheless insufficient and too erratic to mitigate the crunch. No coordinated public action was taken to cope with mounting hunger other than sending extraordinary funding to municipalities, with no strings attached. Most of the time, the resources were used in a discretionary way by mayors, without commitment to food security.

Overall across the different countries I examined, emergency measures translated into providing cash to poor families and the unemployed, in addition to extending furlough schemes to preserve formal jobs and small businesses. Two main dimensions of these packages consisted of, first, special loans offered to small and mid-size firms to maintain employment and wages; and, second, unconditional monetary transfers to eligible households and individuals at risk.

One of the key provisions included in the nearly two-trillion-dollar Coronavirus, Aid, Relief, and Economic Security (CARES) Act[1] adopted in the US — the largest rescue package ever at that time — was the Paycheck Protection Program (PPP). Designed to last for two months, it was comprised of loans to help small businesses and nonprofits cover payroll and benefits expenses and avoid layoffs. Forgivable loans were also offered to millions of small businesses. A budget over USD 600 billion was allocated to the program (US Department of Treasury n.d.). More than five million companies received PPP loans that contributed to increase aggregate private employment by around 2.3 million workers, demonstrating that the program indeed boosted employment at eligible firms. Additionally, 1.5 million jobs were saved (Autor et al. 2020). The unemployment rate dropped from a peak of nearly 15 percent (30.3 million unemployed) in late April 2020 to close to 10 percent in July.

---

1. The CARES Act of March 25, 2020, was a bipartisan bill encompassing a wide array of provisions, from loans to labor-related assistance, to direct payments to families, changes in student loans rules, and health expenditures (US Department of Treasury n.d.).

The US has no national and unified unemployment insurance system, but rather fragmented schemes in each of the fifty-three states and territories that operate with their own rules and procedures, and often rule out various categories of workers. The weekly benefit amount also varies significantly (it barely replaces 45 percent of workers' earnings) and averages USD 330 per week (Bernard and Lieber 2020). To compensate for the absence of a comprehensive national system, two important short-term relief programs have thus been crafted to supplement income benefits. The Federal Pandemic Unemployment Compensation granted an extra USD 600 per week, for four months, for all those eligible for state unemployment benefits, whatever the amount (no income cap). In addition, the Pandemic Unemployment Assistance was tailored to gig, low-paid, part-time workers, and the self-employed and included an extra USD 600 a week. Both benefits also covered those diagnosed with COVID or who needed to care for a family member who had it. The former has reached thirty-one million jobless and the latter, in the range of five to ten million. Finally, the US Congress enacted a one-time stimulus payment of USD 1,200 to single adults with an annual income lower than USD 77,000.[2] Between that level and an annual income of USD 99,000, the benefit amount dropped proportionally until it reached zero.

In Brazil, the far-right government of Jair Bolsonaro, following in Donald Trump's steps, acted recklessly in denying the severity and extent of the coronavirus pandemic. It practically restricted its intervention to the creation of a single relief program. In April 2020, due to initiative and pressure from Brazil's Congress, the federal government enacted the Emergency Basic Income Program. An individual benefit to the amount of BRL 600 (USD 120) was granted for five months, then extended for another three months at half its original value (BRL 300 or USD 60) for 67.2 million people, including Bolsa Família recipients,[3] the unemployed, and all sorts of precarious and informal workers over eighteen years of age with a per capita household income below half the minimum wage of BRL 500 (around USD 100). One of the new features of the Emergency Basic Income Program was the doubling of the benefit value from BRL 600 (USD 120) to BRL 1,200 (USD 240) for single mothers. That expanded benefit, paid to about eleven million poor women, corresponds to six times the average monthly stipend of

---

2. An additional USD 500 was granted for every child aged 16 and under.
3. Bolsa Família is Brazil's flagship anti-poverty cash transfer program.

the Bolsa Família Program and is greater than the current minimum wage. It was the first time that Brazil had set the bar so high regarding compensatory benefits.

The program's expenditure amounted to BRL 293.1 billion (USD 58.5 billion) in 2020, ten times Brazil's previous annual spending on anti-poverty schemes and 4.1% of the GDP. Such atypical and high spending was only possible because the government declared a state of emergency, which allowed an increase in public spending that had been frozen in real terms since 2016.[4] Other measures to preserve jobs, similar to the furlough schemes implemented in many other countries, were taken, including a program to effectively suspend labor contracts and reduce working hours and wages until December 2020 (amounting to BRL 33 billion or USD 6 billion). It is said that 1.4 million companies and 9.7 million workers were covered by these agreements. Both provisions were part of a fiscal stimulus package to the amount of BRL 604 billion (USD 110 billion),[5] approved in April 2020. Nevertheless, a preliminary account released by the Department of Treasury shows that not all of its budget has been executed (TNT 2021).

In the UK, too, an extensive furlough scheme to the amount of USD 102 billion, supporting up to a third of the labor force at the height of the lockdown, covered 80 percent of employee wages up to USD 3,200 (Statista 2021). In nine months, 9.9 million jobs from 1.2 million employers were furloughed as a result of the Coronavirus Job Retention Scheme. Moreover, a Self-Employment Income Support Scheme was put forward to assist those not in salaried relations. Simultaneously, the British government added the equivalent of USD 25 per week to the standard benefit paid under the Universal Credit scheme — the British means-tested safety net that covers the working poor and the unemployed — and suspended conditionalities in relation to work requirements and other controls. These measures are temporary and are planned

---

4. In Brazil, a state of emergency allows extraordinary spending, suppressing the 2016 cap imposed by constitutional amendment that impedes any real increase in social spending until 2036 regardless of economic growth or rise in tax revenues. This is the most draconian measure enacted by the ultraliberal right-wing majority running Congress since former president Dilma Rousseff's impeachment.
5. This fiscal package also included funding for subnational entities and for the health-care sector, financial support for the tourist sector, loans to protect jobs and support the payroll.

to last for twelve months. The total number of those on Universal Credit practically doubled from 3 million in April to 5.8 million in November (Mackley and McInnes 2021).

Without a doubt all of these schemes contributed to lessen the impact of the pandemic on the lives of millions of people, for two reasons. First, they increased unemployment and welfare payments that had been previously capped through successive reforms driven by austerity policies and grounded in particular notions of fairness to taxpayers. The philosophy that had animated these reforms deemed generosity — that is, adequate assistance when necessary — harmful to the labor market, on the grounds that it would prevent jobless claimants and struggling families living on welfare from seeking jobs. The specter of the concepts of economic activation and meritocracy, inoculated in the design of the social policies of the 1990s era, created antibodies that still today hamper major progressive overhauls. Second, these ad hoc schemes have included many who were previously left out of recognition and entitlements. They lifted conditionalities and rigid eligibility criteria whose only purpose had been to curtail demand, making seeking support illegitimate and almost fraudulent and pushing claimants to accept the "bullshit jobs" (Graeber 2018) that have proliferated under finance-dominated capitalism.

But, conceptualized as temporary, these programs were designed with an expiration date and at the margins of the provisions offered by existing social protection systems. And precisely because of this, they have revealed how anachronistic and ineffective the current welfare regimes turned out to be due to cutbacks, defunding, conditionalities, rigidities, and the low value of benefits. The inadequacy of these regimes is all tied to a segmented risk coverage and provisions that were ineffective in filling the gaps of lifetime trajectories that are neither linear nor permanent.

One would hope that the uncontested evidence of the need for these emergency programs in order for the most vulnerable to balance on the tightrope — paying rents to avoid eviction and honoring debts to keep from going into debt (Lazzarato 2012; Lavinas 2020) — would prompt a revamp of social policies after the pandemic, beyond their exclusive focus on poverty. Rather than just addressing market failures, we would be rescuing the social to remake society.

However, criticism soon showered down on the short-lived "grace period" in which replacement incomes were so high that many recipients received more in benefits than in their former wages. A study by the University of Chicago (Ganong, Noel, and Vavra 2020), for example, claimed that 68 percent of unemployed workers under the Federal

Pandemic Unemployment Compensation program were in this situation, arguing that laid-off workers were being discouraged from returning to work after the pandemic. Sawo and Evermore (2020: 4), however, have disputed this claim, finding that "the majority of unemployed Americans could be doing worse, not better, financially in unemployment."

Likewise, in Brazil the emergency aid compensated for 45 percent of wage losses caused by the pandemic and, at the same time, increased the income of the poorest 10 percent of the country by about 2,000 percent. Furthermore, it reduced extreme poverty by half and brought inequality back to levels below those recorded during the Workers' Party administration (Lavinas and Araújo 2020). The enthusiasm with the extraordinary performance of this welfare program even had remarkable political impacts, stimulating an astonishing recovery of popularity for Bolsonaro's government in the most tragic and deadly phase of COVID. Even so, the Bolsonaro administration did not immediately extend the Emergency Basic Income Program after it ended in December. It has also been reluctant to expand the coverage and increase the stipend (which has not even been adjusted for past inflation) of the Bolsa Família Program. With the poverty headcount growing fast, the roster of Bolsa Família recipients is smaller at the outset of 2021 than it was in 2019, prior to the COVID outbreak. A lower take-up rate means growing levels of acute deprivation.

It is worth citing the case of Spain, which eschewed this ad hoc pattern by promoting innovations within its social security system. Indeed, soon after the pandemic hit, the left-wing coalition governing the country since January 2020 approved the creation of a new safety net, the Ingreso Minimo Vital, which guaranteed the right to a monthly benefit ranging from EUR 461 (USD 525) for singles to EUR 1,015 (USD 1,157) for households up to five members.[6] This social welfare reform benefited 850,000 families living below the poverty line at a cost of EUR 3 billion. It reinforced the pillars of social protection.

But elsewhere, the time frames of ad hoc programs are expiring exactly at the moment that countries face second waves of coronavirus infections with no end in sight, thwarting a speedy recovery. Instead of seeing a greater coordination between welfare regimes and the compelling and multifaceted needs of the population, what we see on the horizon is, once again, the adoption of wage-support plans and social-assistance schemes that are even shorter in length and more scaled back.

---

6. An extra EUR 139 (USD 158.5) is given to each additional member.

This is notably the case in the UK and Brazil, where by January 2021 programs were set to turn less generous or be discontinued altogether. The British government was planning to scrap the USD 25 a week uplift added to the Universal Credit,[7] affecting six million beneficiary families (Stewart 2021), squeeze the furlough scheme, and reduce payments of public sector salaries (Toynbee 2020). The retrenchment was seen as inevitable because the ongoing transformations in the labor market had already eliminated hundreds of occupations so that, it was said, there was no reason to continue to protect them. In Brazil, it took five months for the Bolsonaro government to extend the Basic Income Program, this time significantly reducing both coverage (from nearly seventy million recipients to only thirty-nine million) and the value of the benefit (only 40 percent of the original stipend). This downsizing occurred in spite of skyrocketing poverty and unemployment rates.

The Second Wave of COVID: Common and Divergent Response Paths Underway

The surge in infections and death tolls with COVID's second wave made it clear that abiding, unaddressed inequalities had amplified the risk factors that further penalized those deprived groups, poor communities, and ethnic minorities who were incapable of self-isolating. It also unveiled a large number of potential beneficiaries of government aid who had fallen through the cracks of the big relief packages. In Brazil, more than 1.3 million households living in extreme poverty failed to receive the income support (Lavinas 2021) that reached almost seventy million claimants at its peak.

In understanding this landscape one year into the pandemic, it is crucial to note that a significant number of people also committed part of the emergency financial aid to paying off and renegotiating debt, often leading to monthly deductions from these claimants' payments. Household debt, on the rise well before COVID, can explain this drift. Already in 2019 the British Office for National Statistics warned that a context of low unemployment, rising earnings, and economic growth had failed to prevent a steady rise in British household debt levels, which stood per capita at 133 percent of incomes in 2018 (Partington 2019). This

---

7. This extra USD 25 a week was also added to the basic element of the working tax credit.

paradox was explained by the constant increase in the cost of living — transportation, housing, food — which ended up pushing families to take on debts of mounting weight in their budgets. The financial strain provoked by debt repayments has somehow been overlooked as relief packages were laid out. Many of the clientele of social assistance continued for this reason to struggle to afford essential goods, despite the USD 25 a week COVID uplift, because they were repaying the Universal Credit advance loans they took out to cope with the crisis. According to a joint assessment carried out by five universities (Welfare at a Social Distance 2021), over 40 percent of Universal Credit recipients saw their incomes reduced after having to pay back benefit advances. In the UK, generosity did not include a temporary freeze on the debts owed to the state by those targeted for aid by the state. The sharp rise in debt renegotiation during the pandemic has been due to the substantial increase in the value of temporary benefits and to the easy access to loans facilitated by historically low interest rates.

Brazil offers another example. With cash flowing and consumption constrained by lockdowns, credit concessions in order to recompose previous debts — although partial — increased 72.2 percent over 2019 levels (BCB 2020). Not only have state-supported income schemes boosted bankarization, with ten million new accounts being opened in order to receive financial aid, but levels of indebtedness also rose: by the end of 2020, the share of disposable household income[8] engaged in paying off debts to the financial sector surpassed the 50 percent bar for the first time ever (BCB 2020).

The US, for its part, witnessed a shift in the profile of household borrowing from cars, student loans, and consumer credit toward mortgages, breaking records and fueling a housing boom. This was mainly due to government aid and forbearance programs for loans on those same items. Although an uptick in mortgage loans also occurred in Brazil, slightly more than 50 percent of outstanding loans to families in 2020 (BCB 2020) still consisted of consumer credit. People borrowed and spent as they pleased, which underlies the fact that temporary wage-support programs and welfare schemes, though crucial, fell short of reversing trends that have long debilitated working families financially. This continues a dangerous pre-pandemic trend of treating social policy as a means of

---

8. Share of household indebtedness to the national financial system in relation to disposable household income accumulated over the past twelve months. Disposable income means income post-transfer and taxes.

building up collateral (Lavinas 2020), which would grant access to a wide array of financial products and, consequently, fuel indebtedness. In this process, the burden of debt repayment could be loosened in some cases by permissions for new loans and loan extensions, that is, new conditions for being in debt.

On top of this, other mechanisms aimed at renegotiating debts have been expressly created. Student loan debt, which is a major concern in countries like the US, the UK, and Brazil, is among those categories considered for temporary relief. The American CARES Act introduced an important set of provisions that made it possible to pause payments and waive interest on student loans taken out with the federal government, as well as suspend penalties against borrowers in default, notably by stopping collection actions (NCSL 2020). About 95 percent of borrowers (or twenty-two million people) were covered by this measure, which was extended to last through the end of 2020. The suspension of payments on student loan debt, moreover, amounted to over USD 900 billion of the USD 1.4 trillion in debt held by the Education Department.

Similarly, Brazilian student borrowers benefited from a law passed by Congress in July 2020 that deferred payments (principal and interest) during the COVID emergency period, but only for those up to date on their payments or delinquent by less than 180 days. Therefore, the administrative forbearance through December 31, 2020, excluded and penalized over a million defaulted borrowers (40 percent). The law also provided for proportional discounts in moratorium charges for those who agreed to refinance their debt during the period the law was in effect.

But while a student debt forgiveness plan is being seriously considered in the US[9] (though, granted, such is excluded from Biden's COVID relief plan), in Brazil a similar plan seems totally out of line with the government's priorities, with the government instead opting for a restructuring of loans and terms. As in the US (Charron-Chenier et al. 2020), a student debt cancellation policy in Brazil would essentially favor lower-income and black and brown youth in particular, promoting racial

---

9. Democratic senators Bernie Sanders and Elizabeth Warren have campaigned for years for student debt forgiveness, but the Biden administration has not yet decided what form of debt cancellation would apply. One proposal envisions the cancellation of up to USD 50,000 in debt per borrower, whereas the incoming president seems to lean toward a more modest cutback of USD 10,000 and limited to those below a certain income threshold.

equality. In any case, the chances of full or partial debt cancellation being approved in Brazil, and even in the US, seem remote.

Zooming out even further to look at what the pandemic reveals about the wage and social protection architecture of these countries, the crisis has shown that millions of people are continuing to run up debts in order to make ends meet, either because their labor earnings or the social provisions to which they were entitled have proved largely insufficient.

The adequacy of benefits — in both their levels and design — and of minimum wages has come under scrutiny, yielding calls for a new generation of provisions to address both longstanding and fresh problems. What should be done with the 400,000 Americans who, discouraged, have dropped out of the labor force and might not remain eligible for unemployment insurance for long? Likewise, in Brazil, it is estimated that more than six million people have withdrawn from the labor market (IBGE 2019–20). Jobs that at first seemed temporarily lost have been definitively phased out as the silent restructuring of labor markets has progressed, with no clear effort on the part of states to preserve human capital, an asset supposedly cherished by them. Since many of the unemployed are gig and low-skilled workers with backgrounds in the service and retail industries, their chances of returning to the labor market depend critically on a vigorous economic recovery, which promises to occur only gradually in these sectors.

Several traditional occupations may disappear, forcing workers to move into novel positions, especially with the shrinking of the service sector. Ambitious training policies are urgently needed to accommodate this transition and prevent people from being excluded from the labor force. Are such policies a priority? Will training be coupled with valuable income-support schemes, or will these schemes simply be framed as temporary short-term assistance and, for this reason, be rendered ineffective?

The improvement of unemployment insurance has failed to gain prominence in fiscal stimulus packages, and it is unlikely that such a key provision will be revalued and enlarged, given the deep economic contraction and the ongoing structural changes that the pandemic has exacerbated. The UK has set out a USD 3.8 billion plan to provide support for the unemployed, offering some 250,000 government-subsidized jobs. It remains to be seen whether such provisions are responding in advance to the need for boosting skilled labor or whether they are just upholding previously existing workfare schemes. In France, the 2021 unemployment insurance reform announced by President Macron is primarily intended to reduce benefits and slash spending (Hautefeuille 2021), so as to compel those out of work to accept any occupation and remuneration.

Without question, the largest failing in social provisions unmasked by COVID was the dimension of care.[10] Care has never been integrated into social protection systems as a right and has been relegated to the private sphere. When not exercised by women for free as a family assignment, or underpaid in the case of paid domestic work — often marked by racial exploitation — it became a market provision subject to the logic of profit. It is noteworthy that large financial corporations operate many of the long-term care facilities in high-income countries, filling the gap of state provision. In the US, about 70 percent of these facilities are for profit and owned by private equity groups. A study by Gupta et al. (2020) found that nursing home standards fall on average when under private equity ownership. Even before the health crisis began, federal lawmakers were investigating private equity companies with nursing home holdings, which "research has shown often provide worse care than not for profit facilities" (Flynn 2019). COVID cases and deaths in nursing homes in countries like France and the US have recorded rates much higher than those of the overall population. According to *The Times*' tracker (Silver-Greenberg and Harris 2020), 40 percent of all COVID-related deaths in the US until June 2020 occurred in institutions caring for the elderly and disabled, where the staff is generally insufficient, unprepared, overworked, and poorly paid, and where regulations are too slack. It is worth recalling that long-term care was removed from the Patient Protection and Affordable Care Act of 2010 (Obamacare) and residents in general pay for their care (private insurance Medicare or out-of-pocket) or are covered by Medicaid (long-term stays for poor people). Increased life expectancy, changing family profiles, and the absence of public provisions to meet the demands for old-age care have made private nursing homes a business worth millions.

The pandemic, however, uncovered a business model based on neglect and abandonment, which operated with a set of tax and legal advantages

---

10. The definition of "care," elaborated by feminists as a consequence of their reflection about interlocking forces of domination, presupposes labor of an affective and emotional nature, which espouses a concrete response for the needs of others. We can also define it as a relation of service, support, and assistance, implying a sense of responsibility vis-à-vis life and well-being (Hirata 2011).

outside the rules governing welfare institutions, particularly in the healthcare sector. Several abuses in these facilities were reported as the death toll soared. It was even revealed that residents considered less profitable were discharged without previous notice and sent to homeless shelters or other unsafe facilities to make room for more profitable patients with COVID or those who pay above-average fees.

Yet this "eldercide," as Gullette (2021) named it, was not only American; Europe, too, was swept by the same disaster. In December 2020, those housed in long-term care institutions in France accounted for more than four out of ten COVID-related deaths (Sanchez 2020). The French financial group Korian, publicly traded on Euronext and Europe's leader in running nursing homes and care clinics, has performed equally dismally in managing some three hundred Établissements d'Hébergements pour Personnes Âgées Dépendantes (EHPAD or lodging establishments for dependent elderly people) in France. This, however, did not stop the group from issuing follow-on shares amid the pandemic in order to expand its capital and finance the acquisition of other large competitors in the sector.

It is not news that social provisions lie increasingly in the hands of large financial corporations, be they pension funds, insurance companies, or banks, whose returns are independent of the quality of the services provided. Still, it is disturbing that the deaths of and abuses against dependent elderly people have not prompted the immediate establishment of task forces to investigate the care system and enforce key principles of welfare regimes, the first being security. Security and prevention are foundational dimensions in any system of social provision, even those that are market-based, and, as a result, cannot be disregarded. The case of Korian indicates that there is, in the midst of the crisis, a process of concentration underway in the sector, which tends to reinforce the dominance of large private equity firms over hospitals, nursing homes, and geriatric and emergency services, without satisfactory control or compliance mechanisms to regulate their activity.

It is indisputable that the pandemic has changed social perceptions regarding caregivers, who previously toiled in invisibility and whose status was devalued. There is no way to predict whether this recognition will have practical consequences in their lives. The first should be a revaluation of their remuneration, to render it consistent with the irreplaceability of their work. Additionally, the essential workers who have heroically stood on the front lines in the fight against COVID may still not be receiving fair compensation. Aside from a few bonuses paid in appreciation for their dedication and their countless hours of unpaid work, the crisis has not, as a rule, led to a strong revaluation of wage floors. The battle for a significant increase in the real minimum wage has resumed.

In the US, the long-pending Democratic promise to raise the minimum wage from USD 7.25 to USD 15 an hour has been included in the fresh relief package pushed by the Biden administration. It would benefit twenty-seven million workers and pull about nine-hundred thousand out of poverty. This proposal has the greatest potential to immediately curtail food insecurity and the mounting debts of working families. At the same time, it would force the overhaul of welfare benefits, which would tend to slide to pre-pandemic levels after the expiration of extra unemployment payments and expanded safety nets. Given that a rise in wages would cause the number of welfare claimants to drop considerably, public expenditures on social assistance programs would also fall, making room for a revaluation of welfare benefits still compressed by caps.

In Latin American countries, the minimum wage has always stood out as one of the most effective instruments for addressing the income distribution. Its value, however, is currently beginning to lag given both inflation and fiscal rules such as Brazil's staggering spending cap, which has frozen public expenditures there for twenty years.

National minimum wages and national living wages are regulatory provisions that directly impact a country's degree of poverty, food insecurity, and inequality as measured by labor income, while additionally reducing public spending on welfare benefits and stimulating the search for paid jobs. Additionally, a substantial increase in the wage floor would contribute to radically lowering household indebtedness and allowing for the acquisition of essential goods. But traction on the minimum wage coming out of the crisis will depend, on the one hand, on whether the macroeconomic environment will incentivize states to stimulate recovery and, on the other, whether society will show itself capable of advocating for fair pay.

The old clash is once again on the table, between those who espouse fiscal austerity to prevent the return of inflation — the likelihood of which is already overplayed considering the magnitude of the economic downturn — and those who claim that spending should be kept high as long as the labor market and the economy remain anemic. Social provisions in the post-pandemic era, should they materialize, will reflect this cleavage and be shaped according to the prevailing monetary, fiscal, and tax policy options.

Concluding Remarks

The future of social protection systems is difficult to predict, and the paths out of the crisis may take varied routes. The structural weaknesses of welfare regimes tend to produce their fragmentation, creating unprotected voids and reproducing patterns of segregation. It is too early to say whether there will be a profound revalorization of social policies to compensate for the damage caused by the pandemic or to prevent future risks of equal lethality, already foretold in the context of the climate crisis.

With few exceptions — and the Biden administration is one such hopeful case — the generous ad hoc measures that prevailed as an immediate response to the pandemic are already being scaled down or suppressed. Welfare benefits are returning to their pre-pandemic thresholds, regulating levels of deprivation with no commitment to overcoming it. As vaccination campaigns advance, the parenthesis that opened a temporality wherein one's safety was reliant on everyone's safety is closed. For a moment we were all interconnected, and the idea that the future was common to us all seemed unquestioned — a sentiment that seems to be vanishing as normalcy returns.

At this beginning of year II of the pandemic, some common directions can be identified. One of them is the tendency to waive strict conditionalities previously imposed on welfare transfer recipients. That is not exactly a new development but a consequence of the proliferation of minimum-income programs worldwide. Checks can also now be issued more easily via cell phone applications and other controls enabled by new digital technologies.

Second, debt management has clearly become part of the set of social provisions. In extraordinary times, the state jumps in to regulate financial expropriation (Lapavitsas 2013) like it did in the past to oversee working-class conflicts. The first step consists of temporarily suspending the repayment of debts. In countries like Brazil and the US, student debt mortgage payments and evictions have been put on hold to make it easier for households to individually refinance their debts and redefine their relationships with the new providers of welfare. This was possible because governments unleashed floods of cash, resources that served to reduce household debt and the risk of default to financial institutions, rather than providing vulnerable households with food and access to other basic provisions. This is why the fight for debt cancellation is one of the most prominent battlefronts today in the opposition to contemporary finance-dominated capitalism. This is not an easy undertaking.

Among the crucial consequences of debt cancellation would be the securing of gains for debtors, the waiving off of liabilities, and the assumption of losses for asset holders. It would have the cascading effect of causing depreciations in securities and derivatives markets, which could further expose the holders of these assets to the debt of households and nonfinancial corporations and would ultimately endanger the institutional framework that supports financial accumulation and the expansion of fictitious capital.

Third, the flood of cash that has prevailed in COVID policy responses has given new life to the idea that the reorganization of social provisions should occur around the implementation of a universal basic income. Once again, this appears as the one-size-fits-all solution. Not long ago, in the aftermath of the 2008 financial crisis, the deterioration of living conditions for millions of people deprived of jobs and incomes also led to calls for social justice and a widespread interest in the universal basic income. This is a fresh wave. Civil society networks, politicians, policy makers, and scholars across the political spectrum are converging around a solution that is known to be extremely costly if the goal is to completely de-commodify the workforce. With a growing number of people not only unemployed but out of the labor market, it seems crucial to secure an income that guarantees a decent, coercion-free life for all in a market economy.

Despite all of this pressure, no government so far has moved toward adopting a universal basic income program. The most striking example is the American case. The socialist left of the Democratic Party, which had always supported the universal basic income, has concurred with proposals of the Biden administration that privilege job creation along with expanding paid leave for caretakers and introducing a European-style monthly child benefit. However, both are still temporary measures and not permanent provisions for ordinary times. Furthermore, the American Jobs Plan,[11] by which the Biden administration suggested creating jobs under a 2-trillion-dollar infrastructure program extended the notion of infrastructure to encompass the social, conceiving of in-home care as an essential dimension of welfare to be ensured to the elderly and the disabled. To this end it aimed to train and value

---

11. The American Jobs Plan, drafted to create jobs, bolster labor unions, and expand labor rights, has become the second part of President Joe Biden's Build Back Better package. It addresses physical infrastructure and the care economy and led to a bipartisan bill of USD 1.2 trillion in 2021.

care workers. Investments in childcare, preschools, and parental leave to stimulate women's employment are also foreseen in the American Family Plan.[12] Still, it is off the administration's agenda to move toward the public and universal health care system for which the socialist left would advocate.

In the face of a financialized capitalism that squeezes public provision, it is urgent to de-commodify the social reproduction of labor by ensuring that education, health care, childcare, training, housing, and other basic needs will also be fully de-commodified or at least made affordable to the majority. Otherwise cash transfers will serve as a powerful pro-market mechanism, providing collateral, underwritten by the state, for improving people's creditworthiness. Such a move would bolster income-related and highly segmented private services mostly through the financial sector, deepening household debt, discrimination, and inequalities.

The case for Universal Basic Services — a wide array of free basic services (health, social care, education), collectively generated, to serve the public interest (Gough 2019) — stimulates the imagination of those who understand that it is urgent to rethink the social by expanding the public, where collective solutions based on shared choices can meet individual needs. The redemption of public — rather than market-based — systems of provision is the order of the day.

Acknowledgements

This article has profited from the time I spent as a member of the School of Social Science at the Institute for Advanced Study in Princeton during the coronavirus outbreak. I am grateful to economist Pedro Rubin for assisting me in gathering data and information. Marcelo Coelho, Monica Herz, and Guilherme Leite Gonçalves offered generous insights. I am deeply grateful to Catherine Osborn for carefully revising the English manuscript.

---

12. The American Family Plan, which followed the American Jobs Plan, is now the third part of the Build Back Better agenda, and focuses on providing family services (childcare, parental leave, community colleges). It was budgeted at USD 1.8 trillion but has not yet been approved by Congress.

References

Autor, David, David Cho, Leland D. Crane, Mita Goldar, Byron Lutz, Joshua Montes, William B. Peterman, et al. 2020. "An Evaluation of the Paycheck Protection Program Using Administrative Payroll Microdata." Working paper, July 2020. http://economics.mit.edu/files/20094.

Bayliss, Kate, and Ben Fine. 2020. *A Guide to the Systems of Provision Approach: Who Gets What, How and Why*. Cham: Palgrave Macmillan.

BCB (Banco Central do Brasil). 2020. Times Series Data Base. Brasilia.

Bernard, Tara S., and Ron Lieber. 2020. "F.A.Q. on Stimulus Checks, Unemployment and the Coronavirus Plan." *New York Times*, March 28, 2020. https://www.nytimes.com/article/coronavirus-stimulus-package-questions-answers.html.

Blakeley, Grace. 2020. *The Corona Crash: How the Pandemic will Change Capitalism*. London: Verso.

Brown, Wendy. 2019. *In the Ruins of Neoliberalism: The Rise of Antidemocratic Politics in the West*. New York: Columbia University Press.

Butler, Patrick. 2020. "Growing Numbers of 'Newly Hungry' Forced to Use UK Food Banks." *Guardian*, November 1, 2020. https://www.theguardian.com/society/2020/nov/01/growing-numbers-newly-hungry-forced-use-uk-food-banks-covid.

Charron-Chenier, Raphaël, Louise Seamster, Tom Shapiro, and Laura Sullivan. 2020. "Student Debt Forgiveness Options: Implication for Policy and Racial Equity." Working Paper, Roosevelt Institute, August 14, 2020. https://rooseveltinstitute.org/publications/student-debt-forgiveness-options-implications-for-policy-and-racial-equity/.

Dean, Stacy, Crystal Fitzsimons, Zoë Neuberger, Dottie Rosenbaum, and Etienne Melcher Philbin. 2020. "Lessons from Early Implementation of Pandemic-EBT: Opportunities to Strengthen Rollout for School Year 2020–2021." Center on Budget and Policy Priorities, updated October 30, 2020. https://www.cbpp.org/research/food-assistance/lessons-from-early-implementation-of-pandemic-ebt.

Desmond, Matthew. 2020. "The Rent Eats First, Even During a Pandemic." *New York Times*, August 29, 2020. https://www.nytimes.com/2020/08/29/opinion/sunday/coronavirus-evictions-superspreader.html.

Flynn, Maggie. 2019. "Citing Quality Concerns, Senators Demand Answers from Major Private Equity Owners of Nursing Homes." *Skilled Nursing News*, November 19, 2019. https://skillednursingnews.com/2019/11/

citing-quality-concerns-senators-demand-answers-from-major-private-equity-owners-of-nursing-homes/.

Ganong, Peter, Pascal Noel, and Joseph S. Vavra. 2020. "US Unemployment Insurance Replacement Rates during the Pandemic." BFI Working paper, Becker Friedman Institute, August 24, 2020. https://bfi.uchicago.edu/working-paper/2020-62/.

Gough, Ian. 2019. "Universal Basic Services: A Theoretical and Moral Framework." *Political Quarterly* 90 (3): 534–42.

Graeber, David. 2018. *Bullshit Jobs: A Theory*. New York: Simon & Schuster.

Gullette, Margaret M. 2021. "American Eldercide." *Dissent Magazine*, January 5, 2021.

Gupta, Atul, Sabrina T. Howell, Constantine Yannelis, and Abhinav Gupta. 2020. "Does Private Equity Investment in Healthcare Benefit Patients? Evidence from Nursing Homes." NYU Stern School of Business, March 9, 2020, updated November 16, 2020. http://dx.doi.org/10.2139/ssrn.3537612.

Hautefeuille, Cécile. 2021. "La réforme de l'assurance-chômage donne la priorité à la baisse des allocations." *Mediapart*, February 19, 2021. https://www.mediapart.fr/journal/economie/190221/la-reforme-de-l-assurance-chomage-donne-la-priorite-la-baisse-des-allocations?onglet=full.

Hirata, Helena. 2011. "Le Travail du care pour les personnes âgées au Japon." *Informations Sociales* 6 (168): 116–22. https://doi.org/10.3917/inso.168.0116.

IBGE (Instituto Brasileiro de Geografia e Estatística). 2013. Pesquisa Nacional por Amostra de Domicílios. Rio de Janeiro.

IBGE. 2017–18. Pesquisa de Orçamentos Familiares. Rio de Janeiro.

IBGE. 2019–20. Pesquisa Nacional por Amostra de Domicílio Contínua. Rio de Janeiro.

Lapavitsas, Costas. 2013. *Profiting without Producing: How Finance Exploits Us All*. New York: Verso.

Lavinas, Lena. 2020. "The Collateralization of Social Policy by Financial Markets in the Global South." In *The Routledge International Handbook of Financialization*, edited by Philip Mader, Daniel Mertens, and Natascha van der Zwan, 312–23. London: Routledge.

Lavinas, Lena. 2021. "Latin America at the Crossroads yet Again: What Income Policies in the Post-pandemic Era?" *Canadian Journal of Development Studies* 42 (1–2): 79–89. https://doi.org/10.1080/02255189.2021.1890002.

Lavinas, Lena, and Eliane Araújo. 2020. "Programas de renda: entre renda mínima e renda universal, o Brazil na encruzilhada." *A Terceira Margem*, October 6, 2020. https://aterceiramargem.org/2020/10/06/programas-de-renda-entre-renda-minima-e-renda-universal-o-brasil-na-encruzilhada1/.

Lazzarato, Maurizio. 2012. *The Making of the Indebted Man: An Essay on the Neoliberal Condition*. Los Angeles: Semiotex.

Mackley, Andrew, and Roderick McInnes. 2021. "Coronavirus: Universal Credit during the Crisis." UK Parliament, January 15, 2021. https://commonslibrary.parliament.uk/research-briefings/cbp-8999/.

NCSL (National Conference of State Legislatures). 2020. "CARES Act Student Loan Fact Sheet." National Conference of State Legislatures, March 30, 2020. https://www.ncsl.org/Portals/1/Documents/statefed/Student-Loan-Fact-Sheet_v03.pdf.

Partington, Richard. 2019. "UK Households Lose Feelgood Factor Amid Rising Debt — ONS." *Guardian*, February 4, 2019. https://www.theguardian.com/uk-news/2019/feb/04/uk-households-lose-feel-good-factor-amid-rising-debt.

Partington, Richard. 2020. "Two Million in UK Paid below Minimum Wage since COVID Pandemic Began." *Guardian*, November 3, 2020. https://www.theguardian.com/uk-news/2020/nov/03/two-million-in-uk-paid-paid-below-minimum-wage-since-covid-pandemic-began.

Sanchez, Léa. 2020. "Les residents d'Ehpad représentent 44% des morts du COVID-19." *Le Monde*, December 3, 2020. https://www.lemonde.fr/les-decodeurs/article/2020/12/03/les-residents-d-ehpad-representent-44-des-morts-du-covid-19_6062084_4355770.html.

Sawo, Marokey, and Michele Evermore. 2020. "Unemployed Workers and Benefit 'Replacement Rate': An Expanded Analysis." National Employment Law Project — The Groundwork Collaborative, August 2020. https://groundworkcollaborative.org/resource/unemployed-workers-and-benefit-replacement-rate-an-expanded-analysis/.

Silver-Greenberg, Jessica, and Amy J. Harris. 2020. "'They Just Dumped Him like Trash': Nursing Homes Evict Vulnerable Residents." *New York Times*, June 21, 2020. https://www.nytimes.com/2020/06/21/business/nursing-homes-evictions-discharges-coronavirus.html.

Statista. 2021. "Cumulative number of jobs furloughed under the job retention scheme in the United Kingdom between April 20, 2020 and August 14, 2021." Statista, September 2021. https://www.statista.com/statistics/1116638/uk-number-of-people-on-furlough/.

Stewart, Heather. 2021. "Scrap Benefits Cut to Stop Milli9ons Falling into Poverty, Boris Johnson Told." *Guardian*, January 18, 2021. https://www.theguardian.com/society/2021/jan/18/boris-johnson-cannot-level-up-if-he-cuts-universal-credit-top-up-says-thinktank.

TNT (Tesouro Nacional Transparente). 2021. "Monitoramento dos Gastos da União com combate à COVID-19." Tesouro Nacional Transparente, September 17, 2021. https://www.tesourotransparente.gov.br/visualizacao/painel-de-monitoramentos-dos-gastos-com-covid-19.

Toynbee, Polly. 2020. "By Freezing Pay and Benefits, Sunak Will Be Levelling Down, Not Up." *Guardian*, November 24, 2020. https://www.theguardian.com/commentisfree/2020/nov/24/sunak-austerity-raising-taxes-tories.

US Department of Treasury. n.d. "Assistance for American Families and Workers." US Department of the Treasury. https://home.treasury.gov/policy-issues/cares/assistance-for-american-workers-and-families.

Welfare at a Social Distance. 2021. "Accessing Social Security and Employment Support during the COVID-19 Crisis and its Aftermath." Welfare at a Social Distance. https://www.distantwelfare.co.uk/the-research.

CHAPTER 4

Gifts, Grifts, and Gambles

The Social Logics of the Small Business Administration Relief Loan Programs

Sarah Quinn

The numbers were grim. In March of 2020, the stock market tumbled as a record bull market, already shaken by an oil price war, now crashed into a global pandemic and mass lockdown (*Financial Times* 2020; Wells 2020). As social distancing measures disrupted factory floors, global supply chains seized up, and entire industries — leisure, hospitality, transportation — buckled (Falk et al. 2021). In the United States (US), 3.3 million business owners exited the market between February and mid-April, a trend that was particularly devastating to business owners of color; while 17 percent of white business owners reported shuttering their doors, the drop was 41 percent for Black business owners (Fairlie 2020). In March alone 11.4 million people lost their jobs, over five million of which were hotel, food, or retail workers (BLS 2020), with Black and Latine, and teenage workers hit hardest (Fairlie, Couch, and Xu 2020). An economist told the *Washington Post* that she started shaking when she saw that ten million people had applied for unemployment insurance in March. She went on to predict that unemployment would double again by mid-summer (Long 2020); it took less than a month. By April, twenty-six million Americans filed for unemployment insurance, the equivalent a decade's worth of job growth (Iacurci 2020). With the specter of the next Great Depression looming, governments around the world snapped into action.

In all nations, government responses to the global crisis involved some mobilization of existing institutions (Capano et al. 2020). This chapter examines one part of how this worked in the US: the use of the Small Business Administration (SBA) to provide loans that could be forgiven as long as a large portion of the funds went toward payroll. The idea was to prevent joblessness before it started by protecting the small businesses that employ half the US workforce. Yet despite being touted as a life preserver for the nation's most vulnerable and imperiled businesses, the initial rollout of funds systematically advantaged larger, wealthier companies and businesses owned by white people (Hopkins, Johnston, and Rebala 2020).

The SBA loan programs were a state policy of historic proportions. They presented vast opportunities for businesses to survive but also for obfuscation and fraud. They generated a plethora of risks and uncertainties that were disproportionately borne by the most vulnerable businesses, workers, and people of color — the very groups for whom the programs were purportedly designed. Attention to the historical antecedents reveals that these complications were both precedented and predictable. This chapter draws from news reports to reflect on the social logics of the program rollout. For analytical purchase, I discuss the loans as straightforward gift, an opportunity for grift, or a terrible gamble for its intended beneficiaries, though for most people interaction with the program entailed some admixture of all three elements. I conclude that rather than seeing the program's flaws as exceptional or unforeseeable outcomes, we should see them as emblematic of credit programs as a whole, both in terms of their legacy of reproducing inequality and in terms of the complex style of statecraft of which they are a part.

The Historical Context: Why Loans Are a Favored Policy Tool

Credit allocation as a form of disaster support, crisis management, and economic policy has a long history in the US. In other work (Quinn 2019) I trace their origins to the founding era and argue that generations of US lawmakers, across political divides, have turned to credit allocation as a mode of policy making in search of ways to govern an intensely divided populace from within a fragmented political system marked by dispersed power and multiple veto points. In this rocky political landscape, groups that oppose government expansion have an advantage because it is easier to use veto points to prevent new policies than to make them. This has not stopped the US government from expanding but has rather given rise to a particular style of statecraft that relies heavily on partnerships, delegation, tax expenditures, nudges, and credit allocation (Mayrl and Quinn 2016). Market-based policy tools and public-private partnerships advantage business elites and shift risks from states to households. In other nations these features came to prominence after the neoliberal turn of the 1970s (see, for example, Braun et al. 2018; Crouch 2011; Lavinas 2017; Soederberg 2014; Streeck 2014). In the US, they have much deeper roots.

I use the term "political lightness" to summarize a set of qualities or tendencies that help make credit allocation a popular form of governance in the US. Credit programs can avoid or minimize the need to go through appropriations because they can be set up in ways to minimize costs, including being set up off budget, using revolving funds, and relying on guarantees. The US has long provided credit support through guarantees and incentives to private lenders rather than via the direct provision of loans. This allows for cost sharing with private entities and has frequently justified off-budget status and various accounting tricks (Quinn 2017). Since the early twentieth century, credit programs have worked like tax expenditures in that they are more likely to appeal to conservatives as a market-friendly policy form (Ellis and Faricy 2021). In general, credit programs enable a kind of polyvocality that is useful in political contexts, since conservative politicians can plausibly claim that they are solving problems while also deferring to private markets. This duality means that government officials can cater to different audiences by emphasizing different aspects of the policy, alternately playing up private players and market forms on one hand and government intervention on the other, as preferred. Lawmakers of various stripes use the fiscal, budgetary, ideological, and semiotic flexibility of credit programs in various ways to bridge political divides or avoid them entirely.

The SBA coronavirus-crisis loans are rooted in this tradition, and many of the program's eventual problems have historical precedent. The COVID credit programs were organized primarily through the SBA, an agency that was founded as a spinoff of the Reconstruction Finance Corporation (RFC), the legendary financial machine behind the New Deal. Mired in scandal and accusations of in-dealing by the 1950s, the RFC was dismantled under Eisenhower, but many of its functions lived on in other corners of the US federal government (in some cases having been spun off years earlier), such as the Export-Import Bank, the Commodity Credit Corporation, and Fannie Mae. The early SBA included RFC lending officers and took over the work of business lending. The SBA and the RFC both had a long history of critique. From the right, they faced accusations of being inefficient, error-prone, and a quasi-state-socialist experiment (Bean 2001). From the left, they have been attacked for being a form of welfare that helps larger firms at the expense of smaller ones.

The credit programs have enforced and extended racial inequality in the US. On the most foundational level, the long history of white supremacy has meant that white families are disproportionately likely to be business managers and owners, positioning them to disproportionally capture any windfalls generated in the US growth-based model of credit-fueled business development. Beyond this, the lending programs also have a direct history of discrimination against Black, Indigenous, and other borrowers of color. The housing insurance programs by the Federal Housing Administration and Department of Veterans Affairs are the most famous example, their redlining maps helping a generation of white families become wealth-holding homeowners while excluding others from access (Oliver and Shapiro 2006; Massey and Denton 1993; Thurston 2018). But the housing programs are far from alone in this history of racist discrimination. The federal farm loan programs have been derided as "the last plantation" for their long and enduring history of racist exclusion (Daniel 2013; Naylor 2010). The SBA programs also have a history of alternately excluding borrowers and underfunding ill-designed programs for minoritized borrowers (Baradaran 2017; Ture and Hamilton 1992). In view of this history of partnerships, complexity, polyvocality, and inequity, the most troubling aspects of the SBA rollout of March and April 2020 seem less surprising than they would otherwise.

The Policy Design

By mid-March Congress announced that it was in accelerated negotiations over an economic relief bill. In the US, even automatic stabilizers like unemployment insurance require additional congressional authorization when they ramp up (Rocco, Béland, and Waddan 2020). Democrats and Republicans fought over whether or how to shore up existing programs like unemployment insurance as they weighed new options. News reports of these negotiations speak to the useful *lightness of credit* as a policy tool. According to the *New York Times*, Democrats pushed for support for businesses and workers in the form of cash infusions through tax rebates or Treasury payroll processing, whereas "Republicans wanted to steer the program through private sector financial institutions. They won" (Cowley, Rappeport, and Flitter 2020). It is useful to note at this point that all lawmakers anticipated mass loan forgiveness, so private sector partnerships did not imply mass savings. It did, however, mean that the policy would bracket federal administrative capacity, defer to pro-market rhetoric, and reinforce the power of employers and lenders. The reliance on forgivable loans may not have been many Democrats' first choice, but it was an acceptable compromise (Mattingly, Foran, and Barrett 2020).[1] The primary sticking point in the subsequent negotiations over loans was not their use but their oversight. Republicans sought to hide disclosure of recipients (arguing that this would create more instability by stigmatizing the firms) and limit congressional control. Democrats countered that without disclosure and oversight the loans were effectively a slush fund and pushed for businesses owned by members of Congress and the presidential family to be excluded from eligibility entirely (Bresnahan, Levine, and Desiderio 2020; Bresnahan and Levine 2020). In all, the lending programs took a back seat to much more contentious negotiations over direct checks to families.

The Coronavirus Aid, Relief, and Economic Security (CARES) Act, to the value of USD 2 trillion, was signed into law on March 27, 2020 (for a useful summary, see Snell 2020).[2] Among its many provisions,

---

1. This political fragmentation has consequences far beyond the economic policy response. Philip Rocco, Daniel Béland, and Alex Waddan (2020) argue that the US's "patchwork" health programs are responsible for its record-breaking death toll.
2. Among its major provisions, the CARES Act paused repayments on government-held student loans; created a new tax credit for payroll costs; funded food programs (USD 8.8 billion); supplemented unemployment benefits and extended them to gig workers and freelancers (USD 260 billion); authorized relief checks for families (USD 300 billion); authorized funds for local and state governments (about USD 340 billion); and seeded an enhanced national public health response at (USD 100 billion). For larger midsize businesses too small to qualify for the Federal Reserve's existing credit facilities but too large for the SBA programs, the CARES Act provided USD 500 billion toward a new Federal Reserve-administered "Main

the act provided USD 17 billion in bridge loans for current SBA borrowers and added USD 10 billion to the Economic Injury Disaster Loans (EIDL) program, which forgives some smaller loans in low-income neighborhoods and requires collateral for loans greater than USD 25,000. The lending centerpiece of the CARES Act was the authorization of USD 349 billion in low interest loans, under radically new terms, through a new Paycheck Protection Program (PPP). Under the PPP, the SBA waived its requirements for credit worthiness, collateral, and fees. A company with five hundred or fewer employees could apply for loans at an extremely low interest rate of 1 percent, provided it attested that the loan was necessary for its survival. The loan amount could be up to two and a half times the company's monthly payroll, capped at USD 10 million per applicant. In the initial legislation, loans could be forgiven if 75 percent went to payroll over a defined period, with the rest of the funds put toward other qualifying overhead costs like rent and mortgage payments. Inside the SBA, leadership waived existing requirements for the disclosure of demographic information and potential conflicts of interest but kept in place rules excluding landlords, financial institutions, lobbyists, and felons from getting loans.

Four days after being signed into law, lenders were issuing PPP loans. It was a rushed, hectic rollout that involved last minute instructions from the SBA to lenders (Cowley, Rappeport, and Flitter 2020). Smaller banks led the way in the first days. In Oklahoma, for instance, BancFirst set up a "war room" where people worked "around the clock" to issue loans, whereas Citibank waited days to accept applications from small-business clients (Cowley, Rappeport, and Flitter 2020). Within thirteen days of the launch funds were depleted. Congress authorized another USD 310 billion and authorized more fintech lenders (Erel and Liebersohn 2020), and, in an effort to better reach out to underserved borrowers, earmarked USD 60 billion for rural and community development financial institutions (Flitter 2020). In December, Congress authorized another USD 284 billion in lending.

Congress touted the CARES Act loans as a way to prevent joblessness before it started by supporting the small businesses that employ half

---

Street Loan" program. The latter raises interesting questions about the blurring of fiscal and monetary policy, and the changing role of central banks (Braun 2021; Siegel 2020), but in order to keep the scope of this chapter focused, I hone in on the program most closely connected to the history of credit programs in the US, the SBA loans.

of the US workforce. Senator Marco Rubio called the program "an alternative for unemployment and to prevent unemployment," and Treasury Secretary Mnuchin referred to the PPP loans as "job retention loans" (Whoriskey 2020). This framing was both highly resonant and fundamentally at odds with parts of the policy design. Companies had to save jobs to get loan forgiveness but not to get the loans themselves, opening the door for companies to reap the advantage of obtaining an extremely low interest loan without keeping any employees. The term "small business" may invoke the image of the local mom-and-pop store but it often refers rather to larger "small" businesses that employ more people (Stewart 2020) and that the SBA is better positioned to assist. Moreover, for the PPP, entities like hotels and chain restaurants could apply through each subsidiary, a loophole that opened the door for well-financed larger companies to access the funds. Then there is the assumption, built into the framing, that the interests of business owners and employees are aligned. Some small-business owners immediately objected that the support forced them to pay employees who could not work instead of other overhead costs, like rent (Cowley, Rappeport, and Flitter 2020). In response to such objections, Congress later lowered the payroll requirement to 60 percent (Stewart 2020). The extent of the gap between the framing of the policy and the complex reality of its implementation would become clearer as the policy rolled out in early April 2020.

Varieties of Gifts

At a time when businesses were closing at a rapid clip, there was massive demand for access to the program. One article noted that the forgiveness provisions managed to "transform the government loan into a gift" (Whoriskey 2020). Of course, the gift was not just the forgiveness but the low interest loan itself. "The loans are essentially free money," explained one businessman. "They have rock-bottom interest rates and can be forgiven if, among other things, the borrower maintains the size of its work force" (Silver-Greenberg et al. 2020). Add to this the waiver of collateral and credit score requirements, and you have an incredible mobilization of state capacity, with the potential to transform access to credit for Americans who had long been denied such opportunities.

The rollout was fast but not fair. In the act, Congress had instructed the SBA to advise direct lenders to prioritize small businesses and underserved and rural markets, "including veterans and members of the military community, small-business concerns owned and controlled by socially and economically disadvantaged individuals, women, and businesses in operation for less than 2 years." But no such direction was issued in the first rollout, and by the time the SBA disclosed this, most of the initial funds were already spent (Hopkins, Johnston, and Rebala 2020; SBA Office of the Inspector General 2020). What had the banks done instead of reaching out to the underserved? Prioritize their existing customers, thus people who were already advantaged. Keybank went from providing about fifty SBA loans a month before the CARES Act to 37,000 loans in April 2020 alone by reaching out to existing customers first (Liu and Parilla 2020). Bank of America, which issued more loans than any other bank, committed USD 250 million (about 1 percent of the loans it processed) to other community development financial institutions that were to address the underserved and then *exclusively* served existing clients when handling the rest (Hopkins, Johnston, and Rebala 2020).

On the SBA website, the programs were discussed as "relief packages" (Tracy, Day, and Haddon 2020), but initial reports showed that many banks instead provided "concierge" service to their wealthiest clients (Flitter and Cowley 2020). Larger loans generated larger fees for the lenders (Entis 2020). At J P Morgan, customers who had USD 10 million or more in assets got personalized assistance while everyone else queued up. At the end of the first round, with funds rapidly depleted, 280,000 who applied for loans from J P Morgan did not get a loan (Silver-Greenberg et al. 2020). As the first two-week period came to a close, three quarters of the smallest companies who had applied (those who requested loans under USD 50,000) were left waiting for Congress to approve funding in the second round, in contrast to only one quarter of the largest applicants (those requesting loans above USD 5 million) (Hopkins, Johnston, and Rebala 2020). By November 2020, rural communities had received 15 percent of the loans and low- and moderate-income communities had received 30 percent of the loans (Popken and Lehren 2020b).

The use of existing customers and prioritization of the wealthiest customers meant that the gift of a PPP loan was given disproportionately to white borrowers over borrowers of color, even though Black-owned businesses were far more at risk of closure. Black-owned businesses tend to be smaller with thinner profit margins and fewer savings (Brooks 2020). They are also more likely to be situated in underbanked communities, especially those communities of color that had lost more bank branches in a wave of consolidation in the banking industry. Black business owners were also far less likely to have had recent contact with banks than white business owners (Mills 2020; Zhou 2020). One news report quoted Kenneth White, a banker who also serves as board chair of the Maryland Black Chamber of Commerce, saying: "A lot of minority people learned in this process that ... they really didn't have a [banking] relationship, and they didn't have anyone to call. They were left out in the cold" (Hopkins, Johnston, and Rebala 2020). There are a new set of lenders that utilize online and mobile financial technologies, called fintech, to compete with traditional banks and better reach borrowers of color. However, the SBA used these companies less before the onset of the program and did not approve online lenders right away (Liu and Parilla 2020). Waiving collateral and credit score requirements was of little use when the standards had already interrupted the banking relationship and existing ties were used as the basis for access.

This is not just an issue of social network ties, but ongoing discrimination against Black business owners in the administration of the PPP loans. The fact that the SBA, under the Trump administration, stopped collecting demographic data on these loans complicates efforts to measure this, but a matched-pair audit of PPP lenders in Washington DC found that potential borrowers who were Black received less information and more denials (Lederer et al. 2020; Liu and Parilla 2020). A national study found that only 12 percent of Black and Latine small-business owners received the full amount they requested (Color of Change 2020). This is particularly egregious given the context of the denials: *the program had already shifted all credit risk to the federal government through guarantees.* The timing adds insult to injury: between February and mid-April alone, a period that coincided with the initial rollout, 440,000 black business owners closed shop (Brooks 2020; Fairlie 2020).

It is true, as many people have pointed out, that the incredible speed with which this program was implemented caused some unavoidable problems in the rollout of the loans. But one must systematically ignore a long history of racist practices and differential impacts to imagine that the inequities of the PPP were an unforeseeable or exceptional circumstance.

Varieties of Grift

The unequal rollout raised questions about the ethics of the program design, which proved vulnerable to fraud of various types (Davis 2020).

Small-time crooks filed applications for companies that did not exist or formed companies just to get the loan and then spent lavishly on luxury purchases from Gucci and Dior, Lamborghini and Tesla (Billings 2020; Gregg 2020a). By January of 2021, the Justice Department charged fifty-seven people with attempting to secure USD 175 million in false loans (Gregg 2020a).

Other concerns about inappropriate behavior had to do with access to relief funds by the rich, powerful, and well-resourced. Recall that the main debate over the use of these loans leading up to the passage of the CARES Act had to do with oversight (Bresnahan, Levine, and Desiderio 2020). At that time government officials were banned from accessing corporate funds that ran through the Federal Reserve but not the SBA loans. Then during the first rollout, the SBA quietly waived disclosure rules for government officials and members of their households seeking to access loans (O'Connell and Gregg 2020). It was in this context, citing privacy concerns for borrowers, that Secretary to the Treasury Mnuchin insisted that the SBA did not need to disclose information about PPP recipients and, furthermore, that the administration had the power to supervise the CARES Act oversight report (O'Connell and Gregg 2020). Under mounting public pressure for disclosure, in July 2020 the SBA released details, but only about loans over USD 150,000. In November it finally released aggregate data on all SBA and EIDL loans in November, after a judge ruled in favor of a consortium of media outlets who had sued for access (O'Connell et al. 2020; Popken and Lehren 2020b).

As information about the loans was released, news media began reporting about questionable exchanges. The *Washington Post* identified at least seven businesses that had received over USD 150,000 in loans but that were owned by congressional representatives or their family members, including relations of representatives who helped write the ethics requirements for the bill (O'Connell et al. 2020). A Propublica investigation estimated that USD 21 million had flowed into businesses associated with Trump's family members and associates, including a hydroponic lettuce farm owned by Donald Trump Jr. (Gillum et al. 2020). Others noted that Trump donors and tenants of Trump-owned properties received coveted early PPP loans (Fang 2020; Popken and Lehren 2020a). While members of Congress argued that this was all above board, watchdog groups questioned the ethics of allowing potential borrowers to design the legislation, or of allowing relatives of government officials to benefit from a program, when the administration fought so hard against transparency and oversight (Gregg 2020b).

A related issue had to do with large PPP loans issued to well-resourced companies that were large, had alternative sources of funding, participated in stock buybacks, or fired employees. PPP loans were officially capped at USD 10 million, but firms could apply through multiple subsidiaries. The Omni hotel chain, for example, received USD 76 million through thirty-two separate hotels, in some cases making pledges to save jobs that were then abandoned (O'Driscoll 2020). The *New York Times* reported that it "identified roughly a dozen publicly traded companies that had recently boasted about their access to ample capital — and then applied for and received millions of dollars in the federal loans" (Silver-Greenberg et al. 2020). Some first round loans went to private equity-backed companies like the restaurant chains P. F. Chang's and Silver Diner (O'Connell et al. 2020). Restaurant chain Shake Shack was shamed into returning a USD 10 million loan and steakhouse chain Ruth's Chris into paying back USD 20 million in loans secured through two subsidiaries (Tracy, Day, and Haddon 2020; Popken 2020). Other companies accepted loans only to turn around and purchase stock buybacks, settle multimillion dollar court cases, pay down existing debts, or purchase other firms. One company that received a USD 1.4 million loan paid its chief executive officer USD 1.7 million a mere week later (Gregg 2020b; Silver-Greenberg et al. 2020). This was technically legal, since there were no restrictions on how companies used their non-PPP funds, and companies only had to attest in their application that they needed the funds to support ongoing operations in the climate of economic uncertainty (Gregg 2020b). While news media was full of quotes from small-business owners wringing their hands for fear that even if they got a loan it might not be forgiven, wealthier firms were happy to take advantage of an opportunity to get a low interest, 1 percent loan, forgiven or not.

At the time of writing, it is still unclear how many of these loans will be forgiven, or the long-term consequences of these practices. Still, these reports suggest that the big grift here was political in nature — the promotion of a policy as a boon for smaller companies that then gave preferential treatment to firms that were likely to need the support the least.

Varieties of Gambles

The decision to arrange support through loans rather than separate grant programs for businesses and workers added uncertainty to the question of who would get relief and under what terms. In the first two weeks of the rollout, a time when business failures were at their height, small-business owners had little information about whether they would be able to access the funds at all. Business owners reported long waiting times, confusing forms, and unreturned calls from lenders (Stewart 2020). As the Center for Public Integrity noted (Hopkins, Johnston, and Rebala 2020), from the perspective of small-business owners without legal support, the PPP was opaque and confounding. This was a particular problem for Black borrowers who were less likely to have existing relationships with banks to help push them ahead in the line.

Whether a company would get approved for the loan was one uncertainty among many for borrowers. There was widespread confusion reported among potential borrowers who worried whether they could trust that the loan would be forgiven, whether they would be hit with a large tax bill, or whether they would be saddled with debt if the company did not survive in any case. By May, there were days when more money was being returned to the program than borrowed. Reporting on this, the *New York Times* quoted Shelly Ross, an owner of a cat-sitting service that had borrowed USD 75,000: "I cried the day I sent it back. I thought this would save my business, but I was worried about being financially ruined if it wasn't forgiven, and no one could give me any real answers about that" (Cowley 2020). Journalist Brian Thompson (2021) noted that the legacy of confusion was written all over the SBA's webpage, which listed thirty additional rules and eleven pages of frequently asked questions by January 2021.

Then there were the workers, whose access to relief hinged on the decision of their employers. In a story on the funding for the Omni Hotels, NPR quoted Quilcia Moronta, a single mother of two children, who had worked at an Omni hotel for twenty-one years before being fired by them: "As I was struggling to provide for my family, I learned that the Omni had received some PPP money. ... Right now, here we are in December, and we haven't heard anything about Omni using that money to help their employees" (O'Driscoll 2020). At the luxury Fairmont hotel group owned by Dianne Feinstein's private equity executive husband, unemployed and unpaid workers had to send money to their employers to maintain their health insurance, even after the hotel received a PPP loan (Whoriskey 2020). A study from the Center of Public Integrity identified a set of companies that accepted USD 1.8 billion in loans and laid off 90,000 workers (Campbell, Yerardi, and Johnston 2020; Gregg 2020b).

This had wildly divergent ramifications in different states due to the lack of uniformity in the US' decentralized unemployment insurance system. In a state like Mississippi, workers were eager to stay on the payroll. In Washington State, generous unemployment benefits of USD 30 an hour combined with additional weekly federal unemployment assistance of USD 600 meant that lower income employees could earn more if they were fired. CBS News interviewed a spa owner whose employees were devastated to learn that she had received a PPP loan and would continue to hire them. The resentment was returned: "They were pissed I'd take this opportunity away from them to make more for my own selfish greed to pay rent," she said (Iacurci 2020). In other states, workers faced very different set of circumstances.

Conclusion

As the economy collapsed in March 2020, the US turned to credit policies that used lenders to provide support to small businesses and workers. It was a political strategy that held appeal across party lines, that could allow government officials to talk about helping workers without loosening the power of employers, and that could allow a government intervention of epic proportions to be framed in terms of pro-market rhetoric. It was also a program that reproduced the contradictions and inequities of the previously existing credit programs, structuring the way the gift of a government loan was alternately transformed into an opportunity for grift or a gamble of varied proportions.

Never has the US government moved faster to shift credit risks on behalf of small borrowers. Yet even when the government absorbed all credit risk for the loans, racial and income disparities persisted. It turned out that waiving collateral and credit score requirements were of little use when those standards had already interrupted banking relationships and existing ties with banks stood as the basis for access to the loans. Spurred on by critical news reports, the SBA quickly adapted to address these inequities, but we should resist any urge to downplay the importance of those initial weeks, when small businesses were closing in droves. I contend that these inequities were entirely foreseeable and predictable. The lasting lesson of the troubled rollout of the SBA loans is that without deliberate intervention, credit allocation as a form of crisis relief will default to reproducing inequalities built into the system. This is indicative of an even broader lesson: because crises activate existing systems, they reproduce their strengths, their weaknesses, and their inequalities.

The PPP program distributed over five million loans, worth over half a trillion dollars, in 2020. Around 30 percent of those — 1.4 million loans worth over a quarter trillion dollars — have been forgiven so far (SBA 2021). The SBA reported that the program supported up to 84 percent of all small-business employees, saving fifty-one million jobs by June 2020 (O'Connell et al. 2020; Stewart 2020). An early study by economists estimated that the loans saved only 2 percent of jobs because they seem to have gone mainly to companies that would have supported their workforce in any case; still, as the study's authors admit, the PPP may have long-term benefits from saving companies (Chetty et al. 2020). To the extent that is the case, the aftereffects are likely to be felt widely but not equally.

Acknowledgements

The author wishes to acknowledge and thank Roshan Eva Selden for providing excellent research assistance. For helpful feedback and generative conversations, the author also thanks the editors, Didier Fassin and Marion Fourcade, and the other authors in this volume.

References

Baradaran, Mehrsa. 2017. *The Color of Money: Black Banks and the Racial Wealth Gap*. Cambridge, MA: Harvard University Press.

Bean, Jonathan J. 2001. *Big Government and Affirmative Action: The Scandalous History of the Small Business Administration*. Lexington: University Press of Kentucky.

Billings, Kevin. 2020. "Florida Man Used $3.9 Million in PPP Funds from Alleged Fraud Scheme to Buy Lamborghini." *International Business Times*, July 28, 2020. https://www.ibtimes.com/florida-man-used-39-million-ppp-funds-alleged-fraud-scheme-buy-lamborghini-3018041.

BLS (Bureau of Labor Statistics, US Department of Labor). 2020. "Job Openings and Labor Turnover — March 2020." News Release USDL-20-0923, Bureau of Labor Statistics, US Department of Labor. https://www.bls.gov/news.release/archives/jolts_05152020.htm.

Braun, Benjamin. 2021. "Central Banking Beyond Inflation."Transformative Responses to the Crisis, Finanzwende/Heinrich-Böll-Foundation. https://pure.mpg.de/rest/items/item_3288736/component/file_3288737/content.

Braun, Benjamin, Daniela Gabor, and Marina Hübner. 2018. "Governing through Financial Markets: Towards a Critical Political Economy of Capital Markets Union." *Competition and Change* 22 (2): 101–16. https://doi.org/10.1177/1024529418759476.

Bresnahan, John, and Marianne Levine. 2020. "Dems Seize on 'Slush Fund' to Oppose Republican Rescue Package." *Politico*, March 23, 2020. https://www.politico.com/news/2020/03/23/democrats-slush-fund-republican-rescue-package-143565.

Bresnahan, John, Marianne Levine, and Andrew Desiderio. 2020. "How the $2 Trillion Deal Came Together — and Nearly Fell Apart." *Politico*, March 26, 2020. https://www.politico.com/news/2020/03/26/inside-the-10-days-to-rescue-the-economy-149718.

Brooks, Khristopher J. 2020. "40% of Black-Owned Businesses not Expected to Survive Coronavirus." *CBS News*, June 22, 2020. https://www.cbsnews.com/news/black-owned-busineses-close-thousands-coronavirus-pandemic/.

Campbell, Alexia F., Joe Yerardi, and Taylor Johnston. 2020. "These Companies Took $1.8 Billion in Federal Aid to Save Jobs. They Laid off 90,000 Workers Anyway." Center for Public Integrity. December 18, 2020. https://publicintegrity.org/inequality-poverty-opportunity/covid-divide/companies-took-covid-19-aid-they-laid-off-90000-workers-anyway/.

Capano, Giliberto, Michael Howlett, Darryl S.L. Jarvis, M. Ramesh, and Nihit Goyal. 2020. "Mobilizing Policy (In)Capacity to Fight COVID-19: Understanding Variations in State Responses." *Policy and Society* 39 (3): 285–308. https://doi.org/10.1080/14494035.2020.1787628.

Chetty, Raj, John N. Friedman, Nathaniel Hendren, Michael Stepner, and Opportunity Insights Team. 2020. "How Did COVID-19 and Stabilization Policies Affect Spending and Employment? A New Real-Time Economic Tracker Based on Private Sector Data."Working Paper 27431, National Bureau of Economic Research, Cambridge, MA. https://doi.org/10.3386/w27431.

Color of Change. 2020. "First COVID-19 Survey of Black and Latino Small-Business Owners Reveals Dire Economic Future." Color of Change, May 18, 2020. https://colorofchange.org/press_release/

first-covid-19-survey-of-black-and-latino-small-business-owners-reveals-dire-economic-future/.

Cowley, Stacy. 2020. "$130 Billion in Small-Business Aid Still Hasn't Been Used." *New York Times*, June 10, 2020. https://www.nytimes.com/2020/06/10/business/Small-business-loans-ppp.html.

Cowley, Stacy, Alan Rappeport, and Emily Flitter. 2020. "Small-Business Loan Program, Chaotic from Start, Gets 2nd Round." *New York Times*, April 26, 2020. https://www.nytimes.com/2020/04/26/business/ppp-small-business-loans.html.

Crouch, Colin. 2011. *The Strange Non-Death of Neo-Liberalism*. Cambridge, MA: Polity.

Daniel, Pete. 2013. *Dispossession: Discrimination against African American Farmers in the Age of Civil Rights*. Chapel Hill: University of North Carolina Press.

Davis, Michelle F. 2020. "PPP Scammers Made Fintech Companies their Lenders of Choice." *Bloomberg Businessweek*, October 8, 2020. https://www.bloomberg.com/news/articles/2020-10-07/ppp-loans-scammers-used-fintech-companies-to-carry-out-fraud.

Ellis, Christopher, and Christopher Faricy. 2021. *The Other Side of the Coin: Public Opinion toward Social Tax Expenditures*. New York: Russell Sage Foundation.

Entis, Laura. 2020. "The End of the American Dream." *Highlight, Vox*. July 22, 2020. https://www.vox.com/the-highlight/21320361/small-business-closing-covid-coronavirus-ppp-entrepreneur-economy-stimulus-loans.

Erel, Isil, and Jack Liebersohn. 2020. "Does Fintech Substitute for Banks? Evidence from the Paycheck Protection Program." National Bureau of Economic Research, Working paper 27659. https://doi.org/10.3386/w27659.

Fairlie, Robert. 2020. "The Impact of COVID-19 on Small Business Owners: Evidence of Early-Stage Losses from the April 2020 Current Population Survey." National Bureau of Economic Research, Working paper 27309. https://doi.org/10.3386/w27309.

Fairlie, Robert W., Kenneth Couch, and Huanan Xu. 2020. "The Impacts of COVID-19 on Minority Unemployment: First Evidence from April 2020 CPS Microdata." National Bureau of Economic Research, Working paper 27246. https://doi.org/10.3386/w27246.

Falk, Gene, Jameson A. Carter, Isaac A. Nicchitta, Emma C. Nyhof, and Paul D. Romero. 2021. "Unemployment Rates during the COVID-19 Pandemic: In Brief." R46554. Congressional Research Service, January 12, 2021. https://crsreports.congress.gov/product/details?prodcode=R46554.

Fang, Lee. 2020. "Small Business Rescue Money Flowing to Major Trump Donors, Disclosures Show." *Intercept*, April 24, 2020. https://theintercept.com/2020/04/24/coronavirus-small-business-loans-trump-donors-ppp/.

Financial Times. 2020. "A Perfect Storm Wreaks Havoc on Global Markets." March 13, 2020. https://www.ft.com/content/69af7eae-6527-11ea-b3f3-fe4680ea68b5.

Flitter, Emily. 2020. "Few Minority-Owned Businesses Got Relief Loans They Asked For." *New York Times*, May 18, 2020. https://www.nytimes.com/2020/05/18/business/minority-businesses-coronavirus-loans.html.

Flitter, Emily, and Stacy Cowley. 2020. "Banks Gave Richest Clients 'Concierge Treatment' for Pandemic Aid." *New York Times*, April 22, 2020. https://www.nytimes.com/2020/04/22/business/sba-loans-ppp-coronavirus.html.

Gillum, Jack, Isaac Arnsdorf, Jake Pearson, and Mike Speis. 2020. "Trump Friends and Family Cleared for Millions in Small Business Bailout." ProPublica, July 6, 2020. https://www.propublica.org/article/trump-friends-and-family-cleared-for-millions-in-small-business-bailout?token=CpfrqXaMuR8UnJ5-FryRkVwuKl3C98Ae.

Gregg, Aaron. 2020a. "Justice Department Charges 57 People Attempting to Steal $175 Million in Coronavirus Relief Funds." *Washington Post*, September 10, 2020. https://www.washingtonpost.com/business/2020/09/10/ppp-fraud-charges/.

Gregg, Aaron. 2020b. "Publicly Traded Firms Paid Dividends, Bought Their Own Stock after Receiving PPP Loans to Pay Employees." *Washington Post*, September 24, 2020. https://www.washingtonpost.com/business/2020/09/24/dividends-buybacks-ppp-loans/.

Hopkins, Jamie S., Taylor Johnston, and Pratheek Rebala. 2020. "PPP Loans Were Supposed to Prioritize Low-Income Areas during the Pandemic. They Didn't." Center for Public Integrity. December 11, 2020. https://publicintegrity.org/inequality-poverty-opportunity/covid-divide/ppp-loans-did-not-prioritize-low-income-areas-small-businesses-pandemic/.

Iacurci, Greg. 2020. "She Got a Forgivable Loan. Her Employees Hate Her for It." *CNBC*, April 22, 2020. https://www.cnbc.com/2020/04/22/she-got-a-paycheck-protection-loan-her-employees-hate-her-for-it.html.

Lavinas, Lena. 2017. *The Takeover of Social Policy by Financialization: The Brazilian Paradox*. New York: Springer.

Lederer, Anneliese, and Sara Oros; Sterling Bone, Glenn Christensen, and Jerome Williams. 2020. "Lending Discrimination within the Paycheck Protection Program." National Community Reinvestment Coalition. https://ncrc.org/lending-discrimination-within-the-paycheck-protection-program/.

Liu, Sifan, and Joseph Parilla. 2020. "New Data Shows Small Businesses in Communities of Color Had Unequal Access to Federal COVID-19 Relief." *Brookings* (blog). September 17, 2020. https://www.brookings.edu/research/new-data-shows-small-businesses-in-communities-of-color-had-unequal-access-to-federal-covid-19-relief/.

Long, Heather. 2020. "Over 10 Million Americans Applied for Unemployment Benefits in March as Economy Collapsed." *Washington Post*, April 2, 2020. https://www.washingtonpost.com/business/2020/04/02/jobless-march-coronavirus/.

Massey, Douglas S., and Nancy A. Denton. 1993. *American Apartheid: Segregation and the Making of the Underclass*. Cambridge, MA: Harvard University Press.

Mattingly, Phil, Clare Foran, and Ted Barrett. 2020. "Senate Republicans Unveil $1 Trillion Economic Stimulus Package to Address Coronavirus Fallout." *CNN*, March 20, 2020. https://www.cnn.com/2020/03/19/politics/coronavirus-economic-stimulus-senate-republicans/index.html.

Mayrl, Damon, and Sarah Quinn. 2016. "Defining the State from Within: Boundaries, Schemas, and Associational Policymaking." *Sociological Theory* 34 (1): 1–26. https://doi.org/10.1177/0735275116632557.

Mills, Claire Kramer. 2020. "Double Jeopardy: COVID-19's Concentrated Health and Wealth Effects in Black Communities." Federal Reserve Bank of New York, August 2020.

Naylor, Brian. 2010. "Sherrod Debacle Frustrates Black Farmers." *NPR*, July 22, 2010. https://www.npr.org/templates/story/story.php?storyId=128699935.

O'Connell, Jonathan, and Aaron Gregg. 2020. "SBA Exempted Lawmakers, Federal Officials from Ethics Rules in $660 Billion Loan Program." *Washington Post*, June 26, 2020. https://www.washingtonpost.com/

business/2020/06/26/sba-exempted-lawmakers-federal-officials-ethics-rules-660-billion-loan-program/.

O'Connell, Jonathan, Aaron Gregg, Steven Rich, Anu Narayanswamy, and Peter Whoriskey. 2020. "Treasury, SBA Data Show Small-Business Loans Went to Private-Equity Backed Chains, Members of Congress." *Washington Post*, July 6, 2020. https://www.washingtonpost.com/business/2020/07/06/sba-ppp-loans-data/.

O'Driscoll, Bill. 2020. "Omni Hotels Accepted Millions in PPP Funds but Didn't Pay Workers." *NPR*, December 29, 2020. https://www.npr.org/2020/12/29/950902403/omni-hotels-accepted-millions-in-ppp-funds-but-didnt-pay-workers.

Oliver, Melvin L., and Thomas M. Shapiro. 2006. *Black Wealth, White Wealth: A New Perspective on Racial Inequality*. New York: Routledge.

Popken, Ben. 2020. "Which Companies Are Returning their PPP Loans? Here's the List." *NBC News*, April 28, 2020. https://www.nbcnews.com/business/business-news/which-companies-are-returning-their-ppp-loan-here-s-list-n1194566.

Popken, Ben, and Andrew W. Lehren. 2020a. "Release of PPP Loan Recipients' Data Reveals Troubling Patterns." *NBC News*, December 2, 2020. https://www.nbcnews.com/business/business-news/release-ppp-loan-recipients-data-reveals-troubling-patterns-n1249629.

Popken, Ben, and Andrew W. Lehren. 2020b. "Judge Orders Trump Administration to Reveal PPP Loan Data It Sought to Obscure." *NBC News*, November 6, 2020. https://www.nbcnews.com/business/business-news/judge-orders-trump-administration-reveal-ppp-loan-data-it-sought-n1246792.

Quinn, Sarah. 2017. "'The Miracles of Bookkeeping': How Budget Politics Link Fiscal Policies and Financial Markets." *American Journal of Sociology* 123 (1): 48–85. https://doi.org/10.1086/692461.

Quinn, Sarah L. 2019. *American Bonds: How Credit Markets Shaped a Nation*. Princeton: Princeton University Press.

Rocco, Philip, Daniel Béland, and Alex Waddan. 2020. "Stuck in Neutral? Federalism, Policy Instruments, and Counter-Cyclical Responses to COVID-19 in the United States." *Policy and Society* 39 (3): 458–77. https://doi.org/10.1080/14494035.2020.1783793.

SBA (Small Business Administration). 2021. "PPP Data." SBA, updated September 21, 2021. https://www.sba.gov/funding-programs/loans/coronavirus-relief-options/paycheck-protection-program/ppp-data#section-header-0.

SBA Office of the Inspector General. 2020. "Flash Report: Small Business Administration's Implementation of the Paycheck Protection Program Requirements." Report No. 20–14, May 8, 2020. US Small Business Administration.

Siegel, Rachel. 2020. "The Recession Is Testing the Limits and Shortfalls of the Federal Reserve's Toolkit." *Washington Post*, September 15, 2020. https://www.washingtonpost.com/road-to-recovery/2020/09/15/fed-emergency-program-recession/.

Silver-Greenberg, Jessica, David Enrich, Jesse Drucker, and Stacy Cowley. 2020. "Large, Troubled Companies Got Bailout Money in Small-Business Loan Program." *New York Times*, April 26, 2020. https://www.nytimes.com/2020/04/26/business/coronavirus-small-business-loans-large-companies.html.

Snell, Kelsey. 2020. "What's Inside the Senate's $2 Trillion Coronavirus Aid Package." *NPR*, March 26, 2020. https://www.npr.org/2020/03/26/821457551/whats-inside-the-senate-s-2-trillion-coronavirus-aid-package.

Soederberg, Susanne. 2014. *Debtfare States and the Poverty Industry: Money, Discipline and the Surplus Population*. London: Routledge.

Stewart, Emily. 2020. "The PPP Worked How It Was Supposed to. That's the Problem." *Vox*, July 13, 2020. https://www.vox.com/recode/2020/7/13/21320179/ppp-loans-sba-paycheck-protection-program-polling-kanye-west.

Streeck, Wolfgang. 2014. *Buying Time: The Delayed Crisis of Democratic Capitalism*. Translated by Patrick Camiller. London: Verso.

Thompson, Brian. 2021. "Good News for Minority-Owned Businesses: Community Banks Get First Crack at the New Round of PPP Loans." *Forbes*, January 10, 2021. https://www.forbes.com/sites/brianthompson1/2021/01/10/good-news-for-minority-owned-businesses-community-banks-get-first-crack-at-the-new-round-of-ppp-loans/.

Thurston, Chloe N. 2018. *At the Boundaries of Homeownership: Credit, Discrimination, and the American State*. Cambridge: Cambridge University Press.

Tracy, Ryan, Chad Day, and Heather Haddon. 2020. "Small Business Loans Helped the Well-Heeled and Connected, Too." *Wall Street Journal*, July 6, 2020. https://www.wsj.com/articles/u-s-releases-names-of-biggest-ppp-borrowers-11594047600.

Ture, Kwame, and Charles V. Hamilton. 1992. *Black Power: The Politics of Liberation*. New York: Vintage Books.

Wells, Peter. 2020. "S&P 500 Suffers Its Quickest Fall into Bear Market on Record." *Financial Times*, March 12, 2020. https://www.ft.com/content/d895a54c-64a4-11ea-a6cd-df28cc3c6a68.

Whoriskey, Peter. 2020. "PPP Was Intended to Keep Employees on the Payroll. Workers at Some Big Companies Have Yet to Be Rehired." *Washington Post*, July 27, 2020. https://www.washingtonpost.com/business/2020/07/27/ppp-was-intended-keep-employees-payroll-workers-some-big-companies-have-yet-be-rehired/.

Zhou, Li. 2020. "The Paycheck Protection Program Failed Many Black-Owned Businesses." *Vox*, October 5, 2020. https://www.vox.com/2020/10/5/21427881/paycheck-protection-program-black-owned-businesses.

CHAPTER 5

Central Bank Planning for Public Purpose

Benjamin Braun

Since the beginning of this century, the world of financial and monetary policy makers has changed beyond recognition. Reducing net carbon emissions to zero; reducing economic inequality so as to avert social disintegration and democratic backsliding; combating a global pandemic — societies are confronting unprecedented environmental, economic, and social challenges. Tackling these challenges will require states to deploy all economic policy instruments already at their disposal, to develop new ones, and to build a new macro-financial regime to deploy hose instruments in a coordinated way. Several of the most powerful of these instruments are controlled by the central bank — an institution that has been placed beyond the reach of most governments in recent monetary history. The COVID pandemic has catalyzed a debate about whether and how to redeploy these instruments.

The debate has a clear fault line. While (monetary) conservatives have been steadfast in their rejection of any repurposing of central bank instruments away from price stability, progressive voices in politics and civil society are facing a dilemma. On the one hand, they have spoken out against the empowerment of unelected central bankers, especially in the context of the disempowerment of fiscal policy (Dietsch, Claveau, and Fontan 2018; Downey 2020; Van't Klooster 2020). On the other hand, they have increasingly been calling for a reorientation of monetary policy toward green and social purposes (Campiglio et al. 2018; Dikau and Volz 2020).

The progressive concern with the excessive technocratic power of central banks deserves to be taken seriously. It does not, however, imply a return to the *status quo ante*, when central banks enjoyed far-reaching independence while limiting their powers to the pursuit of price stability. Their powers are too formidable not to be wielded. The question is who gets to wield them, for what purposes, and in what kind of macrofinancial architecture.[1] To answer this question, this chapter examines the relationship between technocracy, democracy, and capitalism, with a focus on advanced capitalist economies. Space constraints do not permit a discussion of the implications for developing countries (Maxfield 1998). Nor is there space to discuss the case of the People's Bank of China, which has practiced a form of central bank planning, albeit one embedded in a nondemocratic political system (Bell and Feng 2013).

Capitalism, Democracy, Technocracy

We are used to thinking of capitalism and democracy, if not as a match made in heaven, then at least as a solid marriage. There is a long version of this story in economic history, which emphasizes the deep complementarities between market institutions and political institutions (Acemoglu and Robinson 2012; North, Wallis, and Weingast 2009).[2] Then there is a shorter version, which dates the marriage to the "golden age" of the post-Second World War era of Keynesian social democracy. However, rather than the story of a bilateral marriage, the story of the advanced economies since the mid-twentieth century has been that of an uneasy, triangular cohabitation of capitalism, democracy, and technocracy.[3] The

---

1. On macro-finance as a concept and approach to political economy, see Gabor (2020).
2. For an alternative reading of economic history, see Van Bavel (2016).
3. The experience of the 1970s revived the literature on the relationship between capital and the state. When, following the demise of Bretton Woods, the relationship between "late capitalism" and democracy became more conflict-ridden, social theorists and political scientists re-discovered the state. While (neo-)Marxists debated the modalities and extent of the control of the capitalist class over the state, political scientists began to study the state as a partly autonomous force in advanced capitalist economies. See

three sides of the triangle represent alternative institutional solutions to the problem of organizing and coordinating polity and economy. Each side represents a particular macro-financial regime that marginalizes but does not eliminate the triangle's third corner (see Figure 1). The triangle offers a heuristic to think about the past and future of advanced capitalist economies.

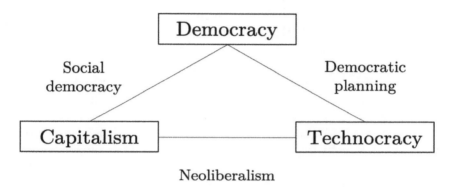

Figure 1: Three ways of organizing the cohabitation of capitalism, democracy, and technocracy.

The decades following the Second World War are said to have marked the "golden age" of democratic capitalism (Marglin and Schor 1990). The social democratic settlement arose from a situation in which the Great Depression and the two world wars had reduced the global economy to a "financially underdeveloped state" (Mehrling 2015: 313). Under the international regime of "embedded liberalism," states kept their borders open to international trade but imposed strict limits on international capital flows and high tax rates on corporations and the wealthy (Ruggie 1982). Keynesian macroeconomic stabilization, industrial policy, and even indicative planning were widespread, and most central banks were subordinated to their governments (Monnet 2018). The state had considerable influence over key sectors of the economy, unions were strong, and managers of large, financially independent and domestically anchored corporations supported the Fordist high-wage, high-consumption growth model. In this mixed economy, capital and

---

Habermas (1975); Offe (1976); Evans, Rueschemeyer, and Skocpol (1985); Miliband (1969); Poulantzas (1973).

democratically elected governments depended on each other. Social democratic capitalism was not a technocratic regime — experts were important but did not rule (Mudge 2018).

Starting in the 1960s, financial globalization gradually eroded this arrangement (Helleiner 1994). From the beginning, central banks — acting with a degree of autonomy that is the hallmark of technocracy — actively paved the way for financial capital to move across borders in large volumes through the Eurodollar market (Altamura 2017; Braun, Krampf, and Murau 2021). The growth and globalization of finance increased the structural power of capital vis-à-vis both labor and the state, undermining the foundations of the social democratic regime (Scharpf 1991). At the same time, governability problems — beginning with inflation and followed by financial instability — led to the delegation of ever more powers to independent technocratic agencies. The near-universal institutionalization of central bank independence took monetary and — by implication — fiscal policy off governments' policy menu, increasing the pressure to generate growth by further liberalizing financial markets and implementing structural labor market reforms (Aklin, Kern, and Negre 2021; Braun et al. 2021). The options available on the democratic menu were significantly reduced (Downey 2020; Van't Klooster 2020). The global financial crisis consolidated this shift toward the capitalism-technocracy axis — most dramatically in the euro area, where national governments received orders from the European Central Bank (Fontan 2018; Jacoby and Hopkin 2019). Some critics have dubbed this new alignment "authoritarian (neo)liberalism" (Bruff 2014; Streeck 2015), but the neoliberal tradition's focus on placing capital and markets beyond the reach of majoritarian politics is long-standing (Madariaga 2020; Slobodian 2018). The neoliberal macro-financial regime minimizes the democratic component of government.

To see why a return to tried and tested social democracy may not be an option, it is important to consider how historical circumstances have changed. Compared to the period of embedded liberalism, financialized capitalism today poses a much greater obstacle to distributive justice, political equality, and climate sustainability. In pursuit of the lowest possible wage and tax bills and the optimal financial and legal structure, corporations have self-fragmented across the globe (Reurink and Garcia-Bernardo 2021). Corporations, and increasingly our homes and infrastructures, are owned by powerful asset management companies who manage retirement savings and the wealth of the global rich (Braun 2021; Fichtner et al. 2017; Gabor and Kohl forthcoming). Whereas managers in Fordism often depended on sustainable relationships with local workers and customers, managers of financial capital seek effective protection *against* local democracy, provided by institutions such as independent central banks and arbitration courts. The scale of the shift of ownership and power from public to private institutions, and from nonfinancial to financial actors, blocks any direct path back to the social democratic capitalism of old.

Can a new path toward a progressive future be forged? Progressives correctly see "actually existing technocracy" as a mode of governance geared toward protecting financialized capitalism against electoral majorities and should be skeptical of naive ideas of "progressive technocracy" within the current macro-financial regime. That said, reclaiming the fiscal and monetary powers of the state and mobilizing them in service of progressive goals is going to be a technocratic — in addition to a political — project. As Daniela Gabor (2021) might put it, the revolutionaries better come armed with a macro-financial blueprint.

Technocracy

Technocrats possess specialized policy knowledge and, unlike mere technicians, occupy positions of power in the apparatus of government. Technocracy itself is "a system of governance in which technically trained experts rule by virtue of their specialized knowledge and position in dominant political and economic institutions" (Centeno 1993). Both authoritarian and democratic states rely heavily on technocratic rule. Prominent cases include authoritarian neoliberalism in Chile, developmental state capitalism in East Asia, and authoritarian state capitalism in contemporary China. In much of the rest of the world, technocracy used to keep a slightly lower profile: the mostly hidden-from-view work of inflation targeting by independent central banks for the West, conditionality imposed by private lenders and the International Monetary Fund for the rest (Deforge and Lemoine 2021; Kentikelenis and Babb 2019). Toward the end of the twentieth century, in a climate of post-Cold War triumphalism on the right and capitulation on the left, an optimistic view of technocracy took hold. The consensus in political science was that the "output legitimacy" produced by higher effectiveness of technocratic government could compensate for losses in the "input legitimacy" that resulted from lower citizen participation (Majone 1998; Scharpf 1997).

Things have changed since then. The area of technocratic governance that has seen the greatest increase of "unelected power" has no doubt been central banking (Tucker 2018). Following the stagflation crisis of the 1970s and Paul Volcker's labor-crushing crackdown on inflation in the United States (US) in the early 1980s, countries around the world transferred the responsibility for monetary policy from those directly accountable to elected representatives to arms-length technocrats governing newly "independent" central banks. By limiting that independence to relatively narrow price-stability mandates, the argument went, this institutional arrangement would strike a balance between the needs of financialized capitalism and the requirements of democracy. That was not, however, how things have played out.

Contrary to the narrative that central bank independence constituted a form of depoliticized welfare-maximizing economic management, central banks retained extraordinary power to determine distributional outcomes. The full scale of that power became apparent in the wake of the global financial crisis of 2008. Central banks' unlimited liquidity operations and asset purchases highlighted their capacity to choose how, and for whom, to do "whatever it takes."

To be very clear, the problem with central banks' policy responses in 2008 and 2020 is not that they acted swiftly and on an unprecedented scale to prevent further economic damage but that those interventions tend to perpetuate a bloated, unstable, and inefficient financial system. In other words, the problem is not the absence of central bank planning but that such planning is carried out as a mere support function, subordinated to the profit-oriented planning capacity of the private financial system (Braun 2018; Gabor 2021; Lemoine 2016). Reversing that hierarchy requires changes not only in the area of monetary policy but also in the areas of fiscal policy and, crucially, financial regulation — in a word, to the broader macro-financial regime.

The Worst of Both Worlds: Central Bank Planning for Private Profit

In theory, the macroeconomic coordination problem has two "pure" solutions. It can be solved either in centralized fashion by a social planner or by Hayekian speculators whose decentralized actions are coordinated via market pricing. These "pure" solutions are ideal types; in practice, we all live in mixed economies: nonmarket institutions and the price mechanism each do a good amount of coordinating. However, much of the capacity to coordinate economic activities across sectors, space, and time — in other words, the capacity to plan — has shifted from public to private institutions, and especially to the private financial sector.

In financialized capitalism, the most important central institution is the central bank. Central banking always carries an element of central planning: monetary policy involves the purposeful manipulation of a key price in the economy, namely the price of short-term liquidity. Since 2008, however, the scale and scope of central bank planning have expanded far beyond that. This expansion has been most dramatically illustrated by large-scale asset purchases ("quantitative easing"), which directly target long-term interest rates while putting a floor under the price of financial assets. Pioneered by the Bank of Japan in the early 2000s, quantitative easing became the policy response of choice to the global financial crisis of 2008 and the ensuing decade of slow growth and low inflation. Central banks launched even larger quantitative easing programs in response to the COVID pandemic. Of the debt issued by the governments of the United Kingdom, the US, the eurozone, and Japan between February and September 2020, their central banks purchased 50, 57, 71, and 75 percent, respectively (IMF 2020). This represents a degree of quasi-monetary financing that until very recently was considered unthinkable.

Less visible but equally consequential are central banks' market-shaping activities. They have built or reshaped money markets and markets for asset-backed securities, as well as the infrastructures for payments and securities settlement. They have further increased their footprints in the financial system by institutionalizing international currency swap lines, by establishing permanent dealer-of-last-resort facilities, and through macro-prudential regulation and stress testing (Birk and Thiemann 2020; Braun 2020; Coombs 2020; McDowell 2019; Thiemann 2019).

The questions are: What strategic vision guides how technocrats wield this formidable instrument of sovereign power? Or, who or what are central banks planning *for*? In recent decades, the answer has generally been: the private financial system. And rather than a decentralized system coordinated by market prices, private finance itself has come increasingly to resemble a centrally planned system: global investment priorities are a function not of the decisions of millions of Hayekian speculators but of the business models of a few dozen extremely large banks and asset managers (Mason 2016). Banks invest in mortgages; asset managers in whichever firms are in market-capitalization-weighted indices; private equity firms in urban real estate; and venture capital firms in scalable rent-extraction models. This sector is highly concentrated at the top, where a few giant companies — banks, hedge funds, private equity funds — control the direction of global capital flows.

Rather than providing a corrective to the inefficiencies and inequities of this mode of capital allocation, central bank planning has long been geared toward expanding and stabilizing it. Indeed, the history of central bank-led financialization is well documented in the political economy literature (Dutta 2019; Gabor and Ban 2016; Krippner 2007; Özgöde 2021; Walter and Wansleben 2019; Wansleben 2020). The 2008 financial crisis and the rise of macro-prudential regulation have not changed that pattern. The shadow banking system will not establish a sufficiently liquid and standardized, pan-European repo market on its own? The European Central Bank (ECB) will help. The private system of securities settlement is inefficient and creates frictions in capital markets? The ECB will build a better, publicly operated system. Asset markets regularly seize up, threatening the expansion of the financial sector? Central banks will create backstops and dealer-of-last-resort facilities, thus effectively underwriting the ability of hedge and private equity funds to gobble up assets amid economic disasters.

Consider the turmoil, in late 2019, in the US repo market, where financial firms borrow and lend cash against securities, pledged as collateral. A major cause of this turmoil was liquidity demand from hedge and private equity funds. These funds are typically levered — in order maximize their returns, they borrow large sums in the shadow banking system, often pledging the assets they acquire as collateral. In order to stabilize the repo market, the Federal Reserve increased its balance sheet by 10 percent, or USD 400 billion, between September 2019 and January 2020. The question "What is the social value of levered hedge funds and private equity buyouts?" was not asked.

The same pattern recurred — on a much larger scale — in the wake of the COVID outbreak in early 2020. In order to prevent the economic shock caused by the pandemic from leading to another systemic financial crisis, central banks across the world chose to backstop not only banks but also the broader shadow banking system. The most audacious measures — in both size and scope — have been implemented by the Federal Reserve. By purchasing so-called "junk bonds" — bonds issued by corporate debtors with lower credit ratings — the Federal Reserve again backstopped private equity funds, which routinely transfer debt to their buyout targets, forcing the latter to issue junk bonds. By backstopping both the money market and the (high-risk) capital market, the Federal Reserve effectively protects both the *liability* side and the *asset* side of levered investors' balance sheets.

In other words, the Federal Reserve ensures that the arsenal of the most predatory actors in the financial system is fully stocked and ready to be deployed — for further financializing currently distressed sectors of the economy, such as elderly care. Shareholders understand — the stock price of firms such as Blackstone and Apollo bounced back spectacularly after the Federal Reserve announced its measures. Unless governments take swift and decisive action to curb the ability of hedge and private equity funds to gobble up assets, COVID will become a major milestone in the long history of central bank-facilitated financialization.

The upshot is that while central bank planning already exists, it is currently geared toward propping up a system in which the planning of investment is in private hands. This system is both unfair and inefficient. Central banks have become the lenders of last resort for a manifestly unsustainable status quo (Fontan, Claveau, and Dietsch 2016; Jacobs and King 2016; Streeck 2014).

Socialize Central Bank Planning

Can central banks be turned into progressive institutions? Among observers from across the ideological spectrum, the overwhelming consensus has been that central banks must be cut down to size and made more democratically accountable. Progressives, however, should consider an alternative path toward democratizing central banking: to cut the private financial system down to size and double down on central bank planning.

It is important to be very clear: while private financial institutions wield extraordinary power in the economy, the ultimate source of that power is the state. Legal scholars Robert Hockett and Saule Omarova (2017) have coined the apt phrase "finance franchise" to describe an arrangement in which private banks act as "franchisees" of citizens, with the power to act with the full faith and credit of the public. This model, which in the US took shape between the establishment of the Federal Reserve in 1913 and President Roosevelt's New Deal reforms of the banking system in the early 1930s, was premised on the twin assumptions that capital was scarce and that private actors were best able to allocate it to its most productive uses. Neither of these assumptions holds today. Capital is abundant, and private capital allocation has created vast inequality within and between nations, while bringing the planet to the brink of catastrophe.

Can the public cut out the middleman? Increasingly, scholars and advocates emphasize "the propriety and the necessity of the public's taking an active role in modulating and allocating its credit aggregates across the economy" (Hockett 2019: 491). Taking such an active role is, of course, a daunting project. Progressives need to think carefully about the architecture of a financial system in which the modulation and allocation of capital is subject to public rather than private planning.

Again, the good news is that central bank planning is already here. The present reality of central bank planning already undercuts the textbook arguments for delegating monetary policy to independent central banks. First, the many ways in which central banks steer, shape, and build financial markets invalidates the market neutrality principle. The notion that monetary policy has (or should have) only a negligible footprint in the economy has long been a myth, which is why proposing to put that footprint to progressive use should not worry us (Van't Klooster and Fontan 2019). Second, central banks have many more tools at their disposal than implied by the so-called Tinbergen rule, according to which a single instrument (such as the short-term interest rate) can only be deployed to achieve a single goal (such as price stability). Applying the Tinbergen rule — long a foundational principle for monetary policy — to central banks is nonsensical. Collateral requirements, targeted asset purchases, regulatory measures, market building, international cooperation — these are only some of the instruments that central banks have been using all along. It is much more accurate to compare the central bank to a Swiss army knife, an apparatus that contains many different instruments and that can therefore be deployed in pursuit of several different goals (Braun and Downey 2020).

Reorienting central bank planning from private profit toward public purpose is both possible and desirable. It is possible only, however, as part of a full-scale overhaul of the financial system. While this is not the place to go into the details, two points are worth highlighting. First, while progressives should think big and bold, it is also important to recognize that we have been here — extreme inequality, financial collapse, economic depression — before. The New Deal period offers many examples of policies and public financial institutions — such as the Reconstruction Finance Corporation — that can serve as guideposts. What is more, key thinkers of the New Deal period had first-hand experience in actual economic planning — Adolf Berle served as legal counsel to the Reconstruction Finance Corporation and John Kenneth Galbraith helped run the government's Office of Price Administration during the Second World War (Lemann 2019). As Sarah Quinn and her colleagues (2019) have shown, Berle's ideas for a "modern financial tool-kit" provide an excellent starting point for thinking about the radical reforms necessary to democratize the financial system today.[4]

The second point worth highlighting is that a progressive agenda for finance must be an international agenda. In retrospect, the 2008 financial crisis did not wipe the slate clean enough (Tooze 2018). Whether the economic and political fallout from the coronavirus pandemic will create a window of opportunity for a renegotiation of the international financial order remains to be seen. The pandemic's repercussions have, however, exposed once more the devastating dependence of the global financial system on the US dollar and hence the Federal Reserve. By late March 2020, capital outflows from emerging market economies had exceeded all previous episodes of capital flight. Lives were on the line already in 2008–9, but the stakes of, for instance, a Federal Reserve swap line were on much starker display during the COVID pandemic. Global warming, environmental degradation, and pandemics are global problems with global feedback effects: there is little prospect of combating these problems without a more balanced, multilateral financial order in which societies have the institutional and economic means to formulate and implement their ideas of the public good.

Conclusion

The reputation of the neoliberal macro-financial regime took a hit in 2008. However, the financial origins of the crisis made it possible to blame the misallocation of capital on the excesses of US mortgage finance. Post-Lehman Brothers, dreaming big was to dream of a well-regulated financial system. Both the climate crisis and the COVID crisis have been different as they have exposed the misallocation, on a planetary scale, of *real* resources. States have failed to protect their citizens, not because of the insufficient regulation of markets, but because of the lack of state capacity to direct resources and production without the intervention of markets (Jones and Hameiri 2021). When the coronavirus

---

4. On democratizing finance today, see Block (2019) and McCarthy (2019).

pandemic eventually recedes, the alternatives for the global economic order could not be starker. While the idea of an enlightened neoliberal technocracy is moribund, neoliberalism will likely survive in its semi-authoritarian and nationalist variants. The alternative is a macro-financial regime that turns finance into a utility-like sector while reorienting the power of central banking towards bolstering the capacity of states for redistribution and green public investment.

References

Acemoglu, Daron, and James A. Robinson. 2012. *Why Nations Fail: The Origins of Power, Prosperity, and Poverty*. London: Profile Books.

Aklin, Michael, Andreas Kern, and Mario Negre. 2021. "Does Central Bank Independence Increase Inequality?" Policy Research Working Paper no. 9522, World Bank. https://openknowledge.worldbank.org/handle/10986/35069.

Altamura, Carlo E. 2017. *European Banks and the Rise of International Finance: The Post-Bretton Woods Era*. Abingdon: Routledge.

Bell, Stephen, and Hui Feng. 2013. *The Rise of the People's Bank of China: The Politics of Institutional Change*. Cambridge, MA: Harvard University Press.

Birk, Marius, and Matthias Thiemann. 2020. "Open for Business: Entrepreneurial Central Banks and the Cultivation of Market Liquidity." *New Political Economy* 25 (2): 267–83. https://doi.org/10.1080/13563467.2019.1594745.

Block, Fred. 2019. "Financial Democratization and the Transition to Socialism." *Politics and Society* 47 (4): 529–56. https://doi.org/10.1177/0032329219879274.

Braun, Benjamin. 2018. "Central Bank Planning: Unconventional Monetary Policy and the Price of Bending the Yield Curve." In *Uncertain Futures: Imaginaries, Narratives, and Calculation in the Economy*, edited by Jens Beckert and Richard Bronk, 194–216. Oxford: Oxford University Press.

Braun, Benjamin. 2020. "Central Banking and the Infrastructural Power of Finance: The Case of ECB Support for Repo and Securitization Markets." *Socio-Economic Review* 18 (2): 395–418. https://doi.org/10.1093/ser/mwy008.

Braun, Benjamin. 2021. "Asset Manager Capitalism as a Corporate Governance Regime." In *American Political Economy: Politics, Markets, and Power*, edited in Jacob S. Hacker, Alexander Hertel-Fernandez, Paul Pierson, and Kathleen Thelen, 270–95. Cambridge: Cambridge University Press.

Braun, Benjamin, Donato Di Carlo, Sebastian Diessner, and Maximilian Düsterhöft. 2021. "Planning Laissez-Faire: Supranational Central Banking and Structural Reforms." SocArXiv Papers, March 16, 2021. https://doi.org/10.31235/osf.io/dp3nv.

Braun, Benjamin, and Leah Downey. 2020. "Against Amnesia: Re-Imagining Central Banking." Discussion Note, Council on Economic Policies. https://www.cepweb.org/against-amnesia-re-imagining-central-banking/.

Braun, Benjamin, Arie Krampf, and Steffen Murau. 2021. "Financial Globalization as Positive Integration: Monetary Technocrats and the Eurodollar Market in the 1970s." *Review of International Political Economy* 28 (4): 794–819. https://doi.org/10.1080/09692290.2020.1740291.

Bruff, Ian. 2014. "The Rise of Authoritarian Neoliberalism." *Rethinking Marxism* 26 (1): 113–29. https://doi.org/10.1080/08935696.2013.843250.

Campiglio, Emanuele, Yannis Dafermos, Pierre Monnin, Josh Ryan-Collins, Guido Schotten, and Misa Tanaka. 2018. "Climate Change Challenges for Central Banks and Financial Regulators." *Nature Climate Change* 8 (6): 462–68. https://doi.org/10.1038/s41558-018-0175-0.

Centeno, Miguel A. 1993. "The New Leviathan: The Dynamics and Limits of Technocracy." *Theory and Society* 22 (3): 307–35. https://doi.org/10.1007/BF00993531.

Coombs, Nathan. 2020. "What do Stress Tests Test? Experimentation, Demonstration, and the Sociotechnical Performance of Regulatory Science." *British Journal of Sociology* 71 (3): 520–36. https://doi.org/10.1111/1468-4446.12739.

Deforge, Quentin, and Benjamin Lemoine. 2021. "The Global South Debt Revolution that Wasn't: UNCTAD from Technocractic Activism to Technical Assistance." In *Sovereign Debt Diplomacies: Rethinking Sovereign Debt from Colonial Empires to Hegemony*, edited by Pierre Pénet and Juan F. Zendejas, 232–56. Oxford: Oxford University Press.

Dietsch, Pieter, François Claveau, and Clément Fontan. 2018. *Do Central Banks Serve the People?* Cambridge: Polity.

Dikau, Simon, and Ulrich Volz. 2020. "Central Bank Mandates, Sustainability Objectives and the Promotion of Green Finance." Working Paper

222, Department of Economics, School of Oriental and African Studies, University of London. https://ideas.repec.org/p/soa/wpaper/222.html.

Downey, Leah. 2020. "Delegation in Democracy: A Temporal Analysis." *Journal of Political Philosophy* 29 (3): 305–29. https://doi.org/10.1111/jopp.12234.

Dutta, Sahil J. 2019. "Sovereign Debt Management and the Transformation from Keynesian to Neoliberal Monetary Governance in Britain." *New Political Economy* 25 (4): 625–90. https://doi.org/10.1080/13563467.2019.1680961.

Evans, Peter B., Dietrich Rueschemeyer, and Theda Skocpol. 1985. *Bringing the State Back In*. Cambridge: Cambridge University Press.

Fichtner, Jan, Eelke M. Heemskerk, and Javier Garcia-Bernardo. 2017. "Hidden Power of the Big Three? Passive Index Funds, Re-concentration of Corporate Ownership, and New Financial Risk." *Business and Politics* 19 (2): 298–326. https://doi.org/10.1017/bap.2017.6.

Fontan, Clément. 2018. "Frankfurt's Double Standard: The Politics of the European Central Bank during the Eurozone Crisis." *Cambridge Review of International Affairs* 31 (2): 162–82. https://doi.org/10.1080/09557571.2018.1495692.

Fontan, Clément, François Claveau, and Peter Dietsch. 2016. "Central Banking and Inequalities: Taking off the Blinders." *Politics, Philosophy and Economics* 15 (4): 319–57. https://doi.org/10.1177/1470594X16651056.

Gabor, Daniela. 2020. "Critical macro-finance: A theoretical lens." *Finance and Society* 6 (1): 45–55. https://doi.org/10.2218/finsoc.v6i1.4408.

Gabor, Daniela. 2021. "Revolution without Revolutionaries: Interrogating the New Politics of Monetary Financing." Transformative Responses to the Crisis, Finanzwende/Heinrich-Böll-Foundation.

Gabor, Daniela, and Cornel Ban. 2016. "Banking on Bonds: The New Links between States and Markets." *Journal of Common Market Studies* 54 (3): 617–35. https://doi.org/10.1111/jcms.12309.

Gabor, Daniela, and Sebastian Kohl. Forthcoming. "My Home is an Asset Class: The Financialization of Housing in Europe." Report for the Greens/European Free Alliance in the European Parliament.

Habermas, Jürgen. 1975. *Legitimation Crisis*. Boston: Beacon Press.

Helleiner, Eric. 1994. *States and the Reemergence of Global Finance: From Bretton Woods to the 1990s*. Ithaca: Cornell University Press.

Hockett, Robert C. 2019. "Finance without Financiers." *Politics and Society* 47 (4): 491–527. https://doi.org/10.1177/0032329219882190.

Hockett, Robert C., and Saule T. Omarova. 2017. "The Finance Franchise." *Cornell Law Review*, no. 102: 1143–1218. http://doi.org/10.2139/ssrn.2820176.

IMF (International Monetary Fund). 2020. *Fiscal Monitor: Policies for the Recovery*. October 2020. Washington, DC: International Monetary Fund.

Jacobs, Lawrence R., and Desmond S. King. 2016. *Fed Power: How Finance Wins*. New York: Oxford University Press.

Jacoby, Wade, and Jonathan Hopkin. 2019. "From Lever to Club? Conditionality in the European Union during the Financial Crisis." *Journal of European Public Policy* 27 (8): 1157–77. https://doi.org/10.1080/13501763.2019.1703791.

Jones, Lee, and Shahar Hameiri. 2021. "COVID-19 and the Failure of the Neoliberal Regulatory State." *Review of International Political Economy*. https://doi.org/10.1080/09692290.2021.1892798.

Kentikelenis, Alexander E., and Sarah Babb. 2019. "The Making of Neoliberal Globalization: Norm Substitution and the Politics of Clandestine Institutional Change." *American Journal of Sociology* 124 (6): 1720–62. https://doi.org/10.1086/702900.

Krippner, Greta R. 2007. "The Making of US Monetary Policy: Central Bank Transparency and the Neoliberal Dilemma." *Theory and Society* 36 (6): 477–513. https://doi.org/10.1007/s11186-007-9043-z.

Lemann, Nicholas. 2019. *Transaction Man: The Rise of the Deal and the Decline of the American Dream*. New York: Farrar, Straus and Giroux.

Lemoine, Benjamin. 2016. *L'ordre de la dette: Enquête sur les infortunes de l'état et la prospérité du marché*. Paris: La Découverte.

Madariaga, Aldo. 2020. *Neoliberal Resilience: Lessons in Democracy and Development from Latin America and Eastern Europe*. Princeton: Princeton University Press.

Majone, Giandomenica. 1998. "Europe's 'Democratic Deficit': The Question of Standards." *European Law Journal* 4 (1): 5–28. https://doi.org/10.1111/1468-0386.00040.

Marglin, Stephen A., and Juliet B. Schor. 1990. *The Golden Age of Capitalism: Reinterpreting the Postwar Experience*. Oxford: Clarendon Press.

Mason, J. W. 2016. "Socialize Finance." *Jacobin*, November 28, 2016. https://www.jacobinmag.com/2016/11/finance-banks-capitalism-markets-socialism-planning.

Maxfield, Sylvia. 1998. *Gatekeepers of Growth: The International Political Economy of Central Banking in Developing Countries*. Princeton: Princeton University Press.

McCarthy, Michael A. 2019. "The Politics of Democratizing Finance: A Radical View." *Politics and Society* 47 (4): 611–33. https://doi.org/10.1177/0032329219878990.

McDowell, Daniel. 2019. "Emergent International Liquidity Agreements: Central Bank Cooperation after the Global Financial Crisis." *Journal of International Relations and Development*, no. 22: 441–67. https://doi.org/10.1057/s41268-017-0106-0.

Mehrling, Perry. 2015. "Elasticity and Discipline in the Global Swap Network." *International Journal of Political Economy* 44 (4): 311–24. https://doi.org/10.1080/08911916.2015.1129848.

Miliband, Ralph. 1969. *The State in Capitalist Society*. New York: Basic Books.

Monnet, Eric. 2018. *Controlling Credit: Central Banking and the Planned Economy in Postwar France, 1948–1973*. Cambridge: Cambridge University Press.

Mudge, Stephanie L. 2018. *Leftism Reinvented: Western Parties from Socialism to Neoliberalism*. Cambridge, MA: Harvard University Press.

North, Douglass C., John J. Wallis, and Barry R. Weingast. 2009. *Violence and Social Orders: A Conceptual Framework for Interpreting Recorded Human History*. Cambridge: Cambridge University Press.

Offe, C. 1976. "'Crisis of Crisis Management': Elements of a Political Crisis Theory." *International Journal of Politics* 6 (3): 29–67.

Özgöde, Onur. 2021. "The Emergence of Systemic Risk: The Federal Reserve, Bailouts, and Monetary Government at the Limits." *Socio-Economic Review*, mwaa053. https://doi.org/10.1093/ser/mwaa053.

Poulantzas, Nicos. 1973. *Political Power and Social Classes*. London: Verso London.

Quinn, Sarah, Mark S. Igra, and Selen Guler. 2019. "'A Modern Financial Tool-Kit': Lessons from Adolf A. Berle for a More Democratic Financial System." SocArXiv Papers, September 27, 2019. https://doi.org/10.31235/osf.io/7e2fc.

Reurink, Arjan, and Javier Garcia-Bernardo. 2021. "Competing for Capitals: The Great Fragmentation of the Firm and Varieties of FDI Attraction Profiles in the European Union." *Review of International Political Economy* 28 (5): 1274–1307. https://doi.org/10.1080/09692290.2020.1737564.

Ruggie, John G. 1982. "International Regimes, Transactions, and Change: Embedded Liberalism in the Postwar Economic Order." *International Organization* 36 (2): 379–415.

Scharpf, Fritz W. 1991. *Crisis and Choice in European Social Democracy.* Ithaca: Cornell University Press.

Scharpf, Fritz W. 1997. "Economic Integration, Democracy and the Welfare State." *Journal of European Public Policy* 4 (1): 18–36. https://doi.org/10.1080/135017697344217.

Slobodian, Quinn. 2018. *Globalists: The End of Empire and the Birth of Neoliberalism.* Cambridge, MA: Harvard University Press.

Streeck, Wolfgang. 2014. *Buying Time: The Delayed Crisis of Democratic Capitalism.* London: Verso.

Streeck, Wolfgang. 2015. "Heller, Schmitt and the Euro." *European Law Journal* 21 (3): 361–70. https://doi.org/10.1111/eulj.12134.

Thiemann, Matthias. 2019. "Is Resilience Enough? The Macro-Prudential Reform Agenda and the Lacking Smoothing of the Cycle." *Public Administration* 97 (3): 561–75. https://doi.org/10.1111/padm.12551.

Tooze, J. Adam. 2018. *Crashed: How a Decade of Financial Crises Changed the World.* London: Penguin.

Tucker, Paul. 2018. *Unelected Power: The Quest for Legitimacy in Central Banking and the Regulatory State.* Princeton: Princeton University Press.

Van Bavel, Bas. 2016. *The Invisible Hand? How Market Economies Have Emerged and Declined since AD 500.* Oxford: Oxford University Press.

Van't Klooster, Jens. 2020. "The Ethics of Delegating Monetary Policy." *Journal of Politics* 82 (2): 587–99. https://doi.org/10.1086/706765.

Van't Klooster, Jens, and Clément Fontan. 2019. "The Myth of Market Neutrality: A Comparative Study of the European Central Bank's and the Swiss National Bank's Corporate Security Purchases." *New Political Economy* 25 (6): 865–79. https://doi.org/10.1080/13563467.2019.1657077.

Walter, Timo, and Leon Wansleben. 2019. "How Central Bankers Learned to Love Financialization: The Fed, the Bank, and the Enlisting of Unfettered Markets in the Conduct of Monetary Policy." *Socio-Economic Review* 18 (3): 625–53. https://doi.org/10.1093/ser/mwz011.

Wansleben, Leon. 2020. "Formal Institution Building in Financialized Capitalism: The Case of Repo Markets." *Theory and Society* 49 (2): 187–213. https://doi.org/10.1007/s11186-020-09385-2.

CHAPTER 6

Authoritarianism and Pandemics

China, Turkey, and Hungary

Latif Tas

Catastrophic events cause people to suffer and die, alone more often than not, although COVID has proven unique. Indeed, in COVID, humanity has experienced a rare and near-universal confrontation with mortality. Even the world wars were not experienced universally. Chernobyl, the fall of the Berlin Wall, and 9/11 likewise had their geographical limits. The plague, the Spanish Flu, and other pandemics, given the lack of easy transport and communication systems, did not create anxiety, panic, fear, and pain among peoples at the same time, in the same way, and on a truly global scale.

The pandemic may have been enormously beneficial to a small group of people either economically or politically, but economic deprivation and authoritarian politics have made conditions more difficult and even unbearable for many others. Human values, advanced technologies, and modern civilizations have been tested. People around the world have been forced to adopt new routines. There have been no exceptions: from north to south and east to west, in capitalist and socialist countries, across differences of terrain and temperature, whether rich or poor, black or white, woman or man, almost everyone has faced this catastrophe. And extraordinarily, despite the cruel inequalities exposed by susceptibility to the contagion, the fear of premature mortality has proven uniform across social boundaries. Indeed, the virus seems one of the few dangers capable of creating almost universal feelings of panic, fear, and the apprehension of death. For the first time in history, world leaders have been afraid to come together for a meeting. The 2020 meeting of the Group of Twenty, like virtually all other meetings during the pandemic, has taken place through teleconferencing.

The COVID crisis has demonstrated how the divide between democracies and autocracies affects the lives of people in both types of societies, in critical ways. Most democratic countries have issued reliable reports of cases and deaths, taken important and meaningful measures against the disease, have had scientists keep publics informed, and have had their leaders hold regular press meetings with journalists. Germany, South Korea, Taiwan, and New Zealand — democratic countries, many of which are (coincidentally) ruled by female leaders — have been models of transparency. Despite its proximity to China, South Korea's early humanistic and scientific approach protected its people. New Zealand and Taiwan were similarly able to mitigate the suffering of their citizens. All have been more successful so far in keeping the virus under control than other countries with autocratic rulers (or would-be autocratic rulers, like Donald Trump in the United States [US] or Jair Bolsonaro in Brazil). While some democratic leaders who took responsible stands were easily reelected (e.g., Jacinda Arden of New Zealand), others lost power, at least in part due to their mishandling of the pandemic (e.g., Trump in the US).[1] However, the pandemic has also had its beneficiaries. Many authoritarian leaders around the world, despite their failed responses to COVID, have further monopolized power and used the crisis for their own benefit.

In this chapter, I focus on how authoritarian governments have responded to the pandemic politically, economically, and socially. Attending to the specific cases of China, Turkey, and Hungary, I examine how the state of emergency induced by the pandemic has served some

---

1. On November 1, 2021, the World Health Organization (WHO) registered 246,594,191 confirmed COVID cases globally, with 4,998,584 deaths, and the administration of 6,893,633,094 vaccine doses on its COVID dashboard. On that day, the US had a total of 45,635,708 cases (739,856 deaths); Brazil 21,804,094 (607,694); Turkey 8,032,988 (70,611); Germany 4,607,208 (95,752); Hungary 874,630 (30,881); South Korea 366,386 (2,859); China 126,078 (5,696); and New Zealand 6,233 (28).

authoritarian regimes, how their power over their populations has increased, and how they have found in COVID a political opportunity.

The Ascendance of Authoritarianism

A story featured in *The Washington Post* on December 7, 2018, entitled "How Democracies Slide into Authoritarianism" (Edel 2018) indicates that global authoritarianism was already on the ascent before the COVID pandemic.[2] As of the early 2000s, there was hope that the world's share of democratic and open regimes, which stood at 46 percent, would increase. However, by 2020 this figure had instead decreased to 39 percent. Democratically elected governments find it difficult to confront the power of authoritarian populists. Compounding the problem in the case of COVID, it is exceedingly difficult to check, challenge, or question the official statistics of authoritarian regimes (Wright 2008; Wright and Escribà-Folch 2012) — critics, indeed, often find themselves jailed for asking the wrong questions. The citizens of authoritarian regimes support lies as truth and lose the very capacity to differentiate between them. Authoritarian regimes, moreover, tend to misrepresent data on minority groups for the unitary benefit of their own majoritarian base of power. These excluded groups — for example immigrants in the Western context, small and powerless religious or ethnic minorities in the Middle East and Asia, progressive democrats in the context of Latin America — serve populist authoritarian regimes as important punching bags, on whom economic, social, and political blame is imputed. Without creating these internal enemies, authoritarian regimes cannot maintain power. Democratic regimes, on the other hand, must address the interests of those who oppose, criticize, and decline to vote for them.

Granted, even the most advanced democratic regimes are not fully safe, and some leaders within such countries may actively be working to transform them into autocracies. As early as 2016 and 2017, the figure of Trump was identified as a potential authoritarian leader (Ball 2016;

---

2. According to the Freedom House Index, 2019 was the fourteenth consecutive year of decline in global democracy and freedom. For data on authoritarianism and democracy around the world, see the Freedom House Index for 2018 and 2019 and Plattner (2015). See, also, Tas (2022) for a detailed discussion of authoritarian governmentality and their increasing global power.

Tenz 2017). He has certainly employed tactics common to autocrats. Authoritarian leaders tend first to spread fear, citing "terror," "migrants," "refugees," "border controls," or "foreign viruses" as threats. They then tell the masses that the means of ending their fear is to transfer it upon others, generating animosity toward particular groups. Their solutions tend to involve erecting walls, removing groups of people, setting up displays of patriotism, purifying the nation. Such measures do not end the fear but only transfer it from one object to another. Populist leaders use conflict to legally justify this transfer, which encourages the masses to unify behind them. People respond to commands from above but at the cost of their judgment, moral values, individuality, and humanity. This is one of the initial signs of the birth of an authoritarian regime.

New technologies can also be controlled for the benefit of these regimes. Autocrats set the limits of and control virtually all information in their countries. Twitter, Facebook, WhatsApp, and Google froze Trump's accounts in reaction to his "incitement of insurrection" (as Congress accused Trump in its article of impeachment) at the Capitol on January 6, 2020, but only after he had lost the election and was departing from office. At this point it was easy for these companies to freeze his accounts given that he had not been able to capture full power, despite the significant damage he had done to democratic institutions. It would, on the other hand, be nearly impossible to freeze the online accounts of Xi Jinping in China, Recep Tayyip Erdoğan in Turkey, or Viktor Orbán in Hungary. In authoritarian countries, social media companies cannot function without permission from, and cooperation with, the regime. In addition to destroying media independence and replacing it with state-sanctioned news sources, autocrats have also increased control over their citizenries through new digital surveillance technology and mass monitoring systems. While in democratic regimes citizens also have the power to use advanced technologies to observe, check, criticize, and contribute to the policies of their governments, this is not possible in authoritarian regimes, and any simple negative remark by a journalist or even a regular citizen can be harshly punished.

The repetition of lies is an essential means by which dictators mobilize support. Additionally, authoritarian governments often begin not by eliminating their opponents but by capturing their own supporters fully and making them dependent on the regime for their economic and physical security. This makes it much easier for autocrats to eliminate their opponents and routinize an "us" versus "them" mentality. Under such a structure, people are no longer represented according to their education, ability, or skills, but by their dress code, the shape and style of their moustache or haircut, the flag they carry, the finger or hand sign they use, the headscarf they wear, the likes or dislikes they express on social media. Without identifiable "others," the "us" cannot be created. Even if the existing enemy is being annihilated, new ones must constantly be invented to ensure the survival of the authoritarian regime.

"Diseases are Deadlier in Non-democracies"

"Diseases like COVID-19 are deadlier in non-democracies" ran a headline in *The Economist* in mid-February 2020 (Economist 2020a). The statement came at a time when authorities in China were deliberately misleading the world about their own coronavirus death toll. Not until almost a month later did the World Health Organization (WHO) label what was occurring a pandemic. By then, three months after the outbreak of the virus, it was already too late for most countries to take strong measures to protect their people from serious illness and death. The WHO had taken Beijing's false reports as fact, ignoring warnings from doctors and scientists around the world — including Li Wenliang, a thirty-four-year-old physician in China who was detained for "spreading false rumours," "seriously disrupting social order," and "putting the public in danger." He was forced to sign a letter that he was "making false comments" and "severely disturbed the social order" (Golley, Jaivin, and Strange 2021). On February 7, 2020, he lost his life when infected by the virus while saving the lives of others. Six weeks after his death, Chinese authorities apologized to his family for the impropriety of their initial response, though it was too late for Li and the rest of the world. Dr Li is seen as a martyr by many Chinese today and his grave receives a large number of visitors (Su 2020). Even after more than a year of global disaster, millions of deaths, and widespread economic collapse, Chinese authorities are still refusing to allow WHO experts to investigate the origins and cause of the COVID pandemic in their country (even though it is still believed to have originated in Wuhan). Unsurprisingly, this attitude has fueled suspicions of a cover-up.

The documentary film *Our World, Wuhan: Life after Lockdown* by Lin Wenhua and Cai Kaihai presents a fascinating look at the lockdown in that city between January and April 2020 (BBC 2020a). By the end of January 2020, all hospitals in Wuhan were already packed and there was no space for new patients. Two military hospitals had to be built urgently to meet the demand, though even this was insufficient. By the end of February, just a month into the outbreak, more than 50,000 people were infected. To compensate for the failures of the state, more than 50,000 volunteers took action by supplying food and medicine to those most in need, often with limited protection for themselves. One of these volunteers featured in the film was Xia Qiyun, a hairdresser, who gave haircuts to more than 2,000 medical and frontline workers during the lockdown.

The documentary showed how COVID affected the lives of regular people, and how Chinese authorities responded in turn. Wang Kui had a well-established florist business that catered for weddings and funerals. After nobody was allowed to attend funerals or have proper weddings during the lockdown, she lost her business and started selling fruits and vegetables to be able to provide for her family. However, police did not allow her and her mother to do business on the street. Wang Kui said: "I understand the police because they are doing their job, but they don't understand that we somehow have to survive." A factory worker, who lost her job and started doing delivery work for survival, said that factory owners and many other people died and that the pandemic did not discriminate between poor and rich: "Rich people of Wuhan have also suffered from the pandemic." Another resident of Wuhan believed that surviving the pandemic "has made people stronger and more positive." A study by researchers at the Chinese Centre for Disease Control and Prevention has shown that during the first quarter of the outbreak, Wuhan alone had more than 500,000 COVID cases among a population of eleven million (BBC 2020b). This figure alone is almost four times higher than the official total of 126,078 infected in the whole of the country announced by the Chinese authorities and submitted to the WHO by November 1, 2021.

Other authoritarian governments around the world have also concealed the truth about the suffering of their people, with some even claiming for weeks after the initial outbreak that their countries had no cases of COVID. These claims, made in defiance of the geographical diffusion of the pandemic, were the subject of many Twitter and Facebook jokes, suggesting that the virus was discerning, able to jump over countries and bypass authoritarian regimes. For example, while by early March 2020 countries that had open border policies with Hungary and Turkey had already reported numerous infections and deaths, the Turkish regime-supporting media outlet *Haber Turk* claimed bold-facedly on March 10, 2020, that Turkey's low totals must be due to the "supergenes" of the Turkish people (Yilmaz 2020). Experts generally suspect that "silent" or "hidden" infection rates generate real totals that are far higher than what these regimes have claimed (Mérieau 2020).

It is thus not a very strange coincidence that on March 11, 2020, the day the WHO labeled COVID a pandemic (after listening to claims and awaiting approval from Chinese authorities for more than three months), many autocratic regimes, including Turkey, Hungary, and Russia, reported very few cases in their countries. After the high death rates reported by Western countries such as Italy, France, Spain, the United Kingdom (UK), and the US, Chinese authorities must have felt embarrassed by their reported fatality numbers, which they had argued for months to be around 3,200 (Wadhams and Jacobs 2020; Kinetz 2021). Despite China's claims that it had control over the virus, Chinese numbers rose sharply on April 16, 2020, when it suddenly declared that COVID had killed 4,632, an almost 50 percent increase in one day. According to the WHO statistics, Chinese authorities declared fewer than two hundred deaths between April 2020 and January 2021, an unbelievably low number given China's large population and the deadly and fast-moving nature of the virus.

Crisis as "God's Gift" for Autocrats

Disasters like COVID are thus "God's gift" to autocrats, given how they provide an opportunity to expand autocratic power and authority. All autocrats aspire to take full control of a legal system and constitution, besides which all else is detail. They attempt to do so through lawfare, rendering legal what is legally, politically, and morally wrong. Falsehood becomes truth and truth becomes falsehood according to the autocrats' laws.

Hungarian Prime Minister Orbán was one such beneficiary of the COVID pandemic, taking every opportunity to expand his power and weaponize the law against his opponents. To this end, the Hungarian parliament, with Orbán's Fidesz party in the majority, voted to suspend its operations, and Orbán seized the power to indefinitely extend the country's state of emergency, to rule by decree, and to jail anyone he claimed to be spreading "false" information about the virus. Those emergency powers were officially rescinded in June 2020, but only with accompanying legislation that codified many of the new powers Orbán had assumed. Newspaper articles from that time are instructive: *The Times* noted that "Victor Orbán's power grab in Hungary heightens fears of dictatorship in EU" (Moody 2020) while the *Telegraph* warned that "if the EU cannot rein in Hungary's dictator Viktor Orbán, it will rot from the inside" (Kelly 2020). *The Economist* (2020b) even averred that "Mr Orbán has in effect become a dictator — in the heart of Europe." In November 2020 Ferenc Falus, Hungary's former medical chief, was cited as follows in a report in the *British Medical Journal*: "There is virtually a military dictatorship in Hungary … It's very fitting that even the hospital directors (previously appointed by the government) were not trusted, and thus soldiers and police officers were assigned to them" (Karáth 2020: 1). The commanders look set to remain in place indefinitely, even after the state of emergency ended in June.

Similar to China's one-party state, the Hungarian government ran a public relations campaign to advertise its "fast solutions" to the pandemic: "On March 20, 2020, Orbán … ordered the construction of a slick, temporary hospital at the premises of Kiskunhalas prison. Under the slogan 'Europe's most modern mobile epidemic hospital' it was finished in just two and a half weeks, providing 150 beds 'to manage the sudden emergence of … a significant patient load,'" in the words of Hungarian secretary of state Zoltan Kovacs (Karáth 2020: 1). However, the facility was officially opened only six months later, on October 1, proving that it had been but a publicity stunt. Instead, in late March the government declared that the pandemic would be over before the summer, and in April Orbán announced that the infections would peak exactly on May 3 and ordered the gradual easing of lockdown measures on that specific day (Karáth 2020). In a similar publicity move, the Orbán government bought around 16,000 ventilators between March and May 2020, with the aim of winning "the ventilators competition" against other countries. Yet there were only an estimated 2,000 doctors and 2,000 intensive care nurses in the country trained to operate them (Karáth 2020: 2). Indeed, the rise of authoritarianism in the country and its crumbling health-care system has led to a brain drain of Hungarian doctors. According to the Union of Hungarian Doctors, between 2010 and 2016 around 5,500 doctors left Hungary to work in other countries (OECD/European Observatory on Health Systems and Policies 2019). This spiked during the COVID crisis: in the first half of 2020, more than 8,000 medical workers, mainly doctors, left Hungary's health-care system (Karáth 2020: 2). Securing its rule for the long term and using the pandemic to fuel the state propaganda machine have been, it seems, more important for Hungary's leadership than responding to the virus according to scientific advice and the needs of the people.

Turkey's Erdoğan had already monopolized power with the 2010 constitutional change and the 2016 military coup, which had crippled parliament. Decisions about wars, cross-border operations, amnesty, taxes, life, and death were decided by a narrow circle. Parliament was only kept informed to pass laws which had already been decided behind closed doors. Erdoğan also did not miss any opportunity to go after those social media accounts and local media sources that held different views about the virus than the regime. In the pandemic, the Turkish regime introduced a broad amnesty for prisoners, though one which disproportionately allowed murderers, rapists, organized crime bosses, and those supportive of the regime to be released. It excluded incarcerated journalists, novelists, Kurdish politicians, activists, outspoken liberal businessmen, and even politicians with serious illnesses. Those who remain imprisoned — mostly unsentenced critics of the regime — are on average sixty years old so that staying in prison represents a significant risk for them under the pandemic. The regime did not tolerate any criticism of its amnesty policy: Özgür Deniz Değer, co-chair of the medical chamber of the eastern city of Van, was arrested by police after giving an interview to the *Mesopotamia News Agency* on March 19, 2020, in which he attacked the government for not including political prisoners in the amnesty (HRW 2020).

Under many autocratic regimes, the concept of public money is flexible. Autocrats can undermine the independence of the central bank and assume the wealth of the people as their own. During the COVID pandemic, many democratic countries, such as the UK, Germany, Belgium, and even the US, provided additional financial support for people and affected businesses. The UK government offered to pay 80 percent of the salaries of all working people, up to GBP 2,500 a month. The US Congress passed a USD 2 trillion economic relief package. Germany, Belgium, and many other European countries took similar measures. In Turkey, however, Erdoğan ordered people to pay the state during the crisis. These funds were then redistributed as handouts in city centers, where TRY 1,000 (USD 144) were distributed, part of care packages along with the signature of Erdoğan so the public could see that it was coming from the leader himself (Euronews 2020; Kuru 2020).[3] This was, incidentally, a risky way for people to receive aid as infection could easily

---

3. President Trump did the same in the US with the Economic Impact Payments where his name was printed on the stimulus checks sent to ordinary Americans. The Turkish Lira subsequently lost 50 percent of its value against the dollar.

be transmitted during these events. But the propaganda was more important. Local authorities who tried to distribute some of their collected funds within the local communities were given a warning: their bank accounts would be frozen and the collected money transferred to the central authority (HRW 2021).

Despite Turkey manufacturing personal protective equipment (PPE) locally, there was a shortage of medical supplies and masks. The regime, meanwhile, engaged in "mask diplomacy," loading up planes bound for Italy, Spain, the UK, and many other countries with PPE to exhibit its power and build international support. Only the national government has the authority to release statistics about COVID infections and deaths, to the exclusion of local authorities, doctors, and civil organizations. Disbelief over the government's official COVID numbers is widespread among doctors in Turkey. Halis Yerlikaya, a physician at a hospital in the south-eastern province of Diyarbakir, told *Reuters* on September 19, 2020, that "the numbers of just one city, or the numbers unveiled by just one or two medical chambers are almost equal to the (official) numbers for the whole country" (Reuters 2020).

According to *Reuters* (2020) and the *British Medical Journal* (Dyer 2020), doctors who shared local COVID figures on social media showing significant differences from the official calculations have faced criminal charges. Many doctors around the country, wearing black ribbons to commemorate colleagues lost in the pandemic, carried out a weeklong protest from September 13 to 20 against the government for hiding the truth. On one placard they declared: "You can't handle it. We're burning out" (Dyer 2020). President Erdoğan's coalition partner Devlet Bahçeli, leader of the Nationalist Movement Party, labeled the protest a "treacherous plot" and asked for the Turkish Medical Association to be outlawed and its leadership prosecuted. He tweeted: "The Turkish Medical Association is as dangerous as coronavirus and is disseminating threats. The medical association which claims the name 'Turkish' should immediately be shut down" (Dyer 2020).

Many doctors have been interrogated on suspicion of "issuing threats regarding health with an aim to create panic and fear among the public" (Article 213 of Turkish Penal Code). The offense carries a possible prison sentence of between two and four years. The cochair of Şanlıurfa Medical Chamber, Ömer Melik, and its secretary general, Osman Yüksekyayla, have on more than one occasion been detained and interrogated by police after posting the number of local cases on the chamber's Twitter account, and after the chamber raised concerns over the safety of health workers and their lack of access to PPE. On June 10, 2020, Human Rights Watch released a report that criticized the Turkish government's response to COVID. Hugh Williamson, Europe and Central Asia director at Human Rights Watch, expressed the concerns thus: "The Turkish authorities criminally investigating medical chamber officials is not only an outrageous attack on free speech but impedes the fight against the deadly COVID-19 pandemic and obstructs their legitimate work. ... Official efforts to discredit and criminalize the association or its provincial affiliates, notably those in the mainly Kurdish southeast and eastern regions, undermines efforts to uphold public health and the right of medical professionals to do their job" (HRW 2020).

The Turkish Medical Association has long been a target of Erdoğan's government. Its entire central committee was arrested in 2018 after it criticized a Turkish military incursion into Syria. Eleven members, including its chair Sinan Adıyaman, received prison sentences of twenty months or more. And after the coup in 2016, more than 3,300 doctors were forced out of their jobs under a new decree. This harsh environment has fueled an accelerating medical brain drain to other countries (Dyer 2020).

The Chinese, Hungarian, and Turkish examples show how authoritarianism has created alternative facts, silenced critics, and prioritized the power of the regime over the public good. Outright lies become truth if the autocrat says so, the media supports it, and the population accepts it (Ho et al. 2019; Greenhouse 2019). Thanks to this work of indoctrination, truth and dissent are cast as false and unhealthy for "the unity of the nation," and criminalized accordingly. In this way, fact-making and totalitarian discipline and education give continuous living power to autocrats and their governments. Hobbes described this at the beginning of his *De Cive*: "man is made fit for society not by nature, but by education" (Hobbes 1991: 110).

Authoritarian governmentality is dangerous. Autocrats almost always prefer silencing criticism and falsifying economic and social data to confronting disasters and saving lives. Some of this is not just typical of authoritarian regimes, of course. It may in fact apply to some democratic regimes where pluralism still exists, where the rule of law is in place, where fair and equal elections are still being held, but where a leader seeks to abuse state power for their own interests and is willing to foster social divisions in pursuit of that goal. Trump has been perhaps the most prominent example of this tendency — with his defiance of congressional subpoenas, his building of the border wall with Mexico without congressional approval, and his calling media outlets that criticize him as producing "fake news." His absurd claim in March 2020 that the virus was "under control" (Collinson 2020) hampered the government's response to the crisis, which led the US to have one of the worst outbreaks of any country in the world, costing more than 400,000 lives during his presidency. In July 2020, the Trump administration launched a concerted effort to discredit the nation's leading infectious disease expert, Anthony Fauci, seemingly because the population in general was trusting the latter more than the president himself — a direct echo of the sort of personality politics that plays out under autocrats in other countries around the world.

Conclusion

The pandemic's ravages have been indiscriminate while also increasing the polarization of social classes and political systems. Which systems have failed, and which have most equitably managed the distribution of the pandemic's burden, will shape the global future.

As Didier Fassin (2009: 47) wrote in his article "Another Politics of Life Possible," "the problem of what is life — or more simply what we should understand here by this word — is complex." Under an authoritarian regime, if one is not part of the autocrat's inner circle, it can be difficult to go about the work of daily life. On the other hand, if one is, one can exercise profound control over other people's lives, wealth, and future. Tyrants punish others under claims of "terrorism" but describe themselves as "defenders of human beings," "God's gifts," and "peacekeepers," which, as Walter Benjamin (1978) stated, puts the "simple fact of living" human life in danger.

While a crisis like COVID might potentially damage the electoral chances of democratic leaders who fail to mount an adequate response, authoritarian leaders find in such crises the opportunity to increase their power and silence opposition groups. And while the fear of death is common across nations, political systems, social classes, and genders, it is compounded for those living under authoritarian regimes, for whom the act of questioning or criticizing authorities can have serious consequences. Even the mere failure of individuals to sufficiently express appreciation to the regime can result in them being punished, alienated, or isolated.

Even the most advanced democratic regimes are not immune to lies and fabricated statistics. Indeed, authoritarianism produces its own "contagion," such that autocratic power can stand to influence not just local but also global politics. It is merely a matter of time: the leadership of Bolsonaro in Brazil and Trump in the US demonstrates that the authoritarian pandemic has already crossed the Atlantic. Just as oceans are not sufficient barriers to stop viruses, they are not sufficient to halt this contagion. As such authoritarian regimes should be challenged not just locally but globally.

The belief that authoritarian regimes can be challenged through normal elections has been a delusion of liberal intellectuals for decades. Once autocrats are in office and enjoy power and control over the judiciary and the media, they are unlikely to leave power democratically, unless there is an equal or stronger force to challenge them.

"What we learn in a time of pestilence: that there are more things to admire in men than to despise," said Camus in *The Plague*. The rising tide of authoritarianism during the pandemic is not inevitable: people can fight to keep or to build humane democracies and habits of the heart. As long as people care for social rights, a free society, scientific knowledge, and truth — as long as they resist the lies of autocrats — they remain a buffer against demagogues who would wrap themselves in falsehood to maintain power.

Acknowledgements

Latif Tas's research project, TRANSNATIONALaw, has received funding from the European Union's Horizon 2020 research and innovation program under the Marie Skłodowska-Curie grant agreement No. 703201. An earlier and shorter version of this chapter was published by *Dissent*, titled "Authoritarian Governance is like a Virus" (July 23, 2020).

References

Ball, Molly. 2016. "Donald Trump and the Politics of Fear." *Atlantic*, September 2, 2016. https://www.theatlantic.com/politics/archive/2016/09/donald-trump-and-the-politics-of-fear/498116/.

BBC News. 2020a. "Inside Wuhan: Life after Coronavirus Lockdown." June 20, 2020. https://www.bbc.co.uk/news/av/world-asia-53106134.

BBC News. 2020b. "China Covid-19: Nearly 500,000 in Wuhan May Have Had Virus, Says Study." December 30, 2020. https://www.bbc.co.uk/news/world-asia-china-55481397.

Benjamin, Walter. 1978. "Critique of Violence." In *Reflections: Essays, Aphorisms and Autobiographical Writings*, edited by Peter Demetz, 277–300. New York: Harcourt Brace Javanovich.

Camus, Albert. (1947) 1967. *The Plague*. Translated by Stuart Gilbert. London: Hutchinson.

Collinson, Stephen. 2020. "Trump Claims Coronavirus is Under Control — Contradicting Reality and His Own Top Expect." CNN, March 16, 2020. https://edition.cnn.com/2020/03/16/politics/coronavirus-us-president-donald-trump-fauci-politics/index.html.

Dyer, Owen. 2020. "COVID-19: Turkey Cracks Down on Doctors who Doubt Official Figures." *British Medical Journal*, no. 370: m3787. https://doi.org/10.1136/bmj.m3787.

Economist. 2020a. "Diseases like COVID-19 are Deadlier in Non-Democracies." February 18, 2020. https://www.economist.com/graphic-detail/2020/02/18/diseases-like-covid-19-are-deadlier-in-non-democracies.

Economist. 2020b. "Would-be Autocrats Are Using COVID-19 as an Excuse to Grab more Power." April 25, 2020. https://www.economist.com/international/2020/04/23/would-be-autocrats-are-using-covid-19-as-an-excuse-to-grab-more-power.

Edel, Charles. 2018. "How Democracies Slide into Authoritarianism." *Washington Post*, December 7, 2018. https://www.washingtonpost.com/outlook/2018/12/07/how-democracies-slide-into-authoritarianism/.

Euronews. 2020. "Erdoğan 65 yaş üstü vatandaşlara mektup yazdı: Sizlere koruyucu maske ve kolonya hediye ediyoruz." April 8, 2020. https://tr.euronews.com/2020/04/08/erdogan-65-yas-ustu-vatanda-slara-mektup-yazd-sizlere-koruyucu-maske-ve-kolonya-hediye-ediy.

Fassin, Didier. 2009. "Another Politics of Life is Possible: *Theory, Culture and Society* 26 (5): 44–60. https://doi.org/10.1177/0263276409106349.

Golley, Jane, Linda Jaivin, and Sharon Strange, eds. 2021. *Crisis*. Canberra: ANU Press.

Greenhouse, Carol J. 2019. "'This is Not Normal': Are Social Facts Finished." *American Anthropologist* 121 (1): 167–70. https://doi.org/10.1111/aman.13185.

Ho, Karen, and Jillian R. Cavanaugh. 2019. "What Happened to Social Facts?" *American Anthropologist* 121 (1): 160–67. https://doi.org/10.1111/aman.13184.

Hobbes, Thomas. 1991. *Man and Citizen (De Homine and De Cive)*. Edited and with an introduction by Bernard Gert. Indianapolis: Hackett.

HRW (Human Rights Watch). 2020. "Turkey: Probes over Doctors' COVID-19 Comments: Investigations into Medical Chamber Leaders Undermine Pandemic Response." Human Rights Watch, June 10, 2020. https://www.hrw.org/news/2020/06/10/turkey-probes-over-doctors-covid-19-comments.

HRW. 2021. "Turkey." In *World Report 2021: Events of 2020*, 666–73. New York: Human Rights Watch.

Karáth, Kata. 2020. "COVID-19: Hungary's Pandemic Response May Have Been Worse than the Virus." *British Medical Journal*, no. 371: m4153. https://doi.org/10.1136/bmj.m4153.

Kelly, Ben. 2020. "If the EU Cannot Rein in Hungary's Dictator Viktor Orbán, It Will Rot from the Inside." *Telegraph*, March 31, 2020. https://www.telegraph.co.uk/politics/2020/03/31/eu-cannot-rein-hungarys-dictator-viktor-orban-will-rot-inside/.

Kinetz, Erika. 2021. "Anatomy of a Conspiracy: With COVID, China Took Leading Role." *AP News*, February 15, 2021. https://apnews.com/article/pandemics-beijing-only-on-ap-epidemics-media-122b73e134b-780919cc1808f3f6f16e8.

Kuru, Ahmet T. 2020. "Turkey Releasing Murderers – but not Political Opponents – from Prison amid Coronavirus Pandemic." *Conversation*, April 23, 2020. https://theconversation.com/turkey-releasing-murderers-but-not-political-opponents-from-prison-amid-coronavirus-pandemic-136466.

Mérieau, Eugénie. 2020. "Covid-19, Authoritarianism vs. Democracy: What the Epidemic Reveals about the Orientalism of our Categories of Thought." SciencesPo Center for International Studies, August 28, 2020. https://www.sciencespo.fr/ceri/en/content/covid-19-authoritarianism-vs-democracy-what-epidemic-reveals-about-orientalism-our-categorie.

Moody, Oliver. 2020. "Victor Orbán's Power Grab in Hungary Heightens Fears of Dictatorship in EU." *Times*, April 2, 2020. https://www.thetimes.co.uk/article/victor-orbans-power-grab-in-hungry-heightens-fears-of-dictatorship-in-eu-83h3g9lpm.

OECD/European Observatory on Health Systems and Policies. 2019. *Hungary Country Health Profile 2019: State of Health in the EU*. Paris: OECD Publishing. https://doi.org/10.1787/4b7ba48c-en.

Plattner, Marc F. 2015. "Is Democracy in Decline?" *Journal of Democracy* 26 (1): 5–10. https://doi.org/10.1353/jod.2015.0014.

Reuters. 2020. "Surge in Turkish COVID Cases Pits Doctors against Politicians." September 19, 2020. https://www.reuters.com/article/uk-health-coronavirus-turkey-idUSKCN26A0N4.

Su, Alice. 2020. "Coronavirus Killed China's Whistleblower Doctor. Now the Virus has Changed how the Country can Mourn Him." *Los Angeles Times*, April 3, 2020. https://www.latimes.com/world-nation/story/2020-04-03/coronavirus-china-doctor-tomb-sweeping.

Tas, Latif. 2022. *Authoritarianism and Kurdish Alternative Politics: Governmentality, Gender and Justice*. Edinburgh: Edinburgh University Press.

Tenz, Courtney. 2017. "What Philosopher Hannah Arendt Would Say about Donald Trump." *Deutsche Welle*, August 16, 2017. https://beta.dw.com/en/what-philosopher-hannah-arendt-would-say-about-donald-trump/a-36766400.

Wadhams, Nick and Jennifer Jacobs. 2020. "China Intentionally Under-Reported Total Coronavirus Cases and Deaths, U.S. Intelligence Says." *Fortune*, April 1, 2020. https://fortune.com/2020/04/01/china-coronavirus-cases-deaths-total-under-report-cover-up-covid-19/.

Wright, Joseph. 2008. "Do Authoritarian Institutions Constrain? How Legislatures Affect Economic Growth and Investment." *American Journal of Political Science* 52 (2): 322–43. https://doi.org/10.1111/j.1540-5907.2008.00315.x.

Wright, Joseph, and Abel Escribà-Folch. 2012. "Authoritarian Institutions and Regime Survival: Transitions to Democracy and Subsequent Autocracy." *British Journal of Political Science* 42 (2): 283–309. https://doi.org/10.1017/S0007123411000317.

Yilmaz, Didem A. 2020. "Türkiye'nin Nabzı: Türk geni koronavirüsten korur mu?" *Haber Turk*, March 10, 2020, video, 2:08:19. https://youtu.be/cPZepBy5GQM.

CHAPTER 7

Stretching Time

COVID and Sudan's Current Transitions

Rebecca Glade and Alden Young

On May 14, the Sovereign Council of the Republic of Sudan issued a statement on its Facebook page announcing the ouster of the Minister of Health, Dr. Akram Ali Eltom. The Sovereign Council is made up of representatives of the military and security services as well as of the main civilian parties. In response to Dr. Akram's sacking, the neighborhood resistance committees, the local manifestations of Sudan's 2019 popular revolution, threatened to return to the streets in protest (Amin 2020). The Forces of Freedom and Change, the main coalition of civilian parties, referred to the sacking as "irresponsible," and the Minister of Information, Faisal Muhammad Salih, came forward to affirm that Prime Minister Abdalla Hamdok, whose office was the only one legally entitled to remove a sitting minister, was currently happy with Dr. Akram's performance (Amin 2020). As the chaos unfolded over where power lay within the transitional government in Sudan, the Sovereign Council edited its Facebook posts at least fifteen times during the course of the night before dropping the matter entirely. Perhaps a small matter, but these repeated edits demonstrated the confusion within the government and how reliant during the height of the pandemic Sudanese officials had become on social media, both for their internal communication and for that with the public at large, in particular the population residing in the major cities like Khartoum, Omdurman and Port Sudan as well as the overseas diasporas.

The confused social media strategy was not merely a communication failure but also underlined the ongoing political conflicts taking place inside of Sudan's transitional government. During the months before the outbreak of the pandemic in Sudan, the transitional government — an uneasy partnership between formerly opposed civilian parties and civil society groups, on the one side, and the security apparatus made up of the Sudanese Armed Forces, intelligence services and government-sponsored militia, on the other — had appeared to be on the verge of a decisive clash. Yet for the duration of the pandemic, the confrontation was postponed even as the tensions over where political authority was located were amplified, as the story of Dr. Akram demonstrates.

As such, the pandemic and policies necessary to respond to it have served to amplify previously existing political dynamics, stretching out the time in which these conflicts have played out. After thirty years of military rule in which political life in Sudan was severely constrained, the fall of the Bashir regime at the hands of a massive country-wide popular mobilization signaled a revival of civil society, and the rise and fall of governments over the next few months brought about an acceleration of political time. Yet, the pandemic has led to a prolongation of the economic, social, and political crises that initially caused Sudan's Revolution of 2018/19. The crises that served as the backdrop of the revolution have not been resolved, they have simply been delayed. As evidence of this continuity and delay, inflation in May 2021 was 379 percent, with water and electricity outages occurring daily. On June 16, 2021, Sudan's transitional Prime Minister Abdalla Hamdok, speaking about the fragmented political situation in the country — whereby both the civilian and the security sectors are internally divided and set against each other — said that this state "can lead us to a situation of chaos and control by gangs and criminal groups, just as it can lead to the spread of conflict among all civilian groups and might lead to civil war" (*Reuters* 2021). The persistence and growth of political fragmentation is one of the consequences of the pandemic. The pandemic became an excuse for Sudanese elites to delay political decisions, even as the attempt to contain ever more groups within the framework of the indefinitely extended transition continues.

Sudan's Revolution began in December 2018 when protesters in cities outside of Khartoum began demonstrations against the lifting of bread subsidies. These events culminated in the burning of the National

Congress Party headquarters in Atbara. The protests then moved to Khartoum where they escalated from weekly to daily rallies calling for the regime led by President Omar al-Bashir to "Just Fall," a translation of the Arabic slogan used on placards, in songs, and on social media to express the demands of the demonstrators for political change. Over the course of four months, leadership in these protests coalesced around various civil society groups, most importantly the Sudanese Professionals Association, a conglomerate of nineteen unions who, alongside a coalition of political parties, signed onto the Freedom and Change Declaration that laid out a path for a peaceful transfer of power.

At the urging of political leaders in this coalition, protesters began a sit-in outside the army's headquarters on April 6, 2019. Withstanding violence from the National Intelligence Security Services, the sit-in grew in size and clout and yielded returns when the Sudanese Armed Forces announced on April 11 the deposition of President Omar al-Bashir and the formation of a Transitional Military Council. While seen as an initial triumph, protesters were not content with this palace coup, and the sit-in continued as protesters demanded a transition to civilian government with calls for *medaniya* (civilian rule) and demands that this government "Fall Again."

The ongoing sit-ins prompted a standoff that lasted for another four months, with the Transitional Military Council negotiating with the Forces of Freedom and Change, the coalition of political parties and civil society groups that gradually came to represent the demands for civilian rule. This standoff and the negotiations that ensued were unstable and violent. On June 3, 2019, the Sudanese security apparatus forcibly cleared the sit-in in a series of violent acts designed to instill fear, killing over one hundred people, raping many, and throwing bodies in the Nile (Salih and Burke 2019). The Transitional Military Council then shut down the internet for the next month as it attempted to stifle public support for *medaniya*. On June 30 civilians nonetheless took to the streets for a protest that was arguably larger than the beginning of the sit-in that ousted Bashir and continued to protest afterwards, maintaining their original demands.

This struggle and the ongoing negotiations between the Transitional Military Council and the Forces of Freedom and Change eventually yielded a Draft Constitutional Declaration in August 2019. This agreement enshrined in law a transitional government that functioned as an uneasy compromise. The executive was to be a Sovereign Council made up of eleven members — five nominated by the security apparatus and five from the Forces of Freedom and Change, with a final member appointed by mutual agreement. This council would be chaired for the first eighteen months of a three-year transitional period by a member nominated by the security apparatus, to then be yielded to a civilian member of the council. Meanwhile, a council of ministers headed up by a Prime Minister would be appointed by the Forces of Freedom and Change, except for the ministries of defense and the interior, to be appointed by the security apparatus.

When COVID came to Sudan in March 2020, Sudan's government functioned as an uneasy transitional government, with all parties involved — both within the security apparatus and within the alliance of Sudanese political movements — advancing different agendas, many with radically different visions of what type of government they wanted to achieve at the end of this period. The Sovereign Council at that point had its locus of power within the security apparatus, especially with its chair, General Burhan of the Sudanese Armed Forces, and its deputy, Mohamed Hamdan "Himeidti" Dagalo of the Rapid Support Forces (RSF), the largest paramilitary force in the country. In contrast, the Council of Ministers and its Prime Minister, Abdalla Hamdok, represented the civilian centers of power, most accountable to the Forces of Freedom and Change and to the local "resistance committees" that had done the work of organizing protests over the eight months of struggle and had become essential to public life in Sudan.

The Sovereign Council's attempt to remove the Minister of Health in May 2020 functioned as yet another step in the ongoing tussle between the parties of the transitional government. Rather than an apolitical move to maximize the country's COVID response, this attempt to remove Dr. Akram was an attempted power grab by the security apparatus that sought to marginalize civilian government.

The confrontation over the Minister of Health came as Sudan faced the worst of the first wave of the COVID pandemic. The day before, 146 new cases of COVID were confirmed, bringing the total number of confirmed cases up to 1,964, with 91 deaths. The week of this confrontation, an average of 168 new cases and 4 deaths were identified each day. In the following week, average deaths would rise to double digits, where they would stay for a month before declining to single digits again in the week of June 18, only to continue to decline from then on.[1]

---

1. All data cited was compiled through Ministry of Health daily reports printed and stamped by the General Director of Public Administration for

Criticism of Dr. Akram's response to the pandemic came despite serious measures undertaken at his direction. Sudan's first confirmed case was announced on March 13, 2020, a Sudanese man who returned from the United Arab Emirates (Middle East Eye 2020). The day after the first case was found, Akram ordered wedding halls and mass gatherings to be closed. Temperature checks were instituted at the airport for all flights, no longer only for the flights arriving from China. After the second case, the Akram and the Ministry of Health ordered universities and schools closed, and selected prisoners were released from prisons. By the time the third case was identified, the government closed the airports, suspended all travel between states, and instituted a 6 p.m. to 6 a.m. curfew — extended several weeks later to a 3 p.m. to 6 a.m. curfew as part of a larger lockdown (Crisis 24 2020). As soon as tests for the virus became available, the Ministry of Health contacted those who had entered the country over the early weeks of March for testing, though they were only able to reach about 50 percent of them (Eltahir, Abdelaziz, and Siddig 2020).

These measures stood out in comparison to other African states such as Kenya, Nigeria, and Burkina Faso, who also instituted lockdowns and took proactive measures, in that the Sudanese response largely avoided the use of state violence (DW 2020; France 24 2020). This decision was critical — so soon after an uprising whose central conflict for much of 2019 was around the need for governance by "civilians," a lockdown enforced by threats of state violence would have served to empower that same security apparatus and undermine the civilians who had just gained a share of power.

To that end, the lockdown put in place in Khartoum in April worked primarily through the control of motorized transportation. Public transportation was suspended and travel via cars or other motorized vehicles was restricted through checkpoints on major roads. Movement by foot remained unregulated — meaning that people could travel from house to house within neighborhoods or go to neighborhood markets. Restrictions on what sort of offices could be open functionally shut down the salaried economy while keeping the informal economy of shops and markets open.

These measures were extensive and necessary given the risks involved in facing a pandemic with a health sector weakened by over thirty years of

---

Emergencies and Combatting Epidemics, then scanned and published as images on the Ministry's Facebook page.

authoritarian mismanagement (Syeed 2014). And yet these government measures may not have been the only reason COVID did not spread in Sudan as extensively as in Europe, for example, during the first wave. As cases declined moderately in early July, the government chose to reduce restrictions, shortening its curfew to 6 p.m. to 6 a.m. and allowing the gradual reopening of offices and certain businesses. That week, Sudan faced an average of eight new cases a day with roughly six deaths. Yet cases continued to decline over the following weeks, going from a daily average of sixty new cases and three deaths during the week of August 13–19 to one of single digit new cases and no deaths beginning with the week of September 12–18.[2]

What accounts then for this dramatic decline in cases, which seems to be similar to the experiences across Africa? Sub-Saharan Africa's reduced mortality rates during the first wave of the pandemic gave rise to several scientific studies trying to offer explanations. These studies typically relied on the concept of "excess mortality." Excess mortality is "as a term used in epidemiology or public health that refers to the number of deaths *from all causes* during a crisis above and beyond what we would have expected to see under normal conditions" (Giattino and Ritchie 2021). According to Sophie Uyoga of the Kenya Medical Research Institute-Wellcome Trust Research Programme, "we don't have an answer" for why excess mortality is so low (Nordling 2020: 756).

Little discussion of the pandemic in Africa has occurred publicly, other than in vague terms. This has led to criticism that analysis of disease in Africa assumes it will necessarily be worse than in Europe and the United States (US). In a prescient piece from May 2020, Mondesire asked: "Given the comparatively slow spread of the novel coronavirus on the African continent, there is nevertheless a marked refusal to entertain the possibility that the facts on the ground in Africa may represent a reversal of the global trajectory of sickness and deprivation. It is incumbent upon us to ask what animates this refusal. Why, in this context, have so many dominant voices refused the facts on the ground in lieu of their own expectations?" (Mondesire 2020). Echoing the question, Nyabola points out that this dismissal of Africa weighs in on the research

---

2. While this decline was pronounced, it was by no means linear. Some weeks had slightly higher numbers than the weeks before, but the pattern over three months was pronounced. No new deaths were reported in Sudan from COVID following the week of September 12 until October 23, when one death was reported in Gezira.

questions being asked about the pandemic there, making it difficult to learn from the experiences of African countries, while Bauer emphasizes the need to move away from a focus on Western perceptions of Africa in order to address the challenges that the pandemic has created for African countries in their own terms (Nyabola 2020; Bauer 2020).

It may not be possible to determine the actual scale of the pandemic in Sudan due to lack of adequate data. Testing in Sudan was always small in scale in comparison with elsewhere, which has made assessing the level of the crisis difficult. Using the Sudanese Ministry of Health data, a small-scale field study across Khartoum, and an online survey, researchers at Imperial College London estimated that between March and November 2020 the reported COVID deaths in Khartoum made up between 2 and 5 percent of all deaths from COVID — with the data suggesting that between 6,000 and 16,000 more people died of the virus than had been reported in the official statistics. They estimate that during that time roughly 38 percent of the capital contracted COVID, warning that should the numbers be lower than estimated in the first wave, the second wave was likely to be more severe (Watson 2020).

While it may not be possible to estimate the full cost of the pandemic itself, the policies put in place in the early period of the pandemic served most prominently to delay elements of the transitional government that had already been lagging previously, such as the appointment of a legislative council and state governors. These appointments should have been processed within months of the agreement being signed. In many ways, these delays stemmed primarily from the fact that few in leadership welcomed the loss or dispersion of authority — the Sovereign Council and security apparatus were in no rush to include more civilian politicians into the government or face the accountability of a legislative council. Hamdok's government was in no rush either, since a legislative council would serve as another center of power with a popular mandate that could challenge the policies adopted by the Council of Ministers. The onset of a lockdown in April served to extend these delays since restrictions on movement made political mobilization in the form of demonstrations difficult, while simultaneously moving attention away from these political conflicts to what now seemed to be a more important health crisis.

Similarly, this period involved an extension of peace negotiations — also delayed prior to the pandemic. Sudan's partition into Sudan and South Sudan in 2011 did not end the civil wars that have marked the country for most of its history since achieving independence in 1956.

Instead, the armed movements in Sudan's peripheries continued fighting, and even after the fall of Bashir's regime in 2019 it remains an open question, up for constant negotiation, how these armed movements will be incorporated. After Sudan's Transitional Agreement was signed in August 2019, formal negotiations began in Juba between the new government and a wide spectrum of Sudan's rebel groups, who had been fighting in Darfur, Kordofan, and Blue Nile — some of Sudan's most marginalized states. For months these negotiations had largely stalled, stuck on issues such as that of secularism, as well as the question of representation within the Sovereign Council and legislative council. But the delays of the pandemic provided more time for an accommodation to be reached, and in October 2020 a fragile peace was signed. Yet the sharing of power in Sudan remains fraught with many decisions simply delayed rather than resolved.

The onset of the lockdown, and the global crisis that the pandemic represented, served to take attention and pressure away from these negotiations, both within Sudan and internationally (Amnesty 2020). The delays caused by the pandemic's early days also served to delay pressure by the international community for Sudan's government to adopt domestically unpopular policies, such as the elimination of food and fuel subsidies. Even before the pandemic the Sudanese economy was facing compounding crises after what the transitional government's first Finance Minister Ibrahim El-Badawi termed "two decades of solitude" (African Development Bank Group 2019). One of the first tasks before the transitional government was to gain emergency financing and to begin the process of debt relief in order to address the mounting economic difficulties in the country, a process that required negotiating with advisers from the International Monetary Fund and the World Bank. International agencies attached stiff demands to any economic assistance, particularly the requirement to lift subsidies for basic goods, including bread and gas, a demand opposed by large segments of the Forces of Freedom and Change coalition.

The international donor conference in which these reforms were expected to be announced was scheduled to occur in April 2020, a month after the COVID crisis had thrown much of the world into a tangled web of lockdowns and restraints. The conference was postponed and eventually held remotely in June, where it garnered pledges of only USD 1.8 billion of the USD 3 billion of aid estimated to be necessary to manage this transition (Arab Weekly 2020). And while discussions of lifting subsidies continued and measures to lift them have proceeded, they were not adopted during the lockdown, which extended opportunities for debate and gave the domestic opposition more time to mobilize.

All of these items came to a head in late June and early July 2020, when protesters took to the streets in an overwhelming sign of political engagement. They showed up in large numbers on June 30, the one-year anniversary of the massive protests that repudiated the political violence of the security apparatus and forced the Transitional Military Council back into serious negotiations with the Forces of Freedom and Change (*Reuters* 2020). The new protests not only called for the appointment of a legislative council and governors but also condemned the preparations implemented toward the lifting of subsidies. The protests were enacted despite disengagement by, and even disapproval from, civilian members of the transitional government, who viewed them as an embarrassment, since they spoke to dissatisfaction with the performance of the government as a whole (DW 2020). The protests were soon followed by further activism as civilians launched a series of sit-ins in Darfur and Kordofan, beginning in Nertiti. These protests made a series of local demands regarding demilitarization, regulation of relations between farmers and herders, and regulations of the security apparatus (Salih 2020).

This activism has been met with mixed success. Soon after the June 30 protests, the transitional government made serious breakthroughs in its peace negotiations with rebel movements, culminating in the signing of a peace agreement with five movements and a declaration of shared principles with the SPLM-North on secularism (Juba Agreement for Peace 2020). This was followed shortly after by a reshuffling of the Council of Ministers, during which fifteen ministers were fired or resigned. This included the resignation of Finance Minister El-Badawi as well as the dismissal of Minister of Health Akram — both of whom faced opposition related less to the immediate circumstances of their firing than other political issues.[3] At the same time, the challenges of the transition continued — while civilian governors were appointed, they faced opposition on various grounds, both tribalist and gender based. A legislative council has yet to be appointed. Meanwhile, as 2021 began,

---

3. Indeed, Badawi's office maintains he was asked to resign due to his request for a full account of the national budget, including oversight of the security apparatus. Dr. Akram, ostensibly facing opposition due to his handling of the pandemic, was also challenged for his management style and attempts to marginalize the pharmaceutical industry, and for pandering to protesters during the June 30 demonstrations.

the government proceeded to lift subsidies and has floated the currency despite adamant opposition across the Sudanese political spectrum.

The early period of the pandemic bought time for conversations and organizing to happen in the absence of extended attention or resources from external powers. With the US, Europe, Saudi Arabia, and the Emirates occupied with combatting the virus and its financial repercussions, and with large-scale movement hindered within Sudan, Sudanese actors — both civilian and security — had time to work internally. For the Vice Chair of the Sovereign Council and militia leader Himeidti and his RSF, this involved a series of charitable works and an expansion of the RSF with active recruitment in order to boost his legitimacy (Mashamoun 2020). In other ministries, this meant the appointment of new staff in lower-level positions within ministries, the promotion of more qualified existing staff, and the drawing up of new plans to be implemented in the future. Among grassroots communities, this meant time for the neighborhood resistance committees to consolidate their organizing, to assist in the distribution of cooking gas, benzine, and bread, and to aid those who faced hardship during the lean times caused by the lockdown (El-Gizouli 2020).

It was in this context that the Sudanese government agreed to pay a USD 334 million settlement to the victims of the 1998 Al Qaeda attacks on the US embassies in Kenya and Tanzania, in exchange for being removed from the state sponsors of terrorism (SST) list in October 2020. While not stated explicitly, this seems to have been linked to US pressure for Sudan to normalize relations with Israel, which was announced by the Sovereign Council soon after (DW 2021). These moves have ostensibly strengthened the security apparatus, giving it credit for negotiating an end to Sudan's presence on the SST list. Meanwhile, the cost of living in Sudan has continued to skyrocket, and daily life has gotten increasingly difficult for the average person.

Currently Sudan finds itself in a period of contestation. It is entirely possible that the security apparatus might gain further legitimacy as this transition continues and might be able to use political opportunities garnered through the financial crisis and tough political choices ahead to grab power, whether through an outright coup or through running candidates in the next elections. At the same time, the ongoing organizing at the grassroots level has thus far served to provide opposition and pushback against power grabs, and the crises may well encourage further socioeconomic solidarities and unite dissatisfied members of Sudanese society, propelling them to further activism in the face of objectionable moves by the transitional government (Malik 2020). It is unclear how these standoffs will end, but the pandemic has bought the different parties in the Sudanese conflict additional time to entrench their positions. By preventing an easy consolidation of power, it has opened the door to the faint possibility that a tense agreement to share power may persist long into the future. In the broader context the pandemic in Sudan fostered a period of continuity even as it decelerated time. Decisions and the resolution of ongoing crises were pushed further and further into the future. Yet daily and political life in Sudan continued. COVID became one unresolved problem amid many others, while in the Global North there is an imagination that the COVID pandemic will end with vaccines and through lockdowns. In Sudan there has for months now been a recognition that the pandemic will not be defeated by vaccines that for most Sudanese people will never arrive. Instead, since the winter months of 2021, Sudanese society began to slowly readjust to life with COVID, as the government decided that it would not reenter a lockdown. In Sudan, as in much the developing world, 2021 has marked the beginning of a life of coexistence with COVID rather than the end of the pandemic.

References

African Development Bank Group. 2019. "Sudan Economic Report: After Two Decades of 'Solitude' Targeted Strategies for Quick Economic Wins." *African Development Bank Group*, September 9, 2019.

Amin, Mohammed. 2020. "Sudanese Activists Threaten Protests if Health Minister Fired." *Middle East Eye*, May 16, 2020. https://www.middleeasteye.net/news/sudan-health-minister-akram-altoum-threat-protests-civil-society.

Amnesty International. 2020. "Sudan: Peace Agreement Must Delivery on People's Quest for Dignity and Justice." Amnesty International, August 31, 2020. https://www.amnesty.org/en/latest/press-release/2020/08/sudan-peace-agreement-must-deliver-on-peoples-quest-for-dignity-and-justice/.

Arab Weekly. 2020. "Western, Arab Donors Pledge $1.8 Billion for Sudan's Transition." *Arab Weekly*, June 25, 2020. https://thearabweekly.com/western-arab-donors-pledge-18-billion-sudans-transition.

Bauer, George K. 2020. "Beyond the Western Gaze." Africa Is a Country, May 29, 2020. https://africasacountry.com/2020/05/beyond-the-western-gaze.

Checchi, Francesco, and Les Roberts. 2005. "Interpreting and Using Mortality Data in Humanitarian Emergencies: A Primer for Non-epidemiologists." Humanitarian Practice Network, Overseas Development Institute, September 2005. https://odihpn.org/resources/interpreting-and-using-mortality-data-in-humanitarian-emergencies/.

Crisis 24. 2020. "Sudan: Government Implements Nationwide Nighttime Curfew March 24 Due to COVID-19/Update 3." March 23, 2020. https://crisis24.garda.com/insights-intelligence/intelligence/risk-alerts/juap5tybcblg2oe6h/sudan-government-implements-nationwide- nighttime-curfew-march-24-due-to-covid-19-update-3.

Deutsche Welle. 2020. "Protestors Hit Sudan Streets Calling for Political Reforms." July 1, 2020. https://p.dw.com/p/3ebVT.

Deutsche Welle. 2021. "Sudan Signs Pact with US on Normalizing Ties with Israel." January 6, 2021. https://p.dw.com/p/3najt.

El-Gizouli, Magdi. 2020. "Mobilization and Resistance in Sudan's Uprising from Neighbourhood Committees to Zanig Queens." Briefing paper, Rift Valley Institute, January 6, 2020. https://xcept-research.org/publication/mobilization-and-resistance-in-sudans-uprising-from-neighbourhood-committees-to-zanig-queens/.

Eltahir, Nafisa, Khaled Abdelaziz, and Eltayeb Siddig. 2020. "Few Ventilators, Little Cash: Sudan Braces for Coronavirus Test." *Reuters*, April 22, 2020. https://www.reuters.com/article/us-health-coronavirus-sudan-idUSKCN22426N.

France 24. 2020. "Security Forces Use Violent Tactics to Enforce Africa's Coronavirus Shutdowns." April 1, 2020. https://www.france24.com/en/20200401-security-forces-use-violent-tactics-to-enforce-africa-s-coronavirus-shutdowns.

Giattino, Charlie, Hannah Ritchie, Max Roser, Esteban Ortiz-Ospina, and Joe Hasell. 2021. "Excess Mortality during the Coronavirus Pandemic (COVID-19)." Our World in Data, Updated October 4, 2021. https://ourworldindata.org/excess-mortality-covid.

"Juba Agreement for Peace in Sudan between the Transitional Government of Sudan and the Parties to Peace Process." October 3, 2020. https://www.peaceagreements.org/viewmasterdocument/2325.

Malik, Nesrine. 2020. "Demise of a Dictator: How Will the World Remember Sudan's Omar al-Bashir." *Prospect*, March 3, 2020. https://www.prospectmagazine.co.uk/magazine/sudan-protests-omar-al-bashir-icc-profile-nesrine-malik.

Mashamoun, Jihad. 2020. "Sudan's Transition to Free Elections Undermined by Hemeti." *Africa Report*, April 6, 2020. https://www.theafricareport.com/25325/sudans-transition-to-free-elections-undermined-by-hemeti/.

Middle East Eye. 2020. "Coronavirus: First Case Reported in Sudan." March 13, 2020. https://www.middleeasteye.net/news/coronavirus-sudan-first-case-reported-returned-uae.

Mondesire, Zachary. 2020. "Predisposed to Chaos." Africa is a Country, May 21, 2020. https://africasacountry.com/2020/05/predisposed-to-chaos.

Nordling, Linda. 2020. "Africa's Pandemic Puzzle: Why So Few Cases and Deaths?" *Science* 369 (6505): 756–57. https://doi.org/10.1126/science.369.6505.756.

Nyabola, Nanjala. 2020. "How to Talk about COVID-19 in Africa." *Boston Review*, October 15, 2020. http://bostonreview.net/global-justice/nanjala-nyabola-how-talk-about-covid-19-africa.

Reuters. 2020. "One Killed in Sudan as Thousands Rally for Faster Reforms." *Reuters*, June 30, 2020. https://www.reuters.com/article/us-sudan-politics-idUSKBN24127Y.

Reuters. 2021. "Sudan's Prime Minister Warns of Risk of Chaos, Civil War." *Reuters*, June 21, 2021. https://www.reuters.com/world/africa/sudans-prime-minister-warns-risk-chaos-civil-war-2021-06-15/.

Salih, Zeinab M. 2020. "Darfur Protestors Call for Action to End Attacks on Civilians by Armed Militias." *Guardian*, July 8, 2020. https://www.theguardian.com/global-development/2020/jul/08/darfur-protesters-call-for-action-to-end-attacks-on-civilians-by-armed-militias.

Salih, Zeinab M., and Jason Burke. 2019. "Sudanese Doctors Say Dozens of People Raped During Sit-In Attack." *Guardian*, June 11, 2019. https://www.theguardian.com/world/2019/jun/11/sudan-troops-protesters-attack-sit-in-rape-khartoum-doctors-report.

Syeed, Nafeesa. 2014. "Sudan's Hospitals: 'Ravaged by Privatisation.'" *Al-Jazeera*, January 6, 2014. https://www.aljazeera.com/features/2014/1/6/sudans-hospitals-ravaged-by-privatisation.

Watson, Oliver, Nada Abdelmagid, Aljaile Ahmed, Abd E. Ahmed Abd Elhameed, Charles Whittaker, Nicholas Brazeau, Arran Hamlet et al. 2020. *Report 39: Characterizing COVID-19 Epidemic Dynamics and Mortality Under-Ascertainment in Khartoum, Sudan*. Imperial College London, December 1, 2020. https://doi.org/10.25561/84283.

Part II. Moral Economies

CHAPTER 8

The Moral Economy of Life in the Pandemic

Didier Fassin

The COVID pandemic has produced an unprecedented global crisis. So go most comments. However, when this assertion is articulated, it does not mean that the disease itself is the worst ever experienced. Without searching as far in the past as the fourteenth-century plague that killed at least one third of the European population, many infections in the modern era have been more severe, measles being more contagious and AIDS more lethal. Compared to the so-called Spanish flu of 1918, which lasted one year, COVID has caused between ten and twenty times fewer deaths worldwide during the first twelve months, probably in good part due to the measures adopted. More accurately, it is the response to the pandemic that has been unprecedented, with complete lockdowns implemented in many places across the globe.

Modalities of this response have certainly differed between countries: authoritarian in China, limited in South Korea, drastic in Australia, fluctuating in Britain, accommodating in Germany, lenient in Sweden, belated and rigorous in Italy, inconsistent and heterogeneous in the United States (US), paternalistic and repressive in France. Beyond these differences in style, however, most governments have decided to discontinue, at least to some degree and for some time, most businesses, restaurants, schools, sports competitions, and cultural events, and the strictest policies have often been implemented in the countries most unprepared and most unreactive to the pandemic. Thus, in France, which at the beginning of the epidemic had neither masks nor tests, where frontline and second-line workers had no protection, where patients were not strictly isolated and contact persons were not traced, a general lockdown was rigidly enforced — with multiple fines for offenders — particularly in disadvantaged neighborhoods. Sanitary policing tended to substitute for the lack of a public health policy. In that regard, it is remarkable that in July 2020 the number of deaths attributed to the coronavirus was, proportional to the population, four times higher in France, where the lockdown had been extremely strict, than in Germany, where no such measure had been taken but where effective preventive policies had been applied earlier with broad testing, contact tracking, and patient isolation.

The lockdowns had two major repercussions. There was, first, a partial suspension of civil liberties and individual rights: freedom of movement, of meeting, of protest, sometimes of expression; the right to education, work, private life, asylum protection, intimacy with loved ones at the end of life, and honoring of the dead at funerals. In many countries, these restrictions were rendered easier by the imposition of states of exception giving broad powers to executive branches, which aggravated the decline in checks and balances already observed before the pandemic. There was, second, a temporary cessation of much of the economy, with predictable deleterious effects: recession, increase of the public debt, bankruptcy of companies (albeit limited by extensive income support and loan programs), expansion of unemployment and underemployment with discontinuation of health insurance and social benefits, pauperization with food insecurities for the most vulnerable categories. Consequences for the people were more tragic where welfare states were weaker.

These are considerable sacrifices for a nation: a withering of democratic principles and an increase in precarity for large segments of society — again, with significant differences between countries determined by political regime, depth of inequality, quality of social protection, and, of course, modality of implementation of the lockdown when there was one. Such sacrifices had only one raison d'être: the reduction of mortality due to the coronavirus. They were deemed the price required to save lives.

What does this tell us about the way one values life in contemporary societies? What are the implications of the recognition of life as the highest good? Which component of life is to be spared, and at the expense of which other? Whose lives are thus spared, and whose lives are neglected or even exposed to risk? In the end, what is the moral economy of life in the pandemic?[1] These are the questions I tackle in this chapter.

Sparing Lives

The primacy of the saving of lives over all other considerations had a very specific translation during the pandemic: it meant that measures were to be taken to avoid the overwhelming of hospitals. Very concretely, the number of patients with acute respiratory distress could not exceed the number of accessible ventilators and the number of unoccupied beds in intensive care units. This indication is important because it shows that the probability of dying depends not only on the severity of the infection, associated with age and comorbidities, but also on the unavailability of medical resources. In France, as in many other countries, there had been over the past decades a reduction of beds and personnel in public hospitals at a time when the population was increasing and aging. Doctors and nurses had been protesting during the year that preceded the pandemic and had even gone on strike to request a reversal of this trend, arguing that they could not meet the needs of patients anymore. The situation was especially difficult in emergency rooms and nursing homes. COVID was the final straw on the camel's back.

Indeed, a major factor to account for the aforementioned low death rate in Germany in the first months of the pandemic is that it had five times more intensive care beds than France, which kept medical

---

1. The expression "moral economy" was coined by Thompson in his works on the English working class in the nineteenth century (1968) and on the English peasantry in the eighteenth century (1971) to refer to a traditional economy grounded on reciprocal obligations between the members of these social groups, but it has been later used independently by Daston (1995) to analyze the web of values and affects that underly the practice of science in the seventeenth century. Based on these two pioneering and seemingly incompatible approaches, I have proposed (Fassin 2009) a new definition, more general, parallel to that of Jean-Baptiste Say for political economy. According to it, the moral economy of a given social question is the production, circulation, distribution, and utilization of values and affects, obligations, and norms related to this question. One can therefore speak, for instance, of the moral economy of crime, of asylum, of poverty, of finance. Here, life is deemed a question that society addresses by mobilizing values and affects.

practitioners from having to select which patients most deserved treatment. Besides, the number of nurses relative to the population in Germany was 23 percent higher, and the growth rate in the number of physicians over the past two decades had been nine times faster, than in France. Finally, the French stock of protective masks had not been renewed by the current health administration, which rendered the country entirely dependent on fierce international competition on the global market dominated by China (Jarreau and Telos 2020). Thus, within the display of the government's will to save lives, the obfuscated reality was this background of austerity measures and product outsourcing.

Neoliberal policies applied to public goods had a human cost (Navarro 2020). In March 2020, French President Emmanuel Macron seemed to admit as much. He conceded that neoliberalism had shown its limits, that "health is priceless," that "certain goods and services should stand outside of the laws of the market," and that, confronted with the pandemic, his government would mobilize "to save lives whatever it takes" (Macron 2020). The latter phrase, borrowed from the former president of the European Central Bank, Mario Draghi, in a very different context, meant that the French president was renouncing the sacrosanct Eurozone dogma according to which the state's budget deficit should not exceed 3 percent of gross domestic product and the national debt should not surpass 60 percent of the latter. In fact, the apparent contrition of the French president mostly served to justify not only exceptionally high expenditures to avoid the crashing of the economy but also major restrictions in individual liberties, basic rights, and the simple quality of life of his constituents. This was the price to pay to correct the failures of neoliberal policies imposed on what can be regarded as public goods.

It is these failures, and the prospect of a hecatomb, that led most governments to intervene energetically, albeit too late, and to declare states of emergency, impose stay-at-home policies, shut down stores and restaurants, put companies on the brink of bankruptcy, isolate entire cities or regions, close borders to workers and tourists, militarize their countries to ensure the implementation of measures, but also to spend exceptional amounts of money for economic relief efforts to the benefit of workers, through paycheck compensations, and of corporations, via grants, loans, and tax breaks, although often not for the neediest. While extremely constraining, these policies were broadly accepted, at least during the first months, in large part because they were publicly justified by the saving of lives in the context of the epidemic's dramatization. Alarming statistics were indeed published and commented upon daily, while televised news showed harrowing images of shrouds being carried from hospitals to swamped mortuaries and presented heartbreaking interviews with relatives of those who had succumbed to the coronavirus. In this context of fear, coproduced by politicians and the media, extreme measures seemed to be the only way to limit the human disaster.

There was, however, a long-hidden predicament: the lives to be spared by this collective effort were mostly those of the elderly. Indeed, during the first months of the pandemic, when the toughest political decisions had to be made, four deaths out of five affected people over 65 and three out of five people over 75 — although at these ages COVID represented less than 10 percent of the total causes of death. In other words, the efforts demanded of children, youths, and active adults were supposed to benefit the elderly. But the facts were thornier. It took weeks, and in some places months, to discover the sinister reality. At least early into the pandemic, many governments, including in France and the US, did little to protect the lives of people residing in nursing homes (Stevis-Gridneff, Apuzzo, and Pronczuk 2020).[2] Clusters in these facilities often had tragic consequences since medical treatment was limited and instructions were given to avoid transferring the sick to hospitals as this would inundate intensive care units with patients that were likely to have long stays and had low chances of surviving.

As a result of this policy, those seriously ill only received minimal treatment in their institution and many of them died. There has been much talk about triage at the expense of the elderly in Italian hospitals, especially in the hard-stricken province of Bergamo. But in many countries, the "tragic choices" regarding life issues in a context of insufficient resources, to use the concept coined by Guido Calabresi and Philip Bobbit (1978), took place not in hospitals (on whether to transfer them into intensive care units) but in the nursing homes (on whether to transfer them to these hospitals in the first place). Triage was thus much less visible. The most disturbing sign of this abandonment was the fact that, during the first weeks, deaths in nursing homes were not even included in the official daily statistics. This was the case in France and in the US, and probably in many other countries, unveiling a dismaying truth: when people's deaths are not counted, their lives do not count for much. The elderly who, by December 2020, died of COVID in nursing homes represent 44 percent of the total number of deaths in France and 39 percent

---

2. See Stevis-Gridneff, Apuzzo, and Pronczuk (2020) and, more specifically for France, Andraca (2020).

in the US.[3] The paradox of the discourse on the superior necessity of saving lives is, therefore, that those for whom this policy was conceived did not in fact receive the care they should have received. In the end, the sacrifices imposed on the general population had a limited impact on the survival of those for whom they were intended.

Biolegitimacy and Its Discontents

Still, governments, physicians, and statisticians, with graphs and figures in hand or on screen, kept repeating that these sacrifices were indispensable to save lives, and, with few exceptions, populations complied with little resistance. Most accepted the Kantian principle repeated by Habermas: "The effort of the state to save every single human life must have absolute priority over a utilitarian offsetting of the undesirable economic costs" (Schwering 2020). Although it is usually unnoticed because it has become part of today's moral economy of life, the primacy granted to people's lives is relatively recent. It even corresponds to one of the major anthropological transformations of the twentieth century. In that regard, the COVID moment can be viewed as the culmination of a historic trend that has given an increasing value to life, making it the most praised good in many societies, notably in the Western world.

Military history certainly offers a spectacular illustration of this evolution. The Great War, with its nineteen million casualties — half of them soldiers, the other half civilians — was only one hundred years ago. At that time the generals, not lacking cynicism, considered that their men could be sacrificed on the battlefields, where trenches defined immobile lines of sovereignty. But behind the frontline it was the entire population, galvanized by propaganda, that supported the soldiers, knowing that they were being massacred for a noble cause. The motto then was not "save lives" but "defend the fatherland." If there had been a "whatever it takes" in those years, it would have been in terms of human sacrifices for this higher good. Conversely, in contemporary asymmetrical wars, the strategy is, on the dominant side, to reduce the number of deaths among the military to a minimum, and even as close to zero as possible, which the use of planes dropping bombs, and even more securely of drones launching missiles, renders possible, while the lives of the enemies, even if they are civilians, can be destroyed by tens of thousands.

---

3. See FranceInfo (2021) for France and Bondy (2020) for the US.

During the 1990 Persian Gulf War, the US army had 154 soldiers killed in battle, mostly on the ground, while casualties among Iraqis numbered up to 100,000 (Helmkamp 1994). During the 1999 Kosovo War, there were no deaths among NATO troops, which were only composed of pilots who, to escape the antiaircraft battery, flew so high that they could not avoid the involuntary killing of several hundreds of civilians (Ignatieff 2000). During the long presence of US military in Afghanistan, drone warfare has allowed operators to kill thousands within the local population, many of those being civilians, while not suffering casualties themselves (Latifi 2019). The valuation of lives is thus completely unbalanced. It only concerns Western soldiers. When then-Secretary of State Madeleine Albright was asked in 1996 about the 500,000 Iraqi children who had died because of sanctions against Saddam Hussein, imposed by the United Nations, she notoriously said: "The price is worth it" (Albright 1996). When George W. Bush decided to intervene in Iraq in 2003 under the fallacious pretext of the presence of weapons of mass destruction, the military operation probably caused more than 500,000 deaths, most of them among civilians, although figures from population-based surveys range from 150,000 to more than 1 million deaths — seeming to give reason to General Tommy Franks when he infamously said: "We don't do body counts," a sentence certainly not applicable to his own soldiers (Broder 2003). Military history thus shows how human life has come to be highly valued in the Western world, on the condition, however, that it is human life on one's own side.

The ideological ground for this evolution has been what Walter Benjamin (1978: 298) has called the "sanctity of life." There is an eschatological foundation to that sanctity. Christianity was established on the sacrifice of Jesus who gave his life, according to the Scriptures, to save humankind. Christ is called the Savior, and it is by dying on the cross that he atones for the sins of humanity. Paradoxically, this message never translated into reality until the legacy of the Enlightenment gave birth to human rights and the inscription of a secular version of the right to life in an increasing number of national constitutions. However, more than these religious and legal frameworks — to the futility of which the massacres of Amerindians, the colonization of Africa, the Atlantic slave trade, the Holocaust, and many other genocides would attest — it is the application of the sanctity of life in a series of effective acts that has given a substance to it: the progressive abolition of the death penalty in 70 percent of the world's countries; the exclusion of lifesaving drugs from the protection of patents for developing nations at the Doha Round of the World Trade Organization; the condemnation of the South African government by a tribunal for not giving access to a preventive treatment to reduce the HIV mother-to-child transmission under the constitutional principle that "everybody has a right to live"; the legalization of undocumented immigrants in France, in the name of "medical rationale," when they can prove that they suffer from life-threatening health conditions that cannot be treated in their country of origin; the legitimation of humanitarian interventions for the "saving of lives" of people at risk of dying due to famine, epidemic, disaster, or conflict; and the recognition by the United Nations of an international "responsibility to protect" for populations under threat of aggression, with, in the latter two cases, the invocation of a primacy of these principles over national sovereignty. All these examples epitomize a major shift, even a disruption, in the assessment of the value of life. The decision to save lives at whatever cost made by most governments in response to the pandemic is thus the climax of a trend corresponding to the rise of a humanitarian governmentality (Fassin 2012). Never before had the superior value of human life been affirmed so explicitly and, for once, on a global scale — whatever ulterior motives governments may have had.

As is well known, Michel Foucault ([1976] 1978) showed that Western modernity is characterized by the advent of what he called biopower, the power over life, which replaced the earlier sovereignty with its power to kill. Biopower is the power to exercise control over bodies and populations via multiple institutions and methods, from education to family planning. Probably for chronological reasons — because the movement was only emerging in the 1970s when Foucault was proposing his compelling argument — his theory missed another dimension that is even more characteristic of contemporary societies: biolegitimacy, or the recognition of life as supreme value. Biolegitimacy does not replace biopower but complements it. Biopower is about the technologies that normalize the conduct of humans; biolegitimacy is about the values that underlie the government of humans. In a certain manner, one could say that biolegitimacy is what gives biopolitics its moral substance. The global response to the pandemic can thus be regarded as the advent of biolegitimacy.

The consequences of this rise in the recognition of life as a supreme good has not been without dissent. Whereas the considerable constraints imposed on populations in the name of saving lives were broadly accepted, at least in the initial phase of the lockdown, some have voiced their discontent on various grounds. Leaving aside those who deny the existence of the pandemic (like Jair Bolsonaro and conspiracy theorists) and those who merely reject any state intervention in their affairs (like Donald Trump and libertarians) — both attitudes often found among the alt-right — criticism of the restrictions relies on two main arguments: one is moral, the other political. The moral argument goes thus: since it is mostly older people who are at risk, it is not acceptable to coerce children, adolescents, and active adults to jeopardize the future generation by undermining the economy. The French philosopher Comte-Sponville expressed it most explicitly: "To sacrifice the youth to the health of the elderly is an aberration. It makes me want to cry" (Lugon 2020). At the age of sixty-eight, he declares that he accepted the possibility of dying and deplored that it has become impossible to envisage death serenely in contemporary societies. The political argument is formulated in these terms: the pandemic, with the suspension of liberties and rights, the multiplication of restrictions in all aspects of life, the vote of states of exception, offers many governments the opportunity to expand their security apparatus and policies of surveillance. The most vocal in this line of thought has been Italian philosopher Giorgio Agamben, who stressed the following paradox: "In the face of terrorism we were told that it was necessary to suppress freedom in order to defend it. Now we are told that it is necessary to suspend life in order to protect it. We live in a society that has sacrificed its liberty to an alleged 'rationale of safety' and that condemns itself to live in a permanent state of fear and insecurity" (cited in Truong 2020). According to him, the measures taken against the pandemic prevent people from living a normal life. Rather, the state of exception has become the normal life.

Which Life? Whose Lives?

The critique I want to develop takes a somewhat different direction as I am not asking whether the economy should be protected or whether the obsession with security should be avoided. I ask instead what "saving lives" actually means. More precisely, I want to answer two questions: Which life is this motto about? And whose lives does it designate? Indeed, certain expressions of life are given less salience than others and certain lives less worth than others.

To the first question, Which lives?, the answer is straightforward. It is to the physical life that governments refer when they justify their policies. Saving lives means keeping people alive by avoiding the transmission of infection and, if they are infected, offering them the best possible conditions to receive treatment. As various authors have argued, life can be considered in two different dimensions. For Georges Canguilhem ([1968] 1994) there is the living and the lived, that is, the matter that keeps us alive and the experience that makes the richness of life. For Hannah Arendt ([1958] 1998) there is the lapse of time between birth and death, which is shared with animals and plants, and the sum of events that occur during this time and can be narrated, which is specific to human beings. One can call the former the biological component of life and the latter its biographical one (Fassin 2018). Of course, the biological component is a necessary condition for the accomplishment of the biographical one. Sparing lives — if it were not to mean spending the rest of one's existence with limited consciousness, breathing via a ventilator, and receiving food through a tube — is therefore a medical imperative. But this condition is not sufficient.

What about the social life, the relationships with one's family and friends, the self-realization through work, art, children, pleasure, in a nutshell everything that gives meaning to the fact of being alive, everything that distinguishes humans from other living beings? For instance, in intensive care units or nursing homes, could the risk of contamination by the coronavirus be a satisfying justification for depriving people of the presence of their loved ones as they lay dying and, after their death, of being honored by their family and friends for what their life had been? In other words, how should mortality and dignity, being alive and having a good life, including a good end of life, be balanced against each other? During the pandemic, especially during the first months of extreme restrictions, the absolute defense of the right to life, understood as the right to be merely alive, led to the tragic denial of another right to life, a right to make decisions on what is good for oneself and what is important, how one wants to live and die, and how one wants to see one's loved ones for an ultimate farewell when terminally ill.

To the second question, Whose lives?, the answer again is manifest: not all lives have received the same attention. Those who had to keep working were all the more exposed, given, at least early in the crisis, that they did not have protective equipment: health personnel, medical transporters, and mortuary workers definitely, but also those working in food delivery, retail sale, correctional institutions, home aid, sanitation, construction, and many others, through their multiple interactions with people during work as well as when commuting to their workplaces. A majority of those who could not perform their jobs remotely belonged to the disadvantaged segment of society and, contrary to physicians and nurses who were celebrated as heroes, remained largely invisible, many not even receiving bonuses as those granted to health personnel. Moreover, in this underprivileged segment where employment is often precarious, many lost their jobs or were put on furlough, which had the effect of dramatically diminishing family resources but also of increasing the number of people occupying the same limited space at home, at a time when children, who could not attend school, were also present.

In France, 50 percent of senior managers worked from home but only 1 percent of blue-collar workers did; only 10 percent of the upper class lived in an overcrowded apartment, but 29 percent of underprivileged households did so. The result of these various risk factors was an excess mortality of on average 118 percent in the poorest French department, Seine-Saint-Denis, and a death rate three times higher in impoverished towns than in rich ones (Bajos et al. 2021). In the US, studies showed that African Americans had a mortality rate three times in excess of their demographic weight of the population. Not only were they more exposed to the risk of being infected for the socioeconomic reasons already discussed, but in a country where the health-care system is so unequal, they were also less likely to get tested, hospitalized, and treated in the most favorable way (CDC 2020). Health disparities preexisted the pandemic, but it revealed and aggravated them. They are the physical expression of "structural violence," to use a phrase coined by Johan Galtung (1969: 175) and used widely since to acknowledge a form of violence corresponding, in his words, to "inequality, above all in the distribution of power." This inequality is embodied. In France, the life expectancy at birth of the wealthiest 5 percent of men is thirteen years longer than that of the poorest 5 percent (Blanpain 2018). In the US, the gap between the top 1 percent and the bottom 1 percent is fifteen years (Chetty et al. 2016). To return to biolegitimacy, the recognition of life, singular, as a supreme good, it is thus an abstract ideal. The reality of the treatment of lives, plural, is a different beast.

The answers given to the two questions about which life and whose lives can be combined in one particularly meaningful context: that of prisons. Correctional facilities present a paradox. There, confinement is the rule, but it is not protective in nature. Whereas the general population was supposed to benefit from being locked down, inmates who were locked up had an increased risk of being infected. This is certainly the case in short-term prisons where inmates are either awaiting trial or have short sentences, and where overcrowding is chronic.[4] In jails in the US, up to sixty prisoners can share a room. In French *maisons d'arrêt*, there are generally two or three in a one-hundred-square foot cell meant to be for one person. But the risk exists also in long-term prisons. During first semester of the pandemic, the two countries had opposite politics.

In the US, most governors did not dare to free prisoners from state correctional institutions, not even the elderly or those with serious illnesses, for fear of the reaction of their constituencies.[5] In the state of New York, the criteria imposed by the governor to free people over fifty-five were so strict that 98 percent of those potentially eligible were excluded, even though the state was described at the time as the epicenter of the pandemic, as 81 percent of those who had died from the infection were Black. In the state of New Jersey, three months after the beginning of the epidemic, the death rate of 16 per 10,000 inmates was by far the highest in the country, a situation paralleled by the fact that the state also has the largest overrepresentation of Black people in prison; yet neither of these elements had any significant impact on the release of at-risk inmates.

In France, on the contrary, where all correctional institutions are centralized under the authority of the national state, the decision was made early to have the health rationale prevail over the traditional security rationale, under pressure from the Defender of Rights, the Controller of Places of Deprivation of Liberty, the International Observatory of Prisons, lawyers' unions, and intellectuals.[6] On the one hand, the prison population was reduced by almost 20 percent because of two combined facts: first, few prison sentences were given since the judicial system was almost shut down and, second, after the issuance of an order by the Ministry of Justice, inmates with less than three months remaining of their sentence were granted an early release, generally with an electronic bracelet. For the first time in half a century, the number of prisoners almost equated the number of spaces in prison, an achievement saluted by the wardens' union and human rights organizations. On the other

---

4. The following discussion is based on observations and interviews conducted in the spring of 2020 in French prisons and, in the fall of that same year, in the US system, based on participation in the New Jersey Criminal Sentencing and Disposition Commission.
5. For updated state-by-state data on coronavirus in prison, see the Marshall Project (2021).
6. For the early evolution of the prison situation, see the analysis of the International Observatory of Prisons (Marcel 2020).

hand, various measures were taken to prevent the dissemination of the virus within the prisons. Some of these measures were restrictive and painful, in particular the interruption of family visits and of educational, cultural, and sports activities. Others concerned isolation of suspected cases and contacts, although it should be added that very little testing took place, thus preventing the correct estimation of the incidence of infection among prisoners. Where these draconian measures were explained to the prisoners, things went relatively well; but in several cases, riots occurred and alleged leaders were severely punished.

By early June, 510 inmates of state and federal prisons in the US had died due to COVID (Saloner et al. 2020) but only one in the French correctional system, an elderly man who was already sick when incarcerated (OIP 2020). Proportional to the respective prison population in the two countries, there were thus twenty-five times more deaths from the coronavirus in the US than in France. If the sociologist Maurice Halbwachs (1913: 94) was right when he wrote more than a century ago that "there are good reasons to think that a society has the mortality that suits it, and that the number of deaths and their distribution at different ages accurately expresses the importance that a society attaches to prolonging the life more or less," then one could infer that France grants twenty-five times more value to the life of its prisoners than the US.

This could certainly have been an achievement for the French Department of Correctional Services if, during the same period, there had not been eighty-two suicides committed by inmates. Indeed, France has the highest prison suicide rate in Europe, a rate six times higher than among the French population at large (L'Union 2020). Approximately 130 prisoners take their life in correctional facilities every year. This alarming situation is the result of a combination of the harshness of the penal system, for which incarceration remains the punishment of reference especially for the working class and for ethnoracial minorities, and of the ruthlessness of the prison system, which adds to the privation of liberty a series of frustrations, humiliations, and violence that inmates have to endure. Solitary confinement, which is the most common retribution for violations of prison rules, generates a risk of suicide nine times higher than stays in regular cells. Beyond this extreme measure, daily attacks on dignity, privacy, and sense of justice generate mental disorders: more than a third of inmates have psychiatric symptoms, most of them being panic attacks and depression — in a situation where in most facilities consulting a psychologist officially takes more than six months. In sum, prisons have been better at protecting prisoners from the coronavirus than they have been at respecting prisoners' rights and ensuring their physical integrity.

When the argument of the "sparing of life" is raised, it is therefore crucial to ask oneself: Which life? And whose lives? These questions often unveil complex and obfuscated realities, as epitomized by the case of the prison. On the one hand, biological life threatened by the pandemic is undoubtedly much better preserved in French correctional facilities than in US ones: in the former, lives have been spared; much less so in the latter. On the other hand, the disregard for the other forms of life, which have been subsumed here under the notion of biographical life, leads in France to another, much less visible, attack on biological life: it is not the pandemic that kills the inmates but the way that certain categories of individuals are treated by the justice and prison systems.

The Aftermath

With the pandemic, the world lives in the present. The whole mobilization of societies and governments to spare lives is focused on the threat caused by the coronavirus, and therefore on the current moment, whatever expansion this moment may have in terms of months probably, years perhaps, until a sufficient proportion of the population has been infected or is vaccinated or both. The present is undoubtedly dilated, but it remains the present. Decision makers have a presentist relation to time: for them, saving lives means saving lives from the pandemic. While this is understandable, both because of the seriousness of the epidemiological situation and because they are convinced that theirs is the only proper reaction to have, there remains an enormous blind spot: the future beyond the pandemic, that is, when one will have to live with the consequences of the response to the pandemic. Of course some try to predict what is coming next, and utopianism has multiplied, mostly during the first months when realism had not yet taken over. Measures adopted by the authorities, especially bailouts to prevent bankruptcies and layoffs, try to anticipate an economic shock even worse than the current one. However, most concerns are about today. Eyes are fixed on the coronavirus, the rate of incidence, the availability of vaccines, the risk of a new lockdown or curfew.

But what about tomorrow? What about the impact of the response to the pandemic? It is as if, when speaking of the lives saved thanks to the policies enacted to control the expansion of the infection, the lives lost thanks to the unpreparedness for and mismanagement of the health crisis have been disregarded. To be fair, the future is not only invisible and untold but is also characterized by an unusual level of uncertainty. The mere observation of the contradictions, hesitations, errors produced at each stage of the pandemic until now, not to mention falsifications and lies, gives an idea of how little is known about what will come next. Yet, as signs of the pandemic's decline are in sight, there is an imperative to reflect on what will be the indirect consequences of the pandemic on people's lives. These consequences can be seen from two different angles: missing lives and injured lives. The former corresponds to the physical expression of life, the latter to its social expression — the biological and the biographical. In both cases, inequalities are predictable.

The social repercussions of the response in terms of missing lives have hardly been publicly discussed so far, probably because such a discussion is feared by both those who govern and those who are governed. Nevertheless, we know from previous economic crises that such events have a high cost in terms of fatalities. This cost has notably been measured via the excess of deaths in a given period after the crisis compared to the average mortality over previous similar periods.[7] In the US, following the 2008–9 financial crisis, there was an increase of 6 percent in the age-adjusted mortality rate among middle-aged adults, corresponding to 33,300 excess deaths of those between the ages of 25 and 64. For the first time in the past half century, this evolution has caused an inversion of the curve of life expectancy, which is now declining. All racial groups follow the same trend, though it is particularly marked among socioeconomically disadvantaged groups. Suicides, alcohol-related diseases, overdoses with opioids, but also cardiovascular diseases are the leading causes in a context of high unemployment and psychological distress. To depict this situation, US economists Anne Case and Angus Deaton (2020) speak of "deaths of despair." Similarly, in Brazil, after the crisis that hit the country between 2014 and 2016 causing a 63 percent growth in unemployment, mortality increased by 8 percent in five years, corresponding to 31,000 excess deaths.

With an even worse economic and social situation, it is inevitable that there will be a high number of missing lives. They will not be those of the elderly, this time, but those of young and middle-aged people. Yet, they will not make the headlines. They will not be counted and announced on

---

7. For the US, see Woolf and Schoomaker (2019); for Brazil, Hone et al. (2019); for more general data, Doerr and Hofmann (2020).

an everyday basis as are the ones that die due to the coronavirus. There will be no emotionally charged stories presented on television. These will be statistical deaths, ignored for the most part, except within academic circles when, by 2030, data will show the increase in mortality across age categories, which will be regarded as an abstract figure. These tens of thousands of lost lives will vanish from the collective memory.

However, life is not just about not being dead. When considering the consequences of the health crisis, it is crucial to take into account the injured lives of those who are still alive but whose quality of life is altered because their worth has declined. The loss of one's job, the eviction from one's home, the devaluation of one's independence via the fall into assistance programs, the disgrace of exposing one's failure to one's children and partner, all these intimate tragedies cause deep damage to many lives, especially among the most vulnerable segments of society — low-income families, minorities, Blacks and Hispanics in the US, Blacks and Arabs in France. In his theory of recognition, Axel Honneth (1997) speaks of "moral injuries," which correspond to situations in which relations with others are affected, harming the three dimensions that allow for self-realization: self-confidence, self-respect, self-esteem. In other words, what makes a person look back at his or her life and say: it was worth living. These injured lives are even more ignored than the missing ones. There are no statistics kept about them, only sometimes vignettes in social science articles and interview excerpts on television or in radio broadcasts, at best ethnographies and documentaries with limited circulation and sparse audiences.

The number of both missing and injured lives depends on the extent of the welfare state. France, as other European countries, still offers its populations some forms of social protection, the legacy of workers' struggles and of the postwar era's belief in a better future, but the safety net is progressively waning under the neoliberal dogma of reducing public spending, which has contributed to the incapacity of the authorities to respond adequately to the pandemic. The US, with its growing inequalities and shrinking benefits, with its federal state's reluctance to aid the poor and its public's distrust of solidarity, may certainly experience once more in the years to come the discrepancy between its idealized American dream and its gloomy US reality. This is to say that governments should not only be held responsible for what happens during the current health crisis, which nourishes most current public debates, but also for what will occur in its aftermath, in particular for the inequality of lives that will have increased.

Conclusion

The pandemic has unveiled a moral economy of life that did preexist but had never been so clearly perceived. Indeed, a signature of the contemporary world is the profound contradiction between the ideal affirmation of life as a supreme value and the actual observation of the unequal worth of lives. Life, singular, abstract, and lives, plural, concrete, are two distinct realities, as physical or biological life differs from social or biographical life. The justification of the major restrictions in liberties and rights as well as the considerable socioeconomic repercussions was the sparing of physical lives, but this biopolitical project only laid bare the disparities between those who could benefit from it and those whose situation only worsened, and, ultimately, the indifference toward the injustices in the treatment of social lives.

The analysis I have proposed has been purposely circumscribed to the Global North, and even often to the Western world. A major feature of the response to the pandemic has unquestionably been the self-centering of the Global North and the lack of concern for the Global South. For months, what was happening in the rest of the world, from repression in Syria to war in Yemen, from famine in South Sudan to demonstrations in Chile, was not even a matter of interest. In October 2020, the World Bank announced that, due to the harsh response to the pandemic in developing countries and the structurally unequal conditions underlying it, extreme poverty, that is, living on less than USD 1.90 a day, had increased for the first time in a quarter of a century, with 100 million more people pushed into indigence. In July 2021, the World Health Organization declared that 1 percent of the African population was fully vaccinated, at a time when this was already the case of half of Western Europe's population. These various news items were hardly noticed. There is indeed a moral geography of the value of life and the worth of lives.

References

Albright, Madeleine. 1996. "The Deaths of 500,000 Iraqi Children was Worth It." YouTube Video, 0: 22. https://youtu.be/bntsfiAXMEE.

Andraca, Robin. 2020. "Accès à la réanimation: des consignes officielles ont-elles été données pour les résidents d'Ehpad?" *Libération*, March 29, 2020. https://www.liberation.fr/checknews/2020/03/29/acces-a-la-reanimation-des-consignes-officielles-ont-elles-ete-donnees-pour-les-residents-d-ehpad_1783370/.

Arendt, Hannah. (1958) 1998. *The Human Condition*. Chicago: University of Chicago Press.

Bajos, Nathalie, Florence Jusot, Ariane Pailhé, Alexis Spire, Claude Martin, Laurence Meyer, Nathalie Lydie, et al. 2021. "When Lockdown Policies Amplify Social Inequalities in COVID-19 Infections: Evidence from a Cross-Sectional Populations-Based Survey in France." *BMC Public Health*, no. 21: 705. https://doi.org/10.1186/s12889-021-10521-5.

Benjamin, Walter. 1978. "Critique of Violence." In *Reflections. Essays, Aphorisms, Autobiographical Writings*, edited by Peter Demetz, 277–300. New York: Harcourt Brace Jovanovich.

Blanpain, Nathalie. 2018. "L'espérance de vie par niveau de vie: chez les hommes, 13 ans d'écart entre les plus aisés et les plus modestes." Institut National de la Statistique et des Études Économique, February 6, 2018. https://www.insee.fr/fr/statistiques/3319895.

Bondy, Halley. 2020. "39% of Covid-19 Deaths Have Occurred in Nursing Homes — Many Could Have Been Prevented: Report." *NBC News*, December 8, 2020. https://www.nbcnews.com/know-your-value/feature/39-COVID-19-deaths-have-occurred-nursing-homes-many-could-ncna1250374.

Broder, John M. 2003. "A Nation at War: The Casualties, US Military Has No Count on Iraqi Dead in Fighting." *New York Times*, April 2, 2003. https://www.nytimes.com/2003/04/02/world/nation-war-casualties-us-military-has-no-count-iraqi-dead-fighting.html.

Calabresi, Guido, and Philip Bobbit. 1978. *Tragic Choices: The Conflicts Society Confronts in the Allocation of Tragically Scarce Resources*. New York: W. W. Norton.

Canguilhem, Georges. [1968] 1994. "La nouvelle connaissance de la vie." In *Études d'histoire et de philosophie des sciences concernant les vivants et la vie*, 335–64. Paris: J. Vrin.

Case, Anne, and Angus Deaton. 2020. *Deaths of Despair, and the Future of Capitalism*. Princeton: Princeton University Press.

CDC (Centers for Disease Control and Prevention). 2020. "Disparities in Deaths from COVID-19: Racial and Ethnic Disparities." CDC, updated December 10, 2020. https://www.cdc.gov/coronavirus/2019-ncov/community/health-equity/racial-ethnic-disparities/disparities-deaths.html.

Chetty, Raj, Michael Stepner, Sarah Abraham, Shelby Lin, Benjamin Scuderi, Nicholas Turner, Augustin Bergeron, et al. 2016. "The Association between Income and Life Expectancy in the United States, 2001–2014." *Jama Network* 315 (16): 1750–66. https://doi.org/10.1001/jama.2016.4226.

Daston, Lorraine. 1995. "The Moral Economy of Science." *Osiris*, no. 10: 2–24. https://doi.org/10.1086/368740.

Doerr, Sebastian, and Boris Hofmann. 2020. "The Recession-Mortality Nexus and COVID-19." BIS Bulletin No. 35, Bank for International Settlements. https://www.bis.org/publ/bisbull35.pdf.

Fassin, Didier. 2009. "Les économies morales revisitées." *Annales: Histoire, Sciences Sociales* 6 (64): 1237–66.

Fassin, Didier. 2012. *Humanitarian Reason: A Moral History of the Present.* Berkeley: University of California Press.

Fassin, Didier. 2018. *Life: A Critical User's Manual.* Cambridge: Polity Press.

Foucault, Michel. (1976) 1978. *An Introduction.* Vol. 1 of *The History of Sexuality*, translated by Robert Hurley. New York: Random House.

FranceInfo. 2021. "Rupture du contrat de sous-marins: la France rappelle ses ambassadeurs aux États-Unis et en Australie 'pour consultations'." September 17, 2021. https://www.francetvinfo.fr/sante/maladie/coronavirus/confinement/COVID-19-taux-dincidence-record-surmortalite-comment-les-ehpad-sont-frappes-par-la-seconde-vague-en-huit-graphiques_4219253.html.

Galtung, Johan. 1969. "Violence, Peace, and Peace Research." *Journal of Peace Research* 6 (3): 167–91. https://doi.org/10.1177/002234336900600301.

Halbwachs, Maurice. 1913. *La théorie de l'homme moyen: Essai sur Quetelet et la statistique morale.* Paris: Alcan.

Helmkamp, Jim C. 1994. "United States Military Casualty Comparison during the Persian Gulf War." *Journal of Occupational Medicine* 36 (6): 609–15. https://pubmed.ncbi.nlm.nih.gov/8071721/.

Hone, Thomas, Andrew J. Mirelman, Davide Rasella, Rômulo Paes-Sousa, Mauricio L. Barreto, Rudi Rocha, and Christopher Millett. 2019. "Effect of Economic Recession and Impact of Health and Social Protection Expenditures on Adult Mortality: A Longitudinal Analysis of 5565 Brazilian Municipalities." *Lancet* 7 (11): e1575–e1582. https://doi.org/10.1016/S2214-109X(19)30409-7.

Honneth, Axel. 1997. "Recognition and Moral Obligation." *Social Research* 64 (1): 16–35.

Ignatieff, Michael. 2000. "The New American Way of War." *New York Review*, July 20, 2000. https://www.nybooks.com/articles/2000/07/20/the-new-american-way-of-war/.

Jarreau, Patrick, and Telos. 2020. "Gestion du Covid-19: la douloureuse comparaison France-Allemagne." *Slate*, May 9, 2020. http://www.slate.fr/story/190353/gestion-coronavirus-COVID-19-douloureuse-comparaison-france-allemagne.

Latifi, Ali M. 2019. "Life in the Most Drone-Bombed Countries." *Technology Review*, October 22, 2019. https://www.technologyreview.com/2019/10/22/132284/afghanistan-warefare-technology-testing/.

Lugon, Laure. 2020. "André Comte-Sponville: 'Laissez-nous mourir comme nous voulons'." *Le Temps,* April 17, 2020. https://www.letemps.ch/societe/andre-comtesponville-laisseznous-mourir-voulons.

L'Union. 2020. "82 suicides en prison depuis janvier, une mission d'inspection lancée par le gouvernement." August 21, 2020. https://www.lunion.fr/id184408/article/2020-08-21/82-suicides-en-prison-depuis-janvier-une-mission-dinspection-lancee-par-le.

Macron, Emmanuel. 2020. "Find Macron's Entire Speech on the Coronavirus." *Web24*, March 13, 2020. https://www.web24.news/u/2020/03/find-macrons-entire-speech-on-the-coronavirus.html.

Marcel, Cécile. 2020. "La prison à l'épreuve du coronavirus: deux mois de crise, et maintenant?" Observatoire International des Prisons, July 1, 2020. https://oip.org/analyze/la-prison-a-lepreuve-du-coronavirus-deux-mois-de-crise-et-maintenant/.

Marshall Project. 2021. "A State-By-State Look at 15 Months of Coronavirus in Prisons." Marshall Project, updated June 1, 2021. https://www.themarshallproject.org/2020/05/01/a-state-by-state-look-at-coronavirus-in-prisons.

Navarro, Vicente. 2020. "The Consequences of Neoliberalism in the Current Pandemic." *International Journal of Health Services* 50 (3): 271–75. https://doi.org/10.1177/0020731420925449.

OIP (Observatoire International des Prisons). 2020. "Coronavirus en prison — L'essentiel." Observatoire International des Prisons, updated June 12, 2020. https://oip.org/COVID19-en-prison-lessentiel/.

Saloner, Brendan, Kalind Parish, Julie A. Ward, Grace DiLaura, and Sharon Dolovich. 2020. "COVID-19 Cases and Deaths in Federal and State Prisons." *Jama Network* 324 (6): 602–3. https://doi.org/10.1001/jama.2020.12528.

Schwering, Markus. 2020. "Jürgen Habermas über Corona: 'So viel Wissen über unser Nichtwissen gab es noch nie'." *Frankfurter Rundschau*, April 10, 2020. https://www.fr.de/kultur/gesellschaft/juergen-habermas-coronavirus-krise-COVID19-interview-13642491.html.

Stevis-Gridneff, Matina, Matt Apuzzo, and Monika Pronczuk. 2020. "When Covid-19 Hit, Many Elderly Were Left to Die." *New York Times*, August 8, 2020. https://www.nytimes.com/2020/08/08/world/europe/coronavirus-nursing-homes-elderly.html.

Thompson, E. P. 1968. *The Making of the English Working Class*. London: Penguin.

Thompson, E. P. 1971. "The Moral Economy of the English Crowd in the Eighteenth Century." *Past and Present*, no. 50: 76–136. https://doi.org/10.1093/past/50.1.76.

Truong, Nicolas. 2020. "Giorgio Agamben: 'L'épidémie montre clairement que l'état d'exception est devenu la condition normale.'" *Le Monde*, March 24, 2020. https://www.lemonde.fr/idees/article/2020/03/24/giorgio-agamben-l-epidemie-montre-clairement-que-l-etat-d-exception-est-devenu-la-condition-normale_6034245_3232.html.

Woolf, Steven H., and Heidi Schoomaker. 2019. "Life Expectancy and Mortality Rates in the United States, 1959–2017." *Jama Network* 322 (20): 1996–2016. https://doi.org/10.1001/jama.2019.16932.

CHAPTER 9

To Kill or Let Die

How Americans Argue about Life, Economy, and Social Agency

Webb Keane

In much of the world, the COVID pandemic brought into sharp relief some fundamental and long-standing tensions among democratic governance, economic reasoning, scientific authority, and moral intuitions. These tensions are especially strong in the United States, given the peculiar coexistence of free market fundamentalism, patriotic communitarianism, libertarianism, social conservatism, positivism, and religiosity so distinctive of this country. The pandemic forced choices whose public expression — which ranged from folksy common sense to austere utilitarian logic — took increasingly stark and dichotomized forms. Eventually even the simple wearing of a protective mask became a simple either/or political statement.

The debates over lockdowns, vaccines, and other measures centered on how we weigh lives against economic well-being. They expressed something fundamental about the way Americans think about economics, the public good, and the legitimacy and powers of social agency. Because of the way these arguments tended to portray the responses in sharply dichotomous terms, they often bore a strong resemblance to the so-called "Trolley Problem" in moral philosophy, which I describe below.

Seeing how this problem was brought to bear on real social policy and people's reactions to it on the ground sheds light on some of the characteristic features, and shortcomings, of the utilitarian rationality that underlies it. Looking in turn from the formality of the trolley problem back to the pandemic can also clarify the broader assumptions that informed the American debates.

Your Granddad or Your Country?

As the United States moved to a scattering of locally variable stay-at-home orders to slow the spread of COVID, some conservatives objected to the orders on the grounds that they would harm the economy. The first lockdowns began in March 2020. Even before many were enacted, the Republican lieutenant governor of Texas, Dan Patrick, spoke on Tucker Carlson's right-wing talk show on Fox TV (Patrick 2020; see also Cole 2020; Livingston 2020). An anti-big government "Tea Party" conservative, Patrick was reacting to the pressure to impose restrictions on businesses and public gatherings in order to slow the spread of COVID. Earlier he had texted Carlson to say that, as a grandfather, he wanted his grandchildren "to have a shot at the American dream. But right now this virus, which all the experts say that 98% of all people will survive, … is killing our country in another way. … [It] could bring about a total economic collapse and potentially a collapse of our society. … So, I say let's give this a few more days or weeks … but after that let's go back to work and go back to living. Those who want to shelter in place can still do so. But we can't live with this uncertainty."

The on-air interview expanded on the theme. Stressing that he was about to turn seventy, and was therefore in a high-risk category, he said:

> I'm not living in fear of COVID-19. What I'm living in fear of is what's happening to this country. Y'know, Tucker, no one reached out to me and said, "As a senior citizen, are you willing to take a chance on your survival in exchange for keeping the American that all America loves for your children and your grandchildren?" And if that's the exchange, I'm all in. … I don't want the whole country to be sacrificed and that's what I see. … I've talked to hundreds of people, and everyone says pretty much the same thing, that we can't lose our whole country. … Let's get back to work, let's get back to living. … And those of us who are seventy plus, we'll take care of ourselves, but

don't sacrifice the country, don't do that, don't ruin this great America dream.
[Carlson]: So you're saying that this disease could take your life but that's not the scariest thing to you? There's something that would be worse than dying?
[Patrick]: Yeah, ... the point is, our biggest gift we give to our country and our children and our grandchildren is the legacy of our country. (Patrick 2020, my transcription)

Patrick's remarks succinctly capture some of the key themes running through the anti-lockdown position: the use of probabilistic reasoning (98 percent will not die); the either/or view of disease (you either die or not); the view of populations as an aggregate (Americans undifferentiated by any relevant characteristic such as race, gender, working conditions, financial precarity, or access to health care — except for age); the decisionism (it assumes that everyone has a choice and those who want to can simply shelter in place); the identification of nation with economy (as they understood it) rather than, say, its people (the American dream); the relative value of life; and the language of sacrifice (an exchange of one's own life for the country). I will return to these below.

Although Patrick spoke with the exaggerated simplicity favored by Fox News, he was not an outlier. About a week before Patrick's interview, Ron Johnson, a Republican senator from Wisconsin and chair of the Senate's Committee on Homeland Security and Governmental Affairs, had said: "97 to 99 percent will get through this and develop immunities and will be able to move beyond this. But we don't shut down our economy because tens of thousands of people die on the highways. It's a risk we accept so we can move about. We don't shut down our economies because tens of thousands of people die from the common flu. ... Getting coronavirus is not a death sentence except for maybe no more than 3.4 percent of our population" (Gilbert 2020).

Tom Galisano, the founder of the information technology provider Paychex, put it in even starker terms: "The damages of keeping the economy closed could be worse than losing a few more people. You're picking the better of two evils" (Reich 2020). And right-wing radio host Glen Beck echoed Patrick's sacrificial language and the equation of the country with the economy: "I would rather die than kill the country. 'Cause it's not the economy that's dying, it's the country" (Richardson 2020). All of these represent the situation as presenting two clear cut options, about which there is a choice to be made: either allow people to die or kill the country (equated with "the economy").

Needless to say, comments like these provoked strong responses. Significantly, however, these tended to accept the dichotomous terms expressed by Patrick — that we are forced to make an either/or choice between granddad and the economy — while reversing the values. Gilberto Hinojosa, the chairperson of the Texas Democratic Party, condemned Patrick's remarks in a statement declaring that "the lives of our families, our friends, and our communities have no dollar amount" (Hennessy-Fiske 2020). Similarly, New York's Democratic Governor Andrew Cuomo tweeted: "My mother is not expendable. We will not put a dollar figure on human life. ... No one should be talking about social Darwinism for the sake of the stock market" (Cuomo 2020). By referring to social Darwinism, Cuomo points out something that probabilistic statements tend to obscure. If you speak of possible deaths as a percentage of the total population treated in the aggregate, you ignore the likelihood that it is *certain kinds of lives* that will be lost. Although Lieutenant Governor Patrick, for his part, does acknowledge the special vulnerability of the old, it is only in order to grant them the dignified status of self-sacrificers. About other vulnerable categories — Blacks, Latinos, Native Americans, the poor, and those who jobs require constant exposure — he remains silent. So too, nothing is said of their capacity — or its lack — to be agents of their own sacrifice, or their willingness to do so were they granted that dignity.

Like Governor Patrick, Governor Cuomo juxtaposes the economy to the image of his mother. This familiar rhetorical move puts the face of intimate affect on the cold numbers of statistical calculation. (By the same token, in the rhetoric of pricing human lives, he is bracketing the economic hardship faced by the most vulnerable during a shutdown.) Like the self-sacrificing Patrick, mother appears here as an individual; unlike Patrick, she is not the willing agent of her own potential demise. But she also stands in for a demographic category: the old. By describing her possible death not as sacrifice (a virtue) but as Darwinism (a eugenic evil), and making her not the agent of her own sacrifice (as in Patrick's imagined death) but its patient, Cuomo points to the possibility of "gerocide" (Cohen 2020, drawing on Servello and Ettore 2020; see also Lewis 2020). The possibility of death by COVID is crystallized into the figure of those who are already most defined by the imminence of death — rather than, say, the wisdom of age or the nurturance of descendants.

Although we might feel that Cuomo's reference to social Darwinism is exaggerated, it seems that there were some public figures who did indeed explicitly call for a policy of "culling the herd" by allowing the elimination of the most vulnerable, such as residents in nursing homes (Law 2020; McLean, cited in Cohen 2020). Although few were willing to follow them to that conclusion, the more general framing of the problem — lives versus the economy — dominated the discussion.

But what is "the economy" such that it can be compared to granddad? Whereas some conservatives spoke of lost jobs, their critics often accused them of merely defending elite interests, such as stock prices and corporate profits. Describing the early period of the outbreak, one critical commentator wrote that "officials expressed skepticism that drastic measures were necessary to avoid an outbreak. If anything, their comments were focused on potential stock market losses rather than public health risks. ... Governments and businesses are now being forced to weigh corporate profits against human life to a newly extreme degree" (Liu 2020). Interestingly enough, as it transpired, the financial sector did remarkably well: it was small businesses like restaurants, bars, hair salons, tattoo parlors, nail salons, and brick-and-mortar shops, along with hotels, theaters, and airlines, that were more visibly hurt. Indeed, recognizing that it is the most vulnerable members of society who were going to be on the frontlines, some on the left were also worried about the economic risks of pandemic lockdowns, something the stark binaries of political argument — and moral decisionism — made it easy to overlook (see Fassin, this volume).

Economies or lives? What we consider to be commensurable weights the scales. We can immediately visualize the hairdresser and the bartender. By contrast, Liu (2020) portrays "the economy" as an abstraction personified by other abstractions, stock prices, and corporations, which are certainly distant from the experience and the personal finances of most Americans.

Taking a different angle, one critic of Governor Patrick treats the economy as everyday consumerism: "If you asked my kids if they would rather have more stuff or have their Grandpa and Nanna, they would choose their grandparents with no hesitation" (tweet by Gene Wu, quoted in Morris and Garrett 2020). The very word "stuff" relegates material interests to the category of unnecessary excess. The implication is drawn out by another critic, for whom the economy simply stands for materialistic values in general: "The decision and subsequent action is people or money. It's really that simple. ... And, not to forget, any who advocate sacrificing others for wealth can no longer claim to be Christian" (Trollman, comment on Hooks 2020). Again, we hear the language of sacrifice, now within a distinctively religious context. Here we enter the expanded sphere of transcendental values. If the position represented by Governor Patrick takes lives and the economy to be the same order of thing, and thus commensurable, that transcendental viewpoint takes them to be incommensurable (see Anderson 1995; Feinberg 2005; Lukes 1997; Zelizer 1994).

Would You Push Granddad in Front of the Trolley?

It is easy to see these statements in the simple terms of left and right, progressive and reactionary, or pro-social and pro-business. Such is the nature of polarized politics in the age of social media. The right-wing focus on economic costs seemed far more audible in public discourse than any similar concerns from the left. But consider how both sides also converge in portraying the options in binary terms: kill granddad to save the economy or kill the economy to save granddad. In the stark imagery of Governor Jay Inslee of Washington: "Going to the bar is fun. ... Been doing it for years. But you might be killing your grandad by going to the bar" (Eldridge 2020).

The way these options are portrayed express something fundamental and distinctive about the way Americans think of the public good and the limits of legitimate social agency. In particular, they display an encounter between rational choice and moralism, both of which are especially prominent in American political discourse. Roughly speaking, rational choice treats ethical decisions in terms of their measurable consequences or expected utilities. Moralism appeals to fundamental deontological principles of duty and obligation, often, but not always, in religious terms (see Keane 2016). To see this more clearly, consider how, when laid out as a morally fraught choice between two, and only two, options — kill granddad or kill the economy — these positions bear a family resemblance to the famous "trolley problem" in moral philosophy.

The trolley problem is a thought experiment originally developed by moral philosophers to clarify their intuitions about agency and responsibility (Foot 1967; Thompson 1976, 1985). Although highly artificial, the trolley problem mimics the dilemmas of medical triage and military situations in which stark choices must be made between clear alternatives, either one of which will inevitably result in harm to someone. In its basic form, it asks you to imagine that you see an out-of-control trolley hurtling toward five people. There is no time to warn them and no way to stop the trolley. The puzzle emerges from the two scenarios that follow. In one, you could pull a switch that diverts the trolley onto another track that has only one person on it. In the other, you could push a man in front of the trolley, whose weight is sufficient to bring it to a stop. The objective outcome is the same in both cases: one life lost in order to save five. The utilitarian calculus that follows seems indisputable: you should pull the switch or push the man. Yet most people who would accept the first option recoil at the second. How do these actions differ?

The debates around this have been unending and intricate. One theme running through them is known as the Doctrine of Double Effect. This doctrine, which dates back to Thomas Aquinas, turns on a distinction between the intended results of an action, on the one hand, and the unintended but foreseeable consequences of an action, on the other. The doctrine holds that whereas it is immoral to *kill* (the result of pushing someone), it is morally permissible to *let die* (the foreseeable but unintended consequence of diverting the trolley to the track with one person). Put in other terms, by pushing the man, you use a person as the *means to an end*, the saving of five lives. In the Western tradition within which this debate takes place, moral philosophers tend to agree that humans should not be treated instrumentally (this is why a doctor should not kill one patient in order to distribute her organs to save numerous other patents). Unlike pushing the man, in diverting the trolley, one person's death is merely collateral damage, ancillary to the means by which lives are saved. Put another way, were there no man on the other track, diverting the trolley would *still* save five lives. In the case of pushing, by contrast, someone *must* die: the body of one man is necessary for stopping the trolley.

Most anthropologists are likely to say that thought experiments like this vastly oversimply a complex world, as well as smuggling in ethnocentric assumptions about autonomous decision-making, anonymity, calculation, and so forth. But even if we were to accept the value of thought experiments for purposes of conceptual clarification, applying them to real life still faces the challenge of finding the right analogies. It seems that the Doctrine of Double Effect can play out in opposite directions, depending on how you see the analogy. For Patrick, the economy is the man we are pushing in front the trolley in order to save the granddads down the track. You are killing the economy. Conversely, for Cuomo, we risk pushing granddad in order to save the economy. You are killing granddad. What are the respective moral alternatives they favor? Patrick would let granddad die (or at least risk dying) in order to save the economy. Cuomo would let the economy die (or at least suffer harm) in order to save granddad.

Sacrificial Exchanges

The virtue of the highly artificial thought experiment is its clarifying simplicity. Of course this is also its weakness, since in real life the devil is in the details. Here are some compounding factors. Recall Patrick's self-proclaimed subject position: he is in the vulnerable category and claims (however tendentiously) to speak on behalf of his age cohort. He repeatedly uses the language of sacrificial exchange. In fact, given the importance of evangelical Christians to his constituency, we might speculate that this has a specifically Christological subtext. More explicitly, however, by equating the economy with the nation (thus denying the global nature of both economy and virus), he portrays himself in patriotic terms, offering to die for his country and for the younger generations that will inherit it. Perhaps we can hear traces of laissez-faire economic reason, which accepts job loss in the present for overall economic gains down the line. But, as John Maynard Keynes remarked when he criticized the equilibrium logic of the laissez-faire economics of his day, "in the long run we are all dead" (Keynes 1923: 80; a perspective elaborated for liberal governmentality overall by Povinelli 2011). In contrast, Patrick's rhetoric accepts the long-run view, portraying sacrifice as an exchange with future generations (a position not entirely confined to the right; see Fassin, this volume). It is as if the man on the diversionary track were to insist that you *allow* the trolley to run him down.

The alternative can also be put in terms of sacrifice. It is not just the stock market that is at risk: saving granddad will push many other financially precarious individuals over the edge. The economy is not just the stock market or corporate profits. As one commentator recalls, during the Great Depression "the problem wasn't the valuation of companies but rather a vast and incalculable accumulation of human misery — suicides, starvation, the dissolution of families, violence both domestic and impersonal" (Hooks 2020). We have already seen the so-called "deaths of despair" (Case and Deaton 2020) wrought by deindustrialization and other effects of neoliberalism. The breathtaking job losses produced by the quarantine orders might be called sacrificial. But just as neoliberalism demanded sacrifices for the sake of economic growth, so too in the case of the virus response: no one is asking the victims of economic crises which way the trolley should go.

To adjudicate between these two sacrificial orders calls for something Cuomo and Hinojosa claim is unacceptable, putting a dollar figure on human lives. Yet, of course, this happens all the time, when federal regulators, insurance companies, manufacturers, hospital administrators, and so forth consider how much to spend on safe buildings and pollution controls, how safe to make cars and planes, what to charge for life insurance, and how much to invest in treating rare diseases. Safety research estimates of the "value of a statistical life" track the lifetime additional wages that workers will demand in order to perform dangerous jobs. Policy makers and citizens are generally willing to finance interventions that provide at least one "quality-adjusted life year," or QALY, for every USD 150,000 spent. QALYs quantify the common-sense notion that we are willing to buy one more year of healthy and happy life, as opposed to a year spent in serious pain or debilitating illness (Pollack 2020). On the basis of such calculations, one sober analysis concludes that, although "proceeding with business as usual would avert a severe recession, it would also cause hundreds of thousands more deaths — and, based on accepted estimates of the cost of a lost life, this increased human toll will more than cancel out the expected economic benefits" (Kellogg Insight 2020). As another puts it, even vulnerable people "have many decades of contributions to the national GDP ahead of them" (Hooks 2020). In order to be persuasive, it seems, even the defense of the elderly must resort not to the moral value of life as such but speak in the hegemonic language of rational choice theory. Turning the tables, then, defenders of the quarantine sometimes resort to the language of *economic* value when countering the sacrificial *morality* of their opponents who defend the economy.

In the end, sacrificial exchange seems to be unavoidable, no matter which direction you take the Doctrine of Double Effect. A glance inside the aggregates of populations and economies quickly shows that differences matter. The switches on the trolley track will favor some over others. One commentator worries that there is already a cultural predisposition toward ageism that will have the effect of turning letting die into killing: "The implication of Patrick's comments was that older people are a burden on society and should be willing to risk being infected by COVID-19 to make sure that all other Americans are able to patronize bars, restaurants, and stores. ... There is already a widespread belief, reflected in our jokes, our films, and our TV programs, that people have a sell-by date when it comes to being valuable and productive" (Wexler 2020; see also Cohen 2020).

Age is indeed a factor in utilitarian ethics. A review of policies from sixty medical centers found that the consensus is to give priority to those who are most likely to survive. As one medical ethicist said, "It would be dishonest if we didn't say age is a driver. Age is correlated with resilience" (quoted in Guarino 2020). Because younger patients, in general, get better faster, they may free up a ventilator more quickly for the next patient. This is the basic logic of triage. As I write this, Los Angeles ambulance crews during a wave of infection have been instructed not to carry to hospitals patients who can be expected not to survive (Lin et al. 2021).

More than that, however, once recovered, the young will on average have more years ahead of them. A report in *New England Journal of Medicine* concluded that when allocating a limited number of ventilators, the highest priority should be to save the most "life-years" (Guarino 2020). In effect, there are two ways of counting lives saved, by numbers of individuals and by numbers of years (Fassin 2018). These are not commensurate: whereas ten individuals saved at any age are, presumably, of equal moral worth, ten individuals saved near the end of life count far less in terms of their economic contribution.

Once vaccines became available in December 2020, the trolley decision reappeared with new variations. Like ventilators, doses of the vaccine were a limited good, and priorities had to be established. After accounting for health-care workers, the choices were again ranged between reducing the sheer quantity of deaths (start with the old) and getting the economy started (start with "essential workers"). Interestingly, within the category of essential workers, which asserts an *economic* logic, recognition was accorded to "frontline workers," those whose jobs most exposed them to other people. Since these people tended to be both the most economically precarious (poorly paid cashiers, transit workers, and so forth) and medically vulnerable (their ranks disproportionally made up of minoritized groups), economic logic converged with the *moral* value of saving lives as such. Yet that moral value has to confront the mathematical logic of triage: the numbers of frontline workers far exceed those of the very old. If there are not enough doses to cover a significant *percentage* of the frontline work force, some argue, then we should instead vaccinate members of the category that is small enough to protect *even if* the latter would not be the top priority on other grounds. As I write, the debate has not yet been resolved, and will, presumably, play out differently in different parts of the country, as did the lockdown and masking measures.

Autonomy, Chance, and Letting Die

Both sides in the debate exemplified by Patrick and Cuomo tend to treat the population as an undifferentiated aggregate or, at most, divided into just two categories: the aged and the rest. Although digitization has been rapidly dividing populations into ever more specific categories (Fourcade 2016), debates like theirs favor pictures with broad outlines. This is not simply an effect of polemics: sometimes aggregates seem to be called for. The Environmental Protection Agency currently values a "statistical life" at about USD 9.6 million, "regardless of the age, income, or other population characteristics of the affected population" (EPA 2020). But a glance inside that aggregate reveals that only about a quarter of the American working population has the kind of job that could be carried out from home. This tends to be people in the better paid sectors, such as professionals and office workers (who are also more likely to be whiter and healthier than average). Service workers simply do not have the choice of working from home and face either unemployment or exposure. As a result, "the best safeguard against the novel coronavirus is the ability to voluntarily withdraw oneself from capitalism" (Liu 2020). It turns out, then, that when the trolley comes barreling their way, some people can just step off the tracks. Others cannot. The tragic irony, then, is that those who are most vulnerable *medically*, such as Blacks, Latinos, Native Americans, and the working poor, also tend to be those who are most vulnerable *financially*. It is as if the very same individuals were on *both* trolley tracks.

It is well known that Americans respond far more easily to rare forms of harm suffered by individuals than to commonplace ones known only through statistics. Heroic efforts to save Thai Boy Scouts trapped in a cave (an incident that captured worldwide attention in 2018; see Beech, Paddock, and Suhartono 2018) or children with rare diseases seem to require no calculation of expense — unlike the public response to car crashes or diabetes. Probabilistic deaths are harder to grasp in terms of personal tragedy and heroic interventions (and of course it is harder to see one's own contribution to large scale effects such as climate change). This may be why, in terms of the Doctrine of Double Effect, they are easier to think of as merely "letting die" rather than "killing." In other words, the relative acceptability of common disease deaths across a population over individual misfortunes may be due to the sense that they are the result of merely letting events take their course (death that just happens to result when I divert the trolley car) rather than purposely undertaking an action (pushing the man onto the tracks).

Some have claimed this is a universal cognitive bias. Whether or not this is the case, the bias is surely amplified and reinforced by the American ideology of individual autonomy (see Cohen, this volume). Discrete events are easily assimilated to the view that the actions of individuals have distinct and identifiable consequences, and that other individuals can actively respond to them. Direct action foregrounds the first-person perspective. We can see this even in the dynamics of the intensive care unit. According to one medical ethicist, doctors compete with one another for scarce ventilators because "each doctor's patient is more important than the other guy's patient" (quoted in Guarino 2020). Probabilities elude this sense of agency, leaving the individual to fend for himself or herself against forces that lie beyond human responsibility.

When Senator Johnson blithely remarks, "getting coronavirus is not a death sentence except for maybe no more than 3.4 percent of our population," he is taking advantage of the distancing effects of probabilistic reason. Lieutenant Governor Patrick translates probability into the ideologically powerful language of American self-reliance. Invoking the logic of self-sacrifice and ignoring the risk he poses to others, he insists (speaking with the hypothetical collective voice of the elderly) that "we can take care of ourselves" in order to oppose the claims of social provisioning and mutual obligation. Paul Bettencourt, a Texas state senator, criticized a proposed stay-at-home order for Houston (whose own libertarian ethos has made it the largest city in the country with no zoning regulations), asking "why are you not asking for voluntary compliance from the public in the spirit of American liberty and Texas friendship?" (Downen 2020; Hooks 2020). Seen this way, a stoic willingness to distinguish between killing and letting die becomes a matter of national identity, all the more patriotic because, seemingly, more hard-headed. Ironically, it is a collective identity that in significant ways denies the collectivity.

The pandemic debates express in accentuated form a more general feature of how Americans think about economy and society. Many Americans tend to resist the idea of formal controls over the distribution of health care. At its starkest, they see such controls as leading to "death panels," small elites deciding who lives and who dies — this is one accusation the right wing made against President Obama's steps toward universal health-care coverage. But fearing *active* interventions, those who fear death panels seem not even to notice that America already has a rationing system, albeit a *passive* one: the marketplace. The agency of the economy is so displaced and naturalized as to be invisible (this seems to hold for *both* sides of the debate sketched out above). It seems to function without anyone needing to take action. This is the logic that allows Americans to reject "death panels" and yet accept the rationing of health care when it is carried out by privatized insurance and medical institutions. Actively making choices looks too much like "killing." In contrast, submitting to the marketplace can be assimilated to merely "letting die."

Acknowledgments

This paper was written during a period of research leave funded by the Institute for Advanced Study and the University of Michigan. I am grateful to my fellow 2019–20 members of the Institute for their comradeship and insights. An earlier, shorter version of this essay appeared in the "Pandemic Diaries" edited Gabriela Manley, Bryan M. Dougan, and Carole McGranahan (Keane 2020).

References

Anderson, Elizabeth S. 1995. *Value in Ethics and Economics.* Cambridge, MA: Harvard University Press.

Beech, Hannah, Richard C. Paddock, and Muktita Suhartono. 2018. "'Still Can't Believe It Worked': The Story of the Thailand Cave Rescue." *New York Times*, July 12, 2018. https://www.nytimes.com/2018/07/12/world/asia/thailand-cave-rescue-seals.html.

Case, Anne, and Angus Deaton. 2020. *Deaths of Despair and the Future of Capitalism.* Princeton: Princeton University Press.

Cohen, Lawrence. 2020. "The Culling: Pandemic, Gerocide, Generational Affect." *Medical Anthropology Quarterly* 34 (4): 542–60. https://doi.org/10.1111/maq.12627.

Cole, Brendan. 2020. "Fox News' Brit Hume Defends Risking Older People's Lives 'to Allow the Economy to Move Forward' in Coronavirus Shutdown." *Newsweek*, March 25, 2020. https://www.newsweek.com/britt-hume-dan-patrick-tucker-carlson-fox-older-people-1494107.

Cuomo, Andrew (@NYGovCuomo). 2020. "My mother is not expendable. Your mother is not expandable." Twitter, March 24, 2020, 5:43 p.m. https://twitter.com/nygovcuomo/status/1242477029083295746?lang=en.

Downen, Robert (@RobDownenChron). 2020. "Sen. Paul Bettencourt wants to know why Harris County leaders are adopting a stay-home order." Twitter, March 24, 2020, 3:13 p.m. https://twitter.com/RobDownenChron/status/1242439334680297473.

Eldridge, Keith. 2020. "'We Can't Rule Anything In or Out,' Inslee Says for COVID-19 Outbreak Measures." *Komo News*, March 18, 2020. https://komonews.com/news/coronavirus/we-cant-rule-anything-in-or-out-inslee-says-for-COVID-19-outbreak-measures.

EPA (United States Environmental Protection Agency). 2020. "Mortality Risk Valuation." EPA, updated November 20, 2020. https://www.epa.gov/environmental-economics/mortality-risk-valuation.

Fassin, Didier. 2018. *Life: A Critical User's Manual*. Cambridge: Polity Press.

Feinberg, Kenneth R. 2005. *What is Life Worth? The Unprecedented Effort to Compensate the Victims of 9/11*. New York: Public Affairs.

Foot, Philippa. 1967. "The Problem of Abortion and the Doctrine of Double Effect." *Oxford Review*, no. 5: 5–15.

Fourcade, Marion. 2016. "Ordinalization: Lewis A. Coser Memorial Award for Theoretical Agenda Setting 2014." *Sociological Theory* 34 (3): 175–95. https://doi.org/10.1177/0735275116665876.

Gilbert, Craig. 2020. "Sen. Ron Johnson Is Telling People to Keep Coronavirus in Perspective." *Milwaukee Journal Sentinel*, March 18, 2020. https://www.jsonline.com/story/news/politics/analysis/2020/03/18/coronavirus-sen-ron-johnson-says-keep-outbreak-perspective/5074145002/.

Guarino, Ben. 2020. "New York's Bioethics Experts Prepare for a Wave of Difficult Decisions." *Washington Post*, March 28, 2020. https://www.washingtonpost.com/world/national-security/new-yorks-bioethics-experts-prepare-for-a-wave-of-difficult-decisions/2020/03/28/4501f522-7045-11ea-a3ec-70d7479d83f0_story.html.

Hennessy-Fiske, Molly. 2020. "Sacrifice the Old to Help the Economy? Texas Official's Remark Prompts Backlash." *Los Angeles Times*, March 24, 2020. https://www.latimes.com/world-nation/story/2020-03-24/coronavirus-texas-dan-patrick.

Hooks, Christopher. 2020. "Dan Patrick to Dan Patrick: Drop Dead." *Texas Monthly*, March 24, 2020. https://www.texasmonthly.com/politics/dan-patrick-coronavirus-tucker-carlson/.

Keane, Webb. 2016. *Ethical Life: Its Natural and Social Histories.* Princeton: Princeton University Press.

Keane, Webb. 2020. "Your Money or Your Life: The Virus, the Economy, and the Trolley Problem." In "Pandemic Diaries," edited by Gabriela Manley, Bryan M. Dougan, and Carole McGranahan, *American Ethnologist* website, April 21, 2020. https://americanethnologist.org/features/collections/pandemic-diaries/your-money-or-your-life-the-virus-the-economy-and-the-trolley-problem.

Kellogg Insight. 2020. "Containing COVID-19 will Devastate the Economy: Here's the Economic Case for Why It's Still Our Best Option, Based on Research of Martin Eichenbaum, Sergio Rebelo, and Mathias Trabandt." March 26, 2020. https://insight.kellogg.northwestern.edu/article/economic-cost-coronavirus-recession-COVID-deaths.

Keynes, John Maynard. 1923. *A Tract on Monetary Reform.* London: Macmillan.

Law, Tara. 2020. "California City Official Ousted after Saying COVID-19 Could 'Fix' Burdens on Society if Allowed to Spread." *Time*, May 3, 2020. https://time.com/5831424/california-city-official-ousted-COVID-19-fix-society-antioch/.

Lewis, Matt. 2020. "The Party of Life Embraces Trump's Death Cult." *Daily Beast*, March 25, 2020. https://www.thedailybeast.com/the-party-of-life-embraces-trumps-gdp-death-cult.

Lin, Rong-Gong II, Luke Money, Soumya Karlamangla, and Alex Wigglesworth. 2021. "Ambulance Crews Told not to Transport Patients who Have Little Chance of Survival." *Los Angeles Times*, January 4, 2021. https://www.latimes.com/california/story/2021-01-04/los-angeles-hospitals-cannot-keep-up-COVID-19-surge-illness.

Liu, Andrew. 2020. "'Chinese Virus,' World Market." *N+1*, March 20, 2020. https://nplusonemag.com/online-only/online-only/chinese-virus-world-market/.

Livingston, Abby. 2020. "Texas Lt. Gov. Dan Patrick Says a Failing Economy is Worse than Coronavirus." *Texas Tribune*, March 23, 2020. https://www.texastribune.org/2020/03/23/texas-lt-gov-dan-patrick-says-bad-economy-worse-coronavirus/.

Lukes, Steven. 1997. "Comparing the Incomparable: Trade-Offs and Sacrifices." In *Incommensurability, Incomparability, and Practical Reason*, edited by Ruth Chang, 184–95. Cambridge, MA: Harvard University Press.

Morris, Alice, and Robert T. Garrett. 2020. "Texas Lt. Gov. Dan Patrick Spurns Shelter in Place, Urges Return to Work, Suggests Grandparents

Should Sacrifice." *Dallas Morning News*, March 23, 2020, updated March 24, 2020. https://www.dallasnews.com/news/public-health/2020/03/24/texas-lt-gov-dan-patrick-spurns-shelter-in-place-urges-return-to-work-says-grandparents-should-sacrifice/.

Patrick, Dan. 2020. "Lt. Gov. Dan Patrick on Tucker Carlson Tonight." Dan Patrick Texas, Lieutenant Governor, March 23, 2020. https://www.danpatrick.org/tucker-carlson-tonight-march-23-2020/.

Pollack, Harold. 2020. "Who Lives, Who Dies, Who Decides." *Washington Post*, March 27, 2020. https://www.washingtonpost.com/outlook/2020/03/27/economy-public-health-virus/?arc404=true.

Povinelli, Elizabeth A. 2011. *Economies of Abandonment: Social Belonging and Endurance in Late Liberalism*. Durham: Duke University Press.

Reich, Robert. 2020. "Ignore the Bankers — the Trump Economy Is Not Worth More Coronavirus Deaths." *Guardian*, March 29, 2020. https://www.theguardian.com/commentisfree/2020/mar/29/bankers-trump-economy-coronavirus-deaths?CMP=Share_iOSApp_Other.

Richardson, Reed. 2020. "Glenn Beck Thinks Older Americans Should Go Back to Work: 'Even If We All Get Sick, I'd Rather Die than Kill the Country.'" *Media Ite*, March 24, 2020. https://www.mediaite.com/news/glenn-beck-issues-call-for-older-americans-to-go-back-to-work-even-if-we-all-get-sick-id-rather-die-than-kill-the-country/.

Servello, Adriana, and Evaristo Ettore. 2020. "COVID-19: The Italian Viral 'Gerocide' of the 21st Century." *Archives of Gerontology and Geriatrics*, no. 89: 104111. https://doi.org/10.1016/j.archger.2020.104111.

Thompson, Judith J. 1976. "Killing, Letting Die, and the Trolley Problem." *Monist* 59 (2): 204–17. https://doi.org/10.5840/monist197659224.

Thompson, Judith J. 1985. "The Trolley Problem." *Yale Law Journal* 94 (6): 1395–415. https://doi.org/10.2307/796133.

Wexler, Celia V. 2020. "Coronavirus has Donald Trump and Dan Patrick Ready to Sacrifice Older People." *NBC News Think*, March 26, 2020. https://www.nbcnews.com/think/opinion/coronavirus-has-donald-trump-dan-patrick-ready-sacrifice-older-people-ncna1169126.

Zelizer, Viviana. 1994. *Pricing the Priceless Child: The Changing Social Value of Children*. Princeton: Princeton University Press.

CHAPTER 10

Protecting the Elderly or Saving the Economy?

Turkey's Ageist Lockdown Policy during the COVID Pandemic

Başak Can and Ergin Bulut

When news of COVID hit Turkey's national agenda in February 2020, journalists asked President Erdoğan about the measures the government was taking. Praising the country's efforts to bring its citizens back from China, he shared his strategy: "Do not catch a cold. Be careful about fever. ... I eat a spoonful of mulberry molasses every morning because it is hematinic food" (Sözcü 2020). On March 11, just over a month later, the country registered its first official coronavirus case, and the effectiveness of mulberry molasses as a treatment was found to be seriously questionable. In mid-March, the country initiated a national campaign called *Hayat Eve Sığar* (Life Fits Inside the Home), banning large meetings, switching to remote education, and shutting down nonessential businesses. These were followed by restrictions on travel to and from thirty-one metropolitan areas within the country. Like many other countries, the Turkish government embraced lockdown as the only strategy to contain the virus instead of widespread testing and tracing (Caduff 2020).

Seeing Spain, Belgium, and France struggle with high death rates in elderly care facilities, the government also introduced a selective lockdown strategy that would target certain demographics as early as

March 22. Accordingly, citizens above sixty-five years of age were not allowed to go outside if they were not part of the workforce, a policy that would negatively impact the elderly on many different levels. When it was first put into place, ageist stereotypes that severely undermined the dignity of the elderly circulated widely on social media, perpetuating discrimination toward senior citizens. The policy also isolated the elderly by restricting their access to their social networks and families, and to health care for routine controls. The policy was discriminatory on the basis of class, given that business owners were exempt from these regulations.

In this chapter we examine the politics of this controversial *#LifeFitsInsideHome* campaign from the perspective of the elderly. We ask: What does it look like to be an elderly citizen and be forced to stay at home in the name of care and protection? How do these communities feel about being the subject of the government's paternal protectionism? What is at stake when, in an authoritarian context, social order within the domestic space is maintained through a medical discourse?

Concerned with preventing a high morbidity rate among the elderly, in the face of the warning by the health authorities that this category was statistically vulnerable, and hoping to protect its national brand in the global struggle against COVID (Bulut and Can 2020), the government placed extreme emphasis on keeping the elderly alive. Yet, during the implementation of this biopolitical policy, the elderly have been inculpated, infantilized, and confined to their houses. Since home confinement produced major physical and emotional difficulties for them, many became resentful, a number of them taking to social media to vocally reject the idea that they lacked the ability to protect themselves and others. The policy was selectively implemented as it applied *only* to the elderly outside the active formal workforce (i.e., those who were retired, unemployed, or non-business owners), even though a considerable number of elderly citizens, despite being officially retired, still work in informal jobs for their livelihoods. Therefore, anyone who was not a business owner or did not work in a formal job was denied the right to mobility. As such, it was the lower- and middle-income elderly, who had already suffered disproportionately over the last two decades from the neoliberal policies of the Turkish government, who were hit especially hard by the policy's effects. The lockdown policy thus revealed who is vulnerable to marginalization in capitalist societies by exposing the insidious relationship between value, productive capacity, and age. This revelation was unsurprising to the elderly themselves, however, as the contradictions in the government's protectionist COVID policies were prefigured in its prior disinvestment in their well-being with its neoliberal welfare policies.

Confining the Elderly to the Home: The Elderly as Objects of Ridicule and Infantilizing Care

At the time of writing, Turkish officials declared 49,774 COVID deaths. Compared to the European context, death numbers were low, especially during the early periods of the pandemic. Despite criticism of the reliability of these figures, a number of reasons can be cited for the low numbers. The government's resistance to conducting widespread testing, the wide availability of beds in intensive care units, computerized tomography, lack of regulation, and the exploitation of health care workers — formerly sources of criticism with respect to the neoliberalization of health services — boosted Turkey's initial ability to keep, or perhaps claim to keep, official numbers relatively low (Balta and Özel 2020; Kayaalp and Işık 2020).

Another widely cited reason for the country's low official fatality rate was the scarcity of nursing homes. Given the inadequacy of formal care institutions for Turkey's elderly and the widespread practice of providing care for the elderly in their own homes (or for families to live with the elderly, especially if the latter were ill), Turkey did not experience COVID outbreaks in nursing home facilities as was observed in several European countries. The centrality of the home to the government's policy response to the virus is thus not a coincidental technical issue but rather a political one, shaped by national peculiarities and Turkey's political-economic context.

However, ageism in the country and widespread misinformation about the relationship between the elderly and the pandemic ultimately not only confined these vulnerable populations to their homes but also perpetuated existing stereotypes. In the early days of COVID, there was indeed nothing short of an "infodemic" in Turkey in which the focus on protecting the elderly created the perception that they were in fact responsible for spreading the disease. The intermingling of the vulnerability of the elderly and the culpability they were assigned stuck in the public imaginary, including both ordinary citizens and senior politicians. For instance, when informing the public, health officials would state exactly how many people above a certain age had died. On March 20, for example, the Minister of Health tweeted: "In the last 24 hours, five old patients with weak immunity lost their lives. Overall, nine people died. *All are elderly. Let's protect them.*" By emphasizing the age of the deceased and pointing to their weak immune system, thus by counting their deaths separately, the Minister of Health implied a causal connection between the elderly and the pandemic.

The minister of health announced the first coronavirus case on March 11, 2020. Only ten days after this announcement, the government imposed a lockdown for those over the age of sixty-five or those who were chronically ill. A month later, the lockdown was extended to people younger than twenty years of age. People from these age groups were allowed to go outside for a limited number of hours and expected to remain indoors unless actively employed. However, the government never closed production facilities, factories, or other types of workplaces if working from home was not feasible. Even when restrictions on public gatherings in cafes, restaurants, or concert halls were lifted, those over sixty-five years of age remained confined to their homes. Age-specific restrictions were lifted only a year later. This age-centric lockdown policy stigmatized the elderly as the viral cause of the pandemic.

In time, the scapegoating of the elderly led to the widespread circulation of ageist harassment on social media. In one video that went viral, a young man, who identified himself as police officer, was filmed reprimanding a senior citizen — a Mr. Ali Ihsan Yavaşça (eighty) — for being in the road, admonishing Mr. Yavaşça that he would let him off the hook this one time. With his shoulders backed up against a shop window, Mr. Yavaşça looked like an embarrassed child, attempting to explain that he was on his way back home from hospital. The young "trickster" was soon arrested, with the court judgment ruling him to stay home for fifteen days and to do community work at an elderly care facility close to his home (Show Ana Haber 2020). This quick state performance aimed to soothe the public outcry directed at both the young trickster and the widespread discrimination against senior citizens that was taking place.

The kind of harassment suffered by Mr. Yavaşça was not an isolated case. His humiliation was facilitated by public authorities whose actions on behalf of elder care had the consequence of demeaning the elderly because they infantilized them and erased them from the public sphere. In one example, police teams wandered across cities making announcements or directly warning senior citizens in the streets that they should be staying indoors. Sometimes police officers would ask for the elderly person's word that they would comply, in others they would give the elderly a ride back home. To limit elderly people from being outdoors, municipalities would remove seating from public parks. In what seems like a cruel joke (see Figure 2), the Uskudar municipality of Istanbul comments on how it uses other tactics to ensure that the elderly remain indoors: "We love you, but please do not push us to do this" (Belediyesi 2020).

Figure 2: Image of an elderly man who wishes to go out but cannot because an excavator is digging a hole right in front of his apartment building. (Source: Üsküdar Belediyesi, "Sizleri çok seviyoruz ama bize bunu yaptırmayın," Twitter, March 21, 2020.)

The government soon formed *vefa timleri* (loyal care teams) with the help of *kaymakamlık* (district governorships), which in line with its protectionist logic would meet the needs of the elderly who were not allowed outdoors. Even after the strictest lockdown restrictions were partially lifted for the general population on June 1, 2020, mobility by the elderly remained limited and was allowed only on Sundays between 2 p.m. and 8 p.m. This was later eased, with the permission to be outdoors daily between 10 a.m. and 1 p.m., though they were barred from using public transportation. These restrictions were finally lifted in May 2021 for those elderly who were fully vaccinated. Although restricting the movement of the elderly was presented as prerequisite for preventing the spread of the disease, in the popular medical discourse the elderly were implicitly depicted as the principal *spreaders* of the virus. Such depictions, and the assignment of an inferior status to the elderly, did not arise in a vacuum but were rather embedded in Turkey's inequitable and paternalistic social policies.

Elderly Care in an Ageing Turkey: Stuck Between the Family and the State

Demographically, Turkey imagines itself as a young member of an old Europe, though this is far from the truth. Turkey is an old country in which people above sixty-five constitute almost 10 percent of the population; once this proportion exceeds 10 percent, as is expected to happen as soon as 2023, the country will officially be "very old" (Arun 2020). That there is immense respect for the elderly is another national myth. In a longitudinal study on the quality of life for the elderly, respondents were asked if they had experienced any discrimination because of their age. The study has found that age discrimination in the country has been growing over the last decade, with the percentage of those responding affirmatively having risen from 4.5 percent in 2013, to 7 percent in 2016, to 10.3 percent shortly before the pandemic (Arun 2020). The government's containment of the elderly thus took place in an old and increasingly ageist country, and one with a neoliberalized welfare system at that.

A strictly centralized and corporatist framework operating under neoliberal principles shapes Turkey's elderly care regime. Governmental bodies (the Family, Labor, and Social Services Ministry, the Social Aid General Directorate, and the Disabled and Elderly Aid General Directorate) work together with public and private institutions but rely significantly on the labor and infrastructures of families to provide care. Along these lines and in a context where the minimum wage is less than TLY 2,500, the government pays around TLY 700 (less than USD 100) to qualifying elderly and makes this monthly payment — *muhtaç yaşlı aylığı* (needy elderly salary) — through the family. In addition, the government provides *yaşlı bakım aylığı* (elderly care salary) at TLY 1,305 (as of 2019) for citizens who undertake care work for their elderly family members. Although this does not necessarily mean that all elderly people live with their children and grandchildren, it does provide a monetary incentive to care for them within the traditional extended family structure. By delegating care services for the elderly to the family, the government has taken the homogeneity of the elderly population for granted, assuming that all have families on which they can rely and that all would find it desirable to make this conscious political — and gendered — investment in the survival of a conservative, home-centered way of life (Can 2019).

The outcome of all this is a care regime that, on the one hand, disregards formal care institutions and, on the other, holds families morally responsible for taking care of their elderly. Central to the state's logic of relying on the family for provision of care services is the belief that strong families enable a strong state. However, in an authoritarian context defined by inequitable access to resources, the protectionist lockdown policy instituted in the pandemic was far from achieving these goals. On the contrary, it not only increased the economic and affective burdens of care providers but worsened senior citizens' economic, bodily, and psychological capacities through an ageist and gendered practice of confinement.

Pandemic Diaries: The Elderly as Criminalized Infants

To understand how the elderly experienced the government's protective care, we carried out interviews with senior citizens in Turkey. We wanted to understand what life feels like when one is unable to leave the house and is turned into an object of popular ridicule. Through snowball sampling and by using our networks in the cities of İzmir and İstanbul, we interviewed sixteen people, mostly from the middle class and mostly baby boomers. All our respondents were between the ages of sixty-five and seventy-five. Most of them were living with their spouses and were taking care of themselves. We talked to nine men and seven women. There were three couples among our respondents. All our research participants preferred phone calls to Zoom or Skype interviews. A considerable number had underlying health conditions. None of them lived with their families but all lived close enough to them to have sustained contact with their children and grandchildren. While their children helped them with their own daily needs, in turn all research participants provided care labor for their grandchildren whenever the need arose. Some of the women we talked to were in fact the primary day-time caregivers of their grandchildren. All respondents disagreed with the enforced lockdown, critiquing the political logic behind the government's strategy, providing critical insights regarding the gendered nature of confinement, and illuminating the relationship between home as a private space and a site of the unfolding of authoritarian politics.

The word "quarantine" has its roots in the Latin word *quadraginta*. Meaning forty, the word stipulates "40 days of segregation, and was derived from Christian theologies of sin and redemption, in which plagues were understood as divine punishment on a fallen world" (Mitropoulos 2020a: 42). Instead of accepting the quarantine's medical protection at face value, the elderly we interviewed foregrounded the idea of punishment and inculpation. Consider Coşkun, a seventy-one-year-old retired man living in Istanbul. With his retired wife, he moved to their summer house in Bodrum, a coastal town, just before lockdown where they rely on their pension funds and the rents coming in from a few homes they own. They are not in the worst situation. However, despite being in their summer house which has a yard and where they can actually go outside without being on the street, unlike their accommodation in Istanbul, Coşkun has faced emotional challenges: "I feel as if I was imprisoned." He is glad to have left Istanbul before the lockdown: "Perhaps we would have argued, [me] with my wife, and gotten a divorce. [I have] no emotions left whatsoever. It's like they're treating sixty-five-plus citizens like a dog." Despite being in the summer house, not enjoying sociality is emotionally trying: "You feel lonely. I am so fed up with experts advising all kinds of different things on television." A particular kind of resentment derived from infantilization is central to Coşkun's experience: "It's not nice that somebody else limits my mobility without my consent. We did go out. I took my wife to the marketplace. Yet, we couldn't dine out. As everyone else was having fun, we had to return home. I resented this. I am really pissed off because I really have no clue regarding the logic."

İbrahim is a seventy-three-year-old man living in İzmir, who has been retired for twenty-six years now. He worked for about ten years following retirement but quit his post-retirement job after breaking his leg. His wife Firdevs is a housewife, and we interviewed them together. On the one hand, the rhythm of their everyday life has not changed much during the pandemic. On the other hand, much has changed insofar as somebody else is dictating to them how they should live their lives — this is why they find themselves so reactive to their situation.

As İbrahim has diabetes and high blood pressure, they pay particular attention to hygiene. They are in fact aware that they may be a bit too cautious, washing paper bills, coins, and everything else coming in from the outside. Once they are back home, they jump in the shower. "Disinfecting everything has been a sort of sickness for us," İbrahim says. The "what ifs" are so many that they avoid going out unless absolutely necessary. In fact, İbrahim delayed a doctor's appointment once, although he soon has to go back. They are aware that certain measures are necessary. For instance, they have not seen any of their grandchildren, daughters, and sons-in-law for the whole summer. Yet, they are heartbroken because of online harassment and the government's targeted lockdown policy: "Why did they target us only? It wasn't necessary."

For the elderly, the repetitiveness of everyday life in lockdown felt like a punishment. Before COVID, Remzi, a retired math teacher, was living "a standard retiree life," going to *kahvehane* (traditional coffee shops frequented by men) every day to play cards. The pandemic broke his routine in such a way that he feels he has been "punished." "I like playing cards. This is major psychological pressure on us. We are free from 10 a.m. till 8 p.m. but I don't understand why we are punished as if we will go to bars at night." He does recognize how the entire world has turned upside down and that changes to one's lifestyle might be necessary. We also see Remzi's internalized ageism in that he cannot imagine his age group going to bars. At the same time, the media and the politicians' overemphasis on the elderly made him feel like a "sacrificial lamb" slated to die first or else to be considered the "cause" of the pandemic. At times, he felt as if he would not ever be able to see his grandchildren again, especially when they asked when they would see him again. Like İbrahim and Firdevs, Remzi underlines how being infantilized and deprived of liberties has hurt him: "Even if you do nothing outside, the idea and practice of being free is beautiful. I mean, you'll be free even if you do nothing. We didn't always go out anyway even during our free times. I should be able to make my decisions as an individual and not be guided by anyone else."

Although significant, the feeling of punishment through enforced immobility was not as severely felt among women, creating a gendered dimension to the confinement. Of course the women were also unhappy about the confinement, but they believed that the men were more severely hit by the lockdown, hinting at the male entitlement to mobility. Nurcan is a sixty-seven-year-old widow living on her own. She refrained from seeing her mother for ten months, though they have moved in together since. For her, "men are no different from kids. They are used to having things done for them. It is more difficult for them to spend time at home. They don't think they belong at home. I'm guessing that they might have gotten bored more than women. Women have responsibilities such as cooking and cleaning that help them pass their time." Kader is also a widow. Now sixty-six years old, she believes not much has changed for her during the pandemic because she was still taking care of her grandchildren despite her physical health problems. Therefore, she was not "bored" at home and, in fact, was quite busy.

Still, the elderly were not willing to countenance their infantilization. By no means did they accept the value regimes assigned to them (Narotzky forthcoming), rejecting the self-ascription of the category "old." We asked our participants if they felt old or would consider themselves to belong to the category of "old." İbrahim, at seventy-three, said he felt like he was fifty-five. His wife Firdevs explained: "It was during the pandemic that they made us feel old." Using a masculine discourse, Remzi contested the view that the elderly were useless: "Listen, the youngsters made fun of the elderly, right? We were told to stay at home and not deal with the pandemic. This is misguided. You could very well benefit from the elderly. I have a functioning body. My brain still works. No amnesia. We could perhaps contribute to resolve this crisis." Nurcan, at sixty-seven years of age, astutely pointed to the pluralities of being old and being in the category of "elderly." As a woman who, before the pandemic, used to provide care labor for her grandchild and mother (aged ninety-two at the time of the interview), she suggested that government policies should consider the multifarious ways of being old and reformulate the policies accordingly.

Ultimately, although the government framed its lockdown policy in the language of care and protection, the policy's outcome has not been much different from the viral harassment video described earlier. The elderly we interviewed did not have to work and had somewhat stable lives. Even so, being controlled as if they were children, and being denied their mobility, were unwelcome developments. In this regard, the fact that their mobility was both restricted by the government and monitored by their concerned children raised insights as to the status of this generation's entitlement to mobility.

Ambivalence toward Protection: Appreciation, Skepticism, and Resentment

Our research participants' response to the lockdown did not simply consist of rejecting culpability, infantilization, or the categorization as "old"; they also provided objective evaluations of the government's pandemic policies. Our respondents appreciated how the chronically ill were able to get their medication from pharmacies without having to go to the doctor's office. For Kader, the government did the right thing in restricting the elderly's mobility by cancelling their free transportation passes. Since her children worked and at times used public transportation, Kader believed that having the elderly out and about in the city would not help limit the spread of the virus. Our informants were also appreciative of the Health Minister's daily COVID briefings. While they did not consider the statistics of cases and morbidity rates that the government provided reliable, they did feel that they were being taken seriously as citizens. For Ali "it was symbolically a good thing for the Minister of Health to take us seriously as human beings and share certain figures." İbrahim agreed that the minister's "behaviors, decisions, interpretations, and advice were all good" but only within their own limits. This is where the skepticism of our respondents became obvious: while they did appreciate receiving a daily briefing, they either did not find the numbers reliable or found the Minister of Health's medical authority was being undermined by the government's desire to limit information.

Perhaps more than appreciation or skepticism, it was resentment regarding the government's failure to respect the elderly that defined their feelings. "We accepted that the elderly are not valued. There are not enough care facilities in this country. We are now convinced that the government doesn't care very much about the elderly," says İbrahim. When asked whether they felt they were being made scapegoats, Firdevs agreed and responded with a policy proposal: "We would have expected them to at least grant us one day for shopping within that entire three-month period of complete lockdown. Or even two hours. I am lucky that I have kids to help out, but others are not as lucky." The government's provision of material services during the crisis was also at the core of our respondents' resentment. Although the government inundated the media with images of free sanitizers and masks being distributed to the elderly, Remzi, for example, never received anything. For him, there was also a double standard in terms of how public life was regulated. As someone who loved playing cards, he simply could not understand how weddings were allowed, even with social distancing, as opposed to playing cards in *kahvehane*s. Remzi also could not understand why younger people were allowed to work while the elderly were in lockdown. This, to him, simply did not add up.

The politics of the quarantine were at the center of Ali's criticism — a lockdown that targeted only the elderly did not make sense. If a lockdown was necessary, perhaps it would also have to be universal. At the same time, the main problem for Ali was the quick shift to quarantines at the expense of widespread testing and tracing. For Ali, this was a political choice that prioritized "resuming the wheels of the economy."

When we asked about their lives at home, the economic dimension of the quarantine emerged as a key issue. İsmail said: "People act according to their income. Right? If I had earned 8,000–10,000 liras a month, I would also like to go out; but because my finances are limited, I feel comfortable at home. This is what life at home means. They only tell us 'life fits inside the home' but this is true only for those who are better off." When asked about the feeling about being stuck at home, Firdevs said: "There are many people who are over sixty-five and don't have a regular income and have to go to work to earn their living, to earn 15 to 20 liras a day. These people suffered a lot. What did they eat during the quarantine?" Indeed, staying at home was an economic privilege as the pandemic exposed the divide between those who can order groceries online and those who cannot. Firdevs attested to these inequalities: "Life is beautiful if you have money. You would place an online order from Migros [a popular grocery store in Turkey]. But we cannot do such things. Because we need to go to the farmer's market and pick our own. Pepper is five liras at Migros but three liras in the market. I save twenty liras in ten kilos. This is the kind of calculation we have to do." As the couple emphasized, there are "different inequalities" among the elderly, a demographic that has been constantly homogenized since the pandemic. These differences impact how the elderly experience the lockdown in social, economic, and psychological terms.

Conclusion: Is There Life at Home?

Although İbrahim and Firdevs started our interview by stating that the pandemic did not disrupt the rhythm of their retiree lives, they ended our interview with these words: "Thanks for this interview. It did make a major change in our everyday lives. We felt we lived a different day today." That İbrahim and Firdevs experienced a different day because we had shown interest in their daily lives during COVID can only be satisfying for us. However, if being interviewed by strangers represents a major change in one's life as an elderly person, then important questions can be raised regarding the mandated domesticity and the inequitable politics of the quarantine.

While the Minister of Health advised adults under sixty-five to declare and practice their own individual state of emergency, elderly people outside the active workforce were forced to stay home. This was problematic both for their health and finances because one would be liable to pay an administrative fine of up to TLY 3,000 for the violation of the lockdown policy. The fact that simply being outside could merit monetary punishment reveals how neoliberalism and authoritarian government have together produced drastic consequences for vulnerable populations during the pandemic.

A contradiction thus emerges regarding the politics of confinement for the elderly. On the one hand, the elderly were aware that confinement worked, scientifically speaking. On the other hand, they were critical of how the young and economically productive, with their mobility intact, could be so dismissive of the virus and in fact endanger the health of others. Similarly, they were aware of a contradiction regarding their worth as people. They understood that they were being forced to stay home because their lives were valued, while they also articulated how they did not feel valued since the lockdown meant they were considered old and economically unproductive.

For these reasons, although the confinement was seen as necessary, it created resentment and intensified ageist inequalities. In other words, it was not simply the confinement but its ageist implementation that was problematic. In sum, the ageist dimension of the lockdown in Turkey reveals a crisis of care, wherein the elderly were ambivalently valued (Narotzky forthcoming). Those employed or those running businesses were seen as deserving of unconditional mobility, whereas the "economically unproductive" were denied this right based on the state's pretext of protection.

Finally, in investigating whether there is life at home, it is worth considering the home in its various dimensions. A home can serve as sanctuary during a pandemic. Indeed, to have a home in which to take shelter is itself a privilege, and, as a bounded space, home does provide security and safety. At the same time, however, the home is also a place where conservatism and authoritarianism can be imposed. Although home is where we are presumably protected against the coronavirus, the confines of the home enable capitalist exploitation, insofar as quarantine at home involves the "suspension of rights over one's own body" (Mitropoulos 2020b) in exchange for the smooth functioning of the economy. Through the legal enforcement of the lockdown, the state not only intrudes upon the private space of the elderly but also makes decisions on their behalf (Suk 2009). The home of the elderly person thus potentially becomes a space of inspection, monitoring, and stigmatization. When confinement, rather than widespread testing, vaccine development, and welfare benefits to the needy, becomes the primary goal of the state, the autonomy of the elderly is reduced. In that regard, home emerges in the case of Turkey as a peculiar place where neoliberalism and a paternal form of authoritarianism have converged upon ageist practices.

Through a critical look at the home as a space of protection, we are able to understand what the government prioritizes (that is, the economy) and is willing to sacrifice (that is, the "economically unproductive" elderly) in its biopolitical game. Ultimately, in order to mask its own interest in social reproduction, and through the deployment of logics that would rationalize keeping the economy open, the Turkish government's protectionism has served to normalize human rights violations against the elderly, adding to the country's broader record on this front.

Acknowledgements

We would like to thank our editors Didier Fassin and Marion Fourcade, the anonymous reviewers, and our colleagues at the Institute for Advanced Study for their feedback and Caroline Jeannerat for her editorial guidance.

References

Arun, Özgür. 2020. "Eşitsiz Yaşlanmak: Türkiye'nin Serüveni, Alanın Niteligi ve Yaşlanma Gündemi." *Cogito* (Istanbul), no. 98: 89–106.

Balta, Evren, and Soli Özel. 2020. "The Battle Over the Numbers: Turkey's Low Case Fatality Rate." Institut Montaigne, May 4, 2020. https://www.institutmontaigne.org/en/blog/battle-over-numbers-turkeys-low-case-fatality-rate.

Belediyesi, Üsküdar. 2020. "Sizleri çok seviyoruz ama bize bunu yaptırmayın." Twitter, March 21, 2020, 10:27 a.m. https://twitter.com/uskudarbld/status/1241280161565245440.

Bulut, Ergin, and Başak Can. 2020. "Rebranding the Turkish State in the Time of COVID-19." *MERIP*, September 29, 2020. https://merip.org/2020/09/rebranding-the-turkish-state-in-the-time-of-covid-19/.

Caduff, Carlo. 2020. "What Went Wrong: Corona and the World after the Full Stop." *Medical Anthropology Quarterly* 34 (4): 467–87. https://doi.org/10.1111/maq.12599.

Can, Başak. 2019. "Caring for Solidarity? The Intimate Politics of Grandmother Childcare and Neoliberal Conservatism in Urban Turkey." *New Perspectives on Turkey* 60 (1): 85–107. https://doi.org/10.1017/npt.2019.4.

Kayaalp, Ebru, and İbrahim B. Işık. 2020. "COVID-19 and Healthcare Infrastructure in Turkey." *Medical Anthropology Quarterly Rapid Response Blog Series.* https://medanthroquarterly.org/rapid-response/2020/08/covid-19-and-healthcare-infrastructure-in-turkey/.

Mitropoulos, Angela. 2020a. *Pandemonium: Proliferating Borders of Capital and the Pandemic Swerve*. London: Pluto Press.

Mitropoulos, Angela. 2020b. "Against Quarantine." *New Inquiry* (blog), February 13, 2020. https://thenewinquiry.com/against-quarantine/.

Narotzky, Susana. Forthcoming. "Caring for the Old and Letting Them Die: A Political Economy of Human Worth." In *Ethnographies of Deservingness: Unpacking Ideologies of Distribution and Inequality.* New York: Berghahn.

Show Ana Haber. 2020. "İhsan Amca: 'Şikayetçi değilim!'" YouTube video, 1: 30 min. March 26, 2020. https://youtu.be/EBBQLMn1tpo.

Sözcü. 2020. "Erdoğan corona virüsünden nasıl korunduğunu açıkladı!" *Sözcü*, February 4, 2020. https://www.sozcu.com.tr/2020/gundem/erdogan-korona-virusunden-nasil-korundugunu-aciklad-5606202/.

Suk, Jeannie. 2009. *At Home in the Law: How the Domestic Violence Revolution Is Transforming Privacy*. New Haven: Yale University Press.

CHAPTER 11

Reflections on Mutual Aid

Z. Fareen Parvez

> The mutual-aid tendency in man ... is so deeply interwoven with all the past evolution of the human race ... that it has been maintained by mankind up to the present time, notwithstanding all vicissitudes of history. ... But when even the greatest calamities befell ... [mutual aid] continued to live in the villages and among the poorer classes in the towns; it still kept them together.
> — Peter Kropotkin, *Mutual Aid: A Factor of Evolution*

The COVID pandemic, arguably one of the great calamities of recent history, has harshly revealed what many disadvantaged and vulnerable communities around the world have always known: that the state will not protect their safety or livelihoods. In the weeks following the global lockdowns, in the midst of unemployment, medical crises, and insecurity, mutual aid movements almost immediately sprang to life to address people's material needs where the state could not or did not. They proliferated to such an extent that for perhaps the first time in the United States (US), "mutual aid" entered the mainstream lexicon and enjoyed coverage in dominant media from the *New York Times* to *USA Today*.

Mutual aid is a method for building solidarity and enacting an alternative vision of social relations. Based on voluntary and nonhierarchical self-organizing, it is "a form of political participation in which people take responsibility for caring for one another and changing political conditions" (Spade 2020: 136). For the Russian anarchist writer Kropotkin, mutual aid, rather than competition, was a law of nature and central to our evolution. Caring for others, he wrote, is beyond mere sympathy; nor is it exactly love. Rather, it is instinct, for animals and humans alike. And in times of crisis, in some contexts it may be the only hope for survival, especially considering the dysfunctions and violence of the structures of states and the capitalist economy.

During the pandemic, the concept of mutual aid has risen to the fore of global justice movements that are struggling to address the combined forces of the ravages of the coronavirus, racial capitalism, and police brutality. They have held out mutual aid as a movement strategy that can over the long run lead to revolutionary transformations in society. To some degree, mutual aid overlaps with the notion of "care," which scholars and activists use to distinguish mutual aid from the world of charity and nongovernmental organizations (NGOs). This essay explores such distinctions and challenges to mutual aid voiced within the political left, the risks of emphasizing voluntarism as well as community, and a potential myopia that stems from applying the term universally instead of reflecting on its substantive meaning across cultures. As Kropotkin himself would have acknowledged, mutual aid is part of everyday life in much of the Global South and was foundational to indigenous ways of life around the world. In the following discussions, I highlight various examples of mutual aid, mostly in the US and, to a lesser extent, in India; present the risks to mutual aid from perspectives within the left; discuss the relevant histories of racial domination; and explore some of the ambiguities and conceptual problems with the concept and practice.

Mutual Aid and the Pandemic

Among the benefits of mutual aid organizing is the conscious avoidance of bureaucratic rules and procedures. This allowed individuals and groups to take action in the early days of the pandemic with great speed. In the US, many thousands of groups throughout the country, in cities and small towns, arose to provide care in their localities. They began either through online platforms like Slack or by simply handing out flyers at the neighborhood level. Nearly every neighborhood in New York City (NYC), for example, developed a mutual aid program (Schlanger 2020). The types of aid included childcare, giving rides, distributing food either directly to individuals or via soup kitchens and food banks, creating neighborhood "pods" in which people organize their mutual care needs, and countless collections of small donations. Much of this support is for the unemployed, often by the unemployed themselves, as well as for those who would not receive benefits from stimulus funds such as sex workers. In the words of one member of NYC United Against the Coronavirus, "I believe we have already passed the point where our governments ... can adequately meet the needs of society under this ongoing coronavirus pandemic. That means that we will need to take care of each other, and we will need to keep each other safe" (cited in Burley 2020).

Many communities were already familiar with or had practiced mutual aid long before the pandemic due to their experience of bitter betrayal by the US state. The movement Cooperation Jackson, in the majority Black city of Jackson, Mississippi, has been building a solidarity economy based on worker cooperatives and a community land trust over several years. Since the pandemic, they produced and distributed their own masks and renewed efforts toward food sovereignty via their ten acres of "Freedom Farms." Members of Cooperation Jackson had already learned from their experiences with the extreme state failure following Hurricane Katrina as well as neglect of the disproportionate impact of HIV on African Americans (P. M. Press 2020).

Similarly, the territory of Puerto Rico, having lived through Hurricane Maria and a devastating earthquake in January 2020, is intimately familiar with government failure and abandonment. During the pandemic, community networks took it upon themselves to produce masks, to actively monitor people's symptoms via phone calls, and even to broadcast coronavirus safety messages through loudspeakers at the neighborhood level (Soto 2020).

The highest per capita infection rates of COVID in the US in fact were in the indigenous Navajo nation. This is the largest land-based reservation in the country, yet it has only thirteen grocery stores, few hospitals, and an unemployment rate of 40 percent (Cheetham 2020; Morales 2020). Thirty percent of residents lack access to running water, electricity, and the internet. Federal relief funds, predictably, were delayed. Several mutual aid organizations raised emergency funds, planned food distribution, and developed a wide distribution network to give masks and other provisions to thousands of people in surrounding indigenous communities. Importantly, mutual aid here is deeply connected with honoring sacred and spiritual traditions, knowing well that their sufferings related to health and food scarcity originate in the many forms of violence that colonialism and capitalism have inflicted.

Just as mutual aid or "radical care" has been part of everyday life in many North American indigenous communities, it is also practiced in neighborhoods and villages across the Global South. Moving to the very different context of India, second only to the US in its total number of coronavirus infections, mutual aid was critical to alleviating the sufferings of migrant workers walking hundreds of kilometers to their villages during the lockdown and to preventing starvation in poor urban neighborhoods as well as villages. With the devastating second wave of infections, mutual aid expanded widely. Examples range from small and local groups to established NGOs providing "ration kits" of oil, lentils, grains, and sugar to poor families; blood donation services; the purchase and distribution of oxygen cylinders; the dissemination of urgent information about hospital bed availability; and the raising of funds for day laborers who lost their incomes. Groups also formed to provide aid to especially vulnerable people, including sex workers, transwomen, and waste pickers, among others. For Muslim minorities, initially blamed for the spread of the coronavirus by Hindu nationalists, mutual aid in some cities facilitated the distribution of medicine, meals, and supplies, and thus allowed some families to bypass bureaucratic obstacles like malfunctioning ration cards. Organizations accompanied the sick to hospital, operated makeshift ambulances, and raised funds to buy PPE for medical workers.

Accustomed to severe and selective government neglect, racialized Muslim communities have long relied on these survival networks. But these networks are often connected to NGOs or rely on the donations of wealthy elites, thus pointing to one of the primary critiques and concerns about mutual aid.

Navigating the State and the "Nonprofit Industrial Complex"

The long-term goals of mutual aid are a prefigurative politics, the creation of new social relations, and self-governed systems of meeting needs such as food and transportation, and even energy and health. The failures of many states (or, as some argue, the exclusions and violence built into their programs) provide opportunities for communities to exercise power by organizing their own basic needs rather than depending on the state to meet them (Spade 2020: 147). The aim of mutual aid is not to assist the state in times of crisis but, rather, to practice autonomy from the state to whatever extent possible (P. M. Press 2020).

While autonomy remains the desired goal, the relationship of mutual aid to states is extraordinarily complex. First, it is worth pointing out the simple fact that not all states are the same, and in some countries the government's welfare apparatus is the only source of support and provision in times of crisis. This is true of some European welfare states like Sweden and France and increasingly of other states like South Korea and Thailand (Ananta 2012; Haggard and Kaufman 2009). Taking a longer historical view, as some have argued, welfare programs in the US and Europe trace their origins to mutual aid societies over the last 300 years. More precisely, modern welfare states emerged as it became clear that mutual aid and philanthropy could not provide for people's needs on a mass scale, especially during economic crises such as the Great Depression (Laville and Eynaud 2019; Konczal 2014). Depending on the context and historical moment, mutual aid has thus been a response to the inadequacy of states as well as a catalyst for the growth of states.

In relating to states, mutual aid groups also face the dual obstacles of state repression and cooptation. Groups that combine emancipatory politics with mutual aid, in particular, may be faced by harassment and violence. These include movements such as the revolutionary Naxalite movement in India, led by lower-caste and tribal villagers (Shah 2019) and combining communist social structures with armed insurgency. Members have been under attack by the Indian state over decades and the organization has faced repression. In the US, one of the most cited examples is the repression of the Black Panther Party and its programs (Nelson 2011); more recently it includes surveillance by the Federal Bureau of Investigation (FBI) of Black Lives Matter activists. At the same time, states may in fact compete with or co-opt the very mutual aid programs that were born in resistance movements or anti-state politics, thus detaching them from a politicized, socioeconomic frame. Most infamously, again, the US Department of Agriculture adopted the Black Panther Party's free breakfast programs for children after identifying the association as a dangerous national threat (Heynen 2009); and the Nixon administration undermined the Black Panther Party's sickle cell anemia prevention efforts but then followed them up by creating its own government program to do the same (Nelson 2011: 148–49).

A second major risk of mutual aid is reinforcing neoliberal ideologies and programs emphasizing voluntarism and private initiatives, thus absolving the state of its responsibilities to provide public goods or, worse, fueling policies such as increased surveillance and policing. In this regard, leftists and conservatives sometimes uncomfortably converge in their support for mutual aid while advocating opposing ideologies. Conservatives have long promoted voluntary initiatives, precisely as an alternative to welfare assistance, which they claim fosters dependency and distributes tax money to the "undeserving" poor (see Tuğal 2017; Konczal 2014; Beito 2000).

At the other end of the spectrum of relating to the state is working with it and accepting government funds. As some argue, in many cases mutual aid has inadvertently reinforced the carceral apparatus by working with the state (see Fleetwood 2020). In the US field of domestic violence, for example, activists have pointed out that working with the state in the era since the passing of the Violence Against Women Act in 1994 has shifted both focus and funding to criminal justice and away from community programs and racial and economic justice. They continued to support VAWA for its many progressive impacts, though it has been unclear to what degree it performed better than past community-based movements of mutual aid. According to Mariame Kaba, a long-time educator and activist against incarceration, the question of the extent to which, and how, mutual aid groups must relate to the state is so complex that it will only yield answers and clarity over the long term, perhaps over generations (P. M. Press 2020).

In the meantime, the more immediate threat to mutual aid projects is the gradual replication of nonprofit methods and structures, or entanglement with the "non-profit industrial complex" (INCITE! 2007). This refers primarily to the effects of seeking funding and competing for grants in accordance with the missions of foundations. Nonprofits invariably end up reproducing the inequality they once denounced. As they begin to align with the ideologies of wealthy funders, they seek the rule of salaried experts, "management" of the poor, and tighter definitions of deservingness rather than serious redistribution and political resistance (Beam 2018). They also tend to focus on single issues and reinforce support for nonconfrontational political tactics like lawsuits and lobbying politicians. The consequence of this is a passivity that goes against the heart of mutual aid and the goal of community self-determination.

At the same time, we must ask: to what degree can mutual aid avoid the hazards of nonprofits? After all, without access to resources, mutual aid remains on a scale that is much too small to lead to economic change. As David Harvey said of mutual aid amid the pandemic, soup kitchens are keeping many people alive and are critically important in the short run, "but can you imagine sustaining a society on the basis of food banks and soup kitchens?"[1] And yet, aiming for larger-scale projects, I suggest, runs the risk of veering toward nonprofits and larger funding goals.

At an international level, where higher levels of poverty persist, such "NGO-ization of resistance" is very difficult to avoid. Arundhati Roy writes that this is not about individual NGOs but the broader neoliberal context in which NGOs "alter the public psyche" by obscuring the root causes of the very problems they serve to address. For her, NGOs are none other than the "secular missionaries of the modern world," steadfast in their beliefs about helping the poor (Roy 2014). Meanwhile, donors and philanthropists of these NGOs gain public admiration, thereby legitimizing an unequal world where a few have much to give, and many have nothing to lose. To cite another example, charitable foundations in the US are exempt from paying taxes' they essentially "rob" the public before handing out donations and gaining admiration in the process (Ahn 2007).

Mutual Aid and Histories of Racial Domination

These concerns, voiced within left movements, become heightened when considering the relationship between mutual aid and racial inequality. Centering histories of racial domination forces a more nuanced understanding than current leftist analyses allow. On one hand, racial minority groups have the sharpest reasons to distrust the state, nonprofits, and foundations. Critics have analyzed, in the context of North America, how white-led social and philanthropic groups have ultimately reinforced racial hierarchies that protect white wealth, as they used their networks and took advantage of unequal power dynamics (King and Osayande 2007). Examining the history of the National Association for the Advancement of Colored People (NAACP) in the US, Megan Francis (2019) shows how in the early twentieth century the organization came to depend financially on white philanthropic organizations that, moreover, did not treat African American leaders as equal partners. The

---

1. David Harvey (2020) used this example to argue for the importance of structural change.

result of this was a process of "movement capture" in which the NAACP shifted its agenda from a focus on racial violence to one on segregation in education, in accordance with funders' objectives. Over the following decades, the asymmetrical and potentially dangerous nature of relationships between external funders and African American justice organizations became even clearer with the FBI surveillance operations of the 1960s (King and Osayande 2007: 87–88).

Today these racial dynamics continue in various ways. For example, considering the world of art activism and mutual aid, Nicole Fleetwood (2020) describes the well-meaning nonprofit organizations that provide arts training to incarcerated populations. This is a relationship marked by "fraught imaginaries," she argues, where primarily white nonprofit groups collaborate with prison organizations and staff in the service of a racialized incarcerated population. In the case of arts activism in Canada, Adam Saifer (2020) refers to this as none other than a "racial neoliberal philanthropy" that uses tools of finance capitalism as it promotes mere survival activities among racial minorities. Again, what began as mutual aid becomes entangled with nonprofits and the reinforcement of racial hierarchies.

The history of white charitable giving to Blacks and other racial minorities, or of global North-South giving, throws into relief the difference between mutual aid and charity. But when it comes to mutual aid *within* racialized communities, the analysis calls for greater nuance and understanding of minority solidarity economies. In the US, mutual aid played an important role historically among African Americans, whose safety, dignity, and sometimes survival under slavery and the Jim Crow regime depended on the confidence and ability to self-organize (Ortiz 2005: 101–2). Mutual aid, whether coexisting with charity within the community or not, was inseparable from opposition to segregation and political action such as boycotts (Ortiz 2005: 120–27). The emergence of a Black middle class during the Progressive era helped facilitate, for example, settlement houses for Blacks in the city of Chicago. The free clinics, employment services, and job training they provided were critical in a city where settlement houses excluded African Americans (Jackson 1978).

The level of economic need of African American organizations, combined with histories of exclusion, has at times necessitated involvement with nonprofits. In the mix of pandemic-related racial injustices and the summer 2020 uprisings against police killings, Black advocacy organizations and bail funds received an astounding volume of donations. The *New York Times* reported the influx as "organic, viral and immense"

(Goldmacher 2020). Color of Change, the largest online racial justice group, for the first time began accepting (and redistributing) corporate donations, while other groups found themselves with the newfound ability to hire paid staff. Among those donating large sums were monopolies/oligopolies like Comcast and SONY Music Group. From the point of view of the racial justice organizations, many of which might be considered part of mutual aid movements, this flood of donations comes with clear dangers. At the same time, in the absence of reparations to African Americans, is this not a miniscule yet urgent reckoning that can at least help advance their work?

In my own research with poor and racialized Muslims in India, I have seen a variety of responses to the risks of cooptation and ideological undermining of mutual aid. In one mosque and madrasa community I studied in the southern Indian city of Hyderabad, members made a conscious decision to reject state subsidies or other financial assistance for madrasas. They chose to forego the support and instead control their own matters, rather than risk state interference in their work. This decision was striking, given the extreme poverty in the neighborhood. Here, mutual aid circulated within the community based on Islamic teachings and with almost no outside resources. In many other cases in the city, however, mutual aid relies on support from the Muslim middle class and elites, and/or through NGOs. For a minority group at the bottom of the socioeconomic hierarchy and uniquely victimized by the state, the choice is often between seeking support from Muslim philanthropists or the state. They generally prefer the former. International NGO support, especially from Muslim diasporas, proved critical to COVID relief work in the poorest neighborhoods. This can be critiqued as NGO-ization, but I argue we might instead understand this within a framework of a minority solidarity economy. In W. E. B. Du Bois' (2007: 97–110) analysis, for example, autonomous economic organizing among Blacks in America was necessary for survival and a stepping-stone to justice in a racial, capitalist state. A similar analysis about what it means to accept money from inside versus outside the community animates the conversation among Muslims in Hyderabad.

The Ambiguity of "Autonomy" and "Charity"

The unique challenges that minority mutual aid associations face help us think about the broader zone of ambiguity in which mutual aid programs dwell. As mutual aid groups seek resources from outsiders in order to sustain their work, they risk the pacifying effects of relying on nonprofits and NGOs and the ideological "corruption" and agenda shifts that can creep into political resistance. This includes the individualizing of suffering and reinforcement of neoliberal ideas about who is most deserving of aid. Mutual aid, as some argue, must be a way of life and not a charitable cause promoted by a foundation.

These long-standing critiques and concerns about mutual aid are crucial interventions. But they tend to dismiss the contradictions that left-oriented mutual aid programs and movements in fact inhabit. Consider the critique of the principle of conditionality perpetuated by NGOs. Many mutual aid projects, I suggest, in fact go into their communities and survey them to determine people's exact needs. This is not the same thing as conditionality, and mutual aid groups would not use the language of deservingness, but perhaps the line separating them is thinner than we think.

From a quite different angle, another ambiguous aspect of mutual aid involves its emphasis on community solidarity. This ultimate ideal can have consequences for individuals who might find such groups and programs coercive and demanding of their loyalty. Whether religious mutual aid societies, immigrant networks, or political groups, they can foster dependency and expect cultural conformity with the norms and expectations of the "community," especially when it provides for its members' material and social needs. The ambiguity of autonomy thus refers to the state and market but, in some cases, also to the relationship between individuals and community.

Considering these types of tensions between leftist critiques and on-the-ground realities, there are two broad areas that require clarity and reflection. One is pragmatic and the other conceptual. Pragmatically, activists have no choice but to confront the twin pressures of states and capitalism, and it can be counterproductive to deny this fact. According to Andrej Grubačić and Denis O'Hearn (2016: 140), solidarity economies operating through mutual aid differ from what they call an "exilic economy," which gains true autonomy from the market. The latter remains a distant goal for even the most radical of movements.

The serious dangers to resistance manifest mostly at certain key moments when groups must "bargain" with external forces. The question, Grubačić and O'Hearn argue, is an empirical one: to what degree do interactions with these forces constrain the movement's goals? They analyze the case of the Zapatista movement in the Mexican state of Chiapas, widely held as a successful example of a resistance movement rooted in mutual aid. Even for the Zapatistas, reliance on remittances from the US, cash from European solidarity groups, and relations with NGOs became necessary for the sustainability of their projects. They have had to participate in certain elements of the market, private property, commodity purchasing, and the hiring of seasonal labor, thereby supporting the very economic practices they in principle reject (Grubačić and O'Hearn 2016: 143–73). On the other hand, the Zapatistas deal with these tensions creatively, using the resources they garner to consciously protect their autonomy (Grubačić and O'Hearn 2016: 143). And the development of their own institutions to meet their basic needs has equipped them to carefully manage the pandemic (Briy 2020).

Beyond these pragmatic issues, I wish to highlight a conceptual problematic in the debate on mutual aid, which has to do with the meaning of charity as it exists across cultures and histories. The Indian Muslim communities I have studied of course operate in their particular cultural, ethical, and religious milieus. For them, the concept of "charity" is sacred regardless of the piety or impiety of individuals, which makes the question of solidarity more complex and the (Western) leftist contempt for charity somewhat jarring. As Cihan Tuğal (2016) argues, the suspicion of charity, explicit in the writings of Marx and Engels, comes out of liberal political economy. For early Christian communities, he shows, the concept of charity originates in the idea of love. (Though Kropotkin, again, distinguished love from instinct.) Tuğal calls for recovering the connection between love and charity as a way to advance resistance and emancipatory imaginaries as opposed to being viewed as nefarious. As he formulates it, "a radically different conception of charity is possible" (Tuğal 2016: 418). In the Islamic tradition, *zakat* (obligatory alms) or *sadqah* (voluntary alms) have various etymologies, including purification, truthfulness, sweetening, and growth. The symbolic meaning of the practice of giving, and therefore the lived experience of those who practice "charity," is arguably more complex than the leftist critiques would have it.

This is not to deny the dehumanization that accompanies some acts of charity, for example, the dumping of consumer waste onto "needy" communities around the world. Indeed, activist critiques of charity have echoes of the anthropological critiques of humanitarianism, its elevation of compassion over justice and benevolence over rights (see Fassin 2011; Ticktin 2014).

While charity and philanthropy are viewed as deeply problematic, activists and scholars seem to have embraced the language of "care" alongside mutual aid — Miriam Ticktin (2020), for example, writes of "reclaiming the political power of care" (Woodly 2020). Amid the pandemic, mutual aid has been not only monetary but has also included cooking, elder care, childcare, nursing, and other caring acts usually devalued as feminine. "Care" obviously avoids the connotations of charity or the hierarchical relations of NGOs; however, I suggest it still bears a good deal of ambiguity. On one hand it clearly refers to concrete everyday actions as well as to professions — indeed, the so-called essential workers of the world. But, on the other hand, is it not also simply circling back to an ethic or a prescribed set of sentiments like compassion, sympathy, or love? What, after all, does it mean to care for someone or about someone?

These tensions and ambiguities, over substance and semantics, get at the crux of mutual aid as prefigurative politics. The risk of reproducing power, inequality, and the structures of capitalism are ever-present, even as prefigurative politics asks us to create a society as though they are not. In other words, how can we enact a world without material inequality when this world does not yet exist? What are the principles by which to relate to one another, as individuals, across difference, and across groups? Care, compassion, and giving are fraught in a world of inequalities just as they might be in a world beyond them.

Conclusion

Anthropologist David Graeber's final essay before his untimely passing in 2020 was a foreword to a new edition of Kropotkin's *Mutual Aid*. In it, he lamented that "both traditional Marxism and contemporary social theory have stubbornly dismissed pretty much anything suggestive of generosity, cooperation, or altruism as some kind of bourgeois illusion" (Grubačić 2020). With the risk of veering from Graeber's exact intention, I read his words as an invitation to find and recognize solidarity in places where we might not see it if one remains too attached to the Western liberal ideal of autonomy and what that must look like. The ambiguities I have pointed to in this essay question why the activist and intellectual left share contempt for the notion or practice of charity (even as it fuels the work of mutual aid) and how this might prevent such recognition. Acknowledging these contradictions and ambiguities also expresses a hope for finding a language to speak about solidarity that perhaps is less burdened by the past. And it is worth the tensions to distinguish mutual aid from the NGO complex, aid industry, and the work of states, which undoubtedly will rush in to take its place.

Despite the concerns raised here, mutual aid in the time of the COVID pandemic carries great potential for transformation if its networks can be sustained beyond the crisis. In the words of Navajo activist Klee Benally, "mutual aid is not just about radical redistribution of resources. It's about radical redistribution of power" (P. M. Press 2020). And as communities become more empowered through mutual aid, they would ideally gain the confidence to attempt bolder forms of politics based on direct action, such as strikes. This requires, however, that the networks developed through mutual aid will be sustained after a crisis has passed, in this case the normalization of life after the pandemic. Rather than weaken and fade until the next crisis, can they become more coordinated and expand into regional networks? There exist many barriers to such longevity and the potentiality of mutual aid networks. Among these, within communities and movements, individuals confront the difficulty of attaining the skills needed to thrive in a mode of free and horizontal organizing. Socialized by and habituated to hierarchical decision-making, where only those at the top make decisions, can individuals continue to take action and practice the type of freedom that mutual aid politics demands?[2]

To summarize the desired principles, mutual aid is about building social relations and organizing horizontally, with the utmost value being placed on community control over its own needs. To avoid severing it from political resistance, communities of mutual aid would incorporate political education and even support for direct action. But for outsiders to a "community," what is the principle that informs the act of giving? This, I argue, remains less clear.

Reflecting on these principles thus remains an important and dynamic endeavor. Thinking comparatively, as I have tried to do, reminds us that social relations and ethics around giving and care mean different things in different societies. And while mutual aid, as Kropotkin insisted, may be a universal instinct, we would be remiss to confine our instinct to a blueprint.

---

2. Dean Spade made this point at the P. M. Press panel discussion, May 21, 2020.

Acknowledgements

I thank Stellan Vinthagen and the authors of this collective volume for their helpful comments.

References

Ahn, Christine E. 2007. "Democratizing American Philanthropy." In *The Revolution Will Not Be Funded: Beyond the Non-Profit Industrial Complex*, edited by INCITE!, 63–78. Durham: Duke University Press.

Ananta, Aris. 2012. "Sustainable and Just Social Protection in Southeast Asia." *ASEAN Economic Bulletin* 29 (3): 171–83.

Beam, Myrl. 2018. *Gay, Inc.: The Nonprofitization of Queer Politics*. Minneapolis, MN: University of Minnesota Press.

Beito, David. 2000. *From Mutual Aid to the Welfare State: Fraternal Societies and Social Services, 1890–1967*. Chapel Hill, NC: University of North Carolina Press.

Briy, Anya. 2020. "Zapatistas: Lessons in Community Self-Organisation in Mexico." *OpenDemocracy*, July 25, 2020. https://www.opendemocracy.net/en/democraciaabierta/zapatistas-lecciones-de-auto-organizaci%C3%B3n-comunitaria-en/.

Burley, Shane. 2020. "Amid the Coronavirus Crisis, Mutual Aid Networks Erupt across the Country." *Waging Nonviolence*, March 27, 2020. https://webcache.googleusercontent.com/search?q=cache: d0AmAkM1JaYJ: https://wagingnonviolence.org/2020/03/coronavirus-mutual-aid-networks-erupt-across-country/+&cd=1&hl=en&ct=clnk&gl=za&client=firefox-b-d.

Cheetham, Joshua. 2020. "Navajo Nation: The People Battling America's Worst Coronavirus Outbreak." *BBC News*, June 16, 2020. https://www.bbc.com/news/world-us-canada-52941984.

Du Bois, W. E. B. 2007. *Dusk of Dawn: An Essay toward an Autobiography of a Race Concept*. New York: Oxford University Press.

Fassin, Didier. 2011. *Humanitarian Reason: A Moral History of the Present*. Berkeley, CA: University of California Press.

Fleetwood, Nicole R. 2020. *Marking Time: Art in the Age of Mass Incarceration*. Cambridge, MA: Harvard University Press.

Francis, Megan M. 2019. "The Price of Civil Rights: Black Lives, White Funding, and Movement Capture." *Law and Society Review* 53 (1): 275–309. https://doi.org/10.1111/lasr.12384.

Goldmacher, Shane. 2020. "Racial Justice Groups Flooded with Millions in Donations in Wake of Floyd Death." *New York Times,* June 16, 2020. https://www.nytimes.com/2020/06/14/us/politics/black-lives-matter-racism-donations.html.

Grubačić, Andrej. 2020. "In Loving Memory of Our Friend, Comrade, and Mentor ... David Graeber." P. M. Press, September 3, 2020. https://blog.pmpress.org/2020/09/03/in-loving-memory-david-graeber/.

Grubačić, Andrej, and Denis O'Hearn. 2016. *Living at the Edges of Capitalism: Adventures in Exile and Mutual Aid.* Oakland: University of California Press.

Haggard, Stephan, and Robert R. Kaufman. 2009. *Development, Democracy, and Welfare States: Latin America, East Asia, and Eastern Europe.* Princeton, NJ: Princeton University Press.

Harvey, David. 2020. "Anti-Capitalist Chronicles: Pandemic, Protests and Economic Disaster." Anti-Capitalist Chronicles (podcast), 37: 04, June 21, 2020. https://youtu.be/Mw32OxBahnA?list=PLPJpiw1WYdTPmOmC2i3hR4_aR7omqhaCj.

Heynen, Nik. 2009. "Bending the Bars of Empire from Every Ghetto for Survival: The Black Panther Party's Radical Antihunger Politics of Social Reproduction and Scale." *Annals of the Association of American Geographers* 99 (2): 406–22. https://doi.org/10.1080/00045600802683767.

INCITE! 2007. *The Revolution Will Not Be Funded: Beyond the Non-Profit Industrial Complex.* Durham: Duke University Press.

Jackson, Philip. 1978. "Black Charity in Progressive Era Chicago." *Social Science Review* 52 (3): 400–17. https://doi.org/10.1086/643652.

King, Tiffany Lethabo, and Evvuare Osayande. 2007. "The Filth on Philanthropy: Progressive Philanthropy's Agenda to Misdirect Social Justice Movements." In *The Revolution Will Not Be Funded, Beyond the Non-Profit Industrial Complex,* edited by INCITE!, 79–90. Durham: Duke University Press.

Konczal, Mike. 2014. "The Voluntarism Fantasy." *Democracy Journal,* no. 32. https://democracyjournal.org/magazine/32/the-voluntarism-fantasy/.

Kropotkin, Peter. (1902) 2017. *Mutual Aid: A Factor of Evolution,* edited and translated by Jhon Duran. CreateSpace Independent Publishing.

Laville, Jean-Louis, and Philippe Eynaud. 2019. "Rethinking Social Enterprise through Philanthropic and Democratic Solidarities." In *Theory of Social Enterprise and Pluralism: Social Movements, Solidarity Economy, and Global South*, edited by Philippe Eynaud, Jean-Louis Laville, Luciane L. dos Santos, Swati Banerjee, Flor Avelino, and Lars Hulgård, 18–43. London: Routledge.

Morales, Laurel. 2020. "Coronavirus Infections Continue to Rise on Navajo Nation." *NPR*, May 11, 2020. https://www.npr.org/sections/coronavirus-live-updates/2020/05/11/854157898/coronavirus-infections-continue-to-rise-on-navajo-nation.

Nelson, Alondra. 2011. *Body and Soul: The Black Panther Party and the Fight against Medical Discrimination*. Minneapolis: University of Minnesota Press.

Ortiz, Paul. 2005. *Emancipation Betrayed: The Hidden History of Black Organizing and White Violence in Florida from Reconstruction to the Bloody Election of 1920*. Berkeley: University of California Press.

P. M. Press. 2020. "Mutual Aid: Building Communities of Care during Crisis and Beyond." Panel discussion with Mariame Kaba, Dean Spade, Klee Benally, and Kali Akukno, moderated by Tim Holland. P. M. Press, YouTube video, 1: 36: 55, May 22, 2020. https://youtu.be/ZTVLYPdF0x0.

Roy, Arundhati. 2014. "The NGO-ization of Resistance." *Massalijn*, September 4, 2014.

Saifer, Adam. 2020. "Racial Neoliberal Philanthropy and the Arts for Social Change." *Organization*, 1–21. https://doi.org/10.1177/1350508420973327.

Schlanger, Zoë. 2020. "Turn Mutual Aid into Meaningful Work." *Dissent* 67 (3): 71–74. https://doi.org/10.1353/dss.2020.0061.

Shah, Alpa. 2019. *Nightmarch: Among India's Revolutionary Guerillas*. Chicago: University of Chicago Press.

Soto, Isa R. 2020. "Mutual Aid and Survival as Resistance in Puerto Rico." *NACLA Report on the Americas* 52 (3): 303–8. https://doi.org/10.1080/10714839.2020.1809099.

Spade, Dean. 2020. *Mutual Aid: Building Solidarity during this Crisis (and the Next)*. London: Verso.

Ticktin, Miriam. 2014. "Transnational Humanitarianism." *Annual Review of Anthropology* 43 (1): 273–89. https://doi.org/10.1146/annurev-anthro-102313-030403.

Ticktin, Miriam. 2020. "Building a Feminist Commons in the Time of COVID-19." *Signs*. http://signsjournal.org/COVID/ticktin/.

Tuğal, Cihan. 2016. "Faiths with a Heart and Heartless Religions: Devout Alternatives to the Merciless Rationalization of Charity." *Rethinking Marxism* 28 (3–4): 418–37. https://doi.org/10.1080/08935696.2016.1243416.

Tuğal, Cihan. 2017. *Caring for the Poor: Islamic and Christian Benevolence in a Liberal World*. New York: Routledge.

Woodly, Deva. 2020. "The Politics of Care." Lecture at the New School, June 18, 2020. https://www.youtube.com/watch?v=ih6F6N9pg-A.

CHAPTER 12

Carceral Contagion

Prisons and Disease

Wendy Warren

> Prisons do not disappear social problems ...
> — Angela Davis, "Masked Racism: Reflections on the Prison Industrial Complex"

The number of people who live in prisons has grown at a staggering rate during the last three decades. This is so particularly and most aggressively in the United States (US), but it is also true of countries such as Brazil, Russia, and China that today incarcerate hundreds of thousands of people. As the prison population has grown, activists and scholars have become increasingly attentive to the injustices of modern imprisonment — both to the increased numbers of people imprisoned and the lopsided racial and economic demographics of the incarcerated population. The strength of protest movements in recent years has enabled such concerns and critiques to reach a broader public than in the past.[1] The movements — what we might loosely categorize as criminal justice

---

1. Scholarship on modern incarceration includes Alexander (2011); Dow (2004); Gilmore (2007); Fassin (2016); Hinton (2016); Murakawa (2014).

reform movements — have identified and denaturalized that violence committed routinely by police forces and legal systems in the US and around the globe. In doing so, they have also succeeded in making the relationship between prisons, race, and poverty increasingly visible, even to segments of the public that have remained largely immune to the sort of policing that has led to mass incarceration.[2]

The coronavirus pandemic thus emerged at a specific historical moment when social movements protesting against unjust policing and legal systems, and, relatedly, against mass imprisonment, had won the support of an unprecedented portion of the public, even in a country such as the US where the mass incarceration agenda had previously seemed to enjoy a broad public endorsement. One result of this temporal overlap was that, with more of the general population newly primed to see prisons as vexed sites of injustice, the linkage of disease and incarceration became obvious, worthy of reportage, and newly relevant. Mass media carried reports of prison outbreaks of the disease, both because those outbreaks threatened the general population and perhaps because the incarcerated population seemed, thanks to the work of activists and others, to include people now meriting sympathy.

But newly visible is not the same as new. In fact, the relationship of prisons to disease has deep roots. There is little that is novel about an infectious disease running rampant inside prisons. Quite the contrary, contagious disease has historically formed a crucial part of the prison experience. Likewise, prisons have historically played a noticeable role in the spread of contagious disease. Long before coronavirus hit, prisons had proven themselves sites of extreme contagion as well as zones incapable of containing diseases within their walls. Diseases in the sixteenth, seventeenth, and eighteenth centuries spread quickly and easily among imprisoned inmates, and diseases at the time also spread quickly into the

---

For critical studies that pose imprisonment as a question, see Davis (2003); Davis (2011); Beckett and Murakawa (2012); Kaba (2021).

2. Criminal justice reform groups include Project NIA, Penal Reform International, the Innocence Project, the Howard League for Penal Reform, the Sentencing Project; projects run by larger groups such as the Southern Poverty Law Center and the American Civil Liberties Union; institutes/think tanks such as the Marshall Project and the Prison Policy Initiative; and many smaller, local organizations, which are probably doing the bulk of the organizing.

general population beyond prison walls. They spread particularly effectively into impoverished communities.

Because the coronavirus pandemic has occurred in the age of mass incarceration, its toll has been greater than if it were to have hit in another, less disciplinary and punitive age. Still, it seems likely that if the pandemic had hit in a season when anti-carceral activism was in retreat, rather than in full mobilization, its effects would have been more severe for those imprisoned. Some communities, authorities, and policy makers now deal with prison outbreaks in ways that might have been unthinkable even a few years ago, and these new responses seem worth exploring.

Of these, perhaps the most telling, unusual, and quietly radical policy has been outright prisoner release, a policy that has had small manifestations in countries around the globe during the pandemic. Part of the rationale for mass incarceration has always been to improve society by extracting from it those who, having committed perceived crimes in the past, are likely to commit further crimes in the future. Society, the argument goes, is served by taking such dangerous individuals (however many hundreds of thousands they add up to) out of circulation. A pandemic shows the fiction of this. In a world beset by COVID, it is hard to imagine that putting a person in prison makes society safer, epidemiologically at least. Epidemiologically, of course, the person in question is not extracted from society; they are just put in circumstances all the more likely to make them sick and contagious to people both inside and outside the prison. Still, despite this, in the past the social reform movements that have emerged to alleviate extreme outbreaks of disease or brutality in prisons have struggled to find mass public support or, where they may have had support, have been suppressed by states.[3]

While it is true that the toll of the coronavirus has been exacerbated because the pandemic occurred in the age of mass incarceration (a Marshall Project study found more than half a million prisoners in the US

---

3. There are historical examples of mass prisoner release. A Prison Policy Initiative report notes that "in 2006, to respond to prison overcrowding, the Italian government released 22,000 people, generally those serving three years or less, except for those convicted of Mafia-related crimes, terrorism, sexual violence or usury." In the Czech Republic in 2013, "outgoing President Václav Klaus gave a mass amnesty/pardon to over 6,000 people, approximately one third of the incarcerated population, as a way to both respond to an overcrowding crisis and to mark the anniversary of Czech Independence" (Wagner 2020).

who had tested positive for the virus by mid-2021, an almost certain undercount because so little testing was done in prisons), it also may be true that its toll has been in some cases and places slightly leavened because it has unfolded under the eye and in the context of long-standing criminal justice reform movements, prison abolitionist movements, and, most visible and contemporaneously in the US and elsewhere, the Black Lives Matter movement (Marshall Project 2021). Whatever sympathy the broader public has displayed for the COVID-afflicted imprisoned is certainly partial and imperfect, but it is all the same historically unusual. More so than anti-carceral social reform movements of centuries past, contemporary criminal justice movements seem to have succeeded in winning some sympathy for, and even social solidarity with, the imprisoned during a public health crisis.

Contemporary Situation

The COVID outbreak of 2020–21 has placed carceral systems around the globe under stress. Even a prison running at its prescribed occupancy level has the characteristics of a perpetual super-spreader event. Overcrowded prisons, however, have become the global norm. According to research by the Institute for Crime and Justice Policy Research at the School of Law of Birkbeck, University of London, prison occupancy in the Democratic Republic of the Congo is at 616 percent of capacity (WPB 2021), making it practically inevitable that the country's prisons have experienced outbreaks. What should not be mistaken for inevitable, or overlooked, though, is that in response Congolese authorities released thousands of prisoners, albeit tentatively, and on a scale much smaller than what prisoners' advocates had in mind (HRW 2020). Those hesitations, though, do not negate the essential character — emancipation as a public good — of the Congo's release policy.[4] Release happened elsewhere, too. In Morocco, King Mohammed VI pardoned more than 5,500 prisoners to mitigate a potential outbreak (Eljechtimi and Potter 2020). In Iran, authorities temporarily released 54,000 prisoners (Zaghari-Ratcliffe 2020).

---

4. For occupancy rates in various countries, see data from the World Prison Brief (WPB 2021). On outbreaks in the Republic of the Congo, see HRW (2020).

To be clear, prison release has not been a universal nor even common reaction, which perhaps makes the fact that it has happened in some places even more noteworthy. Some authorities have, in fact, attempted policies of a very different sort in their efforts to mitigate the virus's spread. In Latin America and the Caribbean, where occupancy rates in prisons can be as high as 360 percent (Bolivia) or even 450 percent (Haiti), COVID outbreaks have flared up throughout the pandemic. Rather than any prisoner release, though, some of these places have tried the opposite approach: isolation and sequestration. One policy answer, for example, that Latin American authorities (but also authorities elsewhere) have tried, has been to ban family visits to prisons. The rationale is the inverse of mass release: instead of decongesting prisons and getting potential contagion carriers out of likely viral epicenters, build up the walls around the prisons and try to seal them off more effectively from the outside world. Beyond the obvious harm to mental health inflicted by such a ban, the policy has material consequences for the nutritional health of the imprisoned: in poorer countries, families are often the primary source of food for inmates.

A similar policy solution has been to restrict medical teams' access to the prisons. The results have been extreme. In Bolivia, frightened, hungry, and angry prisoners have protested their conditions with what national and international media have reported as "rioting." Part of the rioting has consisted of inmates climbing up onto their prisons' roofs to voice their protests to the outside public and to make clear that they were being infected while being denied medical care.[5]

The US has the highest per capita imprisonment rate in the world and, according to data collected by the Marshall Project and the Associated Press, by early December 2020 one in five prisoners in state and federal prisons systems had tested positive for coronavirus. By February 2021, there had been more than 383,000 cases of COVID in US prisons, with 2,446 deaths (almost certainly these numbers are underreported since relatively few prisons have done testing). In New Jersey, one in four prisoners had tested positive for the virus by February 2021, almost three times the infection rate of the state's general population (Marshall Project 2021).[6]

---

5. On outbreaks in Bolivia, see Reuters (2020). On Haiti, see the Charles (2020).
6. For the per capita rate, see WPB (2021). On prisoner infection rates, see Schwartzapfel and Park (2020). On New Jersey rates, see the Marshall

These numbers will surprise no one who has studied the modern carceral system. Modern jails and prisons, notoriously overcrowded and underfunded even in the most wealthy countries, were unhealthy sites even before this pandemic, and their material conditions make them unrivaled amplifiers of airborne infectious diseases like COVID. Prisons offer few possibilities of social distancing; they maintain only few hygiene possibilities; they provide almost no options for open-air activities; prisoners are usually prohibited from masking their faces; and in most of them, inmates share toilets, showers, and sleeping quarters inside poorly ventilated buildings. Food is prepared and eaten in close proximity to others. Prisons and jails regularly transfer prisoners in and out of the institution, largely without testing them for the disease and without quarantine periods. Prison staff also enter and leave the building daily without any testing, meaning both that they potentially carry disease into the prison and also that they can carry it out of the prison and into their communities of residence.[7] Again, epidemiologically speaking, it is a fiction that prisons extract individuals from society.

Making all this worse is the poverty of many prisoners, a reality that makes them more likely to enter prison in poorer health and less able to sustain themselves while incarcerated. In the US context where incarcerated people are charged medical co-payments for physician visits, medications, dental treatment, and other health services, the effects of any disease are exacerbated by poverty. Many low-income prisoners cannot afford health care in the first place and thus do not seek early medical help or even admit ill health.

Indeed, the COVID pandemic has cast a harsh light on the linkage between contagious disease and incarceration, largely because the contagiousness of the coronavirus made the normally difficult circumstances of mass incarceration even more urgent from a public health standpoint. That the linkage has become impossible to ignore has caused usually intransigent institutions to react, even in the US, where imprisonment has long been the answer to social problems. For example, on November 4, 2020, New Jersey, the state with the highest prison death rate from COVID in the US, released 2,258 inmates who were within a year of completing their sentences (and who had not committed murder or

---

Project (2021). Certainly these figures will be higher by the time this article is published.

7. This happened in Chicago, for example (Reinhart and Chen 2020).

sexual assault). New Jersey authorities permitted this in large part to help prevent prison outbreaks of COVID from spreading to the population outside the prison walls. Perhaps most remarkably, a bipartisan bill passed by the state legislature early in the pandemic led to this mass release.

By the end of March 2021, New Jersey was projected to reduce its inmate population by 35 percent. In other words, the state of New Jersey will carry out the largest act of carceral emancipation in its history. The historic nature of the initial prisoner release made some news but may not have been fully absorbed by the public, given the extent to which more general fears of the virus have dominated people's attention. To be clear, recognizing the unprecedented scale of the release is not the same as sentimentalizing the policy. New Jersey, again exemplifying the complicated nature of these moves, completed a release of inmates in December 2020 without guaranteeing that they had either money or shelter, meaning that a good number of the people released went from being imprisoned to being unhoused, in the middle of a global pandemic, as the peak of winter approached. Moreover, the state did not quarantine or effectively test released inmates for the virus before they left the prisons, despite knowing prisons to be central loci of the disease and despite the fact that the release was ostensibly to protect a prison outbreak from spreading via prison staff and released inmates to the larger community (Tully 2020).

But leaving aside the inconsistencies between the goal of releasing the prisoners and the method implementing it, the exceptional situation presented to authorities by the coronavirus pandemic caused a fairly unprecedented reaction in modern prison history: the release of thousands of incarcerated people. What to make of this odd liberation? Without ignoring the fact that the mass carceral regimes of the US and the world are still very much intact (New Jersey was an outlier in its decisions), it seems worth noting that there is something unusual in what we might call the great prison break of 2020 and 2021 and that it is likely that this has something to do with global social movements aimed at criminal justice reform as well as with the particular pathology of the coronavirus. One way to recognize that something historically unusual is afoot is to consider how relatively ineffective attempts in the past had been to remedy the problem of incarceration and disease, even contagious airborne disease with public health impacts. Incarceration and viral contagion have a long-shared history.

Historical Situation

Precisely because outbreaks in prisons lead to outbreaks in the surrounding communities, outbreaks of COVID have drawn new and sustained attention to the unhygienic conditions of US prisons and to the limited medical assistance available to prisoners. But while COVID is new, the problem is long-standing. The spread of HIV/AIDS in the American prison population in the 1980s was well known even at the time, though the relative difficulty of spreading HIV/AIDS, when compared to COVID, meant that public panic was relatively muted. One study in 1988 found that "17.4 percent of male prisoners and 18.8 percent of female prisoners tested anonymously in New York State, the second largest correctional system in the nation, were HIV positive." By the mid-1990s, the rate of HIV infection among incarcerated people was six times the rate of the nation's general population (Kunzel 2008: 227). This transmission was fueled by rape and by drug use; but unlike responses to today's pandemic, the stigmatization of HIV/AIDS and the concomitant popular belief that the disease was limited to marginalized communities meant that there was no strong call to release prisoners early, or to mitigate contagious or violent situations in the prisons. But eventually the link between HIV/AIDS and incarceration grew so great that one study estimated that 15 percent of all HIV/AIDS patients had entered the prison system (along with 40 percent of people with Hepatitis C) (Massoglia 2008: 57). Currently, Estonia, Lithuania, Romania, Slovakia, and the Ukraine have prisons populations where HIV prevalence is over 10 percent (WHO 2021). While public health officials are aware of the situation, there has been little corresponding concern in the general public. Similarly, contemporary prisons have also remained vectors of diseases such as tuberculosis and hepatitis, which are common inside the institutions but seldom excite public conversation.

But the link between incarceration and disease is not a historically recent phenomenon. In the premodern and early modern periods, a defining aspect of imprisonment was close contact with contagious disease. In one prison in Sienna in 1340, a hospital ward was created after twenty-two inmates died in two months, presumably of typhoid (Geltner 2008: 66). In the sixteenth and seventeenth centuries, prisoners frequently complained of fever and smallpox, along with other contagious diseases, running rampant even through small jails. Moreover, throughout the medieval and early modern world, and particularly in Europe and its colonies, prisoners complained of the exorbitant costs of health services such as midwives, doctors, and sanitary equipment, not to mention food, water, and blankets.

In late sixteenth-century England, a spate of outbreaks of something labeled "gaol fever" hit various legal venues around the country. One particularly deadly outbreak caused a panic after more than 300 attendees at what became known as the "Black Assize" of Oxford were reported to have died following the outbreak of a disease brought into the court by, it was believed, diseased prisoners. A later account reported that "suddenly [those in the court] were surprised with a pestilent savour, whether arising from the noysome smell of the prisoners, or from the damp of the ground, is uncertain; but all that were present, within forty hours died, except the prisoners, and the Women and children; and the Contagion went no farther" (Baker, cited in Siena 2019: 101). In this case, the prison was directly below the courtroom. The exact etiology of "gaol fever" is difficult to recover four centuries later, but of relevance here is that observers and commentators understood a disease to be transmittable through the air (via odors), and that prisoners brought it into the larger community. The solution proposed to this problem was not to release the people from the prison, even though they were presumably suffering while incarcerated from the same disease that had been brought to the trial, but rather to isolate the prisoners as much as possible, keeping them from the larger community.

Francis Bacon, the great English philosopher, made clear the relationship between prisons and disease by explaining that "the most pernicious infection next to the plague is the smell of the gaol, where prisoners have been long and close and nastily kept; whereof we have had in our time experience twice or thrice, when both the judges that sat on the gaol, and numbers of those that attended the business, or were present sickened upon it and died" (Bacon 1670: 201; see also Siena 2019: 102). Here, too, the prisoners themselves were blamed for the outbreak — their general and seemingly innate pestilence, understood to have infected others nearby. The proposed solution was not to release the prisoners, nor even to lessen their crowding, but instead to clean their quarters more regularly.

Reform movements attuned to the particular vulnerability of incarcerated people to disease emerged early. Prison reformers launched active and forceful campaigns in the early eighteenth century to eliminate London's crowded and filthy prisons. One worth exploring was led by a London elite named James Oglethorpe (1729). This campaign is instructive because it was much more effective than most of its era in putting the question of prison reform in front of the eyes of the public, and it is also instructive because, even given its relative successes, its effectiveness at curbing carceral excesses was ultimately minimal. In 1729, Oglethorpe chaired a so-called "Gaols Committee," formed by official mandates from both the House of Lords and the House of Commons and composed of ninety-six members tasked with investigating the situation of various prisons in London. Oglethorpe, a gentleman of means and reputation, had personal reason to head the committee: his good friend, the artist Robert Castell, had died in an ancillary jail ("sponging house") of the Fleet, imprisoned for debt and, once in jail, entrapped by spiraling costs. Castell was mistreated by guards and housed, probably deliberately, with a prisoner suffering from smallpox. According to some accounts, Castell had begged the warden to put him among the general population of criminals inside the Fleet rather than face the endemic disease he knew reigned in the ward reserved for debtors. His request was denied. He was promptly infected by his cellmates and died of smallpox within a month of incarceration.

Oglethorpe formed the "Gaols Committee" in large part because of his grief over Castell's death, and the report he and the committee members eventually wrote spared no details. The report focused particularly on two aspects of imprisonment: the ubiquity of contagious disease and the fact that poverty (rather than criminality) had led most inmates to prison. Too many people who ended up in such prisons, Oglethorpe noted, were in prison not because of true criminality; rather, the quickest road to a London prison was paved with debt. They were the "worthy poor," caught in hard times, dependent on credit for survival. When such people found themselves unable to pay their constantly compounding debts, their creditors possessed the outsized social power to have them arrested, an intensely personal form of social domination that historian Joanna Innes (2009: 229) has described as "legalized bullying." Once arrested, their chances of paying their debts dissipated and their situations became dire, as they encountered conditions of disease and squalor they would not have faced outside the prison walls.

Oglethorpe located profiteering at the center of the problem. The lack of restrictions on a warden's ability to personally profit from the miserable inmates meant that conditions could easily be designed to minimize expenses to the warden and maximize costs to the prisoners. Wardens stole from charity boxes intended to feed the truly indigent, and they pressured even those with means into paying extra for any comfort. Extortion was common. Oglethorpe noted that because of a lack of oversight, many wardens had resorted to extralegal measures, including torture, to extort compliance and money from prisoners. In the Fleet, for example, a warden clapped too-small irons around the legs of a prisoner and left them on for three weeks despite the man's screams of agony. The iron cuffs cut off the prisoner's circulation and "mortified his legs," leaving him permanently lame despite a doctor's attention. Oglethorpe emphasized that these "wicked Keepers" went out of their way to intensify prisoners' trauma, for example by locking "Debtors, who displeased them, in the Yard with Humane Carcasses." One man was locked in a yard for six days with two dead bodies that had expired four days prior. As the bodies rotted, the living prisoner spent his days in terror, watching vermin eat the bloating corpses and enucleate their eyes (Great Britain House of Commons [1760]).

All through the prisons, abhorrent conditions ruled. Disease was rampant. In some cells the Oglethorpe committee found, "Persons who are Sick of different Distempers are obliged to lye together, or on the floor." In one particularly egregious case, a woman "had the Small-Pox and two Women were ordered to lye with her," a situation that must have reminded Oglethorpe of his friend's death. In the Marshalsea prison, prisoners in the "Common Side" were divided into rooms called wards and were "excessively Crowded, Thirty, Forty, nay Fifty Persons having been locked up in some of them not Sixteen Foot Square." Of such situations, the committee noted, "the Air is so wasted by the Number of Persons, who breathe in that narrow Compass, that it is not sufficient to keep them from stifling, several having in the Heat of Summer perished for want of Air" (Great Britain House of Commons [1760]).

Many starved to death in the prisons. Once prisoners had run of out charity from friends and sold off any clothes and bedding, they lost their ability to supplement their diet, and they eventually died. When the committee toured Marshalsea, they found entire wards of starving people. Oglethorpe ordered them to be fed, but the health of some had deteriorated beyond saving. He observed that "on the giving Food to these poor Wretches (tho' it was done with the utmost Caution)," one man died because "the Vessels of his Stomach were so disordered and contracted for want of Use, that they were totally incapable of performing their Office" (Great Britain House of Commons [1760]).

Oglethorpe's eventual report on the conditions he found was scathing. He suggested releasing debtors, alleviating conditions, lessening crowds, providing ample sustenance, and offering medical care to prisoners, but nothing came of it. Authorities left the wardens Oglethorpe named as most cruel in charge of their respective prisons. Eventually, Oglethorpe's disgust at the situation in London's prisons would spur him to found, in 1732, the colony of Georgia, the last English colony founded in North America. Now popularly (and incorrectly) known as a colony founded by convicts, Georgia was in fact founded as an anti-penal colony, a place where, Oglethorpe imagined, people might go *instead* of going to prison. He had particular hopes for Georgia as a place for people who otherwise would find themselves in prison only because of poverty and debt. The American colony would offer impoverished English a chance at fresh air, property, and freedom — along with this would naturally come health.

But his dream failed, somewhere along the way. If we fast forward almost three hundred years, we find a story Oglethorpe had hoped to avoid. By 2018 Georgia (now a state) had the fourth-highest poverty rate, and the fourth-largest prison population (in absolute numbers), of any of the US states (Vera Institute of Justice 2019). When the pandemic hit Georgia in 2020, the state did not take up mass release. Instead, the parole board announced that it would review, on an individual basis, the cases of some inmates who were within 180 days of finishing their sentence. The state also suspended family visits and announced it "will be delaying attorney visitation." The Department of Corrections also waived the USD 5 co-payments for inmates with COVID-like symptoms, though it made clear that this duty could be re-established at a later date (Georgia Department of Corrections 2021; Sharpe 2020).

Oglethorpe was a man too far ahead of his time, it seems. Where he saw imprisonment as causing and perpetuating poverty and disease, many of his contemporaries saw poverty as the cause of the other two. A 1778 treatise on fevers and infections noted particularly the existence of "a disease of a contagious nature, the produce of filth, rags, poverty, and a polluted air, which subsists always in a greater or less degree in crowded prisons, and in nasty, low, damp, unventilated habitations loaded with putrid animal steams" (Lind 1778: 3, 306; see also Siena 2019). The author called the disease "jail distemper" and noted that it had "proved very alarming to the judges and court at the Old Bailey, from its frequency in Newgate and in the other jails. ... The influence of his infection is very extensive." In 1795, John Mason Good published "A Dissertation on the Diseases of Prisons and Poor-Houses," on behalf of the Medical Society of London, which explicitly blamed personal habits of the poor for some of the diseases that ran rampant among impoverished communities. "The poor," he wrote, "are, in general, but little habituated to cleanliness; they are liable to a thousand accidents, and a thousand temptations, which every superior rank of life is free from; and they feel not, from want of education, the same happy exertion of delicacy, honor, and moral sentiment, which everywhere else is to be met with." Because of poor hygiene, the poor tended to enter the prison with certain disease, namely "Ulcers, the Venereal Disease," and "the Itch" (Good 1795: 27). Once in prison, they encountered other diseases, the worst of which was tuberculosis. If tuberculosis could be mitigated by a different sort of prison — a reformed institution — the diseases brought into the prison by the poor from the outside world, Good felt, could not be helped. Curing poverty was beyond the scope of that institution's remit.

Similar ills plague prisoners today. In the US, roughly 90 percent of accused criminals cannot afford legal representation. Approximately one-third of the working-class population has a criminal record. Only 49 percent of incarcerated American men were employed in the three years before they were imprisoned, and those who did have jobs had only USD 6,250 in median annual income (Looney and Turner 2018). Despite a national (pre-pandemic) poverty rate of roughly 12 percent, 57 percent of men and 72 percent of women arrested were in poverty before entering prison (Hayes and Barnhost 2020). Adults in poverty in America are three times more likely to be arrested than those who are not. In the US, the burdens of poverty, ill health, policing, legal discrimination, and imprisonment are all concentrated in communities of color.

The relationship of poverty to prisons is clear; what is the relationship of poverty to health? In the US, men in the top 1 percent of income can expect to live fifteen years longer than men in the bottom 1 percent; women can expect a difference of ten years. A 2015 study from the Urban Institute found that "low-income Americans have higher rates of heart disease, diabetes, asthma, and other chronic conditions, including obesity" (this relationship tends to be true in other developed countries, as well) (Woolf et al. 2015). Low-income Americans have the additional burden of limited access to health care, which exacerbates the effects of even manageable chronic conditions. All of this means that low-income people, who are disproportionately affected by the justice system, tend to enter that system in relatively poor health. Once in prison, they find themselves unable to afford medical care and basic necessities such as food, warm clothing, and blankets. This compromised situation puts them at increased risk of contagious disease, especially when they are placed in crowded and unsanitary conditions.

Conclusion

Poor nutrition, endemic disease, poor sanitation: until the advent of the coronavirus pandemic, the situation inside prisons had largely remained the concern of reformers and activists, even if the conditions had of late been slowly coming to the general public's consciousness. But the wily nature of the coronavirus, its efficient spread, its indiscriminate behavior, quickly made what happens inside a prison more relevant to the general public. Indeed, what the pandemic has made clearer than ever before is that prisons also make society, as a whole, more sick; or, expressed differently, if we want a healthy society, we do not want prisons.

Centuries after plagues and smallpox and "gaol fevers" first became known as characteristics of imprisonment, impoverished people still disproportionately populate prisons throughout the world, and many if not most of those prisons are still unsanitary and filled beyond capacity. Contagious diseases still flourish in the cells of modern carceral institutions, and medical assistance remains difficult to obtain. When a situation is fundamentally static for at least four centuries, one must start to ask: are these conditions flaws of the carceral system or part of its design? Michel Foucault (1977: 15–16) took some pains to remind his readers that, though in the nineteenth century "punishment had no doubt ceased to be centered on torture as a technique of pain, ... a punishment like forced labour or even imprisonment — mere loss of liberty — has never functioned without a certain additional element of punishment that certainly concerns the body itself: rationing of food, sexual deprivation, corporal punishment, solitary confinement." To this list we might add disease, the seemingly unavoidable outcome of imprisonment. Foucault argues that "in its most explicit practices, imprisonment has always involved a certain degree of physical pain," or bodily mortification of some sort, including disease. He famously asked, "What would a non-corporal punishment be?" (Foucault 1977: 16).

It seems clear that one of the additional elements of punishment that imprisonment entails is a heightened risk of disease, disease that might be avoided outside the prison walls. This is true as soon as imprisonment begins, whether in pretrial confinement or in post-conviction punishment. What is different in today's pandemic, though, is that, for a variety of reasons, the prisoners themselves have not been blamed (though certainly there was popular displeasure that prisoners might be vaccinated ahead of others). Whether because of the social moment and its heightened awareness of the racial and class disparities in the justice system and the carceral system, or because of public health awareness, or some combination of these and other factors, their environment and living conditions have been seen as the cause of their ill health rather than their own moral deficiencies or personal inadequacies. What is most different today is that some authorities have been pressed into enacting the most obvious, and the most effective, policy available to them, a policy that authorities of the past mostly rejected: to open the prison doors and let people walk out.

References

Alexander, Michelle. 2011. *The New Jim Crow: Mass Incarceration in the Age of Color Blindness*. New York: New Press.

Bacon, Francis. 1670. *Sylva Sylvarum, or, A Natural History in Ten Centuries*. London.

Beckett, Katherine, and Naomi Murakawa. 2012. "Mapping the Shadow Carceral State: Toward an Institutionally Capacious Approach to Punishment." *Theoretical* Criminology 16 (2): 211–14. https://doi.org/10.1177/1362480612442113.

Charles, Jacqueline. 2020. "COVID-19 Has Reached Haiti's Overcrowded Prisons: Some Fear a Human Rights Disaster." *Miami Herald*, May 27, 2020. https://www.miamiherald.com/news/nation-world/world/americas/haiti/article243018516.html.

Davis, Angela Y. 2003. *Are Prisons Obsolete?* New York: Seven Stories Press.

Davis, Angela Y. 2011. *Abolition Democracy: Beyond Empires, Prisons, and Torture*. New York: Seven Stories Press.

Dow, Mark. 2004. *American Gulag: Inside U.S. Immigration Prisons*. Berkeley: University of California Press.

Eljechtimi, Ahmed, and Mark Potter. 2020. "Morocco to Release 5,654 Prisoners amid Coronavirus Outbreak." *Reuters*, April 5, 2020. https://www.reuters.com/places/africa/article/us-health-coronavirus-morocco/morocco-to-release-5654-prisoners-amid-coronavirus-outbreak-idUSKBN21N06R.

Fassin, Didier. 2016. *Prison Worlds: An Ethnography of the Carceral Condition*. Cambridge: Polity Press.

Foucault, Michel. 1977. *Discipline and Punish: The Birth of the Prison*. Translated by Alan Sheridan. New York: Vintage.

Geltner, Guy. 2008. *The Medieval Prison: A Social History.* Princeton: Princeton University Press.

Georgia Department of Corrections. 2021. "Georgia Department of Corrections COVID-19 FAQs for Friends and Family." Georgia Department of Corrections, updated January 28, 2021. http://www.dcor.state.ga.us/content/faq2.

Gilmore, Ruth Wilson. 2007. *Golden Gulag: Prisons, Surplus, Crisis, and Opposition in Globalizing California.* Berkeley: University of California Press.

Good, John Mason. 1795. *A Dissertation on the Diseases of Prisons and Poor-Houses.* London: Printed for C. Dilly.

Great Britain House of Commons. [1760]. *Journals of the House of Commons: From June the 15th, 1727, in the First Year of the Reign of King George the Second, to December the 5th, 1732, in the Sixth Year of the Reign of King George the Second.* Vol. 21. [London]: Samuel Richardson.

Hayes, Tara O'Neill, and Margaret Barnhost. 2020. "Incarceration and Poverty in the United States." *American Action Forum*, June 30, 2020. https://www.americanactionforum.org/research/incarceration-and-poverty-in-the-united-states/.

Hinton, Elizabeth. 2016. *From the War on Poverty to the War on Crime: The Making of Mass Incarceration in America.* Cambridge, MA: Harvard University Press.

HRW (Human Rights Watch). 2020. "DR Congo: Prisons Face COVID-19 Catastrophe." HRW, April 17, 2020. https://www.hrw.org/news/2020/04/17/dr-congo-prisons-face-covid-19-catastrophe.

Innes, Joanna. 2009. *Inferior Politics: Social Problems and Social Policies in Eighteenth-Century Britain.* London: Oxford University Press.

Kaba, Mariame. 2021. *We Do This 'Til We Free Us: Abolitionist Organizing and Transforming Justice.* New York: Haymarket.

Kunzel, Regina G. 2008. *Criminal Intimacy: Prison and the Uneven History of Modern American Sexuality.* Chicago: University of Chicago Press.

Lind, James. 1779. *An Essay on the Most Effectual Means of Preserving the Health of Seamen in the Royal Navy; and a Dissertation on Fevers and Infection; together with Observations on the Jail Distemper, and the Proper Methods of Preventing and Shopping its Infection.* London: Printed for J. Murray.

Looney, Adam, and Nicholas Turner. 2018. "Work and Opportunity Before and After Incarceration." *Brookings Institute*, March 14, 2018.

https://www.brookings.edu/research/work-and-opportunity-before-and-after-incarceration/.

Marshall Project. 2021. "A State-By-State Look at 15 Months of Coronavirus in Prisons." Marshall Project, June 1, 2021. https://www.themarshallproject.org/2020/05/01/a-state-by-state-look-at-coronavirus-in-prisons.

Massoglia, Michael. 2008. "Incarceration as Exposure: The Prison, Infectious Disease, and Other Stress-Related Illnesses." *Journal of Health and Social Behavior* 49 (1): 56–71. https://doi.org/10.1177/002214650804900105.

Murakawa, Naomi. 2014. *The First Civil Right: How Liberals Built Prison America*. Oxford: Oxford University Press.

Oglethorpe, James Edward. 1729. *A Report from the Committee appointed to Enquire into the State of the Goals of this Kingdom: Relating to the Marshalsea Prison; and farther Relating to the Fleet Prison.* In *The Publications of James Edward Oglethorpe*, edited by Rodney M. Baine, 83–119. Athens: University of Georgia Press.

Reinhart, Eric, and Daniel L. Chen. 2020. "Incarceration and its Disseminations: COVID-19 Pandemic Lessons from Chicago's Cook County Jail." *Health Affairs* 39 (8): 1412–18. https://doi.org/10.1377/hlthaff.2020.00652.

Reuters. 2020. "Bolivian Prison Inmates Riot over Coronavirus Exposure." July 27, 2020. https://www.reuters.com/article/us-health-coronavirus-bolivia-jail/bolivian-prison-inmates-riot-over-coronavirus-exposure-idUSKCN24S2O0.

Schwartzapfel, Beth, and Katie Park. 2020. "1 in 5 Prisoners in the US Has Had COVID-19." Marshall Project, December 18, 2020. https://www.themarshallproject.org/2020/12/18/1-in-5-prisoners-in-the-u-s-has-had-covid-19.

Sharpe, Joshua. 2020. "Georgia to Release some Inmates due to COVID-19 Fears." *Atlanta Journal-Constitution*, March 31, 2020. https://www.ajc.com/news/local/breaking-georgia-release-some-inmates-due-covid-fears/np6zhBrlP1oe2jOkUmWVoL/.

Siena, Kevin. 2019. *Rotten Bodies: Class and Contagion in Eighteenth-Century Britain*. New Haven: Yale University Press.

Tully, Tracey. 2020. "2,258 NJ Prisoners Will Be Released in a Single Day." *New York Times*, November 5, 2020. https://www.nytimes.com/2020/11/04/nyregion/nj-prisoner-release-covid.html.

Vera Institute of Justice. 2019. "Fact Sheet: Incarceration Trends in Georgia." https://www.vera.org/downloads/pdfdownloads/state-incarceration-trends-georgia.pdf.

Wagner, Peter. 2020. "Large Scale Releases and Public Safety." Prison Policy Initiative, April 9, 2020. https://www.prisonpolicy.org/blog/2020/04/09/large-scale-releases/.

WHO (World Health Organization). 2021. "HIV in Prisons." WHO Europe. https://www.euro.who.int/en/health-topics/communicable-diseases/hivaids/policy/policy-guidance-for-key-populations-most-at-risk2/hiv-in-prisons.

Woolf, Steven H., Laudan Y. Aron, Lisa Dubay, Sarah M. Simon, Emily Zimmerman, and Kim Luk. 2015. "How Are Income and Wealth Linked to Health and Longevity?" *Urban Institute*, April 13, 2015. https://www.urban.org/research/publication/how-are-income-and-wealth-linked-health-and-longevity.

WPB (World Prison Brief). 2021. "Highest to Lowest — Occupancy Level (Based on Official Capacity)." WPB. Accessed February 2, 2021. https://www.prisonstudies.org/highest-to-lowest/occupancy-level?field_region_taxonomy_tid=All.

Zaghari-Ratcliffe, Nazanin. 2020. "Coronavirus: Iran Temporarily Frees 54,000 Prisoners to Combat Spread." *BBC*, March 3, 2020. https://www.bbc.com/news/world-middle-east-51723398.

Part III. Everyday Economies

CHAPTER 13

Agricultural Day Labor in Spain

The Logics of (Pandemic) Capitalism

Susana Narotzky

Introduction

As the COVID pandemic spread through the world, inequalities became increasingly salient. In an interview in April 2020, Seydou Diop, a Senegalese migrant, explained that while most sectors were locked down, agriculture was considered essential, and that agricultural workers like himself were still working.

> When we come back from work, we have to go get water, shower, go buy food because we have no refrigerator, cook the meal. ... Here in the shack, you can see, some five to eight people live. ... We are a very, very large labor force of this country; we are economically improving this country. ... Now with the coronavirus situation ... all sectors have stopped except for the agricultural sector. ... While people are at home, we wake up early and go to work, to nourish everyone. ... We work and we do not get a better life. ... After we end our workday, they want to know nothing from us, if we eat well, if we sleep well, if we sleep in the street, if we shower or don't shower, they are not interested. What interests them is that we pick the fruit and when it's over we go home. That's all. That is very bad, very bad. ... We want to

regularize our situation, and we want a decent accommodation, and we want to pay for it like the Spaniards do, but they ask for a one or two-year employment contract (*nómina*) but we are temporary workers, that's impossible. We do not ask for preferential treatment. ... Sometimes fire burns the settlements and burns our documents; this is very important ... because the law says that we need three years [of proof of residence] that we can demonstrate. Some people have been here 15 or 20 years and cannot get their papers. ... Politicians don't care about us because we do not vote, but we bring an important economic contribution; some people vote and do not contribute. We need them and they need us. (Moreno 2020)[1]

When the lockdown policies were announced, exceptions were made for "essential workers," which included a wide range of professions. Work in health care, infrastructure, and food provisioning required presence, proximity, and continuity. It transpired that an important sector of the population whose livelihood depends on precarious jobs were considered both essential and worthless, *exemplifying a core characteristic of capitalist accumulation practices*. The confinement of these workers, moreover, was not an option for them as their families in the home countries relied on their remittances.

This chapter charts the relationship between the various ways that people are valued and the specific process of economic valorization, especially as it regards political and economic decisions that have been made at different scales and in different moments. First, I analyze the case of agricultural migrant day laborers who are key actors in food provisioning processes in Spain and in Europe as a whole. In the second section I draw a map of some hotspots during the second wave of COVID and their relation to racialized forms of migrant labor in fruit and vegetable harvesting. I then discuss policy responses to these events and the actions and mobilizations of farmers, day laborers and activists, showing how these highlighted existing tensions rather than pointing to new ones. In this process, the issue of movement (temporary migrant workers, circulation of labor following agricultural campaigns), accommodation (settlement, housing), exploitation (wages, work conditions), and health are tightly knit with symbolic constructions of racial and ethnic worthlessness and disposability. In the final section I draw some conclusions regarding the overlapping ways in which agricultural labor is

---

1. All translations into English are my own.

valued (essential, migrant, gendered, racialized, and ethnicized) and how these interlock with valorization processes.

The picture I present is based on the analysis of documentary material (legal decrees and executive orders, institutional reports, various national and regional daily newspapers, interviews on activist websites and in online magazines), on my ethnographic knowledge of several of the agricultural areas (in Almeria, Alicante/Murcia, Lleida) where some of the COVID hotspots appeared, and on long-term research of a number of influential sociologists and anthropologists.

Food Labor Before and During COVID

For over twenty years, Spain, Europe's main supplier of greenhouse vegetables (grown mainly in the provinces of Almería and Murcia), stone fruit (in those of Lleida and Huesca), and berries (in Huelva province) has operated on the basis of labor exploitation and water extraction systems[2] that are contrary to basic labor rights and environmental regulations. But this racial and gendered exploitation and environmental spoliation has been tacitly accepted by institutions and consumers alike, in Spain and across Europe. These workers became visible and valuable as the COVID lockdown risked breaking the supply chain. For day laborers, COVID made things worse. Even for those with regular residence and work permits, mobility was now legally restricted to going from their homes to the fields, often in overcrowded vans where no distancing was possible. Few masks or gloves were provided at work and distancing was prevented by the pace demanded by the overseers. Workers who were infected had to go into quarantine, thus losing wages and risking not being rehired, so that many concealed an illness if in any way possible. At the same time, the push to productivity led to extensive overtime that was rarely compensated and robbed the workers of their rest days.

Spain is one of the world's leading exporters of fresh strawberries and other berries (OEC n.d.). Most exports go to the European Union (EU), with Germany alone accounting for over 30 percent of these. In terms of world production, its position has varied from third to sixth over the last ten years (FAO n.d.). The abysmal exploitative labor conditions that have been described for strawberry production in California and elsewhere

---

2. Illegal water stealing is depleting aquifers in Huelva, especially those of the Doñana Natural Conservation Park (*La Mar de Onuba* 2019, 2020a).

(Wells 2000) are also found in Huelva. The area has relied on migrant labor of different types as well as on some local day laborers and family labor. In the 1990s an influx of migrants created a pool of both unregulated and regularized labor for the growth of export agriculture (Cachón Rodríguez 1995; Torres Solé, Allepuz Capdevila, and Gordo Márquez 2014; Moraes et al. 2012; Pedreño 1999). Exploitation of unregulated labor and dire living conditions in shanty towns lacking basic infrastructure became the norm. This period was dominated by male migrants, some of whom were already resident in the area. With the intensification of production, the demand for agricultural labor kept growing, parallel to a growing demand from 1996 onwards in the construction industry with Spain's housing bubble. Soon, the racialized conflict between labor and capital in agriculture became blatant (Martínez Veiga 2001). Following two partial regularizations of migrant labor in 1985–86 and 1991–92, by the turn of the century Spain was assertively engaging in new EU policies for channeling labor migration through strictly regulated temporary migration systems framed as co-development strategies meant to transfer resources for development — through remittances — to the home country. Starting in 1993, Spain developed a legal framework for controlled temporary labor migration. The system annually predefined a number of positions offered to laborers of specific nationalities and is still in place with minor changes (Gordo Márquez 2011; Márquez Domínguez et al. 2013). The region of Huelva was to use this system increasingly after 2000, first for the import of female labor from Poland and Romania and later from Morocco (Gualda 2012).

The bursting of Spain's housing bubble in 2008 resulted in skyrocketing unemployment, prompting the government to reduce temporary migrant labor program quotas to a minimum hoping that Spanish unemployed would be attracted to agricultural labor. This did not take place; the jobs were mostly taken by permanent resident migrants with or without papers (CCOO 2019). During this period, employers relied on Romanian workers as Romania was part of the EU since 2007 and therefore movement and contracts fell under the European Economic Area Agreement for EU member countries. As citizens of a EU country, these migrants could move freely, a fact that the employers valued. Yet this freedom also undercut the power of employers as it meant that the migrants were not contractually bound to a particular employer for the entire season as were non-EU migrants that came under temporary migrant programs. By 2016 many employers had reverted to the temporary agricultural migrant labor program which enabled them to have more control over migrant laborers because workers came to Spain under contract to a particular employer which they were not free to leave (Molinero-Gerbeau 2020). Although both informal labor and regular contract labor of Spanish or foreign residents were also present, seasonal worker programs were preferred.

Temporary migrant employment programs produce a form of bonded labor which lacks legal protection of mobility and attaches the worker to a particular employer (although employers do "lend" each other workers). The system contradicts the premises of a free labor market. Moreover, employer associations, local job agencies, or individual farmers who travel to workers' countries of origin to "select" those who will be part of the program's "quota" often illegally impose some defining characteristics on the candidates in a tacit understanding with the sending countries' national employment agencies. Strawberry employers in Huelva, for example, require women from Morocco to be married, divorced, or widowed and to have children under fourteen, so that their family responsibilities will ensure that they will return home once the contract is over (Márquez Tejón and Wilson 2019). This condition had not been required earlier from Romanian women, who were often single and selected for their youthfulness and good looks. Female migrant labor is segmented not only in terms of citizenship and of the legal framework that applies to them but also in terms of their kinship responsibilities, of racial and of sexual characteristics (Reigada Olaizola 2007; Soledad 2020; Carlile 2020). We thus see a shift in the strawberry sector from relying on male migrant workers — often resident, with or without papers — before 2000 to using temporary migration programs increasingly aimed at female labor. Hence, mobility, gender, ethnic, and legal status were some of the frameworks defining the value of laborers before the pandemic.

The main impact of COVID on Spanish strawberry farms was caused by Morocco's border closure. By the time lockdown happened, only 7,000 of the expected 20,000 female Moroccan workers in the migrant labor program had entered Spain; 13,000 were unable to follow. By the end of the harvest, these 7,000 workers were left stranded in Spain because Morocco maintained its border closed, even to nationals. Employers were not contractually bound to pay for accommodation costs during this period and the women had to spend their hard-earned income on living expenses. Because of the nature of their contracts, however, they were not free to move and could not look for work elsewhere. The main employers' association, Interfresa, emphasized the sector's corporate social responsibility and insisted that employers provided good living conditions and care for the stranded migrants while it was negotiating for their return, which was finally accomplished in July (Interfresa 2020). Nevertheless, nongovernmental organizations (NGOs) (Cáritas, Cruz Roja, Women's Link), labor unions (Sindicato Andaluz de Trabagadores-Sindicato de Obreros del Campo [SAT-SOC], the Confederación General del Trabajo [CGT]), and journalists (some by interviewing the migrants themselves) recorded continued exploitation, abandonment, and rent extraction (Vargas 2020a; Kohan 2020; Logroño 2021).

We can draw up a typology of agricultural labor according to the overlap of valuation frameworks that create different vulnerabilities and opportunities for exploitation: (1) formal contractual employment of regular workers, both Spanish and migrants with residence and labor permits; (2) informal employment of Spanish workers; (3) informal employment of permit holding migrants; (4) informal hiring of irregular migrants; (5) seasonal agricultural worker program contracts; and (6) family labor employed in the small farmers' greenhouses (Achón Rodríguez 2013). In addition, valuations attached to gender, race, culture, and skill are pervasive. Legally, all contracts should abide by the collective agreement framing the agricultural sector, but even workers with regular contracts are not paid overtime and other expenses. For most categories, work conditions are hyper-exploitative with long hours, thermic stress (heat over 40°C is not unusual), and various forms of humiliation and sexual harassment, among others (ISTAS-CCOO 2019; Kelly 2019). These circumstances are well known and have repeatedly been exposed by unions, scholars, NGOs, and the media (Palumbo and Sciurba 2018; Pedreño 1999; Martínez Veiga 2001; Barciela Fernández 2013; Cáritas 2018; Cachón Rodríguez 1995). Yet, conditions for laborers have not changed and when the COVID pandemic started to spread in Spain, the only voice that was heard publicly was that of farmers who complained that the closing of the border would bring a labor shortage for the agricultural sector.

Life Conditions and COVID

From January 27, 2020, to February 7, 2020, Philip Alston traveled to Spain as the United Nations Special Rapporteur on Extreme Poverty and Human Rights (Alston 2020). He visited a migrant settlement in strawberry producing Huelva and described the appalling living conditions he found there in a media statement that achieved broad public attention and made the situation widely known:

> In Huelva, workers are living in a migrant settlement in conditions that rival the worst the Special Rapporteur has seen anywhere in the world. They are kilometers away from water and live without adequate sanitation or legal access to electricity. Many have lived there for years and can afford to pay rent but said that no one would accept them as tenants. They are earning as little as 30 euros per day and have almost no access to any form of government support. One person said, "When there's work, Spain needs migrants, but no one is interested in our living conditions." (Alston 2020: 16)

The "illegal" settlements in the town of Lepe, in Huelva province, house around 1,390 residents (as of 2016), with the largest one, located near the cemetery, at different moments accommodating up to 569 people, mostly men, of whom 70 percent held residence and work permits (Hernández Morán 2018: 53–55). In 2020 the Catholic NGO Cáritas counted approximately 2,500 residents living in the shanty towns in Huelva province, all of them working in agriculture (García Padilla, Ortega Galán, and Ramos Pichardo 2020: 13). The shanty structures are built of wood pallets, branches, cardboard, and plastic, and there is no water or sanitation. Of a total of twenty-three settlements in Huelva, only two have access to drinking water; for the rest, residents have to go fetch water that they store in plastic containers — many of them having once held crop pesticides — with the water often sourced from non-potable irrigation systems in the adjacent fields (García Padilla, Ortega Galán, and Ramos Pichardo 2020: 26). When the pandemic began at the end of March 2020, the council of Lepe started distributing water to the settlements in order to keep residents from breaking the lockdown to fetch water, but by mid-June the distribution had already stopped (Europapress 2020a; *La Mar de Onuba* 2020b; Lavozdelsur 2020; La Vanguardia 2020a).

The shanty towns have existed for over ten years on both public and private land and are prone to catch fire, as happened in 2015, 2017, 2019, and twice in July 2020. Often these fires erupt when migrants are at work, so that they lose not only their belongings but also their official documentation and permits. No one has ever been found guilty of arson and the official explanation tends to be that fire results from cooking or from burning garbage.

Proper housing for resident migrant day laborers is elusive all over the intensive greenhouse agriculture area of Andalusia where large and small informal settlements lacking water and/or sanitation have been the norm (Martínez Veiga 1999; Pedreño 1999). Laborers who are brought in under a temporary migrant worker program (*Contratación en origen*), on the other hand, have to be provided such housing by the farmers, as per the program contract. This often applies to strawberry pickers who are hired every year for the harvest in Huelva or to stone fruit pickers in the irrigated fruit orchards in Lleida. Though this accommodation does usually include water, electricity, gas, and sanitation, it is precarious and overcrowded and employees are — illegally — often made to pay for these services.

Similarly precarious and unhealthy living conditions have been the norm in fruit producing areas in Aragón and Catalonia and have been recurrently denounced by local NGOs and by the workers themselves. In the Segrià district in Lleida province, seasonal migrant laborers have been sleeping in the streets of the capital city of Lleida, or in shacks provided by their employers, where access to utilities is also scarce or lacking. The employment of temporary migrant labor from Colombia and Eastern Europe (Achón Rodríguez 2012; Gordo Márquez et al. 2015), together with unregulated labor — mostly from sub-Saharan Africa — is usual. Farmers' associations, local authorities, and even major unions have partially justified or have remained silent in the face of laborers' dire living conditions. Only small, radical unions (such as the CGT and the Confederación Nacional del Trabajo) and some NGOs have publicly condemned the situation. In many cases day laborers have residence and work permits but employers use all sorts of strategies to hire them informally, hence reducing their legal rights and increasing their vulnerability (e.g., nonpayment during illness, nonpayment of social security contributions, unpaid overtime, and so on) (Negro 2020).

The COVID pandemic aggravated the situation. In Segrià — as in Lepe — the presence of these day laborers living in the town square was now considered an imminent risk of contagion for the town's other inhabitants. Different social actors had contrasting views of what the situation entailed. For the neighborhood association of the city center of Lleida, these migrants were a potential danger because of their deficient hygiene, lack of access to health care, disregard of confinement orders, and mobility. Local authorities made available a summer camp hostel in the nearby town of Juneda for day laborers who needed to quarantine and hotel rooms for those who had tested positive and had to be isolated.

Yet many day laborers confided that they would not seek help if they were mildly sick because they needed to work and being quarantined meant a loss of wages. The doctor responsible for COVID containment in the major hospital in Lleida province declared that the health system was intended for residents who were registered in the municipality and could be traced but not for migrant laborers who lacked a proper address and might even be homeless, were mobile, and lived in overcrowded conditions.

Overcrowding in shacks in the shanty towns or in the housing spaces provided by employers made complying with the government's insistently recommended hygiene rules virtually impossible: distancing was impossible, and the regular washing of hands and of laundry was extremely difficult without access to water. And migrants who were not registered in the municipality where they lived had difficult access to health care, even with valid work or residence permits. A Royal Decree issued in 2012 by the right-wing Partido Popular (People's Party) government in the wake of Spain's financial bailout (BOE 2012) introduced a series of austerity measures, one of which was the removal of irregular migrants as recipients of universal health care benefits. In July 2018 the new socialist government overturned this measure by issuing an executive order that reinstated universal public health coverage to irregular migrants (BOE 2018). To qualify for this benefit, however, migrants had to apply for a health card for which they had to provide a number of documents, including an identity document, proof of continued residence in Spain for at least 90 days, usually provided by a municipal register (*empadronamiento*), and proof that no third party was legally responsible for covering their health expenses. Acquiring access to public health coverage was not straightforward and could be impeded by events such as the loss of documentation (e.g., in settlement fires), the inability to prove continued residence, or having the right to public health care through different means (e.g., the seasonal migrant worker program requires an employer to register all workers in the social security system and to inform them of the requisite procedures).

Appalling living and working conditions together with the mobility required from agricultural day laborers seem to explain the second-wave hotspots that were linked to the food provisioning chain in Huesca, Lleida, Murcia, Huelva, and Almeria provinces. Cost-cutting conditions that led to labor exploitation in agriculture had produced work environment that were at once unhealthy (heat stress caused by greenhouses temperatures between 40ºC and 50ºC, dehydration, pesticides, demand for increased productivity, overtime) and unprotected (fraudulent contracts, undeclared labor, sexual harassment). During the first wave of the pandemic, employers provided limited or no protective gear and distancing was often impossible due to the pace of work. During the second wave, masks were distributed more frequently or workers were required to bring their own, though all other conditions remained the same. Social distancing measures were still not implemented: travel to and from work continued to be often carried out in small, overcrowded vans and the pace of work was increased to compensate for the labor shortage. Arguably, contract farming for large distributors such as Driscoll's in the United States (*La Mar de Onuba* 2020c) or supermarket chains such as Tesco in the United Kingdom (De Pablo et al. 2020) also constrains small and medium producers who complain that prices do not cover their higher costs (Reigada et al. 2017).

Institutional Responses and Mobilizations

How have institutions responded to the challenges that COVID has posed to agricultural labor? Early on, the main fear was that mobility restrictions and border closings both within Europe and between EU and non-EU countries, would disrupt a sector that was largely dependent on migrant labor for its harvest season. The exceptions to travel restrictions implemented by the EU guidelines of March 16, 2020, did not include temporary agricultural workers, but by March 30 they were included on the list of "critical" or essential workers that could cross into the EU. Spain followed these recommendations although restrictions to mobility were implemented in a strict lockdown from March 13 until June 21, so that the first migrant workers, from Romania, were allowed to enter the country only in May, for fruit picking (EFE Agro 2020a).

Nevertheless, as early as April 7 the government issued a special decree in reply to claims of labor shortages from agricultural municipalities and farmers' associations.[3] The decree aimed to achieve a balance between the demand for seasonal agricultural labor and the COVID measures of restricting mobility and closing borders (BOE 2020). It reacted to the massive unemployment produced by the lockdown in the hospitality and construction industries, while attempting to contain mobility

---

3. See Alonso (2020: 20) for municipalities' call; La Vanguardia (2020b); Agro Informacion (2020).

by mandating that all hired labor be resident of the same or adjoining municipality to the work place. The government rejected a call from the Defensor del Pueblo (the ombudsman of the people) to address the labor shortage through the regularization of unregulated resident migrants — as was done, for example, in Portugal and Italy — on the grounds that this would not comply with the 2008 European Pact on Immigration and Asylum (Vargas 2020b; Martín 2020). Farmers thus continued to hire irregular migrants on an informal basis for their seasonal harvesting tasks — which was not a novelty — while hardly any unemployed Spanish workers applied. In the end, the call for resident labor led many irregular workers to relocate to the areas where demand for agricultural labor was highest, potentially helping to spread the virus in the first wave (Plaza and Sánchez 2020).

Municipalities supported farmers and had a record of not caring much for workers, even though they — together with autonomous community governments — were responsible for ensuring that all COVID regulations regarding workers' living and health conditions were being complied with. Though this compelled them to check more frequently for exploitative or abusive treatment, the numerous complaints filed by workers during this time suggests that their efforts on behalf of workers were inadequate. And yet many municipalities requested, and obtained, special funds to deal with the risk of contagion generated by settlements and work conditions in agriculture, as well as to deal with the announced loss of income that the COVID agricultural season would entail. Huelva and Almeria provinces each received more than EUR 1 million, and Segrià over EUR 2 million, to provide water, accommodation, quarantine spaces, social mediators, health care, and more for migrant laborers, and to help other sectors of the local economy that were affected. The efficiency with which municipalities used the money seems to have varied tremendously (Europapress 2020b).

Agricultural workers were "essential" and could not stop working: if anything, they were in higher demand. In fact, although work and living conditions became worse, the "critical" aspect of food provisioning gave workers some visibility and leverage during the pandemic. The objective of the laborers was to keep their jobs and wages, but they also found ways to organize, protest, and claim their rights. This happened mostly through associations or unions that included both Spanish workers and regularized migrants. While large NGOs such as Cáritas provided support and helped publicize the precarious work and life conditions of migrant workers, it was the smaller, local movements of migrants *cum* locals that were more effective. There was the Asociación Nuevos Ciudadanos por la Interculturalidad (ASNUCI) in Huelva, the Colectivo de Trabajadores Africanos (African workers collective, CTA) in Almeria, and Fruita amb Justícia (Fruit with justice) in Lleida. Unions followed the same pattern: the major national union Comisiones Obreras (CCOO) and the Unión General de Trabajadores (UGT) were focused mostly on negotiating collective agreements with farmers' associations, even if these were only cursorily applied by employers. Major unions provided research and reports on work conditions (e.g., thermic stress). The smaller SAT-SOC publicly denounced how wages did not comply with the stipulated minimum wage, which resulted in billions in lost wages for workers and tax revenue for the state (Echevarría 2020a; *La Mar de Onuba* 2020e).

The unions that consistently backed day laborers and denounced continuous and concrete exploitation practices in the day-to-day were smaller ones such as the CGT, SAT-SOC, and Jornaleras de Huelva en Lucha (JHL). During the COVID-marked strawberry harvest of 2020, Ana Pinto, a day laborer in Huelva and spokesperson for JHL, often appeared in the media explaining the working conditions (illegal contracts, noncompliance with safety regulations, mistreatment, blacklisting, etc.) of female workers, both temporary migrants and local Spanish workers such as herself. A decidedly articulate young woman, Ana founded this female union of red fruit pickers with Moroccan workers who denounced sexual harassment in 2018: "That year I had been working in a team with fifty Moroccan women and I realized how their lived reality was much worse than ours … yet ours seems terrible to us. I decided to become an activist to expose this situation. And I found other women who denounced the same thing" (Rigol 2020). Asked about JHL's relationship with the major unions, she explained:

> We rejected contact with the major unions [CCOO and UGT] because they have never been in the field. They maintain an absolute silence in the face of the situation we live in. And the minority unions, well, they try to help us, but within them you will find egos, divisions, machismo. … We decided that we are the ones who should lead the struggle, that we are the ones who know it and live it. We are doing our best to be a union, and hopefully at some point we will be able to struggle as one. (Rigol 2020)

The union's main support comes from migrant and feminist collectives and a small local media platform that pays attention to their plight

(Rigol 2020). In another instance she pointed to how exploitation was worse during COVID as laborers were forced to work more hours in an environment that did not comply with the required health safety regulations. JHL filed many complaints to the office for labor inspection but, according to Ana, inspectors enquired into these by speaking only to employers, and only telephonically as it was during the lockdown, and carried out their inspections through video chat.[4]

ASNUCI in Huelva was founded in 2009 as part of an activist network that emerged in the late 1980s with the first waves of Moroccan and sub-Saharan migrants to Andalusia (e.g., Almeria Acoge, an association strongly involved in the defense of migrant labor). During the COVID-marked harvest of 2020 ASNUCI denounced workplace noncompliance with sanitary measures and the aggravated problem of confining laborers to settlements where after work, basic utilities such as water, sanitation, and electricity did not exist (Vivo 2020). In July 2020, after two fires in Lepe, they opposed the municipality's plan of displacing shanty dwellers away from the town center, a move that in their view was meant to isolate migrant workers and render them invisible. They argued that being homeless and demonstrating in the town square was a statement to their deplorable life conditions that could not be ignored by moving it elsewhere (Diario de Huelva 2020a, 2020b). Eventually ASNUCI managed to collect enough money through crowdfunding to build a hostel for temporary migrant workers (Europapress 2020c). Housing has been a recurrent complaint of migrant workers in the settlements, where their demand for *una vivienda digna* (decent housing) underscores everyday racial discrimination and ghettoization (Echevarría 2019).

As a result of intensified mobilization and increasing labor complaints and following the publication of Alston's human rights report about laborers' settlements, Minister of Labor Yolanda Díaz (from the left-wing Unidas Podemos alliance) launched a thorough inspection of agricultural work conditions in May 2020. Protocols mandated on-site visits and included a detailed questionnaire about violence, restriction of movement, legal situation, labor representation, accommodation, and sexual harassment, among others. The stated objective was to detect not only administrative faults but also possible criminal offences such as trafficking, forced labor, servitude, and slavery or similar practices. Farmers'

---

4. Spain has a total of just over 1,000 labor inspectors, a number which is altogether insufficient. The state has begun to consider subcontracting the work to an independent firm (*La Mar de Onuba* 2020d).

associations were incensed while unions and workers strongly supported the initiative (Echevarría 2020b; EFE Agro 2020b; Bocanegra 2020; *La Mar de Onuba* 2021).

Farmers have gone on "strike" several times in recent years, denouncing what they called a structural crisis in agriculture marked by falling prices and increasing costs. They demanded "just prices," pointing to distributors' control of prices, increased labor costs, increased tariffs for exports to the United States, and competition from non-EU countries (EFE Agro 2020c). Recent mobilizations of farmers relate closely to two significant increases in the *salario mínimo interprofesional* (minimum wage, SMI) that the socialist governments had decreed (Ruiz 2019; M. C. 2020). In October 2018 the government under the socialist Partido Socialista Obrero Español vowed to increase the SMI by 22.3 percent to EUR 900 a month, a norm that was approved in December (Gómez 2018); in January 2020 the SMI was increased by another 5.5 percent to EUR 950 (La Vanguardia 2020c). In response, the major farmers' associations — Asociación Agraria de Jóvenes Agricultores (ASAJA, Agrarian Association of Young Farmers), Coordinadora de Organizaciones de Agricultores y Ganaderos (Council of Organizations of Farmers and Stockbreeders), and the Unión de Pequeños Agricultores y Ganaderos (Union of Small Farmers and Stockbreeders) — mobilized all over Spain against a measure they believed would make their farms unviable due to declining prices and unfair competition from third countries (Cordero 2020; Grasso 2020; Gutiérrez 2020). The government responded with a law that prohibited selling at a loss at any stage of the food provisioning chain. In particular contract farming agreements would have to reveal all production costs and set a price above them (Ministerio de Agricultura, Pesca y Almentación, Goberno de España 2020). Indeed, many farmers (especially those owning plots of 5 to 20 hectares in size) suffer from being contract farmers for large distributors (Instituto de Estadístsica y Cartografía de Andalucía n.d.).[5] One aspect of their claims stands out in particular: their understanding of day labor as a "cost," an abstract category they consider only as an agricultural input, and one whose cost threatens their economic viability. When real people are rendered as

---

5. Contract farmers have a contract agreement with distributors such as Driscoll's that sets conditions of cultivation and quality of product and establishes price terms. They often concern labor intensive crops. By setting grade and quality standards, contractors shift risk to producers while retaining pricing privileges outside the market.

abstract costs, it produces a valuation framework that enables practices of human disposability.

Conclusion: Essential and Worthless

A recent international study tentatively places the origin of a mutation of the COVID virus — one that seemed to be responsible for the second wave in Europe — in the fruit picking area of Huesca and Segrià (Hodcroft et al. 2021; see also Torreblanca 2020a). The researchers point to the living conditions of temporary workers as the probable cause of the mutation. In an interview, one of the researchers stated: "This is a very clear message: we need to protect the most vulnerable populations, because afterwards [the virus] spreads to everyone else. [These populations] work and live in very precarious conditions, and we should try to protect them, first for their benefit and second for the benefit of all" (Torreblanca 2020b). So why was this not done? And why did the abysmal work and living conditions of these "essential" workers in the food provisioning chain not just remain precarious but actually worsen during the pandemic?

These workers, who are at the heart of Europe's fresh vegetable and fruit provisioning, have been defined as "essential" or "critical" in the legislation that followed in the pandemic's wake. NGOs, the media, and some recent interviews with day laborers also speak of this work as "essential." And yet, at the same time, migrant day laborers, confined to shanty settlements, have been considered potentially contagious by local residents and authorities, adding an epidemiological "argument" for their isolation. Workers have been caught between immobility and movement: they have been both confined and isolated in the settlements and brought to work every day. They have been asked to provide labor in other harvesting regions around Spain while simultaneously required to reside within an adjoining municipality. They are not protected at work and after work are abandoned and feared. While this had been the "normal" for decades, COVID introduced an important difference: the virus's potential to spread to "other" populations. In this situation, the call to "protect" agricultural workers — such as by the researcher quoted above — emerged not out of a concern for their welfare but out of care for the majority population, thus carrying hidden and unacknowledged discriminatory implications. When the work and life conditions of temporary agricultural workers was suggested as the origin of the virus' second wave, authorities tried to act by setting perimeter closures, allocating money to municipalities to force them to provide quarantine accommodation, asking farmers and municipalities to provide decent lodging for workers, and requiring the health system to test and trace for sick and asymptomatic workers. Despite the allocation of significant financial resources to municipalities, they often were not employed to improve the workers' conditions. Europe's food provisioning depended on these workers' "essential" labor. The workers, in turn, needed work to survive and send income back home as remittances; for them, working was "essential" to social reproduction. The structural contradictions of capitalism become visible in the bifurcated "essential" function of day laborers' work. The work had to be done and workers needed to work, but simultaneously the virus had to be contained.

Global food provisioning chains are notorious for relying on the racial, gender, ethnic, and national segmentation of the labor force, and for resting upon contract farming and distribution firms (Prebisch and Binford 2007; Narotzky 2016). Studies of the horticultural and fruit sector in Spain point to the connection between farmers' contractual relations with distributors and their recourse to migrant day labor, one of the few costs they still control. Migrant labor in its various forms — regular, irregular, migrant program, male, female — produces a flexible labor force, simultaneously available and disposable. This segmentation and precarization is based on the production of social vulnerability where some people are legally and materially set apart from the entitlements that the society they live in provides to citizens (Pedreño 1999; Moraes et al. 2012). There is a political-legal construction of vulnerability that enables a particular kind of exploitation tied to export food production. Legal instruments such as the *Ley de Extranjería* (Law on Aliens), laws regulating temporary migrant programs, or the restriction on universal health coverage are examples of this. A major aspect of the production and reproduction of vulnerable social subjects occurs outside the work environment, in the everyday exclusions that constitute the realities of social reproduction: housing, access to basic utilities, health care, social benefits, and the ability to care for those back home. These material exclusions are entangled with blatant racism together with cultural arguments for discrimination. Migrant workers in the food industry have seen their function upgraded to "essential" with COVID; yet they are denied the basic entitlements and guarantees of constitutional citizenship and are excluded from the body politic. They are produced as fungible.

In 1976 Burawoy described migrant labor systems as political constructions that externalize the reproduction of labor, pointing to the mutual dependence of differentiated spaces of production and reproduction. Likewise, for migrant labor in Spain, Europe's greenhouse, reproduction is materially and ideologically excluded from view. The reproduction of dependents back home is directly excluded in the migrant labor programs that bring Moroccan women for the strawberry harvest, for example, even as it is the main incentive for their work and docility; everyday reproduction is indirectly excluded by pushing migrant workers to live out of sight, in self-constructed shanty settlements on the outskirts of towns. The maintenance and social reproduction of labor is pushed to invisible spaces of abandonment. Production of vulnerability creates the conditions for exploitation, and reproduction is at the heart of it. Most migrant workers accept exploitation because they are responsible for their families abroad through remittances; at the same time, they have to maintain their productivity and their value to the labor force, which requires minimally "decent" spaces of everyday reproduction. There is no divide between production and reproduction for migrant labor: their work is tied to the reproduction of life. On the contrary, for contract farmers, migrant labor should just remain "labor": an abstract cost to be minimized. While workers resent their exclusion from regular housing and their abandonment in spaces of waste, farmers speak about the unsustainable increase in labor costs.

COVID highlights the structural contradictions of an essential but worthless labor force. While the function is essential, the people performing it are disposable. Workers' valuation as "essential" has only emerged publicly with the need to regulate movement during the lockdown period. At the same time, however, the structural vulnerability of migrant workers has increased their probability of spreading contagion, providing arguments for their expulsion from town centers. Control of their mobility intensified while the structural problems that put them at risk by producing them as hyper-vulnerable subjects were not addressed. Indeed, NGOs, the media, and migrant workers themselves have used the paradox of their positive valuation and their abandonment to underline a systemic contradiction.

Epidemiological research of the type quoted above points to the conundrum that COVID has made visible: the vulnerability of these categories of disenfranchized subjects creates conditions that enhance virus mutations that then spread to the "rest" of the population. The condition of being "essential" for food provisioning in Europe seems, paradoxically, to impede any political intervention that would give these workers equal rights. Because food provisioning in Europe is controlled by distribution and pushes contract farmers to minimize labor costs, policy makers seem to be trapped into accepting conditions that rest on having worthless labor carry out essential tasks. Capital accumulation in the global food chain occurs mostly in distribution circuits that feed on contract farming and segmented labor regimes that create disenfranchised hyper-vulnerable subjects. Might COVID have the power to change this?

Acknowledgements

This article has benefited from the insightful comments of colleagues that shared the eventful 2019–20 "Economy and Society" theme-year at the Institute for Advanced Study at Princeton. Likewise, I am grateful to Marion Fourcade and Didier Fassin for their suggestions. The research that started during the lockdown has received funding from the Ministerio de Ciencia e Innovación, PID2020-114317GB-I00, in Spain, and the ICREA-Acadèmia Fellowship Program, Generalitat de Catalunya.

References

Achón Rodríguez, Olga. 2012. "El alojamiento previsto para temporeros gestionado por el sindicato agrícola unió de pagesos. Infraestructura para la disciplina y el suministro de trabajadores." *Athenea Digital* 12 (2): 33–67.

Achón Rodríguez, Olga. 2013. "El empoderamiento de las organizaciones empresariales agrícolas merced la legislación de extranjería y su transformación en agentes ejecutores de la política de control de flujos: El caso de unió de pagesos." *Revista de Ciencias Sociales*, no. 30: 46–73.

Agro Informacion. 2020. "Al campo le falta de mano de obra y el Gobierno solo plantea echar mano de los desempleados nacionales." Agro Informacion, April 2, 2020. https://agroinformacion.com/al-campo-le-falta-de-mano-de-obra-y-el-gobierno-solo-plantea-echar-mano-de-los-desempleados-nacionales/.

Alonso, Florentino. 2020. "El campo espera a los temporeros." *Carta Local*, no. 334: 20–23.

Alston, Philip. [United Nations Human Rights Council]. 2020. "Visit to Spain: Report of the Special Rapporteur on Extreme Poverty and Human Rights." United Nations General Assembly, Human Rights Council, Forty-fourth session, 15 June–3 July 2020, Agenda item 3. A/HRC/44/40/Add.2, April 21, 2020. https://undocs.org/A/HRC/44/40/Add.2.

Barciela Fernández, Sergio. 2013. *La situación social de las personas temporeras agrícolas acompañadas por Cáritas: Informe del año 2012*. Equipos de Inclusión y Estudios Dirección de Desarrollo Social e Institucional, Cáritas.

Bocanegra, Raúl. 2020. "Trabajo ordena indagar abusos laborales y posibles casos de "esclavitud" en el campo y la patronal agraria se indigna." Público, May 14, 2020. https://www.publico.es/politica/ordena-indagar-abusos-laborales-posibles-casos-esclavitud-campo-patronal-agraria-indigna.html.

BOE (Boletín Oficial del Estado). 2012. "Real Decreto-ley 20/2012, de 13 de julio, de medidas para garantizar la estabilidad presupuestaria y de fomento de la competitividad." *Boletín Oficial del Estado*, no. 168, BOE-A-2012-9364, July 14, 2012.

BOE. 2018. "Real Decreto-ley 7/2018, de 27 de julio, sobre el acceso universal al Sistema Nacional de Salud." *Boletín Oficial del Estado*, no. 183, BOE-A-2018-10752, July 30, 2018.

BOE. 2020. "Real Decreto-ley 13/2020, de 7 de abril, por el que se adoptan determinadas medidas urgentes en materia de empleo agrario." *Boletín Oficial del Estado*, no. 98, BOE-A-2020-4332, April 8, 2020.

Burawoy, Michael. 1976. "The Functions and Reproduction of Migrant Labor: Comparative Material from Southern Africa and the United States." *American Journal of Sociology* 81 (5): 1050–87. https://doi.org/10.1086/226185.

Cachón Rodríguez, Lorenzo. 1995. "Marco institucional de la discriminación y tipos de inmigrantes en el mercado de trabajo en España." *Reis: Revista Española de Investigaciones Sociológicas*, no. 69 (95): 105–24.

Cáritas. 2018. *Vulneración de derechos laborales en el sector agrícola, la hostelería y los empleos del hogar*. Estudios e investigaciones, no. 20. Cáritas.

Carlile, Clare. 2020. "If You Don't Want to Work like a Slave, You're Out." Ethical Consumer, April 20, 2020. https://www.ethicalconsumer.org/food-drink/if-you-dont-want-work-slave-youre-out.

CCOO (Comisiones Obreras). 2019. *Flujos migratorios, empleo y formación de la población extranjera*. Madrid: Confederación Sindical de CCOO.

Cordero, Sara. 2020. "En directo: Firma del Salario Mínimo Interprofesional y protestas de los agricultores." ElPlural, January 30, 2020. https://www.elplural.com/economia/directo-firma-salario-minimo-interprofesional-protestas-agricultores_131674126.

De Pablo, Ofelia, Javier Zurita, Annie Kelly, and Clare Carlile. 2020. "'We Pick Our Food': Migrant Workers Speak out from Spain's 'Plastic Sea.'" *Guardian*, September 20, 2020. https://www.theguardian.com/global-development/2020/sep/20/we-pick-your-food-migrant-workers-speak-out-from-spains-plastic-sea.

Diario de Huelva. 2020a. "El Ayuntamiento de Lepe demanda a Asnuci por la 'presión política permanente.'" *Diario de Huelva*, July 28, 2020. https://www.diariodehuelva.es/2020/07/28/ayto-lepe-denuncia-asnuci2/.

Diario de Huelva. 2020b. "Denuncian la marcha de la UME de Lepe sin solución para los inmigrantes." *Diario de Huelva*, July 28, 2020. https://huelvaya.es/2020/07/28/denuncian-la-marcha-de-la-ume-de-lepe-sin-solucion-para-los-inmigrantes/.

Echevarría, Perico. 2019. "Lucha de los jornaleros sin hogar: el CTA propone huelgas de varios días en plena campaña de frutos rojos." *La Mar de Onuba*, November 18, 2019. http://revista.lamardeonuba.es/lucha-de-los-jornaleros-sin-hogar-el-cta-propone-huelgas-de-varios-dias-en-plena-campana-de-frutos-rojos/.

Echevarría, Perico. 2020a. "Cañamero cifra en más de 100 millones de euros el fraude a las arcas públicas y a los trabajadores en el sector de los frutos rojos onubenses." *La Mar de Onuba*, June 7, 2020. http://revista.lamardeonuba.es/canamero-cifra-en-mas-de-100-millones-de-euros-el-fraude-a-las-arcas-publicas-y-a-los-trabajadores-en-el-sector-de-los-frutos-rojos-onubenses/.

Echevarría, Perico. 2020b. "Tensión en el sector de los frutos rojos tras filtrarse el plan de actuación de Inspección de Trabajo en los meses de mayo y junio." *La Mar de Onuba*, May 17, 2020. http://revista.lamardeonuba.es/tension-en-el-sector-de-los-frutos-rojos-tras-filtrarse-el-plan-de-actuacion-de-inspeccion-de-trabajo-en-los-meses-de-mayo-y-junio/.

EFE Agro. 2020a. "España recibe temporeros extranjeros tras el cambio de normativa." EFE: Agro, May 25, 2020. https://www.efeagro.com/noticia/espana-temporeros-extranjeros-cambio-normativa/.

EFE Agro. 2020b. "La inspección de Trabajo recibe críticas de agricultores y respaldo de sindicatos." EFE Agro, May 15, 2020. https://www.efeagro.com/noticia/inspeccion-trabajo-agricultores-sindicatos/.

EFE Agro. 2020c. "Agricultores al límite: ¿Por qué protesta el campo español?" EFE Agro, January 29, 2020. https://www.efeagro.com/noticia/por-que-protesta-campo-espanol/.

Europapress. 2020a. "Un camión cisterna llevará agua potable a los asentamientos en Lepe (Huelva)." EpHuelva, March 31, 2020. https://www.europapress.es/andalucia/huelva-00354/noticia-camion-cisterna-llevara-agua-potable-asentamientos-lepe-huelva-20200331133441.html.

Europapress. 2020b. "Junta destina 2,2 millones para asentamientos de inmigrantes en Almería y Huelva." Europapress, April 14, 2020. https://www.europapress.es/andalucia/noticia-junta-destina-22-millones-asentamientos-inmigrantes-almeria-huelva-20200414161749.html.

Europapress. 2020c. "Asnuci pide ayuda para crear el primer albergue de temporeros inmigrantes de la provincia de Huelva." EpHuelva, April 22, 2020. https://www.europapress.es/andalucia/huelva-00354/noticia-asnuci-pide-ayuda-crear-primer-albergue-temporeros-inmigrantes-provincia-huelva-20200422183414.html.

FAO (Food and Agriculture Organization). n.d. "Countries by Commodity." FAO. http://www.fao.org/faostat/en/#rankings/countries_by_commodity.

García Padilla, Francisca M., Ángela M. Ortega Galán, and Juan D. Ramos Pichardo. 2020. *Análisis de la situación de salud de los/as inmigrantes de los asentamientos de Huelva*. Huelva: Cáritas diocesana de Huelva.

Gómez, Manuel V. 2018. "La subida del salario mínimo será la más alta en los últimos 40 años." *El País*, October 11, 2018. https://elpais.com/politica/2018/10/11/actualidad/1539254597_107378.html.

Gordo Márquez, Mercedes. 2011. "Los contratos en origen de temporada a las 'marroquinas': estrategia empresarial para sustituir a las trabajadoras del Este de Europa tras la incorporación de estos países a la UE." In *Cooperación Transfronteriza Andalucía-Algarve-Alentejo: Actas del XI Congreso de Ciencia Regional de Andalucía, Universidad de Huelva, 2009*, edited by Juan Antonio Márquez Dominquez, 573–93. Huelva: Servicio de Publicaciones, Universidad de Huelva.

Gordo Márquez, Mercedes, Rafael Allepuz Capdevila, Juan Antonio Márquez Domínguez, and Teresa Torres Solé. 2015. "La gestión colectiva de los contratos en origen de temporeros colombianos en la provincia de Lleida." *Boletín de la Asociación de Geógrafos Españoles*, no. 68: 233–52.

Grasso, Daniele. 2020. "De los precios al clima: nueve claves que explican la rebelión del campo español." El País, February 1, 2020. https://elpais.com/economia/2020/01/31/actualidad/1580484923_205608.html.

Gualda, Estrella. 2012. "Migración circular en tiempos de crisis. Mujeres de Europa del Este y africanas en la agricultura de Huelva." *Papers* 97 (3): 613–40. https://doi.org/10.5565/rev/papers/v97n3.436.

Gutiérrez, Maite. 2020. "¿Por qué protestan los agricultores españoles?" La Vanguardia, January 31, 2020. https://www.lavanguardia.com/economia/20200131/473224065195/agricultores-protesta-jaen-andalucia-salario-minimo-aceite.html.

Hernández Morán, Mariá. 2018. *2017: Realidad de los asentamientos en la provincia de Huelva; Análisis, diagnóstico y propuestas.* Sevilla: Asociación Pro Derechos Humanos de Andalucía.

Hodcroft, Emma. B., Moira Zuber, Sarah Nadeau, Timothy G. Vaughan, Katharine H. D. Crawford, Christian L. Althaus, Martina L. Recihmuth, et al. 2021. "Spread of a SARS-CoV-2 Variant through Europe in the Summer of 2020." *Nature*, no. 595: 707–12.

Instituto de Estadístsica y Cartografía de Andalucía. n.d. "Propiedad de la tierra." Atlas de Historia Económica de Andalucia, SS XIX–XX. https://www.juntadeandalucia.es/institutodeestadisticaycartografia/atlashistoriaecon/atlas_cap_12.html.

Interfresa. 2020. "Interfresa hace balance de una campaña histórica que reafirma el papel determinante del Prelsi en el sector de los frutos rojos." Interfresa, August 5, 2020. https://www.interfresa.com/interfresa-hace-balance-de-una-campana-historica-que-reafirma-el-papel-determinante-del-prelsi-en-el-sector-de-los-frutos-rojos/.

ISTAS-CCOO (Instituto Sindical de Trabajo, Ambiente y Salud; Comisiones Obreras). 2019. *Guía de estrés térmico por calor en invernaderos: Prevenir y proteger.* Valencia: EDIPAG.

Kelly, Annie. 2019. "Rape and Abuse: The Price of a Job in Spain's Strawberry Industry?" Guardian, April 14, 2019. https://www.theguardian.com/global-development/2019/apr/14/rape-abuse-claims-spains-strawberry-industry.

Kohan, Marisa. 2020. "Denuncian a España ante la ONU por violar los derechos humanos de las temporeras de la fresa en la pandemia." Público, June 3, 2020. https://www.publico.es/sociedad/trabajadoras-fresa-coronavirus-denuncian-espana-onu-violar-derechos-humanos-temporeras-fresa-pandemia.html.

La Mar de Onuba. 2019. "Doñana: los frutos que condenan el paraíso." June 16, 2019. http://revista.lamardeonuba.es/los-frutos-condenan-el-paraiso-de-donana/.

La Mar de Onuba. 2020a. "El Seprona detecta hasta 562 pozos y 146 balsas ilegales que esquilman el agua de Doñana." January 14, 2020. http://revista.lamardeonuba.es/el-seprona-detecta-hasta-562-pozos-y-146-balsas-ilegales-que-esquilman-el-agua-de-donana/.

La Mar de Onuba. 2020b. "Comienza a llegar el agua a los asentamien- tos chabolistas de trabajadores de Lepe." March 30, 2020. http://revista.lamardeonuba.es/comienza-a-llegar-el-agua-a-los-asentamientos-chabolistas-de-trabajadores-de-lepe/.

La Mar de Onuba. 2020c. "El Relator de la ONU sitúa el origen de los asentamientos de trabajadores sin hogar en el enorme crecimiento de la in- dustria de los frutos rojos." February 9, 2020. http:// revista.lamardeonuba.es/el-relator-alston-pedira-a-la-multinacional- driscolls-que-se-pronuncie-respecto-del-chabolismo-laboral-en-torno-a-la-industria-de-los-frutos-rojos/.

La Mar de Onuba. 2020d. "Ep. 5. — Finaliza la campaña de frutos rojos en Huelva." YouTube video, 32: 34, July 1, 2020. https://www.youtube.com/watch?v=eK3S9LBttfY&feature=emb_rel_pause.

La Mar de Onuba. 2020e. "Los trabajadores del campo dejaron de percibir 440 millones de euros en 2019 por la negativa de los empresarios agrícolas a aplicar el SMI." October 18, 2020. http:// revista.lamardeonuba.es/los-trabajadores-del-campo-dejaron-de-perci-bir-440-millones-de-euros-en-2019-por-la-negativa-de-los-empresari-os-agricolas-a-aplicar-el-smi/.

La Mar de Onuba. 2021. "La ministra Yolanda Díaz acertó: sancionadas siete de cada diez explotaciones agrícolas inspeccionadas desde mayo de 2020." January 10, 2021. http://revista.lamarde-onuba.es/la-campana-de-inspecciones-ordenada-por-la-ministra-diaz-detecto-y-sanciono-infracciones-en-el-715-de-las-empresas-agricolas-visitadas/.

La Vanguardia. 2020a. "Denuncian la suspensión del reparto de agua potable en asentamientos de Lepe." June 14, 2020. https://www.lavanguardia.com/vida/20200614/481771454033/denuncian-la-suspension-del-reparto-de-agua-potable-en-asentamientos-de-lepe. html.

La Vanguardia. 2020b. "El campo alerta de falta de mano de obra por el cierre de fronteras." April 1, 2020. https://www.lavanguardia.com/economia/20200401/48251809408/campo-temporeros-mano-de-obra-parados-agricultura.html.

La Vanguardia. 2020c. "Así ha cambiado el salario mínimo en España los últimos años." January 23, 2020. https://www.lavanguardia.com/economia/20200123/473090819346/salario-minimo-smi- espana-evolucion-subida-950-euros-cambios-gobierno.html.

Lavozdelsur. 2020. "Denuncian que el ayuntamiento de Lepe ha dejado de repartir agua potable en los asentamientos chabolistas." June 14, 2020. https://www.lavozdelsur.es/actualidad/sociedad/denuncian-que-el-ayuntamiento-de-lepe-ha-dejado-de-repartir-agua-potable-en-los-asentamientos-chabolistas_182883_102.html.

Logroño, Inmaculada Montero. 2021. "Otra investigación constata las vulneraciones de derechos que sufren en Huelva las temporeras marroquíes de los frutos rojos." *La Mar de Onuba*, May 17, 2021. https://web.archive.org/web/20210517134327/http://revista.lamardeonuba.es/otra-investigacion-saca-a-la-luz-las-vulneraciones-de-derechos-que-sufren-las-temporeras-marroquies-en-la-recolectas-de-frutos-rojos/.

Márquez Domínguez, Juan A., Mercedes Gordo Márquez, Jesús Felicidades García, and José Díaz Diego. 2013. "Evolución de los contingentes de trabajadores extranjeros en España (1993–2011): Las actividades agrícolas." In *Desarrollo regional sostenible en tiempos de crisis, Vol. 2*, edited by José A. Camacho Ballesta and Yolanda Jiménez Olivencia, 757–80. Granada: Editorial Universidad de Granada.

Márquez Tejón, Aintzane, and Hannah Wilson. 2019. "Temporeras marroquíes en la agricultura onubense: Condiciones de trabajo y estancia de las trabajadoras contratadas en origen." *Women's Link Worldwide*, March 13, 2019.

Martín, María. 2020. "El defensor del pueblo pide autorizaciones de trabajo para immigrantes que puedan emplearse en el campo." El Pais, April 3, 2020. https://elpais.com/espana/2020-04-03/el-defensor-del-pueblo-pide-autorizaciones-de-trabajo-para-inmigrantes-que-puedan-emplearse-en-el-campo.html.

Martínez Veiga, Ubaldo. 1999. *Pobreza, segregación y exclusión especial: La vivienda de los inmigrantes extranjeros en España*. Barcelona: Icaria.

Martínez Veiga, Ubaldo. 2001. *El Ejido: Discriminación, exclusión social y racismo*. Madrid: Los Libros de la Catarata.

M. C. 2020. "Cómo esquivar la huelga agrícola de hoy en Almería capital." Ideal, January 29, 2020. https://www.ideal.es/almeria/almeria/esquivar-huelga-agricola-20200128143643-nt.html.

Ministerio de Agricultura, Pesca y Almentación, Goberno de España. 2020. "El Gobierno aprueba medidas urgentes para modificar la ley de la cadena alimentaria y prohibir la venta a pérdidas." February 25, 2020. https://www.mapa.gob.es/es/prensa/ultimas-noticias/el-gobierno-aprueba-medidas-urgentes-para-modificar-la-ley-de-la-cadena-alimentaria-y-prohibir-la-venta-a-p%C3%A9rdidas/tcm: 30-526739.

Molinero-Gerbeau, Yoan. 2020. "Dos décadas desplazando trabajadores extranjeros al campo español: Una revisión del mecanismo de contratación en origen." *Panorama Social*, no. 31: 141–53.

Moraes, Natalia, Elena Gadea, Andrés Pedreño, and Carlos de Castro. 2012. "Enclaves globales agrícolas y migraciones de trabajo: Convergencias globales y regulaciones transnacionales." *Política y Sociedad* 49 (1): 13–34. https://doi.org/10.5209/rev_POSO.2012.v49.n1.36517.

Moreno, Rafael. 2020. "Así se vive el confinamiento en los asentamientos de inmigrantes de Huelva." Diario de Huelva, April 29, 2020. https://www.diariodehuelva.es/2020/04/29/huelva-inmigracion-con-coronavirus/.

Narotzky, Susana. 2016. "Where Have All the Peasants Gone?" *Annual Review of Anthropology*, no. 45: 301–18. https://doi.org/10.1146/annurev-anthro-102215-100240.

Negro, Merche. 2020. "Temporero con papeles pero sin derechos." El Pais, August 22, 2020. https://elpais.com/espana/catalunya/2020-08-22/temporero-con-papeles-pero-sin-derechos.html?ssm=TW_CC.

OEC (Observatory of Economic Complexity). n.d. "Strawberries, fresh." OEC, https://oec.world/en/profile/hs92/2081010.

Palumbo, Letizia, and Alessandra Sciurba, A. 2018. *The Vulnerability to Exploitation of Women Migrant Workers in Agriculture in the EU: The Need for a Human Rights and Gender Based Approach*. PE 604.966. European Parliament's Committee on Women's Rights and Gender Equality.

Pedreño, Andrés. 1999. "Construyendo la 'huerta de Europa': Trabajadores sin ciudadanía y nómadas permanentes en la huerta murciana." *Migraciones*, no. 5: 87–120.

Plaza, Analía, and Raúl Sánchez. 2020. "El desastre de los temporeros que "faltaban" en el campo: aumento de la movilidad, gente sin techo y rebrotes." *El Diario*, June 14, 2020. https://www.eldiario.es/economia/prematura-vivienda-movilidad-contagios-temporeros_1_6016362.html.

Prebisch, Kerry, and Leigh Binford. 2007. "Interrogating Racialized Global Labour Supply: An Exploration of the Racial/National Replacement of Foreign Agricultural Workers in Canada." *Canadian Review of Sociology* 44 (1): 5–36. https://doi.org/10.1111/j.1755-618X.2007.tb01146.x.

Reigada, Alicia, Manuel Delgado Cabeza, David Pérez Neira, and Marta M. Soler Montiel. 2017. "La sostenibilidad social de la agricultura intensiva almeriense: una mirada desde la organización social del trabajo." *Ager: Revista de Estudios sobre Despoblación y Desarrollo Rural*, no. 23: 1–26. https://doi.org/10.4422/ager.2017.07.

Reigada Olaizola, Alicia. 2007. "Trabajadoras inmigrantes en los campos freseros: hacia una segmentación sexual y étnica del trabajo y la vida social." Pensamiento Crítico. http://www.pensamientocritico.org/alirei0407.html.

Rigol, Meritxell. 2020. "En Huelva se da toda la explotación posible: racismo, machismo y destrucción del medio ambiente." *CTXT Contexto y acción*, no. 261. https://ctxt.es/es/20200601/Politica/32487/campo-racismo-machismo-ana-pinto-huelva-en-lucha-explotacion-meritxell-rigol.htm.

Ruiz, José E. 2019. "Cierre total en el sector hortofrutícola en Almería." Ideal, November 19, 2019. https://www.ideal.es/almeria/provincia-almeria/cierre-total-sector-hortofruticola-almeria-20191119101157-nt.html.

Soledad, Carlos. 2020. "Jornaleras en lucha: "Se debe saber lo que hay detrás del fruto rojo que se compra a precio de oro." El Salto, June 12, 2020. https://www.elsaltodiario.com/temporeros/jornaleras-en-lucha-se-debe-saber-que-hay-detras-fruto-rojo-que-se-compra-a-precio-oro.

Torreblanca, Marina E. 2020a. "Un estudio sitúa en España el origen de una variante del virus de la COVID que se ha extendido por Europa." El Diario, October 29, 2020. https://www.eldiario.es/sociedad/estudio-situa-espana-origen-variante-virus-covid-extendido-europa_1_6371986.html.

Torreblanca, Marina E. 2020b. "Iñaki Comas, investigador: 'La nueva variante de COVID demuestra que hay que saber tomar a tiempo medidas para evitar una propagación tan rápida.'" El Diario, October 29, 2020. https://www.eldiario.es/sociedad/inaki-comas-investigador-nueva-variante-covid-demuestra-hay-tiempo-medidas-evitar-propagacion-rapida_1_6373642.html.

Torres Solé, Teresa, Rafael Allepuz Capdevila, and Mercedes Gordo Márquez. 2014. "La contratación de mano de obra temporal en la agricultura hortofrutícola española." *Ager: Revista de Estudios sobre Despoblación y Desarrollo Rural*, no. 16: 7–37. https://doi.org/10.4422/ager.2013.03.

Vargas, Jairo. 2020a. "La cárcel de fresa de Fatima." Público, July 12, 2020. https://www.publico.es/sociedad/temporeras-atrapadas-huelva-carcel-fresa-fatima.html.

Vargas, Jairo. 2020b. "¿Por qué España no puede regularizar migrantes como Italia o Portugal?" Público, May 20, 2020. https://www.publico.es/sociedad/regularizacion-migrantes-covid-19-espana-no-regularizar-migrantes-italia-portugal.html.

Vivo, Al Rojo. 2020. "Sin agua ni luz y "con mucho miedo": así se vive el confinamiento en un asentamiento de temporeros." La Sexta, April 14, 2020. https://www.lasexta.com/programas/al-rojo-vivo/entrevistas/sin-agua-ni-luz-y-con-mucho-miedo-asi-se-vive-el-confinamiento-en-un-asentamiento-de-temporeros_202004145e95aa1131c6450001eedb48.html.

Wells, Miriam J. 2000. "Politics, Locality, and Economic Restructuring: California's Central Coast Strawberry Industry in the Post–World War II Period." *Economic Geography* 76 (1): 28–49. https://10.1111/j.1944-8287.2000.tb00132.x.

CHAPTER 14

Making a Living, Resisting Collapse, Building the Future

Livelihood in Times of Pandemic and Lockdown

Isabelle Guérin, Nithya Joseph, and G. Venkatasubramanian

What does lockdown mean for people who depend on mobility, debt, and sociability to make a living and build their dignity? Drawing on an ethnography of three villages from the central-eastern coast of Tamil Nadu, South India, this chapter explores how the first lockdown (March–September 2020), even more than the pandemic, destroyed and then rebuilt — at least temporarily — local village economies and what underpins them: relationship to time, space, and sociality.

In a region where we have been working for twenty years, we followed sixty families from different backgrounds for six months, by phone and then face-to-face. The objective was to grasp the lived experience of the crisis, the different tactics and strategies deployed to face it individually and collectively, and the consequences in terms of inequalities and social and power relations.

As in many other contexts, the first stage of lockdown provoked a kind of astonishment, combining a feeling of collapse — the term comes up again and again in the testimonies — and withdrawal into oneself.

And then over time, as often observed during severe crises (Shipton 1990), life resumes its course — people adapt, resist, organize, help each other, and transform, at least temporarily, their own aspirations and values. Whereas movement and "elsewhere" was previously the symbol of progress and emancipation, the village now appears as a space of refuge and protection. While off-farm employment, the city, and agribusiness seemed the only way forward, the benefits of subsistence agriculture now come to light. While a consumer society was emerging beforehand, spending is now reduced to a minimum. Meanwhile, social relations are being severely tested. Certain forms of solidarity are disappearing. Relationships of kinship and friendship retract. Old forms of patronage reappear. New forms of sharing emerge. As economic anthropology has shown since its beginnings, social interdependencies, whether they are based on power and hierarchy, solidarity and mutual aid, or sharing, are the structural condition of livelihoods. The crisis reveals both the strengths and fragilities of these social interdependencies.

Unsurprisingly, the absence of a future is probably the most irretrievable loss. The most destitute, who are still predominantly Dalits (formerly untouchables) and landless, suffer the most. Nevertheless, the villagers are able to deploy various tactics to temporarily rebuild a local economy. This is particularly true for women. Even more than usual they are proving to be the pillars of livelihoods and social reproduction. This local economy, tinkered with to offset the disaster of confinement, could serve as an inspiration to build a more humane economy. Unfortunately this is not at all the path taken by the current Indian government.

An Unprecedented Crisis

On March 24, 2020, the Indian prime minister announced that workers had four hours to return home. And yet several tens of millions of workers are internal migrants, working hundreds or thousands of kilometers from home. During the following months, excessive police forces are deployed to prevent people from moving, including in rural areas. The Modi government uses the pandemic as an opportunity to strengthen two pillars of its policy since coming to power. The first is a relentless attack on the informal economy of the poor. After the brutal demonetization of November 2016 and the introduction of a very unfair consumption tax — the Goods and Services Tax — in July 2017, the imposition of a lockdown without any concern for migrants is a further step

(Harriss-White 2020). Meanwhile, the criminal economy, embedded in mafia businesses and political networks, is proliferating (Michelutti et al. 2018). The second pillar of the Modi policy is to assert the supremacy of the Hindu upper classes and castes. Very quickly, Muslim Indians, North-East Indians (from one of the poorest regions from which many migrant workers originate), tribals, and Dalits are accused of spreading the virus.

The shutdown of the economy causes an unprecedented economic recession, one of the strongest in the world. The gross domestic product contracts by a quarter in the first half of 2020 and by 8 percent for the entire year. In the early days of lockdown, hundreds of people die by suicide, hunger and thirst, police brutality, and lack of treatment for other diseases. Employment falls drastically. Even according to the most optimistic estimates, only 15 percent of workers are able to work from home (Chatterjee, Dey, and Jain 2020).

While the brutality of the lockdown caused unprecedented panic, the government announces a few days later (March 26) a few anti-poverty measures: strengthening the subsidized food scheme (one of the pillars of Indian social policy since the 1960s), introducing cash transfers and subsidized loans, and restarting and strengthening the National Rural Employment Guarantee Act of 2005 (NREGA), an existing employment program. The ambition, however, is derisory compared to the scale of need — the aid package represents at best 2 percent of the country's gross domestic product, which is quite low compared to what has been done elsewhere. Above all, its implementation is inefficient, and the region studied here is no exception (Harriss 2020).

Researchers and activists have rightly denounced the lack of compassion shown by the Indian government (Aiyar 2020; Harriss 2020), its attempts to "destroy" the informal economy of the poor (Harriss-White 2020), and its "political strategy of cumulative inequality" (Breman 2020). The lived experience of the crisis shows how these different trends translate into the everyday and how people cope with them. Even though Tamil villagers have experienced multiple crises and some of them are living in a state of permanent crisis, the ban on movement — and therefore on work — and the extent of police repression are unprecedented. Estimated at several tens of millions, the flows of migrants are believed to be greater than those generated by the partition of 1947 (Harriss 2020). Apart from regular cyclones, Tamil villagers have recently experienced two major crises which people spontaneously refer to for comparison: the Indian Ocean tsunami of December 2004 and the demonetization of November 2016. The COVID crisis and its lockdown are, however, difficult to compare to these. The tsunami only affected coastal villages, though, admittedly, it ravaged houses and took many lives. Within a few hours, the tsunami had caused around 8,000 deaths in Tamil Nadu. If the horror of the tsunami tragedy was very real, the disaster provoked a massive influx of money and multiple sorts of aid: very quickly it seemed possible to rebuild a future. Similarly, in November 2016 the immediate elimination of the two most widely used bank bills caused massive panic, especially since it took the government more than three months to put new bills into circulation. Again, the economic and social costs, especially for the poorest, were real and well documented. But the crisis was temporary, and people knew it. The lockdown, on the other hand, causes absolute uncertainty. At the time of writing (January 2021), ten months after the first lockdown, the economy is still partly at a standstill. No one knows when things will return to normal and if they ever will. The official COVID death toll stands at about 12,000 in Tamil Nadu. At its peak in August 2020, the daily death toll was 127, for the regional population of around 68 million. And yet, even if the official data is probably underestimated, COVID deaths are hardly visible on a daily basis: for ordinary citizens, the maintenance of livelihoods is much more worrying than the protection of biological life, and it is often the first thing people say: "Who cares about our livelihood?" (see Fassin, this volume).

We focus here on three villages in a region we have been studying for almost twenty years, located in central-eastern Tamil Nadu, on the border between the districts of Villipuram and Cudallore. This prior knowledge of the region and of the people was a guarantee of trust and encouraged people to confide in us by telephone. We followed up with sixty families by phone over a period of six months from June to November 2020, with an average of three interviews per family. From September onwards, one of us visited the villages regularly and returned to a classic ethnography, combining immersion, observation, and face-to-face interviews.

The lived experience of the pandemic is shaped by a specific local political economy that must be described briefly. Over the past two decades, the region has undergone profound changes, due to the combined effects of economic growth, male migration, and debt. The gains of this transformation were very uneven but nevertheless visible to the naked eye in the pre-pandemic period: improvement of road infrastructure, construction of private schools, but also of wedding halls and temples, including in the *ceri*, the hamlets reserved for the Dalits. Housing was also improved, but often unequally, with thatched huts built next to colonnaded and two-story houses — and here too the *ceri* were no exception. Many houses were equipped with satellite antennas. Some still had outdoor wood-burning ovens, others were fitted with gas stoves. Shelters normally intended to provide shade for livestock were increasingly used to house motorcycles and sometimes cars. Many agricultural fields were left abandoned. Most adults and youth, both male and female, had a cell phone, sometimes a smartphone. The consumer society had gained ground, even in the most remote areas. These transformations were based on three pillars: movement through the circulation of male labor, confidence in the future made possible by easy access to credit (and its counterpart, debt), and, finally, a broadening of social relations. With COVID these three pillars were suddenly and severely disrupted.

Men Back Home and the Contraction of Space

Over the last two decades, villages in Tamil Nadu have been emptied of many of their men. Before the pandemic, most were working elsewhere while regularly commuting back home. For those without education, interpersonal skills, and capital, this usually meant daily manual labor as masons' assistants or brick molders on construction sites, sweepers, cleaners, or security guards for big firms or restaurants, and sugar cane harvesters or coconut pickers on the big farms of agribusiness companies. One of the pillars of India's economic growth is its cheap, vulnerable, and circulating labor force, which moves back and forth according to the needs of private capital (Breman 2007; Picherit 2018; Shah et al. 2018). It is estimated that these nomadic workers number more than 100 million and account for about a quarter of the total Indian workforce (Srivastava 2020; Breman 2020). "Informal" (thus unregulated and unprotected) employment accounts for 80 to 90 percent of work arrangements for these laborers (Harriss-White 2020). In the region studied here, circular migrants represent roughly 60 percent of the labor force and "formal" employment is the exception. By choice or necessity, leaving agriculture — as a daily wage earner or even a small farmer — and working "outside" (*veliyurila vela*) had become the norm. As in many other contexts of deprivation, immobility is an "inaccessible luxury, synonymous not with life but death" (Neiburg 2020).

The movement of male workers profoundly transformed their relationship to space. The circulation of male labor was an essential link in the labor chains of capitalist exploitation. At the same time, circulating and leaving the village has always been experienced as a possible vector of emancipation, albeit fragile and partial, from agrarian caste hierarchies. To be exploited elsewhere, anonymously, does not have the same meaning as local, humiliating exploitation, which many Dalits no longer want.

With the lockdown, this relationship to space is turned upside down. Most migrants return, sometimes in deplorable conditions. A symptom of modernity, they are suddenly considered useless, sometimes as pariahs. More fundamentally, the very status of migration is called into question: whereas leaving and "working outside" was perceived in itself as a source of improvement (*munnetram*), now the elsewhere becomes a hell, whose future is unknown.

Migrants quickly understand that the crisis will last, that construction — the sector that provides most employment opportunities — will operate in slow motion for months or even longer. They are right — by the end of 2020, the construction sector declines by 12 percent. Most urban workers see their wages cut overnight. The inequalities between protected permanent jobs and unprotected daily jobs are strikingly apparent. Between these two extremes, however, the line is often blurred: some employers in the informal economy, out of generosity or interest, continue to pay their employees or provide them with wage advances. Among the few permanent workers in the "formal" sector, it is not uncommon for wages to be cut, sometimes by half or even completely. As usual in India, the employers act with impunity, as if labor laws do not concern them.

Clearly, while the non-farm economy collapses with the lockdown, agriculture shows some resilience. Over the last decades, many high-caste landowners turned away from farming, either selling or leasing their land to lower castes. Men also turned away, leaving women to do the arduous and poorly paid day labor on the farms and sometimes even take on their management. Now, agriculture regains value, either because it feeds families or because it is the only source of employment. Agriculture becomes again what it had always been, says a peasant: the *achani*, the central axis of the wheel of the bullock-cart, that is to say, the center of life. In the first stage of lockdown, however, working and living off the land mean defying the omnipresent police. It did not matter that produce was rotting in the fields, the rule was to "stay at home." "We're going to starve to death," says V., describing how the police threaten to beat women sorting out groundnuts. Selling, even locally, is also a challenge. Some people cycle dozens of kilometers a day to sell their produce, bag by bag. Cycling allows villagers to use side roads that are less frequented by the police and not risk losing their driving licenses, a threat brandished by the police. Others are forced to entrust their produce to strangers who are allowed to travel because they deliver essential goods. Police presence in rural areas is unusual. Usually it is possible to smile, negotiate, pour a bribe. Now the instructions are strict, and the power of the police seems unlimited. It's like a "state of war." "We feel shame. The police treat us as culprits," the villagers explain. Women, usually spared from police violence, are no longer ignored.

Then again, agriculture has been resilient only when it comes to subsistence crops. Under pressure from of the agribusiness industry, subsistence agriculture has been significantly reduced over the last decades in favor of cash, commercial, and often less labor-intensive agriculture. Casuarina, cotton, fruit, and especially sugar cane — the main local cash crop — have replaced rice, millet, and peanuts. Even rice, the subsistence crop par excellence, is increasingly sold. Self-consumption has decreased drastically. As in the rest of the world, the lockdown exposes the contradictions of commercial agriculture. Not only does sugar cane not feed people, but it cannot be sold. Commercial agriculture requires distribution and transport networks, but most of these are stopped with the lockdown. As a consequence, most sugar mills have closed. Farmers let the stalks rot in the ground. What's the point of picking them if they cannot be sold and processed? For watermelon and jackfruit, other widespread cash crops, farmers eventually distribute them for free. Raising dairy cows also proves to be very useful — "Our cow is like the God for us," we were told — both for self-consumption and for sale, since each rupee is precious. But the cows still need to be fed, and some families are forced to sell them to get cash for food or to pay off debts.

Very quickly, the peasants understand the extent of the crisis and react. Where they have unused land, they start subsistence farming, mainly vegetables such as pumpkins, lady fingers, ginger. For small farmers, who had abandoned agriculture for urban activities, doing so is a question of survival. For larger farmers it is a question of cash, but it is also a response to pressure from landless women who are desperately looking for jobs. Individually or collectively, women ask farmers to return to manual and therefore more labor-intensive techniques, whether for irrigation, ploughing, or harvesting. Women also reinvent local sales channels. The closure of markets, which lasts more than six months, leads to the proliferation of itinerant or temporary roadside sales. Some men also give a hand, and others leave this survival business, which is often limited to a few baskets, to the women.

The local labor force is abundant, so wages drop, and women agree to share work. Whereas women used to be paid INR 120 (around EUR 1.36) for three hours of work, they must now work double or triple that and in different locations. It also happens that wages are paid late or in kind, a reminiscence of a feudal past from which agricultural workers, often Dalits, had managed to escape. But it is better than nothing. Questions of prestige are put aside, the Dalits rake in their pride and agree to return to the old patronage economy where landowners provide protection but also impose exploitation. While landlordism had almost disappeared in this region, the crisis is making it rise from the ashes, even though landowners are also suffering greatly from the crisis (see also Carswell et al. forthcoming).

Since the mid-2000s, the NREGA rural employment program dedicated to the "poor" was supposed to address the needs arising from the agrarian transition, which it did very unequally depending on state and local political contexts. Over time, this became mainly a women's program, providing significant supplemental income to them, both rich and poor. With the COVID crisis, the program is transformed: nonexistent for the first two months, even though the need was immense, it slowly begins to recover in May. It attracts not only women but also men, who are now completely idle. Due to local political pressure, it sometimes starts first in the non-Dalit (and richest) neighborhoods. Nevertheless, it provides a very valuable cash flow in the face of the COVID shortages. As for the promise of cash transfers made by the central government, almost none of the families interviewed receive anything (Guérin et al. forthcoming).

The Burden of Debt and the Contraction of Time

Surviving the day and being able to put food on the table are obviously the central concern. For men and children, now at home and idle, meals are an essential distraction. Women complain that the crisis distends men and children's stomachs. As usual, women eat last and make do with the leftovers. Women must thus be creative and resourceful to appease their hunger, diversify meals as much as possible to limit complaints, and to do all this while spending the bare minimum. Tricks include returning to wood-burning stoves (when gas had become the norm for many); reducing or even discontinuing meat, fish, eggs, and dairy products; giving up "snacks" — salty or sweet cookies loved by the children; cooking only once — heavy eaters get bored and eat less; reducing vegetables by making do with seasonings of chopped onion and tomato; collecting wild plants, an old but abandoned practice; sharing gravies with neighbors (with some variation about whether it is reciprocal or charity); getting gravies or other food from employers; doing small jobs in wealthy people's houses and be paid in rice; buying lower quality rice and breaking it in the mill to get a finer grain; stopping making *idli-dosa* pancakes (which are expensive because of the oil, dal, and chutney required); last but not least, making massive use of the government food distribution system, including for people who usually despise this type of food, reserved for the poor and needy. From June, children's lunches are added to the family expense in place of the meal usually distributed at school (closed since the first day of the lockdown and still closed ten months later). Ration food is basic (rice, oil, sugar), insufficient in quantity (the distribution is monthly but fills only two weeks of need), and poor in quality. For many families, the quality of the meals is much lower than usual. "We are hungry from the Corona," as we were told, or "Since corona we forget to eat food with side dish." Here it must be acknowledged, however, that government help (more at the state than the federal level) has been decisive in ensuring food security.

While meeting the needs of daily life requires a lot of time and energy, especially for women, preparing for the future is an equally important concern. A difficulty that adds to the lack of employment and job prospects is the burden of debt. Getting into debt is nothing new in the context of labor migration, but the extent and terms of debt were radically transformed over the last two decades. A longitudinal survey conducted in neighboring villages shows that the average amount of debt owed by families has increased significantly since 2010, because of both a massive supply of credit and insufficient real income — insufficient either to make a living or meet growing aspirations (Guérin et al. 2020). For many families, debt flows represent the same weight on their daily cash flow as income, and debt repayments often account for more than half their expenses. In many families, it is precisely urban employment — of the husband, or frequently of one or more sons — that makes it possible to pay off debt, as well as enable the contraction of new debts. Without urban employment, repayment is unthinkable.

How are we going to pay the "finance" (local term for market debts, those that do not tolerate any delay in repayment), or how the "EMI" (equated monthly instalment, the bank jargon that people use to talk about their repayment bills), were questions frequently asked in our interviews. When the lockdown is announced, this is the first source of anxiety, especially for women, since they are most often responsible for putting aside the repayment money and facing the moral pressure of lenders. It is a matter of honoring one's due but also of preserving one's solvency for the future, since they know that debt will now, more than ever, be the only way out.

The degree of anxiety depends on the type of debt. Anxiety is much more pronounced with market debts, which have expanded widely over the last two decades. Market debts have a particularity: the maturities are fixed and nonnegotiable. Until recently good relations with the credit agent made negotiation possible. With the introduction of a biometric credit-score system, negotiation is no longer an option. Quite soon after the lockdown, the Central Bank of India announced a moratorium on repayments, first until June and then until August. This announcement provokes respite and relief, although lenders do not always act in line with it. Financial companies need liquidity and try to recover their debts, bypassing the moratorium. Women borrowers must thus regularly — sometimes through collective action — assert their rights and refuse to repay. Other women repay even when they are not obliged to do so, regardless of the sacrifices involved — selling an asset, tightening one's belt, borrowing elsewhere — to avoid accumulating interest, which has not been suspended.

Market debt represents only a small part of family debt. Most families juggle loans from pawnbrokers, local elites, employers, labor recruiters, friends, neighbors, lovers. Despite the diversity of their sources, a major characteristic of these nonmarket debts is their negotiability. Subject to moral standards of protection and reputation, lenders must be patient and tolerant. The way they respond to the crisis is uneven. Some demand repayment but nevertheless wait a few months, unless they are informed that their debtors have a source of income. Some erase debts altogether. Others postpone repayment but will later demand heavy interest charges. At the same time, none of the lenders, market-based or not, takes the risk of lending (if they do have liquidity) without collateral. The only way to obtain cash is to pledge assets, but with limited hope of recovering them. Another option is to sell assets directly. Gold, which in normal times already plays the role of a quasi-money, is often what people pledge first. Families who have nothing to pledge sell trees, livestock (goats, cows, poultry), household equipment. They pledge their title deeds or their insurance savings account.

Of course, situations are very unequal. "It isn't even possible to see money with our eyes," some say to account for this shortage of money. Some families immediately sell their few possessions because they have nothing to pledge, "not even a *mukku kutti*," a nose ornament, one of the smallest pieces of jewelry that can be pledged. Some gradually lose all their assets, while others are able to leave their assets untouched. One interviewee, a *Naidu* (high-caste) woman who works as kindergarten assistant in a government school, continues to receive her salary (INR 4,000 monthly, around EUR 45). Her brothers are engineers in Bangalore, and she knows that she can count on them, even though they have their own obligations. When we asked her in June whether she has pledged her gold, she answers that neither she nor the other women in her neighborhood had done so. Asking naively "who would pledge gold since there are no agricultural expenses?" — her husband is a farmer — she fails to imagine that others might need to pawn their gold for food.

With cash becoming a scarce resource, the cost of debt rises. While monthly interest rates rarely exceed 5 percent per month in normal times, now they reach 10 or even 15 percent, although they vary greatly depending on the situation. Bank loans remain cheap (around 1 percent per month), but they are accessible only to the minority that owns valuable farmland or houses. Wealthier women, most often of high caste, organize among themselves to circulate their savings. Poorer women also organize themselves, but their lack of cash limits the potential for mutual help. Rich (and high-caste) women also have easier access to government soft loans set up specifically for the crisis. Government officials insist that these are loans, not grants: only those with small businesses or capital (thus wealthy and high-caste women) are eligible. In our three villages, almost no Dalit woman receives such a loan. NGOs, which could support and strengthen local mutual help efforts (see Parvez, this volume), no longer exist in this region. Like the rest of civil society, they were eradicated by the Modi government and its financialization of development policies.

The debt burden reverses the relationship with time. If debt levels were high before the pandemic, it is first because debt has always been a necessity in the face of the vagaries of daily life. As elsewhere, however, the debt boom was also shaped by and constitutive of confidence in the future and aspirations of social mobility (James 2015). Here this means that debt was also used to finance luxurious weddings, expensive private schools, and nice houses. Many of these projects, however, were more akin to "social speculation" (Zaloom 2019) than real investments. With lockdown, the fragility of this social speculation becomes apparent and faith in the future falls apart. Up until now, high indebtedness was seen as a symbol of respectability, courage, self-confidence, and optimism. Now, indebtedness becomes like a "jackfruit on the head of a crow," as we were told, something impossible to hold on to and that blocks any projection into the future.

Many projects collapse. G. is the mother of four children, indebted to the tune of 15 lakhs (around EUR 17,000) which she used to pay for the private education of her children and to send one of them — a boy — to Singapore. He had barely arrived when COVID struck. He had only been able to remit INR 40,000 (around EUR 450) before he lost his job. In June, she does not even have 30 rupees at hand (EUR 0.35) to prepare a meal. She feels crushed by the debt, with no possibility of repayment. G. and her husband had started to build a permanent house. They had to stop the work but the interest on their debt continues to accumulate. At the end of November, their outstanding debt stood at over 1 lakh, or roughly EUR 1300). As in this example, most of the projects for which people went into debt — education, marriage, housing — have been set aside. "Even after the lockdown we can't come up to the normal situation and normal life," says V, indebted to the tune of several hundred thousand rupees with rapidly accumulating interest. For families with daughters, gold was gradually accumulated to prepare for their marriages. The loss of this gold due to the COVID crisis calls into question the very prospect of marriage for a young woman, a matter that probably affects many families.

In early September, when the debt moratorium is lifted, many men decided to leave home in order "to find something." They have no idea what they will find, they expect that the wages will be low, but they have no choice: debts must be paid. By mid-January 2021, while the urban economy is still in slow motion and jobs remain scarce, the pressure becomes oppressive. V., a Dalit woman, overindebted, hides every time the loan officer passes — she risks blacklisting but she has no choice. For the past few months she has been taking antianxiety medication. As for many others, late payments are piling up. Some pay their debt by selling goods, saving on food, going into debt elsewhere. Some hope for a debt cancellation, but this option does not seem to be on national government's political agenda or the agenda of financial companies, which by now are themselves running out of liquidity.

The Collapse of Trust and the Contraction of Sociability

The broadening of social relations was a profound marker of social change in recent decades. Caste discrimination persisted, but Dalits' dependency upon local high castes had declined. Diversifying jobs and debt sources had only been made possible through a broadening of social relations, patiently built up over the years, away from agrarian caste-based relations of patronage and sometimes away from kinship circles. The crisis, in turn, undermines this trust and shrinks this sociability.

"Corona closes the doors," we heard repeatedly in the first stage of the lockdown. The doors are closed to maintain physical distancing. But also, and above all, because mutual aid and debt — the cement of local sociability and economy — are seriously weakened. While during the demonetization of the second half of the 2010s we observed an extension of networks (and people often compare the two situations), here the opposite takes place. And it is first and foremost uncertainty in the future that narrows relationships and causes the "collapse of trust" (*nambikai pochu*).

People all describe this climate of permanent suspicion, highly marked at the beginning of the lockdown. Even good friends avoid each other so as not to be solicited for money and forced into the embarrassment to refuse. Those who have the reputation of being rich "quarantine themselves," not to avoid the virus but to avoid solicitations. Kinship as well as friendship are built around reciprocal relations of indebtedness where cash, food, grain, and gold constantly circulate.

The collapse of trust is expressed in several ways, with more or less dramatic consequences. Some women confess to immediately eating what they have cooked to avoid any solicitation. It is harder to refuse to share a prepared meal than unprepared food. As we were told: "Some people say, 'Don't come to my home with borrowing motive'." For some, the situation seems unsurmountable. G., a young man, is a job recruiter in the brick kiln industry, in charge of distributing wage advances to kiln workers, many of whom are his relatives. The advance money is given to him by the brick kiln employer. In early 2020, at the start of the season, production forecasts are high, and the advances per pair of workers go up to 1.3 lakh (around EUR 1,500). With lockdown, production stops, and the workers return to the village, unemployed and owing the advances as debt. Fearing that he would lose his capital, the owner of the brick kiln instructs G. to demand from the workers their property titles, as guarantee for the debt, which he does. The workers are offended by this demand, finding it fundamentally unjust, and believe that G. is not playing his role as mediator: he should be convincing the employer to trust them. Overwhelmed by the pressure from all sides, aware that he has lost the trust of both his workers and his employer and seeing no way out, G. tries to commit suicide.

During the early stages of lockdown, expenses are kept to a minimum, the first tactic for managing shortages. Apart from food, other expenses are reduced or cut: debt repayments, school expenses (since the schools are closed), nappies, entertainment (cinema, restaurants for those who could afford it), phone cards, petrol, as well as a key item of expenditure, ceremonies. For the first few months, most ceremonies are cancelled. But ceremonies are at the heart of the entanglement of debts and entitlements that forge socialities and local economies. As time passes, ceremonies resume. Beyond their social and symbolic significance, ceremonies are also a purely material issue. Since ceremonies are financed through a complex system of gifts and counter-gifts, cancelling a ceremony is like losing money: there is the risk that gifts given in the past may never be returned. "If we don't have anything to eat, we will manage with porridge. But we must do something for people who have already done for us," explains A., a young Dalit man who, like many, borrows to contribute to a ceremony of one of his relatives. Ceremony organizers do not hesitate to knock on doors to claim their due. Depending on the circumstances there are of course possibilities for negotiation, as in the case of a widow with young children: people easily understand that she cannot contribute anything. Individuals make calculations and trade-offs: Is it better to organize now and recover liquidity at the risk of getting little, or to postpone to better days in order to optimize the gift? Holding ceremonies can be a strategy to cope and to recall capital that is scattered in this dispersed hoard. People check their account books carefully — ceremonial gifts are accurately accounted for — and are relieved when they see that they are at the end of their cycle with a particular person and therefore do not have to start a new one. But stopping the chain of gifts and counter-gifts also means ending, at least temporarily, social relationships. While in the pre-pandemic period ceremonies had become an opportunity to showcase and broaden relationships — seen both as new friendship and as strategic support in the future — the crisis narrows ambitions and networks. Most ceremonies take place in small circles, at home rather than in prestigious and expensive halls.

Over time, social relationships change. Kinship and friendship become more selective and reconfigure themselves around small circles. The circulation of cash, food, and gold once again becomes a key coping strategy. Those who manage to earn some cash lend easily, as much out of generosity as out of speculation — even in times of crisis, even among relatives or friends, very few loans are free of cost. In this economy of scarcity and uncertainty, the slightest opportunity is seen as a possibility of "marginal gain" (Guyer 2004). While there is nothing new in this, the pandemic context gives much more value to the slightest gain, however marginal it may be.

What Future?

In documenting how, day after day, men and women, rich and poor, reorganize their lives and manage to get by, our aim is certainly not to romanticize resistance, nor is it to simply conclude that villagers are "resilient." The resourcefulness of the poor should not mask the "poverty of resources" (González de la Rocha 2020). People survive, but they do not come out unscathed. They adapt, but at what cost, whether in terms of material loss, erosion of social relationships and trust, emotional stress, humiliation, and suffering? As in other crises such as war and famine, women are at the forefront. Due to the shutdown of the urban economy, the main source of male employment, the women often turn into breadwinners. They scramble to find work, beg for vegetables, queue up at the subsidized food shops, do child-minding, negotiate relations with the police and neighbors, and put food on the table. This pivotal role does not seem to give them any particular respect. They are simply doing what is expected of them: ensuring the physical and social reproduction of the family. The pandemic is an unprecedented crisis of social reproduction (Mezzadri 2020), which here takes on a very singular face. Undoubtedly, social inequalities are increasing. This is obvious nationwide, between the few well-off who have managed to make the "online migration" (see Fourcade, this volume) and the villagers described here. This is also partially true at the local level, and we have given several examples for it. Local divisions are less clear, however, since even some of the big landowners have lost much.

For many, the lack of a future is an irremediable loss. Whereas the pre-pandemic period was marked by confidence in the future, fueled by economic growth and easy access to credit, now the belief in a better future collapses. Debt, until now a possible vector of projection into the future and of social mobility, turns to dispossess debtors of their hope in view of the accumulation of unpaid debts.

But, even if the future is uncertain, the villagers keep on thinking about it, regardless of their status. For farmers, is this not an opportunity to move away from commercial farming and dependence on agribusiness? When informal meetings resume, in the teashops or in front of temples, this is a question that comes up again and again. Returning to subsistence farming is hardly conceivable for larger farmers. Commercial farming, which is not very demanding in terms of presence in the fields and monitoring of the labor force, allows them to engage in urban activities (moneylending, transport), which are much more profitable. Many smaller farmers also want to move away, knowing very well that commercial agriculture is a trap. They wonder whether the labor force, which today is abundant and badly needed for subsistence farming, still be there in the future? And what is the absorptive capacity of local markets, flooded with cheap vegetables from other Indian states, often of hybrid varieties? Farmers are also very lucid about the economic power of agribusiness, whether it be in subsidies, prepurchase, or soft loans. Workers have similar concerns. Once back home in the early days of the lockdown, they take the opportunity to rest, and some come to question their lifestyle. They realize that the village is a safe place: it is not opulence, and times are hard, but at least no one is starving. Would not this be an opportunity to look for local employment and stop this incessant and exhausting circulation, which is a source of perpetual uprooting? As the lockdown eases, many struggle to find local jobs, getting at most a few hours or days of work here and there as drivers, sales assistants, or brick molders in artisanal brickkilns. Others turn to activities that had almost disappeared, such as fishing in ponds. But the opportunities remain meagre. Above all, and although families are able to make do with a frugal diet, they are caught up by the debts that need to be paid: the financialization of their social reproduction needs condemns them to proletarianization.

The pandemic could certainly be conducive to a structural transformation of agricultural and rural economies, rehabilitating subsistence farming, short food supply chains, and "hundred-miles communities" (Bhatt 2015). But this presupposes structural conditions and strong political will, which the Indian government has not displayed. At the time of writing, the country is experiencing large-scale farmers' demonstrations against an agricultural reform project that will strengthen the power of agribusiness. The pandemic could represented the beginning of a more responsible economy, something that the villagers are calling for and have managed to implement temporarily. Sadly, the pandemic is likely to do the exact opposite, reinforcing a predatory and inhumane economy.

Acknowledgements

We are firstly very grateful to the many respondents that willingly gave up time to speak with us and share their stories and experiences. We are also grateful to Vivek Raja, Antony Raj, and Radhika Kartikeyan who were key to enabling us to undertake data collection. We also thank the editors and authors of the book for their helpful and constructive comments on an earlier version of the chapter. The research used in this article was funded by the UK Research and Innovation Global Challenges Research Fund (Ref: ES/T003197/1). Access requests to the data underlying this article should be addressed to rdm@royalholloway.ac.uk.

References

Aiyar, Yamini. 2020. "The State Needs to Step up, Urgently." *Hindustan Times*, April 16, 2020. https://www.hindustantimes.com/columns/the-state-needs-to-step-up-urgently-opinion/story-UQhi5oyhA61C-52vU7fDxJO.html.

Bhatt, Ela R. 2015. *Anubandh: Building Hundred-Mile Communities*. Ahmedabad: Navajivan Publishing House.

Breman, Jan. 2007. *Labour Bondage in West India: From Past to Present*. New Delhi: Oxford University Press.

Breman, Jan. 2020. "The Pandemic in India and Its Impact on Footloose Labour." *Indian Journal of Labour Economics*, 63: 901–19.

Carswell, Grace, Geert De Neve, Nidi Subramanyam, and S. Yuvaraj. Forthcoming. "Lockdown and Livelihoods in Rural South India: Rethinking Patronage at the Time of COVID-19." In *How to Live Through a*

Pandemic, edited by S. Abram, H. Lambert, and J. Robinson. London: Routledge.

Chatterjee, Partha, Soma Dey, and Shweta Jain. 2020. "Lives and Livelihood: An Exit Strategy from Lockdown." *Economic and Political Weekly* 55 (22): 7–8.

González de la Rocha, Mercedes. 2020. "Poverty and Resilience in Mexico." In *Oxford Research Encyclopedia of Anthropology*, edited by Mark Aldenderfer. Updated October 2020. Oxford: Oxford University Press. https://doi.org/10.1093/acrefore/9780190854584.013.214.

Guérin, Isabelle, Sébastien Michiels, Arnaud Natal, Christophe J. Nordman, and Govindan Venkatasubramanian. 2020. "Surviving Debt, Survival Debt in Times of Lockdown." CEB Working Paper no. 20-009. Brussels: Centre Emile Bernheim.

Guérin, Isabelle, Vincent Guermond, Nithya Joseph, Nithya Natarajan, and Govindan Venkatasubramanian. Forthcoming. "COVID-19 and the Unequalizing Infrastructures of Financial Inclusion in Tamil Nadu." *Development and Change*.

Guyer, Jane I. 2004. *Marginal Gains: Monetary Transactions in Atlantic Africa*. Chicago: University of Chicago Press.

Harriss, John. 2020. "'Responding to an Epidemic Requires a Compassionate State': How Has the Indian State Been Doing in the Time of COVID-19?" *Journal of Asian Studies* 79 (3): 609–20. https://doi.org/10.1017/S0021911820002314.

Harriss-White, Barbara. 2020. "The Modi Sarkar's Project for India's Informal Economy." *Wire*, May 20, 2020. https://thewire.in/political-economy/the-modi-sarkars-project-for-indias-informal-economy.

James, Deborah. 2015. *Money from Nothing: Indebtedness and Aspiration in South Africa*. Stanford: Stanford University Press.

Mezzadri, Alemezzadri. 2020. "A Crisis like No Other: Social Reproduction and the Regeneration of Capitalist Life during the COVID-19 Pandemic." *Developing Economics* (blog), April 20, 2020. https://developingeconomics.org/2020/04/20/a-crisis-like-no-other-social-reproduction-and-the-regeneration-of-capitalist-life-during-the-COVID-19-pandemic/.

Michelutti, Lucia, Ashraf Hoque, Nicolas Martin, David Picherit, Paul Rollier, Arild E. Ruud, and Clarinda Still. 2018. *Mafia Raj: The Rule of Bosses in South Asia*. Stanford: Stanford University Press.

Neiburg, Federico. 2020. "Life, Economy, and Economic Emergencies." *SASE Newsletter*, July 13, 2020. https://sase.org/newsletter-summer-2020/life-economy-and-economic-emergencies/.

Picherit, David. 2018. "Rural Youth and Circulating Labour in South India: The Tortuous Paths towards Respect for Madigas." *Journal of Agrarian Change* 18 (1): 178–95. https://doi.org/10.1111/joac.12196.

Shah, Alpa, Jens Lerche, Richard Axelby, Delel Benbabaali, Brendan Donegan, Jayaseelan Raj, and Vikramaditya Thakur. 2018. *Ground Down by Growth: Tribe, Caste, Class and Inequality in Twenty-First Century India*. London: Pluto Press.

Shipton, Parker. 1990. "African Famines and Food Security: Anthropological Perspectives." *Annual Review of Anthropology*, no. 19: 353–94. https://doi.org/10.1146/annurev.an.19.100190.002033.

Srivastava, Ravi. 2020. "COVID-19 and Circular Migration in India." *Review of Agrarian Studies* 10 (1): 164–80.

Zaloom, Caitlin. 2019. *Indebted: How Families Make College Work at Any Cost*. Princeton: Princeton University Press.

CHAPTER 15

Crisis as Preexisting Condition

Yemen Between Cholera, Coronavirus, and Starvation

Nathalie Peutz

On May 20, 2020, a Yemeni woman living near Aden notified me that she and her daughter had contracted the "virus." Accompanying Salma's WhatsApp message were photographs of her COVID-stricken daughter and of her own right hand bandaged with an intravenous cannula, evidence that she had received medical treatment of some kind. An unknown number of COVID-inflicted persons in Yemen have not been and will not be as fortunate as Salma and her daughter were. Even before the outbreak of the coronavirus pandemic in Yemen, the country's health facilities were gutted. More than five years of armed conflict, economic collapse, water scarcity, and a population weakened by hunger and disease had set the stage for the novel coronavirus to explode. Salma later told me that nearly everyone in her family had been infected. Suffering from high fevers and extreme exhaustion, they self-administered intravenous fluids that her medically connected brother had purchased from a pharmacy. Hospitals were turning people away. In their neighborhood, and across Aden, elderly people were dying, as many as fifty to sixty a day, Salma estimated, during the end of Ramadan.[1]

I first met Salma and her daughter in Djibouti's Markazi camp for refugees from Yemen, where she and her family had landed after fleeing the battle between the Houthi militia and pro-government forces in Aden in April 2015.[2] Like many of the refugees I met in Markazi, Salma had sought to escape not only the war but also the tribalism, corruption, and discrimination she had suffered in Yemen (Peutz 2019). For four years she lived in a makeshift shelter on an arid plain in northern Djibouti hoping for third-country resettlement and a "future" for her daughter. But after securing a divorce from her abusive husband, she was pressured by her natal family to return to Yemen. In 2019, Salma and her daughter traveled back to Aden by cattle boat chaperoned by another returning family that had become "exhausted" (*ta'bān*) by life in the camp. Worn down by daily stressors and indignities, hundreds of refugees have returned from Djibouti to Yemen despite the country's ongoing conflict and food insecurity. "In Yemen, people die quickly; here, we die slowly," was a common refrain. "People say if we had stayed in Yemen," Salma told me in October 2017, "we may have died of a bullet, but it would have been immediate. When we came to Djibouti, we died slowly. [Here,] we die every day, every day, every day." This sense of dying slowly — day-by-day or over and over again — is exacerbated during the summer months when the heat index exceeds 40°C (104°F) and hot sandstorms whip through the tents. "It is because of these difficulties that many refugees returned to Yemen," a refugee from Taiz told me in March 2018, "preferring a quick death over a slow death."

When COVID kills, it kills quickly. Not as rapidly as cluster bombs or ballistic missiles, but quicker than starvation, one of Yemen's many

---

1. Government burial statistics indicate that deaths in Aden had reached up to eighty per day in late May, compared to an average of ten deaths per day before the outbreak (Hincks 2020). Data from Yemen's Ministry of Public Health and Population for the southern governorates shows that the highest number of confirmed COVID cases and deaths in 2020 occurred during epidemiological weeks twenty-three and twenty-four (May 31–June 13), following Ramadan (GoY and WHO 2020).

2. I visited the camp ten times between December 2016 and January 2020, interviewing members of more than one hundred households and maintaining close connections with several families. Personal communications and accounts are drawn from this fieldwork.

overlapping calamities. For years the country has been in the grip of what the United Nations (UN) has been calling the world's "worst humanitarian crisis." By the end of 2020, more than twenty-four million Yemenis — 80 percent of its population — required humanitarian assistance or protection. 45 percent of the population did not have enough food to eat and were at high risk of acute malnutrition or starvation (OCHA 2020b). And, in 2020 alone, authorities reported 235,000 suspected cases of cholera across the country (UNICEF 2020). In comparison with these figures, and contrary to expectations, the number of laboratory-confirmed COVID cases in Yemen has been astonishingly low: 2,101 cases and 611 deaths at the end of 2020 (OCHA 2021). So low, indeed, that the COVID situation in Yemen attracted scant media attention internationally. Yet, it is exactly these low numbers that are indicative of both widespread silent (asymptomatic) spread and a hidden (underreported, undertested) epidemic in a country already incapacitated by multiple critical situations.

This chapter reflects on the immeasurable impact of the SARS-CoV-2 pandemic in a setting where COVID represents just one of many acute threats to people's livelihoods and lives. Not only has the spread of COVID in Yemen been overshadowed by the country's other crises, but it also appears to have been eclipsed in some Yemenis' experiences by both "quick death" exacted through explosions and "slow death" induced by hunger and despair.[3] When I asked Salma whether she had been afraid during her COVID illness, she said she had feared for her daughter but not for herself. "Afraid of the virus? If I had died, it would be [like] heaven!" she sighed, depressed by the ongoing toll of everyday day life in war-torn Yemen where there is "no water, no electricity, no food, no future — no hope" (pers. comm., November 10, 2020). Challenging the Western media's framing of the pandemic as a singularly disruptive or exceptional event — a planetary-wide crisis — this chapter discusses its emergence and representation in a context where crisis is a preexisting

---

3. "Slow death," as my interlocutors define it, is akin to the "slow violence" that "occurs gradually and out of sight" (Nixon 2011, 2) and may result from the kind of long-term environmental catastrophes Nixon describes. However, it may also result from structural conditions such as poverty and inadequate health care. In contrast to "deaths of despair" (Case and Deaton 2020), slow death is not associated principally with suicide or substance abuse. An emic term, "slow death" combines aspects of both "slow violence" and "deaths of despair" but with a focus on the embodied experience of vulnerability.

condition that renders entire populations vulnerable to the pandemic's viral effects. Yet, despite the majority of Yemen's population being at high risk for COVID on account of the country's chronic stressors, the severity of the pandemic is masked by the fact that COVID is but one of many untimely ways to die. At the same time, COVID has not been killing Yemenis "quickly" enough for the country to attract the international attention and aid it would need to avert a looming famine. In this sense — and like crisis narratives in general — our focus on the pandemic creates a "blind spot, or a distinction, which makes certain things visible and others invisible" (Roitman 2013, 40). Exposing structural inequalities across the globe, the pandemic has obscured other epidemics and crises that are contemporaneous with it. In fragile contexts, as in Yemen, this obscuration may result in inadequate political decisions or humanitarian assistance and even more fatalities.

Crisis within a Crisis

Crisis is commonly perceived in the Western tradition as a critical turning point or as a traumatic but temporary rupture in the "normal" order of things. Crisis is often depicted as a bounded, abnormal event — the 1962 Cuban Missile Crisis, the 2001–2 Argentine crisis, the 2007–9 global financial crisis, the 2015 refugee crisis in Europe — even though some events are of such magnitude (the climate crisis) that they call into question "the temporality of crisis itself" (Masco 2017, S72). Crisis, or the narrative of crisis, can also be deployed politically and discursively to justify military and humanitarian interventions (Fassin and Pandolfi 2013) as well as to engender certain kinds of critique (Roitman 2013). The COVID pandemic obtains elements of "crisis" in that it has sparked what is already now being viewed as a critical turning point in our relationship to technology, work, consumption, and the social. It is also conceived (perhaps optimistically) as a bounded, temporary disorder in the sense that, for those in confinement, it "constitutes a liminal instance" during which "time is perceived as 'stagnant,' 'stopped,' 'frozen'" (Visacovsky 2017, 9, 12). Those whose lives have not been shattered may expect some return to the "normal" once so-called herd immunity is reached. Yet, as Henrik Vigh (2008, 5) notes, for many marginalized, ill, and poor people around the world, "crisis is endemic rather than episodic and cannot be delineated as an aberrant moment of chaos or a period of decisive change." In this context, crisis is not a temporary disorder but a chronic condition resulting from "persistent instability and uncertainty" (Vigh 2008, 18). This does not mean that people become inured to crisis. Yet, for people like Salma and other refugees, "whose lives are trapped in situations of structural, social and existential crisis" (Vigh 2008, 21), it can be difficult to envision a future beyond the seemingly stagnant present.

The SARS-CoV-2 pandemic is but the most recent of numerous upheavals afflicting Yemen. Even before its emergence, Yemen was one of the poorest and hungriest nations in the world. When war erupted in March 2015, over half of Yemen's population was living below the poverty line, over 40 percent was malnourished, and more than 60 percent required humanitarian assistance to meet the daily basic needs (WFP 2014). Moreover, the country was beleaguered by corruption, political instability, Sunni militant and Shia rebel forces, and deep-seated tensions between the north and the south. In late 2014, an Islamic political and armed movement called Ansar Allah (often referred to as "Houthis") took control of Yemen's capital Sanaa and, in February 2015, announced a full government takeover. After fleeing to the southern city of Aden, Yemen's transitional president Abd Rabbuh Mansur Hadi called for international support to restore his government. Meanwhile, the Zaydi (Shia) Houthis expanded their control into the predominantly Sunni southern governorates. On March 26, 2015, a day after Houthi forces reached the outskirts of Aden, Saudi Arabia and a coalition of Sunni Arab nations launched a full-scale military campaign in Yemen. The Saudi-led coalition — which received logistical and intelligence support from the United States (US) and the United Kingdom — expected a quick victory. Instead, the war between the Saudi-backed, internationally recognized government and the Iranian-aligned Houthi Supreme Revolutionary Committee is ongoing, fractured into multiple conflicts across numerous fronts.

Yemeni civilians have borne the brunt of this prolonged war. Five years into the conflict(s), more than 112,000 Yemenis had been killed or injured by airstrikes, armed clashes, and shelling (ACLED n.d.). These conservative estimates do not include the thousands of civilian deaths from hunger, communicable diseases, and other indirect causes. The war has also been a major driver of displacement. Since March 2015, approximately four million Yemenis — more than 10 percent of the population — have been internally displaced in temporary settlements throughout the country. Far fewer were able to flee Yemen due to the closure of the country's airports, visa restrictions, and the expense of travel. Still, in the first two years of the war, more than 38,000 Yemenis took boats to Djibouti from where they embarked to places such as Egypt, Malaysia, Europe, and the US (UNHCR 2018) — if they were lucky enough to enter the latter before the Trump administration instituted the "Muslim Ban" (Executive Order 13769). As one of the few countries to grant Yemenis refugee status on a prima facie basis, Djibouti established the world's only camp for refugees from Yemen, Markazi camp, which has housed between 1,200 and 3,000 refugees over the past six years. The camp is located just south of the small coastal port of Obock, where every year thousands of Ethiopian migrants congregate to be smuggled across the Red Sea to Yemen and, eventually, to Saudi Arabia in search of work.

In what follows I discuss three waves of epidemics sweeping through Yemen during the past five years — cholera, starvation, and COVID — with a particular eye to the Yemeni refugees and Ethiopian migrants languishing in Djibouti. These are not the only afflictions plaguing Yemen, but each of these has been cast in the superlative: the world's largest cholera outbreak, the world's largest food security emergency, and the world's highest case fatality rate for COVID. Here, the affective language of crisis is invoked to draw international attention and mobilize humanitarian support, even though each new epidemic diverts attention from the preceding (though persisting) one. Neither temporally nor spatially distinct, these crises within a crisis — "the world's worst humanitarian crisis" — underscore the connections between mobile bodies, pathogens, and diseases in a transnational setting. They also show why, in places where crisis is endemic, the SARS-CoV-2 pandemic may not be the worst, and is certainly not the only, present-day scourge.

Cholera

During my first visit to Markazi camp in December 2016, I came down with amoebic dysentery. The camp's Yemeni doctor who treated me was distracted and distressed by news of a cholera outbreak in his natal village near Taiz. His brother, whose daughter had contracted the illness, thought the outbreak had started at school — thus threatening nearly every household in the village. Visibly shaken, the doctor worried about an impending catastrophe (*kāritha*). "We have two governments [the Houthi government in Sanaa and the Hadi government in Aden] and no one is doing anything! What other country has two governments?" he railed. Administering medical advice through WhatsApp, the doctor instructed his brother to gather together the village's "educated" residents to teach them how to implement quarantine measures. Without medicines or functioning public hospitals, the "citizens" (*muwāṭinīn*) were left to fend for themselves, he said.

Yet by this point Médecins Sans Frontières (MSF) and other humanitarian agencies working in Yemen were quite aware of the cholera outbreak in northern Yemen. Beginning in Sanaa in September 2016, the first wave lasted until April 2017, to be followed immediately by a larger wave that swept through the entire country (Al-Mekhlafi 2018). By September 2017, the cholera epidemic had surged to 750,000 cases and soon exceeded the approximately 800,000 cholera cases recorded in the wake of the 2010 earthquake in Haiti (Snyder 2017). Yemen's cholera outbreak thus became the largest and fastest-growing cholera epidemic since the World Health Organization (WHO) began recording cholera cases in 1949. And the outbreak continued. By early 2018, it had exceeded one million cases, waning a little and then surging again in September 2018 and April 2019 (Federspiel and Ali 2018). By the end of December 2019, as news of SARS-CoV-2 was beginning to emerge, Yemen had suffered nearly 2.2 million cases of cholera and 3,750 deaths (far exceeding the 9,500 cases counted in Somalia and 350 in Sudan during this same period) (WHO 2019). And yet, the case fatality rate for cholera in Yemen was unusually low — 0.17 percent compared to 0.51 percent in Somalia and 3.25 percent in Sudan — a likely indicator that Yemenis, especially children, were dying at home, untreated, and uncounted (Snyder 2017).

Continuing into 2021, Yemen's cholera outbreak was aggravated if not catalyzed by the war. Airstrikes have destroyed Yemen's water, sanitation, and hygiene infrastructure. By 2017, half of the country lacked access to safe drinking water or sanitation. Moreover, with only 50 percent of its hospitals fully functioning, Yemen did not have targeted response teams or an oral vaccination program in place until September 2017, when the outbreak had already reached its peak (Spiegel et al. 2018). Recurring Saudi-led blockades and Houthi obstructions have disrupted Yemen's food and aid supply, hampering humanitarian relief efforts. Refugees living in Djibouti's Markazi camp were relieved to have escaped their villages where they had been worried about contracting cholera, with garbage rotting in the street and even in heaps in the produce markets. "Here [in the camp], my children can play outside," Amina, a woman from another village outside of Taiz, told me shortly after her arrival in the fall of 2017. "We don't have to worry about cholera or bombs."

But Amina's relief would soon be shaken by a cholera outbreak right outside the camp's perimeter. In June 2018, tens of Ethiopian migrants traversing Djibouti's desert en route to Obock, and from there to the Arabian Peninsula, died of cholera and acute diarrhea. Already, many of the camp's residents, including Salma and Amina, had become accustomed to bundling up their family's leftovers for the young Ethiopians who entered the camp to beg for food. That summer refugees circulated photographs of corpses lying on the road to Obock, some within meters of the camp. Not only was the epidemic not confined to Yemen, but it now became evident that cholera was spreading through and alongside the people moving between the Horn of Africa and Yemen. In January 2019, scientists established on the basis of genomic sequencing that the strain of cholera causing the outbreak in Yemen had been circulating in the Horn of Africa in 2013–14 before entering Yemen in 2016 (Weill et al. 2019). While the study attributes the spread of cholera to Ethiopian migrants, it could have been carried — as it has been historically (Serels 2020) — by other mobile bodies, including the Yemeni refugees returning to their homeland.

Starvation

Although Yemen's cholera epidemic was recognized in the fall of 2017 as the worst cholera outbreak in history, it would soon be eclipsed by reports of the country's near famine. What made the international news now was that Yemenis were not just "going" hungry; they were being pushed into starvation by the Saudi-led blockade. Aid organizations' immediate concern was the Saudis' November 2017 blockade of Yemen's air, sea, and land ports after the Houthis fired a ballistic missile northwards toward the Saudi international airport in Riyadh. Despite a long history of terraced agriculture, Yemen was importing around 90 percent of its commercial and staple food. This full blockade threatened to strangle a country that was now fully reliant on imported food, fuel, and humanitarian aid. Even though many of the ports were reopened to humanitarian assistance within weeks, the blockade caused food and fuel prices to skyrocket. By the end of 2017, Yemen was facing "the world's largest food security emergency" (Oxfam 2017, 4). By January 2018, more than eight million Yemenis were on the brink of starvation (OCHA 2018).

But the November blockade was not a one-time occurrence; rather, it was part of an already ongoing wider "food war" against Yemeni civilians

(Mundy 2018). After initially targeting military and government installations in areas under Houthi control, in August 2015 the coalition shifted to bombing civilian and economic targets, "including water and transport infrastructure, food production and distribution, roads and transports, schools, cultural monuments, clinics and hospitals, fields and flocks" (Mundy 2018, 7). Millions were forced to flee their homes, abandoning sources of local food production. The majority of those who fled across the sea and came to reside in Markazi camp were fishermen whose boats had been destroyed by coalition-fired, US-made munition. This included much of the population of Dhubab, a fishing village north of the strategic Bab al Mandeb strait that was struck multiple times in 2015–16. It also included most of Wahija, where airstrikes in September 2015 killed more than forty villagers attending a wedding party (Al-mosawa and Fahim 2015). Fishermen who remained in the area were prohibited from going out to sea. In addition to destroying local means of production and distribution, the coalition constrained Yemen's food imports by placing restrictions on all container ships delivering cargo through Hodeidah, Yemen's largest Red Sea port, and by closing the Sanaa airport to all commercial flights in August 2016, including to persons in need of medical treatment.

Yemen's "food security emergency" was not, then, simply the result of a lack of food. It was a disaster that was "entirely man-made" (Oxfam 2017, 5). Import restrictions, taxation at multiple checkpoints, and damaged infrastructure increased food and fuel prices significantly at the same time that millions of Yemenis lost their income. In September 2016, the Hadi government relocated the Central Bank of Yemen from Sanaa to Aden, creating a liquidity crisis. It then suspended the government's Social Welfare Fund, which had disbursed monthly cash payments to vulnerable families, and stopped paying the salaries of government employees in Houthi-controlled territories. The devaluation of Yemen's currency further increased the prices of imports, making it that much more difficult for those without salaries to purchase ever more expensive staples. This was the situation before the November 2017 blockade of Yemen's ports, a move that was widely condemned. And by June 2018 it had deteriorated even further when coalition-led forces and Emirati-backed pro-Hadi fighters began aerial attacks and a ground advance on Hodeidah, which the Houthis had captured in 2014. Within two months, as clashes between the coalition and Houthi forces intensified, more than half of Hodeidah's 600,000 residents were displaced (IOM 2018). An all-out battle for the Hodeidah port, through which

70 percent of all commercial imports and aid entered Yemen, threatened to propel the entire country toward famine.

Finally, after more than three years of deafening silence with regard to this US-supported war, the media in the US began to take notice. On October 26, 2018, the *New York Times* published a photograph of 7-year-old Amal Hussain, a Yemeni child emaciated from starvation (Walsh 2018). Her gaunt figure put a human face to the dire situation in Yemen, one that cholera sufferers had not. Three days earlier, UN humanitarian chief Mark Lowcock had warned the UN Security Council that "there is now a clear and present danger of an imminent famine engulfing Yemen: much bigger than anything any professional in this field has encounter[ed] during their working lives" (UN 2018). Aid organizations reported that an estimated 85,000 children under five years of age had died already from malnutrition between April 2015 and October 2018 (BBC 2018). Circulated within weeks of the killing and dismemberment of Saudi Arabian journalist Jamal Khashoggi at the Saudi consulate in Istanbul, the haunting image of Amal Hussain and other starving Yemeni children galvanized public opinion in the US and Europe against their governments' unchecked support for the Saudi regime. On October 27, in response to its readers' requests, the *New York Times* published a list of aid organizations still active in Yemen under the title "How to Help" (Beirne 2018).

The Trump administration came under renewed pressure to answer for US involvement in the war. On October 30, 2018, US Secretary of Defense James Mattis and Secretary of State Michael Pompeo called for a cessation of hostilities and a resumption of peace talks. Even the refugees living in Markazi camp were newly hopeful that the Trump administration would reverse its "Muslim Ban" and begin accepting refugees from Yemen. It was during this period of slight international political will that the UN managed to broker the December 2018 Stockholm Agreement between the warring parties. This cease-fire agreement for the city and ports of Hodeidah and the influx of humanitarian aid that followed helped Yemen avert the imminent famine Lowcock had warned about in October.

But for Amal — and thousands of children like her — it was too late. Discharging her the clinic's doctors referred Amal's family to a more suitable clinic fifteen miles away. But her family could not afford the transport costs. So they brought Amal home to the camp to which they had moved after fleeing from Saada, the Houthi stronghold, to escape the coalition airstrikes. There, in one of Yemen's many camps for internally displaced persons, Amal — whose name in Arabic means *hope* — died of starvation, on the day the *Times* story broke (*The Daily* 2018). Amal may have been gasping her last breath at the very moment that its readers encountering her image were moved to write comments like, "How can I help feed this child?" (Johanna Schulte-Hillen, from Aachen, Germany, October 26, 2018, comment on Nagourney and Slackman 2018).

As for the Stockholm Agreement, its implementation was stalled as both parties disagreed over its terms and continued their airstrikes against one another. As per agreement the United Arab Emirates withdrew the bulk of its forces from Hodeidah in June 2019 but redeployed them in the south of Yemen in support of the Southern Transitional Council (STC), a secessionist group formed in May 2017. Escalating tensions between the Emirati-backed STC secessionists and Saudi-backed Hadi loyalists nearly erupted into a civil war within a civil war when the STC took control of Aden and parts of other southern governorates in August 2019. Finally, in November 2019 Saudi Arabia brokered the Riyadh Agreement, a power-sharing agreement between Hadi and the STC. But, again, the two sides to the agreement disagreed on the process and the sequencing of the deal. Few steps had been achieved before April 26, 2020, when the STC declared "self-rule" in Aden and the southern governorates. Three days later, the first cases of COVID were detected in Aden.

COVID

During my latest visit to Markazi camp in January 2020, one of the residents told me about a twenty-day-long "bone-breaking" fever he had recently suffered: "It's not a normal fever. ... It's new here and I think it came from Ethiopia or something. All of Djibouti [the capital] is sick." "It's an epidemic there," a bystander confirmed, drawing my attention to a small poster affixed to the walls of the food distribution center warning of an outbreak of dengue fever. The poster advised the camp's inhabitants to cover their skin, apply mosquito repellent (as if this was available), and discard or keep away from stagnant water. As we scrutinized the poster, the still-recovering refugee said something that only caught my attention a year later, in January 2021, when I relistened to our recorded conversation. Disputing the proclamations that this fever was mosquito-borne, the man explained: "When I went to Djibouti [city], I stayed one day. So we had someone who came from Yemen by airplane. He had the fever. We took him to the emergency [room], me and another guy. They gave him a shot. He got better. But when we came back here [to Obock], the both of us, ... everyone got sick."

We may never know when the coronavirus first reached Djibouti, or Yemen — or whether there is any possibility that this unusual fever "epidemic" in Djibouti city could have been an early, undetected outbreak of COVID. Djibouti confirmed its first case on March 17, 2020, brought into the country by a member of the Spanish special forces three days earlier. Although the government closed its ports and borders on March 18 and imposed a nationwide lockdown on March 23, community transmission was already occurring (Elhakim, Tourab, and Zouiten 2020). Within a month, Djibouti had the highest prevalence of confirmed COVID cases in Africa, though it was also conducting the most per capita tests on the continent (Aljazeera 2020). Djibouti's three neighbors all confirmed their first cases in the same month — Ethiopia on March 13, Eritrea on March 21, and Somaliland on March 31 — all brought into their territories through air travel. It is evident, however, that the virus had already been circulating in the region (Serels 2020).

The commencement and scale of Yemen's coronavirus outbreak is even less certain. Yemen's internationally recognized government in Aden reported the country's first laboratory-confirmed case of COVID on April 10, 2020: the patient, a port official in the southern region of Hadramawt. So combustible was the situation in Yemen that Saudi Arabia declared a unilateral two-week cease-fire on April 8, a day after this man was first tested (BBC 2020). (The coalition resumed its airstrikes on Houthi forces the following week.) Two weeks passed before additional cases were confirmed: five, in Aden, on April 29. That same day, the STC announced a seventy-two-hour curfew in Aden and the closure of mosques, restaurants, and *qāt* (a mild narcotic) markets for at least two weeks (Mukhashaf and Ghobari 2020).[4] In Yemen's southern and eastern governorates, the internationally recognized Hadi government instituted a COVID surveillance system aided by rapid response teams. Aid agencies activated community-based and mass-media awareness campaigns and supplied medical and personal protective equipment from abroad. Even so, by the end of May, authorities confirmed 327 infections

---

4. In late July 2020, the STC abandoned its position of self-rule to implement the stalled 2019 Riyadh Agreement. Talks broke down again a month later. In December 2020, the two sides began implementing the power-sharing agreement and established a new cabinet.

across Yemen, including 81 COVID deaths (OCHA 2020a). What these numbers do not reveal was the surge of COVID-like illnesses and excess deaths in Aden and other Yemeni cities that month. On May 11, the Hadi government's coronavirus committee declared Aden an "infested city" and barred movement from Aden to other regions (Ghobari 2020). Satellite images of burial activity across cemeteries in the governorate of Aden reveal significant excess mortality in April to July 2020 (Koum Besson et al. 2020). In the Houthi-controlled northwest, the authorities tried to suppress the extent of the outbreak. After reporting the first case of COVID in Sanaa on May 4 — a Somali man found dead in a hotel — and three more infections that month, the Houthi authorities stopped releasing numbers of the cases and deaths in the territories under their control. Yet, leaked videos of nighttime burials performed by grave diggers wearing protective gear indicated that the pandemic was exploding in northern Yemen, too (Michael 2020). On June 18, 2020, the London School of Hygiene and Tropical Medicine estimated that up to one million Yemenis — a thirtieth of the population — had been already infected (UK Government 2020).

What is clear from the epidemiological data is that the first wave of the epidemic had peaked in Yemen's southern and eastern governorates by September 2020, with the numbers of confirmed cases declining through the end of the year (GoY and WHO 2020). The second wave hit Yemen in March 2021 — just as it was entering its seventh year of war — and lasted through May, once again overwhelming the country's debilitated medical facilities. Yemen received its first batch of vaccines on March 31, 2021: 360,000 AstraZeneca doses of the measly 1.9 million doses that it is due to receive in 2021 through COVAX (HRW 2021).[5] Yet, the country's testing capacity and data collection remains woefully inadequate. The statistics compiled by the Yemen government do not include data from the northwest regions controlled by the Houthi interim authority, which as of September 2021 continues to withhold information ("Yemen receives its third batch" 2021). And Yemen's four million

---

5. Yemen's total allocation through COVAX is fourteen million doses, sufficient to vaccinate all persons over sixty-five, 23 percent of its total population (Nasser and Zakham 2021). In June 2021, the first ten thousand doses arrived in Sanaa for use in the Houthi-controlled territories, home to the majority of Yemen's population (Barrington 2021). By September 2021, when Yemen was in the midst of its third wave, only 0.1 percent of its population had been fully vaccinated (UNFPA 2021).

internally displaced people, many of whom live in crowded camps where they are especially vulnerable to COVID, have little access to testing, let alone vaccines. Especially striking is that, in contrast to the country's unusually low case fatality rate for cholera, its case fatality rate for COVID remains extraordinarily high. Nearly one-third (29.08 percent) of all Yemenis who tested positive in 2020 died, making Yemen the country with the highest COVID case fatality rate in the world.[6] This suggests that the virus has been spreading undetected as well as underreported; that only people in critical condition are seeking medical treatment at clinics or hospitals; and that many more already vulnerable Yemenis are suffering, if not dying, at home (Hincks 2020; Oxfam 2021).

Reports from humanitarian organizations, journalists, and social media corroborate these deductions. Although SARS-CoV-2 appears to have swept through much of Yemen in the spring of 2020, the majority of infected patients could not or would not access medical care. When doctors in Aden started falling ill and dying, most hospitals closed their doors or refused to accept patients with respiratory illnesses. One hospital was designated as an official COVID treatment center, but it lacked the necessary staff, beds, and equipment until an MSF team arrived in May (Al-Maghafi 2021). In Sanaa, where the medical system was already overrun, fear of hospitals as sites of infection and fear of being stigmatized by the community if one tested positive for COVID inhibited people from seeking medical attention (MSF 2020). And across Yemen, rumors spread through social media that doctors were injecting patients with the virus or that they were euthanizing COVID patients by lethal injection. Such theories are reflected in the following June 2020 tweets, first from a male journalist based in front-line Taiz and then a response from a woman in the southern region of Hadramawt:

> In #Yarim [in northern Yemen], one patient was admitted with a #cold to a clinic, and when one of the patient's relatives went to bring a sum of money to pay the remainder of the costs of the tests, he returned to find the patient a lifeless body. … The tribes and the blood

---

6. By July 15, 2021, Yemen's case fatality rate had dropped to 19.62 percent, but was still the highest worldwide, among countries with over 1,000 reported cases (on the reasons for this, see Noushad and Al-Saqqaf 2021). By comparison, Sudan and Syria had a case fatality rate then of 7.54 and 7.37, respectively (Statista 2021). As of November 2021, the COVID death rate in Yemen remains the highest in the world.

relatives rallied together and the clinic closed after it became clear that a doctor was involved in killing the patient with a poisonous injection … on the basis that he had #corona (Alameri 2020).
Unfortunately, this talk is all over the republic, even here in Mukalla [in southern Yemen] we have the same cases that they inject them with something and they die so that they are on the corona death list. (Emeli 2020)

Misinformation and xenophobia spread alongside the virus. In mid-March 2020, before any cases of COVID were officially detected in Yemen, several people in Taiz insisted that the virus was either a "Christian" or an Asian disease that would never reach (Muslim) Yemen or that it was part of a biological warfare program aimed against China (Yemen Shabab TV 2020). Six months later, even after Yemen's first wave had peaked, various residents in Sanaa's Old City maintained that there was no coronavirus in Yemen (Crawford 2020). Coronavirus denialism in Sanaa and other northern governorates is likely sustained by the lack of mandated hygiene protections and the suppression of official statistics in the Houthi-controlled territories. A spokesman for the Houthi health ministry told a reporter in June 2020 that their reason for not releasing COVID numbers is "because such publicity has a heavy and terrifying toll on people's psychological health" (Michael 2020). Ostensibly worried about their population's mental health — or, as some Yemenis suspect, worried about keeping their war economy running and their fighters from absconding — Houthi officials have both spread disinformation and allowed conspiracy rumors to proliferate (HRW 2021). Predictably, some Houthi supporters blamed "America" for spreading SARS-CoV-2: in this view, "corona" is another weapon in the US-supported, Saudi-led "siege" of Yemen and "genocide" of its people (see, for example, Mohammad 2020).

As in other countries, migrants and refugees in Yemen have been stigmatized as disease transmitters. In April 2020, Houthi fighters rounded up thousands of Saudi-bound Ethiopian migrants from a temporary settlement area near the Yemeni-Saudi border on the pretext that they were carrying the coronavirus. As the Houthis expelled the Ethiopians across the Saudi border by shooting at them, Saudi border guards fired at them from the other side for entering illegally. Thousands of surviving migrants became stranded in the mountains between Yemen and Saudi Arabia. Those who entered Saudi Arabia were detained in inhumane conditions and eventually deported to Ethiopia

(HRW 2020a). Meanwhile, between May and December 2020, more than 6,000 Ethiopian migrants stranded in Yemen returned to Djibouti where, due to border restrictions, many were stranded once again (IOM 2020). In Yemen, this deadly stigma may have found fertile ground owing to previous narratives of Ethiopian migrants carrying cholera — if not by the convenient detection of northern Yemen's "first" COVID case in the body of a Somali refugee.

As scarce as the data is about the spread of SARS-CoV-2 in Yemen in 2020 and through the first half of 2021, we know even less about the trajectory of the virus in the months and years ahead. Yemen may well experience an even more deadly COVID outbreak before vaccinations become widely available to its relatively young population. Even before the country's second wave, however, many Yemenis appeared to have become resigned to the inevitable spread of the disease. One detects this in the gallows humor circulating via social media, quips that underscore Yemenis' resilience in the face of chronic crisis, the government's feeble response, and the recognition of another "wave" — soaring food insecurity — to come:

> The #coronavirus forced Italy to close the Vatican, forced America to close Disneyland, and forced Saudi Arabia to close the Grand Mosque in Mecca, but it was not able to force #Yemen to close the Qat markets!! (Naif 2020)
> The country in the world that dealt best with #corona is #Yemen. #Corona arrived, found the health system dead … and died along with it so we are delivered from #corona. (Albarakani 2020)
> The new corona virus causes colic. | Britain: stay tuned for the 24-hour curfew | Europe: stay tuned for the suspension of all flights | Yemen: stay tuned for the rise in the price of yogurt. (Al Fathli 2020)

An even better indication of Yemeni resignation — and resilience — in the face of yet another epidemic in the context of chronic crisis is when people do not single out the coronavirus by name. In the coastal villages from which many of the Markazi refugees fled, Yemenis refer to the infection that raged through their communities as "the passing one" (*al-gāzi'a*): a scourge, like many others, that passes to and through every body. An Adeni refugee explained that *al-gāzi'a* connotes an unfamiliar disease, microbes, and other "invisible creatures" carried along by insalubrious winds. The "visible" form of this, he explained, were the "unfamiliar, weak, and frightened" Oromo migrants passing through on their way to Yemen (WhatsApp message to author, January 29, 2021).

Conclusion

When refugees living in the Markazi camp distinguish between "quick" and "slow" deaths, they know, of course, that all manners of death occur on both sides of the sea. Many have ready examples of how their own family members have died "quickly" in Yemen, including those who had sought refuge in Markazi. A thirty-three-year-old engineer from Wahija lost his mother in the wedding strike — she had returned from Markazi to Yemen days before the celebration. A widow's twenty-one-year-old son, tired of languishing in the camp and despairing over his nonexistent "future" there, returned to Aden and enlisted with "the resistance" (government forces) to earn a salary. Within weeks of completing his training, the army vehicle in which he was traveling exploded on its way to the Marib front. Other families experienced "quick" deaths in the confines of the camp. A father suffered a heart attack, his wife and teenaged children thereupon returning to Yemen without him. And then there are people like Salma who returned to Yemen where she continues to feel herself dying slowly, day by day. When "people find themselves caught in prolonged crisis rather than merely moving through it" (Vigh 2008, 8), quick deaths can be merciful. It is the slow deaths — from hunger, trauma, untreated illness, displacement, the absence of any viable future, and the daily annihilation of the soul — that can inflict an even greater anguish.

This Yemeni categorization of death contains both a temporal and a visual dimension. Exceptions notwithstanding, quick deaths are dramatic and eventful. Often, they are publicly visible and enumerated, by the government or the media, such as the deaths resulting from the bombardment of the wedding party in Wahija. The slow deaths that occur in family after family due to chronic crisis are harder to see and count. Yemen's five-year-long cholera outbreak continued into 2021. The official number of cases in 2020 was significantly lower than in 2019, though the fact that Yemenis were avoiding seeking medical assistance from health centers out of concern of contracting COVID means that the true scope of this epidemic is likely to remain hidden. Even more alarming is the renewed threat of imminent famine. Of the sixteen million people expected to go hungry in Yemen in 2021, five million people are in danger of starving to death and 50,000 were already living in famine-like conditions at the start of the year (Lowcock 2021). Yet, whether due to donor fatigue, frustration with Houthi obstructionism, or the country not gaining visibility as a COVID hotspot because of a lack of registered cases, Yemen did not attract the same level of international attention and aid in 2020 as it did, briefly, in 2017 at the peak of the cholera epidemic and in 2018 when it was on the verge of famine (HRW 2020b). In 2020, funding for necessary health programs and humanitarian assistance dropped to a three-year low. Aid agencies received only 50 percent of the donations they required and less than half of what they had received in 2019. As a result, fewer Yemenis are receiving food aid and those who do receive half the calories they used to (OCHA 2021).[7]

Meanwhile, the full threat and impact of the coronavirus pandemic continues to be buried under the weight of Yemen's many other crises, reducing its visibility to the "outside" world — but also within. Disproportionally affecting low-income communities and racial and ethnic minorities, the coronavirus pandemic has exposed the catastrophic effects of socioeconomic inequalities and health disparities even in the world's wealthiest nations. Still, in the Global North people with ready access to vaccinations can anticipate that their lives will, eventually, return to (a new) normal. In places like Yemen, where crisis is a preexisting condition, the coronavirus is just one of many scourges "passing" through. Here, and around the globe, the enduring effects of the SARS-CoV-2 pandemic may not be the quick deaths from COVID but the protracted deaths and invisible suffering of the world's most vulnerable, day after day. It is these slower deaths the world over — the ones that are both multiplied and hidden by the pandemic — that may never be properly counted and accounted for.

Acknowledgements

I began writing this chapter as a Wolfensohn Family Member in the School of Social Science at the Institute for Advanced Study in Princeton, with additional funding from the American Council of Learned

---

7. In March 2021, international donors' pledges for humanitarian aid to Yemen fell short again, by more than 55 percent of the UN request (UN 2021). As of November 2021, this large funding gap has not been met (UNFPA 2021).

Societies (2019–20), and completed it as a Berthold Leibinger Fellow at the American Academy in Berlin (Spring 2021). I am grateful to these institutions for supporting my scholarship and to the New York University Abu Dhabi (NYU Abu Dhabi) for funding my field research. I thank Didier Fassin, Marion Fourcade and my colleagues in the School of Social Science and in the Economy and Society seminar for their generous feedback and warm company during the 2019–20 year, especially as we entered the pandemic. I thank Sara Thabet, student at NYU Abu Dhabi, for research assistance. And I am profoundly grateful to the refugees from Yemen who have shared their experiences with me.

References

ACLED (Armed Conflict Location and Event Data Project). n.d. "Research Hub: War in Yemen." Accessed November 5, 2021. https://acleddata.com/research-hub-war-in-yemen/.

Alameri, Arafat (@Ye2020Alameri). 2020. " في #يريم تم إدخال أحد المرضي #بالزكام إلى أحد المشافي وحينما ذهب أحد أوليا المريض لجلب مبلغ مالي," Twitter, June 5, 2020, 4:18 p.m. https://twitter.com/Ye2020Alameri/status/126891005587 0672898.

Albarakani, Majid (@majedAlbarakani). 2020. " أفضل دولة في العالم تعاملت مع #كورونا #اليمن ... #كورونا وصل و لقى النظام الصحي ميت" Twitter, December 26, 2020, 3:43 p.m. https://twitter.com/majedAlbarakani/status/13428282 929 49348355.

Al Fathli, Ziad (@ziadfathli). 2020. " فايروس كورونا الجديد يسبب المغص بريطانيا ... ترقبوا خطر التجوال على مدار ٢٤ ساعة أوروبا ترقبوا تعليق كافة الرحلات اليمن" Twitter, December 29, 2020, 1:11 a.m. https://twitter.com/Ziadfathli/status/1344 058471713529856.

Aljazeera. 2020. "Coronavirus Surges in Djibouti as Population Ignores Measures." April 24, 2020. https://www.aljazeera.com/news/2020/4/24/coronavirus-surges-in-djibouti-as-population-ignores-measures.

Al-Maghafi, Nawal. 2021. "Yemen: This Doctor Saw COVID Hospital Empty after Fake Death Text." *BBC News*, January 18, 2021. https://www.bbc.com/news/world-middle-east-55563798.

Al-Mekhlafi, Hesham M. 2018. "Yemen in a Time of Cholera: Current Situation and Challenges." *American Journal of Tropical Medicine and Hygiene* 98 (6): 1558–62. https://doi.org/10.4269/ajtmh.17-0811.

Almosawa, Shuaib, and Kareem Fahim. 2015. "Airstrikes in Yemen Hit Wedding Party, Killing Dozens." *New York Times*, September 28, 2015. https://www.nytimes.com/2015/09/29/world/middleeast/airstrikes-in-yemen-hit-wedding-party-killing-dozens.html.

Barrington, Lisa. 2021. "WHO to Start COVID-19 Vaccination in Houthi-Run North Yemen." *Reuters*, June 1, 2021. https://www.reuters.com/world/middle-east/who-start-covid-19-vaccination-houthi-run-north-yemen-2021-06-01/.

BBC News. 2018. "Yemen Crisis: 85,000 Children 'Dead from Malnutrition.'" November 21, 2018. https://www.bbc.com/news/world-middle-east-46261983.

BBC News. 2020. "Yemen 'Faces Nightmare' as First Coronavirus Case Confirmed." April 10, 2020. https://www.bbc.com/news/world-middle-east-52249624.

Beirne, Aodhan. 2018. "Yemen's Humanitarian Crisis: How to Help." *New York Times*, October 27, 2018. https://www.nytimes.com/2018/10/27/world/middleeast/yemen-how-to-help.html.

Case, Anne, and Angus Deaton. 2020. *Deaths of Despair and the Future of Capitalism*. Princeton: Princeton University Press.

Crawford, Alex. 2020. "Coronavirus: Yemen in Denial about COVID-19 — and Worse Still, there's a Fog of Mystery over How Many Are Dying." *Sky News*, September 18, 2020. https://news.sky.com/story/coronavirus-yemen-is-in-denial-about-covid-19-and-worse-still-theres-a-fog-of-mystery-over-how-many-are-dying-12073435.

Elhakim, Mohamed, Saleh B. Tourab, and Ahmed Zouiten. 2020. "COVID-19 Pandemic in Djibouti: Epidemiology and the Response Strategy Followed to Contain the Virus during the First Two Months, 17 March to 16 May 2020." *PLoS ONE* 15 (12): e0243698. https://doi.org/10.1371/journal.pone.0243698.

Emeli 296-02141 (@Emeli_6). 2020. "الكلام للأسف في جميع انحاء الجمهوريه حتى عندنا في المكلا نفس الحالات يحقنونها بشي و يموتو عشان و يكونو بلائحة" Twitter, June 5, 2020 (suspended account, accessed January 17, 2021). https://twitter.com/Emeli_6/status/1268933066417999874.

Fassin, Didier, and Mariella Pandolfi, eds. 2013. *Contemporary States of Emergency: The Politics of Military and Humanitarian Interventions*. New York: Zone Books.

Federspiel, Frederik, and Mohammad Ali. 2018. "The Cholera Outbreak in Yemen: Lessons Learned and Way Forward." *BMC Public Health* 18 (1): 1338. https://doi.org/10.1186/s12889-018-6227-6.

Ghobari, Mohammed. 2020. "Yemen Declares Aden an 'Infested' City as Coronavirus Spreads, Clashes Erupt." *Reuters*, May 11, 2020. https://www.reuters.com/article/us-health-coronavirus-yemen/yemen-declares-aden-an-infested-city-as-coronavirus-spreads-clashes-erupt-idUSKBN22N07K.

GoY (Government of Yemen) and WHO (World Health Organization). 2020. "Epi Situation Report of COVID-19 2020/Yemen." COVID-19 Surveillance Team, December 22, 2020. https://reliefweb.int/report/yemen/epi-situation-report-covid-19-2020-yemen-covid-19-surveillance-team.

Hincks, Joseph. 2020. "Yemen Officially Has One of the Middle East's Lowest COVID-19 Counts: In Reality, the Virus Is Spreading Unseen and Unchecked." *Time*, May 28, 2020. https://time.com/5843732/yemen-covid19-invisible-crisis/.

HRW (Human Rights Watch). 2020a. "Yemen: Houthis Kill, Expel Ethiopian Migrants." Human Rights Watch, August 13, 2020. https://www.hrw.org/news/2020/08/13/yemen-houthis-kill-expel-ethiopian-migrants.

HRW. 2020b. "Deadly Consequences: Obstruction of Aid in Yemen During COVID." Human Rights Watch, September 14, 2020. https://www.hrw.org/report/2020/09/14/deadly-consequences/obstruction-aid-yemen-during-covid-19.

HRW. 2021. "Yemen: Houthis Risk Civilians' Health in COVID-19." Human Rights Watch, June 1, 2021. https://www.hrw.org/news/2021/06/01/yemen-houthis-risk-civilians-health-COVID.

IOM (International Organization for Migration). 2018. "Yemen: Hudaydah Displaced Population Now an Estimated 336,846." International Organization for Migration, August 17, 2018. https://www.iom.int/news/yemen-hudaydah-displaced-population-now-estimated-336846.

IOM. 2020. "Ethiopian Migrants Returning from Yemen to Djibouti: A Qualitative Study." IOM Djibouti, October 1, 2020. https://migration.iom.int/reports/ethiopian-migrants-returning-yemen-djibouti-qualitative-study.

Koum Besson, Emilie, Andy Norris, Abdullah S. Bin Ghouth, Terri Freemantle, Mervat Alhaffar, Yolanda Vazquez, Chris Reeve, Patrick J. Curran, and Francesco Checchi. 2020. "Excess Mortality during the

COVID-19 Pandemic: A Geospatial and Statistical Analysis in Aden Governorate, Yemen." *BMJ Global Health* 6 (3): e004564. http://dx.doi.org/10.1136/bmjgh-2020-004564.

Lowcock, Mark. 2021. "Briefing to the Security Council on the Humanitarian Situation in Yemen." UN Office for the Coordination of Humanitarian Affairs, January 14, 2021. https://reliefweb.int/sites/reliefweb.int/files/resources/210114_Yemen_USG%20SECCO%20statement%20_FINAL.pdf.

Masco, Joseph. 2017. "The Crisis in Crisis." *Current Anthropology* 58 (S15): S65–S76. https://doi.org/10.1086/688695.

Michael, Maggie. 2020. "Yemen's Rebels Crack Down as COVID-19 and Rumors Spread." *AP News*, June 9, 2020. https://apnews.com/article/677a1fc12d864cd37eea57e5f71614a2.

Mohammad, Yahya (@yaayha2013). 2020. " جريمة إبادة جماعية بحق الشعب اليمني ترتكبها #أمريكا والدول المتحالفة في العدوان على #اليمن فأمريكا وراء نشر فيروس #كورونا" Twitter, June 13, 2020, 12:06 a.m. https://twitter.com/yaaahya2013/status/1271927072311644165.

MSF (Médecins Sans Frontières). 2020. "As COVID-19 Spreads, Fear Drives People away from Hospitals in Yemen." Médecins Sans Frontières, July 9, 2020. https://www.msf.org/covid-19-spreads-fear-drives-people-away-hospitals-yemen.

Mukhashaf, Mohammad, and Mohammad Ghobari. 2020. "Yemen Records Multiple Coronavirus Cases for First Time; U.N. Fears More." *Reuters*, April 29, 2020. https://www.reuters.com/article/us-health-coronavirus-yemen-idUSKBN22B2CJ.

Mundy, Martha. 2018. "Strategies of the Coalition in the Yemen War: Aerial Bombardment and Food War." World Peace Foundation, October 9, 2018. https://sites.tufts.edu/wpf/files/2018/10/Strategies-of-Coalition-in-Yemen-War-Final-20181005-1.pdf.

Nagourney, Eric, and Michael Slackman. 2018. "Why We Are Publishing Haunting Photos of Emaciated Yemeni Children." *New York Times*, October 26, 2018. https://www.nytimes.com/2018/10/26/reader-center/yemen-photos-starvation.html#commentsContainer.

Naif, Anas bin (@AnasBnNaif). 2020. " فيروس #كورونا أجبر إيطاليا تقفل الفاتيكان وأجبر امريكا تقفل ديزني لاند وأجبر السعودية تقفل الحرم المكي" Twitter, May 9, 2020. https://twitter.com/AnasBnNaif/status/1259205432343760897.

Nasser, Abdullah, and Fathiah Zakham. 2021. "A Strategy for SARS-CoV-2 Vaccination in Yemen." *Lancet* 397 (10291): P2247. https://doi.org/10.1016/S0140-6736(21)01016-3.

New York Times. 2018. "The Photo of the Yemeni Girl." *The Daily* (podcast), December 7, 2018. https://www.nytimes.com/2018/12/07/podcasts/the-daily/yemen-saudi-arabia-amal-hussain-photo.html.

Nixon, Rob. 2011. *Slow Violence and the Environmentalism of the Poor*. Cambridge, MA: Harvard University Press.

Noushad, Mohammed, and Inas Shakeeb Al-Saqqaf. 2021. "COVID-19 Case Fatality Rates can be Highly Misleading in Resource-Poor and Fragile Nations: The Case of Yemen." *Clinical Microbiology and Infection* 27 (4): P509–510. https://doi.org/10.1016/j.cmi.2021.01.002.

OCHA (Office for the Coordination of Humanitarian Affairs). 2018. "Yemen Humanitarian Bulletin, Issue 30." January 28, 2018. https://reliefweb.int/report/yemen/yemen-humanitarian-bulletin-issue-30-28-january-2018-enar.

OCHA. 2020a. "Yemen: COVID-19 Preparedness and Response Monthly Report (May 2020)." June 18, 2020. https://reliefweb.int/report/yemen/yemen-covid-19-preparedness-and-response-monthly-report-may-2020-enar.

OCHA. 2020b. "Yemen Situation Report." December 9, 2020. https://reliefweb.int/report/yemen/yemen-situation-report-9-dec-2020.

OCHA. 2021. "Yemen Humanitarian Update, Issue 12 (December 2020)." January 11, 2021. https://reliefweb.int/report/yemen/yemen-humanitarian-update-issue-12-december-2020.

Oxfam. 2017. "Missiles and Food: Yemen's Man-Made Food Security Crisis." Oxfam Briefing Note. https://reliefweb.int/sites/reliefweb.int/files/resources/bn-missiles-food-security-yemen-201217-en.pdf.

Oxfam. 2021. "Yemen at Tipping Point as COVID-19 Second Wave Hits amid Renewed Fighting and Famine Fears." Oxfam, March 23, 2021. https://www.oxfam.org/en/press-releases/yemen-tipping-point-covid-19-second-wave-hits-amid-renewed-fighting-and-famine-fears.

Peutz, Nathalie. 2019. "The Fault of Our Grandfathers: Yemen's Third-Generation Migrants Seeking Refuge from Displacement." *International Journal of Middle East Studies* 51 (3): 357–76. http://dx.doi.org/10.1017/S0020743819000370.

Reuters. 2021. "Yemen Receives Third Batch of COVID-19 Vaccines." September 23, 2021. https://www.reuters.com/business/healthcare-pharmaceuticals/yemen-receives-third-batch-covid-19-vaccines-2021-09-23/.

Roitman, Janet. 2013. *Anti-Crisis*. Durham: Duke University Press.

Serels, Steven. 2020. *Epidemics in the African Red Sea Region: A History of Uneven Disease Exposure*. Rift Valley Institute. https://riftvalley.net/publication/epidemics-african-red-sea-region-history-uneven-disease-exposure.

Snyder, Michael. 2017. "Unanswered Questions from Yemen's Cholera Outbreak." *Outbreak Observatory*, September 28, 2017. Johns Hopkins Bloomsberg School of Public Health. https://www.outbreakobservatory.org/outbreakthursday-1/9/28/2017/unanswered-questions-from-yemens-cholera-outbreak.

Spiegel, Paul, Ruwan Ratnayake, Nora Hellman, Daniele Latagne, Mija Ververs, Moise Ngwa, and Paul Wise. 2018. "Cholera in Yemen: A Case Study of Epidemic Preparedness and Response." Johns Hopkins Center for Humanitarian Health. December. http://hopkinshumanitarianhealth.org/assets/documents/CHOLERA_YEMEN_REPORT_LONG_Low_Res_Dec_4_2018.pdf.

Statista. 2021. "Coronavirus (COVID-19) Death Rate in Countries with Confirmed Deaths and over 1,000 Reported Cases as of July 15, 2021, by Country." https://www.statista.com/statistics/1105914/coronavirus-death-rates-worldwide/.

UK Government. 2020. "UK Calls for Drastic Action in Yemen as Coronavirus Infections Reach One Million." UK Government, June 18, 2020. https://www.gov.uk/government/news/uk-calls-for-drastic-action-in-yemen-as-coronavirus-infections-reach-one-million.

UN (United Nations). 2018. "International Community Must Take Action to Stop Catastrophic Famine in Yemen, Top Humanitarian Affairs Official Tells Security Council." Security Council SC/13550, 8379th meeting, October 23, 2018. https://www.un.org/press/en/2018/sc13550.doc.htm.

UN. 2021. "Yemen Pledging Conference: Severity of Suffering 'Impossible to Overstate' Says Guterres." UN News, March 1, 2021. https://news.un.org/en/story/2021/03/1086042.

UNFPA (United Nations Population Fund). 2021. "UNFPA Response in Yemen: Situation Report." Issue No. 2, July–September 2021. https://reliefweb.int/report/yemen/unfpa-response-yemen-situation-report-issue-2-july-september-2021.

UNHCR (United Nations High Commissioner for Refugees). 2018. "Djibouti — Response to the Yemen Situation." Inter-Agency Operational Update, March 2018. https://reporting.unhcr.org/sites/default/files/Djibouti%20Inter%20Agency%20Operational%20Update%20Response%20to%20Yemen%20Situation%20%5BENG%5D%20-%20March%202018.pdf.

UNICEF (United Nations International Children's Emergency Fund). 2020. "Yemen — 2020 AWD/Cholera Response Dashboard, Weeks 1–52." Updated December 21, 2020. https://reliefweb.int/report/yemen/yemen-2020-awd-cholera-response-dashboard-weeks-1-52.

Vigh, Henrik. 2008. "Crisis and Chronicity: Anthropological Perspectives on Continuous Conflict and Decline." *Ethnos* 73 (1): 5–24. https://doi.org/10.1080/00141840801927509.

Visacovsky, Sergio Eduardo. 2017. "When Time Freezes: Socio-Anthropological Research on Social Crises." *Iberoamericana* 46 (1): 6–16. http://doi.org/10.16993/iberoamericana.103.

Walsh, Declan. 2018. "The Tragedy of Saudi Arabia's War." *New York Times*, October 26, 2018. https://www.nytimes.com/interactive/2018/10/26/world/middleeast/saudi-arabia-war-yemen.html.

Weill, François-Xavier, Daryl Domman, Elisabeth Njamkepo, Abdullrahman A. Almesbahi, Mona Naji, Samar Saeed Nasher, Ankur Rakesh, et al. 2019. "Genomic Insights into the 2016–2017 Cholera Epidemic in Yemen." *Nature*, no. 565: 230–33. https://doi.org/10.1038/s41586-018-0818-3.

WFP (World Food Program). 2014. *Yemen: Comprehensive Food Security Survey (CFSS)*. November 2014. Sana'a: World Food Program. https://documents.wfp.org/stellent/groups/public/documents/ena/wfp269771.pdf.

WHO (Regional Office for the Eastern Mediterranean, World Health Organization). 2019. "Arbovirus Diagnostics." *Weekly Epidemiological Monitor* 12 (50), 1. December 15, 2019. http://www.emro.who.int/pandemic-epidemic-diseases/information-resources/weekly-epidemiological-monitor-2019.html.

Yemen Shabab TV. 2020. "الشعب اليمني يتحدى كورونا ... شوفوا ايش قالوا على الفيروس | اخبار اليوم" YouTube video, 3: 35, March 21, 2020. https://youtu.be/HBZqo9Aha88.

CHAPTER 16

Searching for Life in Times of Pandemic

Federico Neiburg and Handerson Joseph

This chapter deals with how the COVID pandemic becomes embedded in the flow of life of people who inhabit the Haitian diasporic universe, organized by movement within the national territory and foreign routes of mobility. The key to observing these moving landscapes is the Creole expression *chache lavi* ("searching for life"). It unlocks ways of dealing with the materiality of life in extreme poverty and reveals processes of care, even at a distance. The chapter also discusses how, in times of pandemic, *chache lavi* is modulated by memories and practical knowledges acquired over time in the long history of Haitian crises. Thus, Haitian landscapes offer a privileged point of view to observe the dynamics of (im)mobility and care that inform the pandemic as a human experience beyond the Haitian world. We do not seek here anything that resembles a description of the "effects" of the pandemic. Our goal is to use this unprecedented process of uncertain temporality (when we finish this text, it will still be with us) to think about dynamics that structure the Haitian social universe far beyond the pandemic, as well as the relationships between life, care, and (im)mobilities.

During 2019, Haiti's cycles of endemic crises escalated, as several times in history before. Massive demonstrations with barricaded streets protested the high cost of living and demanded the resignation of President Jovenel Moïse, accused of corruption and of being responsible for the country's economic and humanitarian collapse.[1] Inflation had been on the rise since late 2018, accompanied by the devaluation of the national currency, the gourde. In October of that year, the Food and Agriculture Organization of the United Nations (FAO) issued a warning that, with the food crisis, almost 40 percent of the country's population needed urgent intervention in order to survive (IPC 2020). For months on end, people stayed at home for fear of street violence. Before anyone had even heard of SARS-CoV-2, or of "lockdowns," the media and social networks were already complaining that Haiti was paralyzed — *peyi lòk*, literally "a locked country" (see Bulamah forthcoming; and Danticat 2019).

On March 19, 2020, the president reported the first two cases of COVID, declaring a national health emergency, imposing a curfew, closing ports, airports, schools, universities, and places of worship, and banning travel and meetings of more than ten people. Haiti's only land frontier, with the Dominican Republic, was subject to strict restrictions, with an imposed limit to the cross-border comings and goings that feed markets and families. Few celebrated the president's presumed "reestablishment of authority" over the fate of the country. Most criticized him severely. For some, the measures arrived too late, for others, they were precipitated (Haiti Libre 2020a; Popovic 2020). Many people scurried to ensure provisions, further amplifying the instability of the price of basic goods and the turbulence of ongoing street violence (see, for example, Le Nouvelliste 2020d).

The measures were only partially enforced, and then gradually relaxed, after July 2020, but their economic impact began to be felt immediately, deepening the crisis that the country was already facing. Remittances from Haitians in diaspora diminished. The health crisis and the slowing down of the global economy also resulted in the return of a significant number of Haitians who had lived abroad. Between March and September approximately 200,000 Haitian migrants returned, mostly from the Dominican Republic, Brazil, Chile, and the United States (US), resignifying mobility and aggravating the impact of the circulation of the

---

1. In the early morning of July 7, 2021, just as we were finishing the final version of this chapter, President Moïse was assassinated in his Port-au-Prince residence.

virus, as well as the management of the pandemic within the national territory.[2]

A little over eleven million people live in Haiti, at least three million more live abroad. In 2019, 37 percent of the gross national product was composed of remittances of Haitians who live in, or were passing through, other countries. Most of the money is received monthly in quantities that vary between USD 50 and USD 200, making up a substantial portion of a family's income.[3] For decades observers have noted that this Caribbean country has socioeconomic indicators that are very similar to those of countries in sub-Saharan Africa. More than 60 percent of the Haitian population subsists on under USD 60 a month. The centuries-old crises of the rural areas worsened in the last decades, as a result both of environmental degradation and of the opening up of the market to foreign foods; today, 80 percent of food comes from abroad (see PNUD 2014). In cities, particularly in the capital where 2.5 million people live, wage earnings are marginal in personal and family incomes. Most men work in so-called "informality," obtaining their money through temporary jobs, working in the streets in precarious activities or in the services sector. A significant proportion of women works as street vendors, selling cooked food and other items in the streets and markets, and on the roads that link the hinterland to Port-au-Prince and the Haitian commercial capitals outside of the country, such as Santo Domingo, Miami, or Panama.

Restrictions on mobility within the country and in Haitian transnational circuits, including hundreds of thousands of returnees and diminishing remittances, had immediate effects on the existing crisis and on people's suffering, despite the actual number of confirmed cases of COVID remaining relatively low. In July 2021, at the time of writing this chapter, the official numbers from Haiti are of 450 dead and a little over 180,000 infected. In recent months, with the arrival of new variants, the situation seems to have worsened. Nevertheless, even considering obvious underreporting, the number of deaths and infected people are thus far going against all prognoses of a health tragedy of epic proportions. Predictions in March 2020 were of 300,000 COVID deaths by the end of the year, and with every wave of the pandemic, and the emergence

---

2. Estimates based on data from the Groupe d'Appui aux Rapatriés et Réfugiés (https://www.garr-haiti.org/). See also Fortin (2020).
3. On remittances, Ratha et al. (2015); on Haiti, Duroseau and Jean (2019); on the region, Caruso et al. (2021).

of new, more aggressive variants of the virus, apocalyptic projections that are constantly renewed but have not, until now, materialized.[4]

We know that the COVID pandemic has dramatically expanded social inequalities: between people who inhabit the same national territory, as well as between nations, widening the gulf that separates those who can afford to stay at home and those who need to move to make money; between places with robust health infrastructures and those in which they are almost inexistent; and, in the last few months, between those who have access to vaccines and those who do not. In this chapter, we look at these dynamics of inequality across Haitian landscapes, both within the country and in the diaspora, focusing on the articulations of (im)mobilities and care thematized in the Creole expression *chache lavi* (searching for life). *Chache lavi* conflates care with life itself and with the life of those who are not necessarily physically but affectively and morally close, and the process of making do during a life on the move with the search for a better life (*chache lavi miyò*): the identification of the quest for money and sustenance with the exploration of paths (*voye chache*) that others may later follow thus become integrated into activities in movement and the circuits of mobility.

The pandemic of the novel coronavirus recalls memories, practical knowledges, and an ethics of care which are constitutive of the morality of persons and the good life. Memories, knowledges, and moralities, which have been cultivated in the long durée of the Haitian crises, marked by catastrophes like the earthquake of 2010 (which left at least 250,000 dead) or the cholera epidemic that followed it (killing at least another 20,000). Loaded with morality, the use of the expression *chache lavi* also sheds light on singular forms of experiencing the daily proximity of death in the flux of ordinary life.[5]

(Im)mobilities

On March 4, 2020, three days after a state of emergency was declared in Haiti, a video was disseminated and watched by thousands showing a saleswoman expressing her indignation at how the government was

---

4. See, for example, Bourcier (2020). An example of public debates on these projections on Haiti can be seen in Pierre (2020).
5. On the relations between the permanence of the *kriz* (crisis) and *chache lavi*, see Beckett (2019, 2020).

dealing with the pandemic. Such accounts illustrate the suffering and feelings of frustration which we find, of course, in many other places beyond this Caribbean country. The woman complains:

> The President asks us to stay at home, but under what conditions? I have six children, I support my mother, my father, and I have a younger brother I also support. This is where I get by. Do you think I can stay at home wringing my hands? ... He asks us to stay at home, are we to die? If we stay home, it's not the coronavirus that's going to kill us, but hunger, misery. ... Just imagine, I'm used to cooking eight kilos of rice to sell on the streets, but now there's no movement here, I had to cook only two kilos. If I stay at home, I will die. If I die, I'll die in the streets.

Along with the restrictions to street trading, the economic effects of the pandemic soon intensified. Globally, remittances to Haiti were reduced by 15 percent throughout 2020, but if we focus on low-value remittances the slump is even greater.[6] As with migrants in other places, many Haitians take up devalued and precarious positions in the job market. This is particularly evident with those who live in the US, which is host to the largest proportion of the diaspora and from which most of the remittances come. In a dynamic that is typical of other diasporic landscapes, the interdependence of Haitians at home and those in the diaspora intensifies the crisis provoked by the pandemic.[7]

In May 2020, in New Jersey, the Haitian migrant Ralph, who had been in the US for just over five years, expressed his concerns to one of the authors of this chapter, whom he has known for a long time: "Federico, I can't live like this. I don't know how I will send money to my family in Haiti next month. They need it! The car [Uber] has been parked for two months, people don't leave their houses. This disease may not kill us, but if I can't continue to search for life, it will destroy life"

---

6. According to World Bank, the decline in low-value remittances may be as high as 20 percent (World Bank 2020a). According to a report by the Banque de la République d'Haïti (Duroseau and Jean 2019), March saw 8.17 percent fewer remittances in relation to the same month in 2019 (see also Banque de la République d'Haïti 2020).
7. See also Cela and Marcelin (2020) and the webpage of the Global Knowledge Partnership on Migration and Development (KNOMAD), a think tank on migration.

(*Si m pa ka kontinye chache lavi, sa ka detwi lavi m*). The destruction of life is less about biological death than about the destruction of the landscapes where life is sought out.[8]

In July 2021, one of our interlocutors, who lives in Port-au-Prince, described as follows some of the effects of the decrease in remittances to Haiti:

> As you know, Handerson, I myself live off the diaspora. If it were not for the diaspora, I could be begging for money today. During the coronavirus, the remittances decreased because they [the diaspora people] complain [that] they lost their jobs. When they received aid from the US government, they sent me three hundred dollars. I used it for food, bought large quantities to store at home, so I can live. Remittances decreased for all families. … Some people in [the] diaspora work in the care sector, and the people they care for passed away, so they ended up losing their jobs.

Faced with the high value of the US dollar in relation to the gourde, and the Haitian government's determination to prevent the receival of remittances in foreign currencies, some people, particularly those that live close to the border with the Dominican Republic, move to the neighboring country to receive remittances in US dollars.

The COVID pandemic highlighted, on a global scale, the associations between immobility, suffering, and death. For our Haitian interlocutors in the *katye popilè* (shanty towns) of Port-au-Prince and in the diaspora territories, there is nothing exceptional about these associations. They are part of the everyday and they are part of history. In Plantationocene landscapes (Haraway and Tsing 2019), immobility elicits captivity, sorcery, and death. As Rodrigo Bulamah (forthcoming) carefully explains, *bare* (holding), *kenbe* (tying), and *kanpe* (restraining), among other terms, speak of bodies, moralities, and emotions. Following Lauren Derby (2015), he also remarks that witchcraft can take the form of illnesses that are sent to someone or someone's kin or property, and it is an instrument of power that can prey on or halt and cease movement. Mobility, on the contrary, is always synonymous with life and vitality, as stated in a popular proverb we were often told: *Kote ki gen grangou, kabrit*

---

8. As we can see in many creole proverbs and songs, such as the beautiful and sad poetry of Haitian troubadour (twoubadou) Beken. The title of one of his songs is, precisely, *Chache Lavi Detwi Lavi* (Search for life destroying life).

pa mouri nan kòd (Where there is hunger, no goats die tethered to their ropes). The condition of slavery drives one to escape, to become a *mawon* (maroon). Poverty also drives one to move to *pran wout la* (take to the road), a synonym for life and hope (Montinard 2020).

The semantic field covered by the concept of *chache lavi* has movement at its core. People *chache lavi* daily, making ends meet on city streets, on country roads, along the paths of the diaspora, looking for a livelihood for oneself and those who are emotionally and morally close, persons who are "one of the others," even at a distance.[9] This permanent movement, attending to one's own expectations and to those of others (Audebert 2012; Baptista 2019; Evangelista 2019; Glick Schiller and Fouron 2001; Joseph 2015 and 2019; Richman 2008), is morally constitutive of the person. As we learned from our interlocutors, movement stabilizes relations between those at home, and it upholds bonds with kin and ancestors, between those residents in a place and those moving within and across national borders — even if it achieves all of this at a physical distance. As we have shown elsewhere (Joseph 2020; Neiburg 2021), in these unstable landscapes, houses (in the country and the diaspora) are inhabited by people in motion, and mobile people inhabit many houses. Even children grow up in relation to several houses, accompanying their parents, or spending time with others while the parents are on the move. Movement is morally and relationally productive — while the moralities of relationality are the condition of possibility for movement.

Both people (Sheller and Urry 2006) and money (Maurer 2012) move: money is always circulating, for most people through small transactions between part-time jobs and marketplaces, slight gains, loans, and debts. Monies permanently mutate, moving between places and across scales, among gourdes, US dollars, Dominican pesos, euros and, in the last few years, Brazilian reais and Chilean pesos. Units of monetary value are at once moral, physical, and yet imaginary (Neiburg 2016). Monies and people cross geographical barriers and legal borders, technico-politically regulated by companies that facilitate monetary circulation (Western Union, Wise, MoneyGram) and by laws and devices that hinder the circulation of people (de Genova and Peutz 2010; Domenech 2017; Fassin 2011; Marcelin, Cela, and Dorvil 2017; Sheller 2018).

The pandemic altered global regimes of human mobility. Never before in the history of Haitian mobility has there been a movement back

---

9. On the category *moun mwen* (my person) and the languages of familiarity and kinship, see Dalmaso (2019).

to the country like the one we have been witnessing since the start of 2020. The land border with the Dominican Republic became turbulent soon after the outbreak of the pandemic. With the help of the International Organization for Migration, the Haitian Embassy in Santo Domingo and the Dominican Embassy in Port-au-Prince drew up a "Plan for Assisted Voluntary Return," allowing more than 120,000 Haitians to return to Haiti. There were also reports of some additional 20,000 undocumented people being deported from the Dominican Republic at the same time. Among the reasons for these returns was the propagation of the virus in the Dominican Republic and the undocumented status of most Haitian migrants there, which prevented them from accessing government benefits and put them in a situation of extreme vulnerability (see, for example, Haiti Libre 2020b; GARR 2020).

Returnees suffered twice over. First, for the fact that their return was associated with the moral failure of searching a life in the diaspora, both for themselves and their relatives who remained in Haiti. Second, for the stigma of bringing the disease back to Haiti. Some became doubly isolated, through the quarantine demanded by the health authorities, and the moral and social shunning that accompanied their return. Moral dilemmas and health risks were frequently expressed in social networks, as when someone declared, "Dyaspora pa vinn propaje kowona nan peyi a" (Diaspora, don't come and spread the virus in the country), which was countered by, "Pa gen pwoblèm, nou pa p antre nan peyi a, men nou pa p voye lajan tou" (Well, then we won't return to the country, but we also won't send any more money).

These tensions between life in the diaspora and the possibility of returning were a cause of constant anguish for people like Bernadette, a Haitian woman who has been living in Rio de Janeiro for nine years and who now suffers the double threat of the virus and the growing economic crisis affecting her South American host country. Speaking to one of us, Bernadette explained her plight: "There is no life here, there is no way I can stay in Brazil. If I stay, how am I going to help my family in Haiti?" She expressed her sense of failure and the moral risk of returning, as well as the stigma that is associated with the *moun diaspora* (diaspora person) who returns as a potential vector of contagion.

In early 2021, the change in government in the US brought hope (sadly not to be confirmed) for a politics less hostile to migrants, reactivating in South America the so-called *wout Miami* (road to Miami) (Montinard 2020) through which Haitians living in Brazil and Chile undertook a long journey by land toward the US in the hope of settling there, economic conditions permitting; or else that they could attempt to return to Haiti. This journey would lead them across frontiers lying in the Amazonian forest, the same frontiers that only a decade earlier were their entry routes into South America during the first wave of migration that brought the continent into the Haitian diasporic geography (Joseph 2015). With COVID, people now wanted to move in the opposite direction, yet border guards in Peru and Colombia had put up barriers in the forests to contain the passage of Haitians — mostly men, but also women and, in some cases, whole families — trying to escape disease and a recession that was heavily affecting Brazil. The pandemic instated a new regime for the government of frontiers (Álvarez Velasco 2020; see also, for example, Delfim 2021).

Caring

There is great risk involved in writing about a process that is still developing. Countries that at first seemed to be models of how to manage COVID later faced situations of extreme gravity. Others, for which high mortality rates had been predicted, such as Haiti, have not yet produced those numbers.

Speculations as to the reasons for the low incidence of the pandemic in the Caribbean country rely on four arguments: (1) underreporting; (2) a low proportion of old people among the population (life expectancy in Haiti is 63 years); (3) the stigma surrounding the disease, which favors concealment of the illness as cause of death; and (4) care among those who are close, particularly among kinspeople and within the home; and (5) the use of traditional medicine combined with the positive agency of the Christian God and the Vodou entities (*Iwa*).[10]

In August 2020, Haiti was one of the three countries (along with France and Mauritania) qualified as a model by the World Health Organization (WHO) because of its "domestic administration" of the disease (WHO 2020). The WHO' assessment concerned not so much Haitian state policies but rather the efforts of a set of agents — including nongovernmental organizations (NGOs), international agencies, local civic organizations, families, and *medsen fèy* (plant doctors). In Haitian

---

10. For a general overview of speculations concerning the "mystery" of low rates of infection during the pandemic in poor countries (for now, at least), see Cash and Patel (2020) and Mukherjee (2021).

public debate, and in international debates concerning Haiti, a positive relation was thus established between the government of the disease and *jeni ayisyen* (traditional culture), in stark contrast to what Paul Farmer (2006) described for the HIV epidemic in the 1980s. At that time the media and renowned experts wrongly identified Haiti as the global center for the dissemination of AIDS due to its customs and cultural traits, Vodou practices, a supposedly uncontrolled sexuality, and a lack of proper care. Now this very same cultural tradition was said to be responsible for the low rates of SARS-CoV-2 in Haiti.

This is reenforced in the marked contrast between Haiti and neighboring countries. In the Caribbean, the only country that had numbers as low as Haiti was Cuba, which has a robust public health system that scores much more highly on social indexes than that of Haiti. When compared to the neighboring Dominican Republic, Haiti's low numbers stand out more starkly: with 333,000 infected and more than 3,800 deaths, the Dominican Republic had ten times more deaths per million people than Haiti, according to figures (by Worldometer and the Johns Hopkins COVID-19 Dashboard) from July 2021, in a population of about the same size as that of Haiti.

Despite Haiti's ongoing economic and political crisis, and contrary to the prevailing view of the "nonexistence" or "bankruptcy" of its health infrastructure, investment in health has been on the rise since the 2010 earthquake, through efforts by the state, NGOs, and international agencies. The latest report from the World Bank shows that investment in health in Haiti reached USD 13,100 per capita, slightly above the regional average, with 20 percent of this amount contributed by the government and 80 percent by international agencies and NGOs (Cavagnero et al. 2017). Haiti founded the Center for Permanent Information on the Coronavirus (CPIC) and the Multi-Sector Commission for Managing the Pandemic in March of 2020 to monitor the pandemic. During that year, Haiti received medical equipment from foreign countries, mainly from China. The World Bank promised to donate USD 20 million (World Bank 2020b). As the authorities continued to clamor for more international aid, they were berated by the population that was dissatisfied with the value of the benefits and the poor and corrupt management of the resources that were available.

Even so, these agencies ran educational campaigns in the media and social networks on hygiene (washing hands, wearing masks) and social distancing. Drawing on health agents in the communities and *medsen fèy*, they also encouraged people to take care in their homes, particularly in densely populated contexts such as the popular neighborhoods and "ghettos" of Port-au-Prince. This happened in collaboration with the authorities of the country's administrative divisions and international agencies, such as the Mirebalais University Hospital, which received the first COVID patients in March 2020,[11] or the Zile Foundation, which supplied one hundred doctors to the Dominican and Haitian governments in the border area (*El Día* 2020). In September 2020, echoing the WHO's positive view of the Haitian model for managing the pandemic, Doctors Without Borders closed its health-care center in the Hôpital des Grands-Brûlés de Drouillard in the deeply impoverished neighborhood of Cité Soleil in Port-au-Prince. Cuba's Henry Reeve International Medical Brigade, which had been present in the country since the 2010 earthquake, left one month later (Le Nouvelliste 2020a). During the same period, the scientific committee of the Université d'État d'Haïti released a widely circulated report that identified seventy-two plant recipes used by the population for preventing and treating COVID and reinforcing immunity (*Le Nouvelliste* 2020b).

The emphasis on traditional medicine and home care recalls forms of dealing with collective sanitary calamities that have become incorporated through memories of other tragedies, such as the AIDS pandemic and the cholera epidemic, the 2010 earthquake and the devastating seasonal hurricanes. We can think of these episodes as "acute-on-chronic events," extending a concept proposed by Farmer (2011, 21) in his analysis of the earthquake. Such events — or "quasi-events," in Veena Das' (2015) terms — offer coordinates for action and care that incorporate issues like hygiene, which are just as critical for the control of the coronavirus. These forms of care can be better understood through the semantic field of *chache lavi* (searching for life).

At the start of the pandemic, the fear that gripped the streets when the first cases were announced was transformed into feelings of concern for the self (*chak moun pran swen tèt yo*) and for mutual care (*pran swen youn ak lòt*). In Haiti, as one of our interlocutors said, "it is necessary to always search for life. If you let your arms down, you die" (*an Ayiti, ou oblije chache lavi, si w bese bra w, w ap mouri*). People thus mobilized, even when in many cases they were forced to remain in a state of immobility, in order to search for life by caring for one another.

---

11. The Mirebalais University Hospital was founded in 2010 in collaboration with Partners in Health (called Zanmi Lasante in Haiti).

The Haitian diaspora, like all diasporas (Hage 2021), took on a singular density during the last decades through the use of digital social networks. "Remote communication" was part of diasporic landscapes long before the pandemic, fostering extreme familiarity with mutual experiences of being (Sahlins 2012) at a distance. Thus joy, expectations, and sadness are shared; help is offered; obligations are fulfilled; or projects are discussed, such as opening up paths for others to become part of the contact networks (*fè pati rezo kontak*), or acquiring documents such as passports and visas, or engaging in small business in Haiti and/or abroad. Care among those who are socially proximate and physically separated is constitutive of diasporic landscapes, shaped by the circulation of information and care, aid and money.

News on the pandemic first reached Haiti through the media but also, and above all, through the networks of Haitians in Europe, the US, the Caribbean and, later, South America.[12] The dilemma lived by those who considered a return or who began movements of return was accompanied by and molded through existing networks, as with everything in the routes of the diaspora. As Mélanie Montinard (2020) shows, during travel people accompany each other and care for each other. For instance, those who are permanently or temporarily established at points of the diaspora monitor relations with the *ajans* and *raketè* who mediate border crossings (and are usually generically, and mistakenly, identified with "coyotes"). Unexpected longer stays at certain stopovers may require financial help, sent by family or friends situated at other points in the diaspora — as when, for example, family members in the US, France, or Canada sent money to those held up at the border between Brazil and Colombia or Peru, or to the hundreds of Haitians who had to wait in the airports of Santiago for humanitarian repatriation flights (*Le Nouvelliste* 2020c).

Those who remain in Haiti or who move abroad are tormented by the possibility of not having funds due to the economic crisis generated by the pandemic, or the fear of disease and death far from close ones, with

---

12. "Kowona sou nou" (coronavirus is upon us), people would say. For a description of aspects of the "arrival" of the pandemic in Haiti, see Mézié (2020). Bulamah (forthcoming) describes similarities between views of the arrival of SARS-CoV-2 (thrown through the air from US airplanes, for example) and other pathogens, such as those that in the 1970s decimated Haiti's indigenous Creole pig population, which had been central to family sustenance, evoking Haitian forms of conceptualizing interspecies relations.

little possibility of fulfilling the proper funeral rites. All of this disturbs regimes of mobility, intensifying feelings of suffering and frustration (on *fristrasyon* see Braum 2019; Neiburg 2017).

We followed closely, for example, a young Haitian woman who, after many years of planning, successfully joined her mother in Rio de Janeiro a little before the start of the pandemic. Just as she was finding her footing in the city, managing a small street shop that allowed her to finish her nursing studies and send remittances to family members in Haiti, she was infected by the novel coronavirus and died. Her mother's immeasurable pain was only mitigated by the arrival on the very same day of her sister and niece, who had begun their journey from Haiti to the south long before the pandemic.

Stories such as this one traversed the paths of Haitian mobility prior to the pandemic, strengthening bonds between those who remain in the country and those who move to points in the diaspora. People take care of each other — affectively, spiritually, and economically — and help each other in Haiti and in the diaspora circuits, sharing practical knowledge and taking decisions that are simultaneously individual and collective: to remain where and with whom, to leave when and how, to return when and how. These are daily dilemmas lived by diasporic subjects, exponentially intensified by the pandemic and increasingly aggravated by scarce resources, in Haiti and elsewhere, brought about by the economic crisis that has accompanied it.

While those that are outside of Haiti send information on their own fate and the course of the pandemic in various places around the globe, those in Haiti mobilize available resources to make do during the crisis in their search for life. In the shanty towns of Port-au-Prince and even in rural regions, markets are visited in a search for medicinal plants that increase immunity and offer protection from the disease; in some places *medsen fèy* go door-to-door to offer their remedies. Everyone moves, searching for life, taking care of those near and far, finding their way in streets and on routes. On their journey, people find their way in the "absence" of the state, activating narratives that constitute relations between people and government, fed by the memories of the country's endemic crises: "Nou pa ka konte sou gouvènman an, se Bondye k ap pwoteje Ayiti ak pèp la, nou oblije ap pran swen kò nou jan nou kapab, fòk nou chache lavi" (We cannot count on the government. It is God who is protecting Haiti. It is the people, it is us, who must take care of our bodies in our own way, who must search for life) (see also Beckett 2019; Kivland 2020; Trouillot 1990, 1995).

Final Thoughts

This chapter is based on long-term research by the authors, one an Argentinian/Brazilian and the other a Haitian/Brazilian, conducted in Haiti and in the Haitian diaspora. As we make clear in our account, the use of remote communication is integral to the landscapes we study. It has also allowed us to maintain, in these endless months of lockdown, our connections with family members, friends, and interlocutors. These connections have contributed data to the research on which this text is based. It has also contributed to the acute feeling of contemporaneity, synchronicity, and simultaneity (Fabian 1983) at a distance, which is proper to these pandemic times, and to the sense of a shared atmosphere of emergency (Beckett 2020; Neiburg 2021).

As we conclude, some countries have started to speed up vaccination against SARS-CoV-2, in the hope that this will provide protection against the new variants of the virus. The unequal availability of the vaccine in different countries reinforces social and economic inequality on a global scale. A number of voices claims that the disease may become endemic in poorer countries, which would heighten centuries-old inequities. Haiti's hope for vaccination at the moment includes the COVAX initiative, a partnership between the WHO and the Pan-American Health Organization announced in December 2020, and a promise by the Cuban government to donate vaccines from those they are producing for use in Caribbean countries.[13] While they wait for the start of vaccination, the main preoccupation of Haitians in Haiti remains not so much the virus but the daily violence and political and economic crises that stem from the global effects of the pandemic, which have significantly increased the prices of basic foodstuffs.

As with other crises, protests against *lavi chè* (expensive life) are spreading throughout the country. These protests aim at more than the high food prices. They also involve a moral judgment of inequality and a demand for justice. The protesters denounce the impossibility of life for some and the exaggeration of life for others — an abnormality

---

13. As we finish this text, the first vaccines from the WHO consortium are arriving in Haiti. Meanwhile, vaccination in the Dominican Republic, which excludes Haitians, reinforces feelings of discrimination and inequality amongst the migrant population.

normalized and condemned for its immorality, as in one of the many Creole sayings that speaks to the relationality of poverty: *gran nèg jete, malerèz ranmase* (what the big fish discards, the little fish enjoys). Young people and adults demonstrate, children *dlo kreyòl* (distribute water by bringing it in buckets and serving it in small mugs), women make food in the streets (*fritay, chen janbe*) which they sell or even give away. *Lavi chè* celebrates life, collectively, even when it places life at risk in the context of the pandemic, the fire and smoke of the barricades, and the always latent possibility of violence. Or, as Omar Ribeiro Thomaz (2010) described when he was caught in the midst of the incommensurable catastrophe of the January 2010 earthquake, when it was impossible to see amid the dust that hovered over the city, and when people were calling to *Jezi* (Jesus) and *Bondye* (God) and communicated with the *lwa* (spirits): in that catastrophe women traders ensured the arrival of basic products and made and distributed food in the ruined streets, ensuring the supply of food, thus preventing widespread hunger and celebrating solidarity. Commensality, substances exchanged between persons and more-than-human entities, life in motion. As Michael Jackson (2011) wrote, hunger is also a metaphor for life and for drive, underlining the movement against stasis. Demonstrating against *lavi chè* is also a means to *chache lavi miyò*, to search for worthy and full life.

Haiti is distant from the international debates on the COVID pandemic. The position of the Caribbean country seems to reactualize durable images of silence that mix the odd with the extraordinary (Trouillot [1990] 2000) and that express moral judgments and political stances that accentuate inequalities. Our Haitian interlocutors in Haiti and in the diaspora inhabit inequality, searching for life. And by *chache lavi miyò* they experience and thematize the events that mark the ordinary flux of daily life. Periodization ("the time of the pandemic," "the time of the earthquake," "the time of Hurricane Matthew") marks events and inserts them into an open-ended temporality, into a horizon of movement.

Acknowledgements

Parts of this chapter are elaborations of Joseph and Neiburg (2020a, 2020b). We thank Luiz Costa for the translation. We also thank Isabelle Guérin, Rodrigo Bulamah, and Susana Narotzky for their careful reading and insights.

References

Álvarez Velasco, Soledad. 2020. "(In)movilidad en las Américas em tiempos de pandemia." *Lasa Forum* 51 (3): 17–23.

Audebert, Cédric. 2012. *La diáspora haïtienne: territoires migratoires et réseaux transnationaux.* Rennes: Presses Universitaires de Rennes.

Banque de la République d'Haiti. 2020. "Note sur la politique monetaireé 2éme trimester de l'exercise fiscal 2020 (Janvier–Mars 2020)." https://www.brh.ht/wp-content/uploads/note_polmon2t20.pdf.

Baptista, José Renato C. 2019. "Misturas." In *Conversas etnográficas haitianas,* edited by Federico B. Neiburg, 159–92. Rio de Janeiro: Papéis Selvagens Edições.

Beckett, Greg. 2019. *There is No More Haiti: Between Life and Death in Port-au-Prince.* Oakland: University of California Press.

Beckett, Greg. 2020. "Unlivable Life: Ordinary Disaster and the Atmosphere of Crisis in Haiti." *Small Axe* 24 (2): 78–95. https://doi.org/10.1215/07990537-8604502.

Bourcier, Nicolas. 2020. "Haïti désarmé face au risque d'une catastrophe due au coronavirus." *Le Monde*, March 27, 2020. https://www.lemonde.fr/international/article/2020/03/27/haiti-desarme-face-au-risque-d-une-catastrophe-due-au-coronavirus_6034582_3210.html.

Braum, Pedro. 2019. "Frustração." In *Conversas etnográficas haitianas,* edited by Federico B. Neiburg, 131–58. Rio de Janeiro: Papéis Selvagens Edições.

Bulamah, Rodrigo. C. Forthcoming. "Lòk: Pandemics and (Im)mobility in Northern Haiti." *Global Perspectives.*

Caruso, German Daniel, Maria E. Cucagna, and Julieta Ladronis. 2021. "The Distributional Impacts of the Reduction in Remittances in Central America in COVID-19 Times." *Research in Social Stratification and Mobility*, no. 71: 100567. https://doi.org/10.1016/j.rssm.2020.100567.

Cash, Richard, and Vikram Patel. 2020. "Has COVID-19 Subverted Global Health?" *Lancet* 395 (10238): P1687–P1688. https://doi.org/10.1016/S0140-6736(20)31089-8.

Cavagnero, Eleonora Del Valle, Marion J. Cros, Ashleigh J. Dunworth, and Mirja C. Sjoblom. 2017. *Mieux dépenser pour mieux soigner: Un regard sur le financement de la santé en Haïti.* Washington, DC: World Bank Group. Accessed August 27, 2020. https://documents1.worldbank.org/curated/

en/835491498247003048/pdf/116682-WP-v2-wb-Haiti-french-PUBLIC-fullreport.pdf.

Cela, Tony, and Louis H. Marcelin. 2020. "Haitian Families and Loss of Remittances During the COVID-19 Pandemic." *INURED* (blog), Interuniversity Institute for Research and Development, May 18, 2020. http://www.inured.org/blog/haitian-families-and-loss-of-remittances-during-the-covid-19-pandemic.

Dalmaso, Flavia. 2019. "Família." In *Conversas etnográficas haitianas*, edited by Federico B. Neiburg, 53–80. Rio de Janeiro: Papéis Selvagens Edições.

Danticat, Edwidge. 2019. "Demonstrators in Haiti Are Fighting for an Uncertain Future." *New Yorker*, October 10, 2019. https://www.newyorker.com/news/news-desk/demonstrators-in-haiti-are-fighting-for-an-uncertain-future.

Das, Veena. 2015. *Affliction: Health, Disease, Poverty*. New York: Fordham University Press.

De Genova, Nicholas, and Nathalie Peutz. 2010. *The Deportation Regime: Sovereignty, Space, and the Freedom of Movement*. Durham: Duke University Press.

Delfim, Rodrigo B. 2021. "Imigrantes no Acre vivem limbo em meio à Covid-19 e clima tenso na fronteira." MigraMundo, February 25, 2021. https://migramundo.com/imigrantes-no-acre-vivem-limbo-em-meio-a-covid-19-e-clima-tenso-na-fronteira/.

Derby, Lauren. 2015. "Imperial Idols: French and United States Revenants in Haitian Vodou." *History of Religions* 54 (4): 394–422. https://doi.org/10.1086/680175.

Domenech, Eduardo. 2017. "Las políticas de migración en Sudamérica: elementos para el análisis crítico del control migratorio y fronterizo." *Terceiro Milênio: Revista Crítica de Sociologia e Política* 8 (1): 19–48.

Duroseau, Fritz, and Edwige Jean. 2019. "Haiti — The Productive Use of Remittances." Presentation to the Comisión Económica para América Latina y el Caribe, Mexico, June 14, 2019. https://www.cepal.org/sites/default/files/presentations/brh_haiti-the_productive_use_of_remittances.pdf.

El Día. 2020. "Diáspora haitiana ofrece médicos, enfermeras e ideas para enfrentar COVID19 en la isla." April 20, 2020. https://eldia.com.do/diaspora-haitiana-ofrece-medicos-enfermeras-e-ideas-para-enfrentar-covid19-en-la-isla/?fbclid=IwAR01SOZJLGDzCJyfuHjoL QRzQKKCnh2G5W6wqNZFIWRImdyx-NY-v4xFA_k.

Evangelista, Felipe. 2019. "Comércio." In *Conversas etnográficas haitianas*, edited by Federico B. Neiburg, 101–30. Rio de Janeiro: Papéis Selvagens Edições.

Fabian, Johannes. 1983. *Time and the Other: How Anthropology Makes its Object*. New York: Columbia University Press.

Farmer, Paul. 2006. *AIDS and Accusation: Haiti and the Geography of Blame*. Berkeley: University of California Press.

Farmer, Paul. 2011. *Haiti After the Earthquake*. New York: Public Affairs.

Fassin, Didier. 2011. "Policing Borders, Producing Boundaries: The Governmentality of Immigration in Dark Times." *Annual Review of Anthropology*, no. 40: 213–26. https://doi.org/10.1146/annurev-anthro-081309-145847.

Fortin, Olriche. 2020. "COVID-19 et la migration de retour force en Haïti." *INURED* (blog), Interuniversity Institute for Research and Development, January 1, 2020. http://www.inured.org/blog/covid-19-et-la-migration-de-retour-forcee-en-haiti.

GARR (Groupe d'Appui aux Rapatriés et Réfugiés). 2020. "Covid-19 Update." Facebook post, October 15, 2020. https://www.facebook.com/garrhaiti/posts/2696523450609303/.

Glick Schiller, Nina, and Georges E. Fouron. 2001. *Georges Woke Up Laughing: Long-Distance Nationalism and the Search for Home*. Durham: Duke University Press.

Hage, Ghassan. 2021. *The Diasporic Condition: Ethnographic Exploration of the Lebanese in the World*. Chicago: University of Chicago Press.

Haiti Libre. 2020a. "Le Président Moïse déclare l'état l'urgence sanitaire (texte de l'Arrêté)." March 20, 2020. https://www.haitilibre.com/article-30311-haiti-flash-le-president-moise-declare-l-etat-l-urgence-sanitaire-texte-de-l-arrete.html.

Haiti Libre. 2020b. "Haïti — Ouanaminthe: 'Plan de retour volontaire assisté' pour les haïtiens en RD." May 25, 2020. https://www.haitilibre.com/article-30859-haiti-ouanaminthe-plan-de-retour-volon- taire-assiste-pour-les-haitiens-en-rd.html.

Haraway, Donna, and Anna Tsing. 2019. "Reflections on the Plantationcene: A Conversation with Donna Haraway and Anna Tsing." By Gregg Mitman. *Edge Effects*, June 18, 2019. https://edgeeffects.net/haraway-tsing-plantationocene/.

IPC. 2020. "IPC Alert on Haiti, October 2019." Integrated Food Security Phase Classification, IPC Alert 14. http://www.ipcinfo.org/ipcinfo-website/ipc-alerts/issue-14/en/.

Jackson, Michael 2011. *Life within Limits: Well-Being in a World of Want.* Durham: Duke University Press.

Joseph, Handerson. 2015. "*Diaspora*: Sentidos sociais e mobilidades haitianas." *Horizontes Antropológicos* 21 (43): 51–78. https://doi.org/10.1590/S0104-71832015000100003.

Joseph, Handerson. 2019. "Diáspora." In *Conversas etnográficas haitianas*, edited by Federico B. Neiburg, 229–49. Rio de Janeiro: Papéis Selvagens Edições.

Joseph, Handerson. 2020. "Maisons diasporas et maisons locales: mobilités haïtiennes et réseaux transnationaux." *Etnográfica* 24 (3): 749–74. https://doi.org/10.4000/etnografica.9566.

Joseph, Handerson, and Federico Neiburg. 2020a. "I'm Going to Die in the Street: Haitian Lives in the Pandemic." *City and Society* 33 (2). https://doi.org/10.1111/ciso.12314.

Joseph, Handerson, and Federico Neiburg. 2020b. "A (i)mobilidade e a pandemia nas paisagens haitianas." *Horizontes Antropológicos* 26 (58): 463–79. https://doi.org/10.1590/S0104-71832020000300015.

Kivland, Chelsey L. 2020. "The Spiral of Sovereignty: Enacting and Entangling the State from Haiti's Streets." American Anthropologist 122 (3): 501–13. https://doi.org/10.1111/aman.13344.

Le Nouvelliste. 2020a. "Médecins sans Frontières sort de la Covid-19 faute de patient." August 11, 2020. https://lenouvelliste.com/article/219690/medecins-sans-frontieres-sort-de-la-covid-19-faute-de-patient?fbclid=IwAR2r2Pmm-h8MADmgCtO7W8Y79NpLHh_FOhjEuqs2uXKUo50eZhb58n06-ns.

Le Nouvelliste. 2020b. "UEH: Environ 72 recettes traditionnelles recen- sées pour prévenir et combattre la COVID-19 en Haïti." August 8, 2020. https://lenouvelliste.com/article/219774/ueh-environ-72-recettes-traditionnelles-recensees-pour-prevenir-et-combattre-la- covid-19-en-haiti.

Le Nouvelliste. 2020c. "COVID-19: des Haïtiens en difficulté au Chili impatients d'être fixés sur leur date retour en Haïti." August 10, 2020. https://lenouvelliste.com/article/219511/covid-19-des-haitiens-en-difficulte-au-chili-impatients-detre-fixes-sur-leur-date-retour-en-haiti?fbclid=IwAR3-KUcR1-7FKAXzVOu6MgM6oVCauKgApU0sXFQ_n_O5mAp1djDkq9jYBwA.

Le Nouvelliste. 2020d. "Nouvelle manifestation violente de policiers." March 9, 2020. https://lenouvelliste.com/article/213174/ nouvelle-manifestation-violente-de-policiers.

Marcelin, Louis Herns, Toni Cela, and Henry Dorvil. 2017. *Les jeunes Haïtiens dans les Ameriques*. Québec: Presses de l'Université du Québec.

Maurer, Bill. 2012. "Mobile Money: Communication, Consumption, and Change in the Payments Space." *Journal of Development Studies* 48 (5): 589–604. https://doi.org/10.1080/00220388.2011.621944.

Mézié, Nadege. 2020. "A água sanitária e a Bíblia: o coronavirus em Porto-Príncipe (Haiti)." *Observatório CEMI COVID-19*, no. 9.

Montinard, Mélanie. 2020. "*Pran wout la:* expériences et dynamiques de la mobilité haïtienne." *Vibrant: Virtual Brazilian Anthropology*, no. 17: e17503. https://doi.org/10.1590/1809-43412020v17d503.

Mukherjee, Siddhartha. 2021. "Why Does the Pandemic Seem to be Hitting Some Countries Harder than Others?" *New Yorker*, February 22, 2021.

Neiburg, Federico. 2016. "A True Coin of their Dreams: Imaginary Monies in Haiti; The 2010 Sidney Mintz Lecture." *HAU* 6 (1): 75–93. https://doi.org/10.14318/hau6.1.005.

Neiburg, Federico. 2017. "Serendipitous Involvement: Making Peace in the Geto." In *If True be Told: The Politics of Public Ethnography*, edited by Didier Fassin, 170–98. Durham: Duke University Press.

Neiburg, Federico. 2020. "Life, Economy and Economic Emergencies." *SASE Newsletter*, July 13, 2020. https://sase.org/newsletter-summer-2020/life-economy-and-economic-emergencies/.

Neiburg, Federico. 2021. "Multiscale Home: Shifting Landscapes and Living-in-Movement in Haiti." *Cultural Anthropology* 36 (4): 548–55. https://doi.org/10.14506/ca36.4.02.

Pierre, Hancy. 2020. "Les chiffres et les choses: Entre exceptionnalité et catastrophisme, un débat ouvert dans le contexte de la pandémie du COVID 19 en Haïti?" *Le Nouvelliste*, May 22, 2020. https://lenouvelliste.com/public/index.php/article/216137/les-chiffres-et-les-choses-entre-exceptionnalite-et-catastrophisme-un-debat-ouvert-dans-le-contexte-de-la-pandemie-du-covid-19-en-haiti.

PNUD (Programme des Nations Unies pour le Développement). 2014. "Programme des Nations Unies pour le Développement, République d'Haïti." https://www1.undp.org/content/undp/es/home/librarypage/hdr/2014-human-development-report.html.

Popovic, Caroline. 2020. "Couvre-feu et état d'urgence sanitaire en Haiti après les deux premiers cas de coronavirus." *FranceInfo*, March 20, 2020. https://la1ere.francetvinfo.fr/martinique/couvre-feu-etat-urgence-haiti-apres-deux-premiers-cas-coronavirus-814452.html.

Ratha, Dilip K., Supriyo De, Ervin Dervisevic, Sonia Plaza, Kirsten Schuettler, William Shaw, Hanspeter Wyss, Soonhwa Yi, and Seyed Reza Yousefi. 2015. "Migration and Remittances: Recent Developments and Outlook. Special Topic: Financing for Development." *Migration and Development Brief*, no. 24. Washington, DC: World Bank. https://openknowledge.worldbank.org/handle/10986/25478.

Richman, Karen E. 2008. *Migration and Vodou*. Gainesville: University Press of Florida.

Sahlins, Marshall. 2012. *What Kinship Is — and Is Not*. Chicago: University of Chicago Press.

Sheller, Mimi. 2018. *Mobility Justice: The Politics of Movement in an Age of Extremes*. London: Verso.

Sheller, Mimi, and John Urry. 2006. "The New Mobilities Paradigm." *Environment and Planning A: Economy and Space* 38 (2): 207–26. https://doi.org/10.1068/a37268.

Thomaz, Omar R. 2010. "O terremoto no Haiti, o mundo dos brancos e o Lougawou." *Novos estudos CEBRAP*, no. 86: 23–39. https://doi.org/10.1590/S0101-33002010000100002.

Trouillot, Michel-Rolph. 1990. *Haiti: State Against Nation: Origins and Legacy of Duvalierism*. New York: Monthly Review Press.

Trouillot, Michel-Rolph. 1995. *Silencing the Past: Power and the Production of History*. Boston: Beacon Press.

Trouillot, Michel-Rolph. (1990) 2020. "The Odd and the Ordinary: Haiti, the Caribbean and the World." *Vibrant: Virtual Brazilian Anthropology*, no. 17: 1–7. https://doi.org/10.1590/1809-43412020v17j553.

WHO (World Health Organization). 2020. "Home Care for Patients with Suspected or Confirmed COVID-19 and Management of their Contacts: Interim Guidance, 12 August 2020." World Health Organization, no. WHO/2019-nCoV/IPC/HomeCare/2020.4. https://apps.who.int/iris/handle/10665/333782.

World Bank. 2020a. "Selon la Banque mondiale, les remises migratoires devraient connaître un repli sans précédent dans l'histoire récente." World Bank, April 22, 2020. https://www.banquemondiale.org/fr/news/

press-release/2020/04/22/world-bank-predicts-sharpest-decline-of-remittances-in-recent-history.

World Bank. 2020b. "La Banque mondiale approuve un don de 20 millions de dollars pour soutenir la réponse d'Haïti face au COVID-19 (Coronavirus)." World Bank, April 1, 2020. https://www.banquemondiale.org/fr/news/press-release/2020/04/01/world-bank-approves-us20-million-grant-to-support-covid-19-response-in-haiti.

Part IV. Knowledge Economies

CHAPTER 17

The Great Online Migration

COVID and the Platformization of American Public Schools

Marion Fourcade

Everywhere around the world, the public health policies associated with the COVID-19 pandemic have turned the economic world upside down. The consequences of disease, social distancing, and halted physical mobility, whether forced or voluntary, suspended entire industries — from transportation to tourism, from restaurants to personal services, from entertainment to worship, from aeronautics to automobiles. Without governmental support, stores that relied on foot traffic would have tottered on the brink of bankruptcy — and many still do. Other sectors, deemed more essential, have had to profoundly reorganize their operations. Hospitals recentered their activities around the monomaniacal goal of treating wave after wave of coronavirus patients, while doctors rapidly expanded virtual office visits. Services that rely on in-person interactions and resources, such as foster care, mental health, or hospice, have been paralyzed, unable to meet citizens' basic needs.[1] Meanwhile, all public and private workplaces have been forced to adapt to the abrupt

---

1. See Cray (2020) on foster care.

rolling out of a sometimes long-foretold virtuality. In the United States (US), the share of people working from home jumped from 15 percent before the pandemic to nearly 50 percent in April 2020 (Brynjolfsson et al. 2020). As of September 2021, 45 percent of full-time employees still worked from home, 25 percent all of the time and 20 percent part of the time (Saad and Wigert 2021).

As societies grew fearful of contagion, digitality seemed to offer a reasonable substitute for everything — education, work, physical sustenance, social connection, learning, spirituality, play, business, and politics. This "great online migration" was uneven, but what it implied — the renovation or build-up of digital infrastructures, the restructuring of supply chains, the reconfiguration of jobs, occupations, and all forms of social experience — touched every country, to some degree. The fix was thought to be temporary — but with the pandemic stretching into an uncertain future, digital resettlements began to look more permanent. The transition felt like a brutal leap into an uncertain modernity, but will that modernity become a new normal? After all, fears have already been overcome. New habits and ambitions have already been developed. Major investments were made — and ought to be recouped.

This chapter explores the cultural package of the great online migration through the lens of the virtualization of American public education. The reason for this focus is that schools (elementary and secondary, or K-12 in the American lingo) stand at the center of controversies over the legitimacy of public closure mandates. They are also one of the sites where the online transition has been the most radical — and the most problematic. Most significantly, schools' transformation during the pandemic reveals in stark fashion the latent dependency of basic public good provision on an increasingly complex field of technology vendors, all eager to "disrupt" and reinvent them. And so schools offer a particularly useful window to think about the pains, promises, and long-term implications of the COVID-19-driven leap into digitality.

Accelerations

The great online migration did not begin with COVID-19, of course. But the pandemic dramatically accelerated the inevitable mutation of capitalism through digitality and the economic and political ascent of the technology industry and its leaders. At the broadest level, this mutation supercharges the processes of natural exploitation and energy consumption that make the earth increasingly inhabitable and intensify the social partitioning of the world (Mbembe 2021). Some of the changes implemented by organizations both large and small during the pandemic may be hard to reverse in the future. For the select few in e-commerce, cloud computing, online advertising, cybersecurity, fintech, and more, the devastation brought about by the worldwide circulation of the virus was an unexpected boon. Online platforms, whether established firms or digital upstarts, were quick to capitalize on the collapse of the offline economy and to press massive digital reorganizations onto every sector. The future they had been hoping to design had arrived, years ahead of schedule. As the economy slumped, people filed for unemployment, and state budgets took a nose-dive, tech stocks, investment, and profits soared. Facing hot demand for their hardware, software, and services, the five biggest US tech companies (Alphabet, Apple, Amazon, Facebook, and Microsoft) saw their combined revenue grow by a fifth in 2020 — and their combined market capitalization by a half (see Wall Street Journal 2021). Between mid-March 2020 and mid-July 2021, the collective wealth of America's 713 billionaires rose by more than USD 1.8 trillion, up nearly 60 percent in just sixteen months — with much of the increase driven by a small number of tech owner-executives (Collins 2021).[2] Further down the income ladder, other social divisions have been amplified or reactivated. For instance, the rapid expansion of tech jobs has primarily benefited men, who are more concentrated in the computer and data science sectors, while women — and especially mothers — stayed behind or exited the workforce en masse. Another trend is a rise in labor precariousness. As digital platforms started taking over the management of workforces, long-term employees of brick-and-mortar businesses[3] were fired and rehired as autonomous contractors, with fewer job benefits and protections, much greater difficulty to unionize, and an increased exposure to competition from each other (Rosenberg 2021).

The implications of the precipitous turn to digitality extend well beyond growing distributional inequalities, however, as shocking as the current wealth accumulation, or gender and class dynamics, may be. It has also hastened a profound transformation in lifestyles, with more

---

2. This figure included Tesla and SpaceX's Elon Musk (at a +562 percent increase), Amazon's Jeff Bezos (+88 percent), Facebook's Mark Zuckerberg (+131 percent), Google's Larry Page and Sergey Brin (+115 percent).
3. Brick-and-mortar businesses are defined as businesses with at least one physical store.

dramatic changes on the horizon. When the situation eventually improves, shopping and leisure could still be durably affected, with newly formed habits keeping people away from street-side outfits — stores, cinemas, restaurants — in favor of online entertainment, virtual reality, or a highly concentrated delivery service industry. The same is true of work organization. Early in the pandemic, several tech companies located on the west coast of the US (Twitter, Square, Google, Facebook, etc.) announced that work from home arrangements could become permanent (Pardes 2020). Entire real estate markets started shifting on the prospect, with people deserting city centers and relocating to cheaper and more spacious sub- and exurbs. As they left the famously expensive San Francisco Bay Area, housing prices and rents dropped sharply from pre-pandemic levels (the latter by as much as a third in six months in San Francisco itself). But these local reorderings may soon give way to other, much more disruptive movements: the global tele-migration of service labor to places around the world where its cost is lower. As Richard Baldwin and Rikard Forslid (2020) put it, "the digital transformation forced by COVID has radically lowered the barriers of trade in services — specifically to people sitting in one nation yet working in offices in another nation." In other words, the pandemic could well offer, in miniature, a rehearsal for the already announced "globotics upheaval" that will see the online migration (and thus possible globalization) of many traditionally offline workforces (Baldwin 2019).

Migration, however, does not simply mean displacement. Digital *enrollment* is on the march, too, powered by venture capital, solutionism, necessity, and rapidly changing behaviors. In the early weeks of the pandemic, there were worries that the physical infrastructure of the internet would not be able to withstand the charge. These concerns were misguided. Rather than bringing the internet's infrastructure to its knees, the great online migration has made it more ubiquitous and formidable. Living outside of technology's orbit has become even more inconceivable, and terribly marginalizing. The online exodus has brought into sharp relief the relevance of the digital divide to inclusion and basic social rights such as work, education, and sometimes the distribution of income supports. The inability of poor populations, both urban and rural, to access the necessities of digital life has become increasingly visible, and increasingly unacceptable. The digital solutions aggressively peddled by both industry power players and opportunistic upstarts fit into an already well-established narrative about technology as a solution to exclusion and marginality.

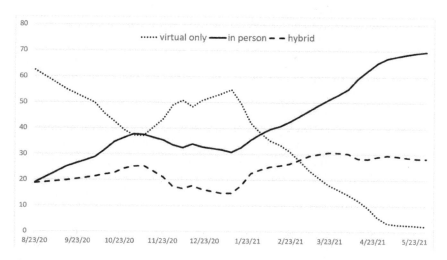

Figure 3: Estimated percentage of US K-12 public school students attending school in virtual-only, in-person, or hybrid mode. (Source: Burbio's K-12 School Opening Tracker (https://cai.burbio.com/school-opening-tracker/). Reproduced by permission from Dennis Roche, Burbio.com.)

The Virtualization of American Classrooms

Education offers an especially potent illustration of this dynamic. At the end of 2020, some 320 million children worldwide were still "locked out of schools." In the US, where education policy is heavily decentralized, an estimated 62 percent of school districts started the 2020–21 academic year virtually. By January 2021, only 39 percent were back in traditional school full time, with the remainder split equally between online education or some sort of hybrid solution (see Figure 3). Millions of school children were forced to stay at home to comply with local COVID-19 mandates or with teachers' legitimate fears of contagion, relayed by labor unions and often supported by local school boards.[4] With the pandemic stretching indefinitely, however, the pressure to reopen the schools intensified rapidly. Administrative authorities insisted that poor

---

4. In the United States, the educational policy of small regional areas such as cities and counties is determined by an independent elected body often called a "school board." The board usually hires the district's administrator or "superintendent." Other authorities in educational matters include the state government and (to a lesser extent) the federal government.

families rely on schools for many matters beyond education (e.g., subsidized meals or health care). After supporting the closures, public health authorities reverted their position and sounded the alarm about the catastrophic social and emotional toll of remote instruction on students. The showdown between political authorities (at the local, state, and federal level) and teachers' unions escalated, with public opinion shifting rapidly, though somewhat unevenly (as will become clear below). In the city of Chicago, for instance, the school district chief threatened to lock teachers who refused to teach in person out of their classroom account (K.-Y. Taylor 2021). In February 2021, the city of San Francisco, which enjoyed some of the lowest virus rates among the nation's urban areas, sued its own school board to force a reopening. An agreement with labor unions immediately staved off the threat, but the schools remained effectively closed until August of the same year or eighteen months after the beginning of the pandemic.

While the consequences of "distance learning" dragging on are potentially serious for all pupils, those with poor internet access, inexistent hardware, and digitally unskilled parents struggle much more. Many students in traditionally vulnerable categories (the homeless, foster children, non-English mother-tongue speakers, of low-income families) saw their absenteeism rates go up or simply vanished from the school rolls. Data from one national panel survey of American households shows that as of mid-January 2021, only 33 percent of White children but 62 percent of Black and Hispanic children attended school with the "remote only" option (USC Dornsife 2020: UAS280 Wave 23, Crosstabs)[5] (including a whopping 17 percent of parents of low-income students, and 18 percent of those of Black students, who reported that their child attended a "virtual" school).[6] Furthermore, ambivalence toward school reopenings consistently ran high among these families: in the same survey,

---

5. By May 2021, the virtual school numbers had slightly increased, to 20 percent and 19 percent respectively (USC Dornsife 2020: UAS264, Wave 27). Also see Meckler (2021) for similar figures.

6. Note that a virtual school (which may be for profit, charter, or district-operated) is different from a district or private school in (temporary) virtual mode. While it is not inconceivable that some parents may have mixed-up these two possibilities as they answered the survey question, it is unlikely that Black parents would have been *uniquely* confused. Furthermore, the numbers reported here seem consistent with the trend, discussed below, of rapidly rising enrollments in charter schools, and especially virtual charter

only 14 percent of Black parents, but 46 percent of non-Hispanic White parents and 29 percent of Hispanic parents expressed a preference for an "in-person only" education. These figures are very much consistent with findings from parents' surveys and press reports from around the country as well as with my own analysis (with David Joseph-Goteiner) of school board meetings in various cities in Alameda County, California.[7] As sociologist Keeanga-Yamahtta Taylor pointed out in an article in *The New Yorker* (2021), the aversion of poor, often nonwhite families to sending their children back to school builds on a long history of distrust and anger toward institutions (public health, education) that have often served communities of color poorly, as well as on their own awareness that the pandemic has taken a heavier toll on them.[8] And it has persisted, even after repeated reassurances by public authorities — including the Centers for Disease Control — about the safety of schools and a national moral panic over the severe learning losses and mental health challenges now faced by low-income and especially minority children.

Meanwhile, better-off, predominantly White children experienced the pandemic differently. They were not only less exposed to virus contagion, but their parents were also more likely to pressure local school boards to design hybrid solutions or resume normal education altogether. And where school closures were prolonged (as in much of California), the most privileged in this group had alternative solutions to work with — from moving to rural areas to in-person instruction in private schools (often exempt from stay-at-home orders) or homeschooling "pods" relying on private tutors and teams of educated parents. Wealthy families, in other words, reverted to familiar domestic and commercial strategies — somewhat reminiscent of how the children of social elites were educated prior to the advent of mass education.

Private schools and privately operated charter schools (including evangelical schools), in turn, have faced a surge in enrollments. Various

---

schools, over the 2020–21 school year. Still, in the absence of more data, these figures must be taken with caution.

7. For example, Shapiro, Green, and Kim (2021) on New York City; Nierenberg and Taylor (2021) on Chicago.
8. As of January 2021, people of color were about four times more likely to be hospitalized, and nearly three times more likely to die from the virus than Whites. People of color here means Native Americans, African Americans, and Hispanics. Corresponding death rates for Asians are similar to Whites (CDC 2021).

types of virtual schools, instructional platforms, and online tutoring services seem to have benefited from this exodus. And as students, both rich and poor, withdrew or transferred to other systems, public school enrollments dropped, threatening to defund public education for years to come.[9] The effect is particularly noticeable in the entry grades, with kindergarten enrollments dropping by 9.3 percent nationally between 2019 and 2020 (13.6 percent in low-income neighborhoods) (Goldstein and Parlapiano 2021).

The flagrant escalation — and renewed visibility — of educational inequalities as school districts moved to online platforms in the midst of the pandemic initially prompted many states and cities to invest heavily to expand broadband coverage and access to connected devices, sometimes with the inducement of tech philanthropists.[10] Educational consultants, foundations, and nonprofit organizations, both national and international, urged renewed efforts at fostering "digital equity and inclusion," all the more since the populations left behind tend to be poor and nonwhite. Injunctions about "closing the digital divide," first aired in the 1990s, were suddenly revived, echoing familiar citizenship claims about other infrastructural divides (Fourcade 2021).

The task, however, was daunting on many levels, and the decentralized nature of American education complicated matters enormously. The most impacted districts were also the least resourced, and thus the least likely to be able to invest. For many educators, transitioning to online teaching was anything but natural. The digitally illiterate had no choice but to adapt on the fly, often with little training, little guarantee of privacy, and little consideration for personal circumstances, such as family responsibilities. Some organizations, such as the California Teachers' Association, tried to stem the transition to remote instruction. It was soon apparent that the new mediations, which enable recording and digital analytics on both students' and teachers' practices, would profoundly change work practices and invite increased scrutiny by supervisors,

---

9. This is especially relevant since, in the US, federal and state allotments to schools depend on the number of students enrolled.
10. In Oakland, California, Twitter CEO Jack Dorsey pledged USD 10 million to ensure that students have computers and internet service at home. Gifts from private parties, including cash donations from wealthy individuals and philanthropic foundations, donations of tablets and computers from hardware companies, and free hotspots provided by mobile companies, are part of the California strategy and that of many other localities.

administrators, parents, and possibly the larger public. Students' screen fatigue, poor demonstrated effectiveness, and the need to preserve the confidentiality of classroom interactions initially provided strong arguments against distance learning. For the younger grades the number of hours of instruction was sharply reduced from the offline benchmark. In some American cities, teachers initially fought against *both* school reopenings *and* the rushed deployment of online alternatives — an untenable answer to an unsolvable dilemma (Goldstein and Shapiro 2020).

By and large these resistances did not last, though they may return in a post-pandemic future. Teachers' unions (initially with significant public support) came to embrace virtualization as the lesser evil, given the continued risk of virus exposure. During the pandemic, teachers' "number one" concern, one administrator reported, was "how am I going to teach my kids this year?"[11] And thus the social conflicts one might have expected over virtualization — fears about deskilling, job losses, or data-driven surveillance — did not happen, were muted, or momentarily deferred. If anything, prolonged exile from schools had made everyone hungry for physical interactions, so the perspective of a radical transformation still seemed quite distant. But perhaps that was a misconception. COVID-19 accelerated an ongoing structural transformation,[12] and, with massive investments at stake, many public education officials felt there would be "no going back" from remote and hybrid learning (Herold 2021). In San Antonio, Texas, the superintendent vowed to make hybrid education permanent. Iowa City is accelerating the transition to a permanent online option, starting with high schools.[13] A national survey of American school districts found that "about two in ten districts have already adopted, plan to adopt, or are considering adopting virtual

---

11. Interview, Bruce Kaminsky (pseudonym), Alameda county, CA, February 26, 2021 (conducted jointly with David Joseph-Goteiner).
12. The use of online instructional platforms (such as the nonprofit Khan Academy) with prerecorded learning blocks largely predates the pandemic.
13. Higher education, where pre-pandemic pressures for online instruction already ran high, offers a model of sorts. As Lossin and Battle (2020) argue, "distance learning figures into a decades-long trend of greater administrative oversight of university teaching by promising not just a change in protocol but a wholesale material reorganization of learning. In short, online learning is the fulfillment of managerial desire," a desire from which universities — and perhaps also post-pandemic schools — may never fully recover.

schools as part of their district portfolio after the end of the COVID-19 pandemic" (Schwartz et al. 2020). Some do it out of necessity, to meet a growing demand from families, often unvaccinated, or a shortage of teachers, discouraged by the pandemic. Others see a promise of cost reduction, economies of scale, and flexibility. Virtual academies and educational startups are popping up everywhere to serve these ambitions, backed by a rush of venture capital. Digital educational capitalism is on the march.

Appropriations

Education is just one among many sectors that the pandemic has primed for an overhaul. The symbolic and material opportunities opened by the global public health catastrophe were not lost on tech executives. In the early weeks of the pandemic, many confidently proclaimed their industry's capacity to solve the various emergencies unfolding throughout the world. On an April 14, 2020, livestream of the Economic Club of New York, Eric Schmidt, former CEO of Google and executive chair of Alphabet, stated matter-of-factly: "Think about what your life would be like in America without Amazon, for example. The benefit of these corporations — which we love to malign — in terms of the ability to communicate ... the ability to get information, is profound — and I hope people will remember that when this thing is finally over. ... So, let's be a little bit grateful that these companies got the capital, did the investment, built the tools that we're using now and have really helped us out. Imagine having the same reality of this pandemic without these tools" (cited in Schleifer 2020). Similarly, Facebook's Mark Zuckerberg (2020) wrote in a *Washington Post* editorial at the beginning of the pandemic: "I've always believed that helping people come together as a community will help us address our greatest challenges — not just by sharing our experiences and supporting each other in crises but also by working together at scale to solve problems. The world has faced pandemics before, but this time we have a new superpower: the ability to gather and share data for good. If we use it responsibly, I am optimistic that data can help the world respond to this health crisis and get us started on the road to recovery." Not to be left behind, Microsoft chief executive Satya Nadella (2020) offered his company's services to a business-government alliance and wrote: "We at Microsoft view ourselves as digital first responders."

Political leaders latched onto these inflated promises of tech as so many Hail Mary's. In the early weeks of the pandemic, US President Donald Trump invoked an obscure subsidiary of Alphabet (the parent company of Google) as a solution to help slow the spread of coronavirus — but the project was not ready, and the product was never delivered. Likewise, COVID contact-tracing apps never quite took off in the US or Europe, in spite of their widely trumpeted unveiling, which involved a rare collaboration between Google and Apple. The simple truth is that these technologies were possibly less effective than the detective work performed by human contact tracers; and without proper privacy safeguards, they were not trusted (Soltani, Calo, and Bergstrom 2020). In other words, six months into the pandemic, the great problem-solving hopes placed in big data and artificial intelligence had failed to materialize (Heaven 2021). But the mirage remained alive, and the big tech firms thrived anyway, for other obvious reasons.

The US technology sector is already one of the most concentrated in a heavily concentrated economy, for reasons that have to do with the historically lenient enforcement of antitrust law in the US (see Stiglitz 2019; Cohen 2019; Kahn 2019; Philippon 2019) and with the nature of digital technologies.[14] Before the pandemic, Amazon commanded half of US e-commerce and half of global cloud computing revenues. Facebook owned WhatsApp and Instagram, cornering much of the social media experience. Google had YouTube, Waze, and Nest. Skype belonged to Microsoft. Google and Apple had the two most popular mobile operating systems in the world. In other words, large firms already controlled the most important gateways into the digital economy. To be sure, the great online migration also prompted a creative rearticulation of local, brick-and-mortar economies through web-based tools and empowered some newcomers. Zoom, for instance, emerged from the "great lockdown" as a ubiquitous tool for facilitating meetings and virtual instruction. And as people found it increasingly hard to interact with

---

14. As Morozov (2015) puts it, "the more people on Facebook, the more valuable it becomes, and it doesn't really make sense to have five competing social networks with twenty million people on each; you want all of them on one platform. It's the same for search engines: the more people are using Google, the better it becomes, because every search is in some sense a tinkering and improvement in the service." The first advantage is known as "network effects." The second is a direct consequence of the way cybernetic feedback/machine learning works.

their bank at a critical time, fintech companies started feeding on online spending, government stimulus checks, and automated credit, displacing more established providers. A World Bank and Centre for Alternative Finance study (2020) mentions the rapid increase in the use of fintech products (including digital payments and remittances) throughout the world, particularly in jurisdictions with stringent COVID-19 containment measures.

How long these smaller upstarts will survive is unclear. Instead, they might be targeted by the largest companies' infinite appetite for acquisition — a familiar pattern in periods of economic crisis. With boundless cash at their disposal, the GAFA (a new acronym for Google, Amazon, Facebook, and Apple) have already used the pandemic to launch into a spending frenzy, "laying the groundwork for a future where they will be bigger and more powerful than ever" (Isaac 2020). In China, Alibaba has followed the same strategy (Horwitz 2020).

The great online migration has allowed the digital behemoths and newcomers to expand their reach quickly into new populations, or to intensify the exploitation of existing users. As people holed up at home, digital interfaces became the nearly obligatory point of passage for communication, economic exchange, and leisure. Social media and streaming and messaging platforms — including Netflix, YouTube, Facebook — exploded again.[15] By some measures, the digitality that has accompanied the COVID-19 pandemic increased the flow of data creation by as much as 50 percent (Foroohar 2020). The immediate result is that tech firms accumulated ever more voluminous, ever richer troves of financial, text, and image/video data — from personal, governmental, and corporate sources. This data, in turn, has now been stored for future uses that even the most cunning digital capitalists do not yet fathom. But from those servers it now threatens to re-entangle itself into people's lives in ways no one fully expects. What we know of the proliferation of visual data, for instance, is that once there it can be mobilized and repurposed to demand new forms of accountability or enable new forms of evidence that are increasingly recognized in court (Brayne, Levy, and Newell 2018).

Even more than the urgency, perhaps, the fog of the pandemic has opened a narrow window for digital capitalism to reimagine government with more machines and fewer people, and for governments to learn from what Adam Przeworski (2020) has called a "laboratory of

---

15. Facebook's Messenger Kids, a texting app for children under 13, became wildly popular at the start of the pandemic.

experiments." It has already offered a unique opportunity to impose a new normal of digital surveillance onto populations and workforces, often with troubling implications for human rights, privacy, and the growth of corporate power (SSRC 2021). And it has accelerated the reform of many public operations in the name of modernization, efficiency and, increasingly, the need to recoup the costs of recent digital investments. In May 2020, Andrew Cuomo, governor of New York, signaled his willingness to follow the prescriptions of tech executives, rather than policy experts, in defining how technology can become more thoroughly integrated into post-COVID-19 public life. Schools, again, were high on the agenda. Naomi Klein (2020) describes the tenor of Cuomo's press conference as "something resembling a pandemic shock doctrine": "Calling [Bill] Gates a 'visionary,' Cuomo said the pandemic has created 'a moment in history when we can actually incorporate and advance [Gates's] ideas ... all these buildings, all these physical classrooms — why, with all the technology you have?' he asked, apparently rhetorically." Unsurprisingly, the comment drew fire from the state's teachers' union, which countered that nothing will ever replace the personal relationship between a teacher and their students.

Appropriation and Valuation in the Virtual Classroom

The stakes of the great online migration are indeed particularly high with populations in the care of the state, such as children, prisoners, the aged, and the poor. In the old technology battleground of K-12 education, the "Googlification of the classroom" (Singer 2017) was already far along before COVID-19, with the Bay Area company dominating both the provision of hardware (Chromebooks, or cheap computers outfitted with Google's Chrome operating system) and cloud software specific to educational use (Google Education, upgraded during the pandemic to include a video meeting platform, Google Meet). Still, COVID has supercharged this power: the number of Google Classroom users worldwide multiplied almost fourfold in a little over a year (from 40 million in 2019 to 150 million in 2021), and the platform was reorganized as a gateway through which all online interactions (including with other edtech vendors) must pass (Perrotta et al. 2021).

The pandemic has truly transformed education into a "seller's market" (Teräs et al. 2020) and acted as a catalyst for an emergent network of financial investors eager to frame edtech as the next digital cash cow. Scrambling and resource-starved school districts found themselves harassed by edtech carpetbaggers selling untested tools. Following a well-established business model in tech (Fourcade and Kluttz 2020), education start-ups offer basic apps for free (often directly to teachers, students, or parents) to generate interest and word-of-mouth virality, but districts face steep pricing schedules if they want to adopt the school-wide option (Clifford 2020). Some of these tools are all-encompassing and resemble social media platforms. The app Seesaw, popular in elementary schools, is thoroughly gamified, for instance, with users (teachers, students, parents) encouraged to upload content (audio, voice, video; homework or lesson) through the app, like and comment on the child's work, and possibly share it with the rest of the class, with the teacher's consent. Additional features, such as grading or analytics, require a subscription.

The edtech sector, like the rest of the tech industry, has a history of using data as an invisible currency. Before the passage of federal and state data privacy laws, data could be bargained away to vendors without real democratic oversight (Lupton and Williamson 2017). Many of the more restrictive policies implemented after the mid-2010s still contain significant loopholes (Alim et al. 2017) and in many states it is schools, rather than tech companies, who are responsible for establishing privacy protocols. In 2018, and again in 2020, the US Federal Bureau of Investigation issued a warning about the privacy and cybersecurity risks of edtech services (see FBI 2018). In 2020, the state of New Mexico sued Google for collecting the personal data of school children under the age of 13 through its G Suite for Education software and Chromebooks, in violation of federal law. But these laws are difficult to enforce, especially given the lack of a unified policy framework throughout the country. COVID-19 has sent America's 13,506 school districts scrambling to organize their mission in a pandemic world, with possibly as many local approaches to privacy and surveillance and as many contracts with edtech firms (K. Taylor 2021).[16] Most find that they do not have the expertise, nor the resources, to survey the vast offering of online services, let alone negotiate individualized data privacy agreements with providers. Finally, edtech companies often target teachers directly, who then ask students to sign up for new apps in an ad hoc manner. Not only is such decentralized diffusion inherently difficult to control, it habituates both

---

16. For instance, a September 2020 report by the American Civil Liberties Union of the state of Rhode Island found that out of 36 public school districts, "24 districts allow officials to access the microphone or camera on a school-loaned device at any time" (see ACLU 2020).

children — including very young children — and parents to a medium that often provides a "gateway into social media" (Chang 2020). Most of these apps collect data from anyone who is logged in, use browser cookies to follow users outside the digital classroom (where privacy protections are much weaker), and encourage parents (who are not covered by the strictest laws) to enroll as well. As Perrotta and his colleagues (2021) put it, the pipes of online learning are built to be structurally "leaky." The data being primed for collection thus dramatically overflows the student population and the confines of educational technologies, and a much broader range of online behaviors may suddenly become accessible, surveilled, analyzed, and, of course, monetized.

Furthermore, the edtech sector has increasingly reframed data production as an analytical solution to increase the legibility of school activities to students, parents, teachers, and administrators. The new generation of edtech proposes flashy data dashboards with analytics designed to disaggregate the learning and teaching processes into easily commensurable and quantifiable bits — time on site, response to assignments, instructor comments, scores and grades, and much more. By encouraging audiences to buy into the business in the name of convenience, transparency, or productivity, edtech companies legitimate their own data collection processes and normalize an infrastructure of generalized digital surveillance.[17]

Once unleashed, these dynamics take a life of their own, however, and the consequences are profound. The collection and use of data generated through online learning is largely unregulated and no one knows for sure what is retained, for what purpose, and what it is worth. Today *all* organizations assume they should sweep up as much of it as they can, as a matter of course.[18]

In addition to a dizzying array of startups, the sector is teeming with financial actors that specialize in the production of "valuation claims" about the edtech field and thus "make [it] intelligible and attractive to investors," from venture capitalists to asset managers worldwide (Williamson 2020a). The agency HolonHQ, founded in 2018, predicts that

---

17. Universities, again, are leading the way, with a rapid acceleration of student surveillance technologies, from smartphone location software to virtual proctoring systems that can monitor students' video, audio, screen, and computer mouse (Harwell 2020).
18. This is what Healy and I have called "the data imperative" (Fourcade and Healy 2017).

the "global education market" will reach USD 10 trillion by 2030 and sells detailed "intelligence" into a complex and crowded field, including a list of the "global edtech unicorns" (companies with a valuation over USD 1 billion) (Williamson 2020a). According to financial analysts everywhere, the COVID-19-related school closures dramatically boosted predictions of future "market growth" for the edtech sector, leading to the creation of global exchange traded funds designed specifically to support companies "in the business of transforming education" (Williamson 2020b).[19] In these imaginaries of capital, what was once the quintessential public good has already been remade into a bundle of assets yielding future streams of income (Leyshon and Thrift 2007; Birch and Muniesa 2020). And that process is substantive as much as it is infrastructural: it is not simply the delivery of education that is being transformed and privatized but also its content and its philosophy (Williamson 2017).

Digital Crossroads

So where does this leave us? The time since the beginning of the pandemic has been paradoxical for the tech sector. On the one hand, COVID was a boon. It sharply accelerated the seemingly inexorable digitization of all industries, inviting massive streams of state and private capital in a rush to bring about the digital future sooner than expected while nearly obliterating social resistance to virtuality. On the other hand, tech is now facing its most important political challenges to date. Having rendered technology a social necessity, COVID helped reorient the debate toward latent questions of inequality, fairness, and democracy. The matter is no longer whether to use technology at all, but how to build and govern digital infrastructures. Landmark antitrust actions in Europe and the US, initiated in 2020 and 2021, have revealed a new willingness, on the part of both legal thinkers and political leaders, to question and possibly reverse the untrammeled expansion of digital monopolies: just like earlier industrial "trusts" — in the railroads, oil, or telecommunications — the tech behemoths have been called to give account of matters of privacy, profit, economic justice, democracy, and job displacements.

---

19. The rise of passive investors, notably in the form of exchange traded funds, is part of a general transformation of finance in twenty-first-century capitalism (for example, see Braun 2016).

These concerns are especially acute in the domain of education, where public institutions under duress have been forced to collaborate with, sometimes outsource their entire mission to poorly regulated private corporations with little track record.[20] Yet, whatever misgivings parents, students, and teachers may have, a return to the status quo ante looks unlikely. The customizability and auditability of e-learning may appeal to some populations, especially in the US where children's education is often seen as a matter of family or personal discretion. The economies of scale may seduce policy makers, administrators, and some teachers, especially in cash-strapped districts. As an institution, the public school is, therefore, in flux, both because the digital disruptors are looking to dissolve it into technology, in the name of efficiency and modernity, and because part of the "public" concurs, in the name of choice. Through these material and cultural upheavals, it is the very notion of public and universal good that is at play — and the political struggles of the twenty-first century that are looming on the horizon.

Acknowledgements

The author is grateful to David Joseph-Goteiner, Molly Jacoby, Jack Vallentine, and Amanda Yao for their research assistance on the broader project of which this chapter is a part, and to members of the Institute for Advanced Study's "Economy and Society" seminar for their useful comments and suggestions.

References

ACLU (American Civil Liberties Union). 2020. "ACLU of RI Report Shows Alarming Lack of Privacy Protection for Students on School-Loaned Computers." ACLU, September 21, 2020. https://www.aclu.org/press-releases/aclu-ri-report-shows-alarming-lack-privacy-protection-students-school-loaned.

---

20. Some countries, such as France, developed their own e-learning platforms to maintain control over what they see as an essential prerogative of the state. China has cracked down on online tutoring firms that that advantage wealthier students (Koenig 2021).

Alim, Frida, Nate Cardozo, Gennie Gebhart, Karen Gullo, and Amul Kalia. 2017. *Spying on Students: School-Issued Devices and Student Privacy*. April 13, 2017. San Francisco: Electronic Frontier Foundation. https://www.eff.org/wp/school-issued-devices-and-student-privacy.

Baldwin, Richard. 2019. *The Globotics Upheaval: Globalization, Robotics, and the Future of Work*. London: Weidenfeld and Nicolson.

Baldwin, Richard, and Rikard Forslid. 2020. "COVID 19, Globotics, and Development." VoxEU, Centre for Economic Policy Research, July 16, 2020. https://voxeu.org/article/covid-19-globotics-and-development.

Birch, Kean, and Fabian Muniesa. 2020. *Assetization: Turning Things into Assets in Technoscientific Capitalism*. Cambridge, MA: MIT Press.

Braun, Benjamin. 2016. "From Performativity to Political Economy: Index Investing, ETFs and Asset Manager Capitalism." *New Political Economy* 21 (3): 257–73. https://doi.org/10.1080/13563467.2016.1094045.

Brayne, Sarah, Karen Levy, and Bryce C. Newell. 2018. "Visual Data and the Law." *Law and Social Inquiry* 43 (4): 1149–63. https://doi.org/10.1111/lsi.12373.

Brynjolfsson, Erik, John J. Horton, Adam Ozimek, Daniel Rock, Garima Sharma, and Hong-Yi Tu Ye. 2020. "COVID-19 and Remote Work: An Early Look at US Data." Working Paper 27344. Cambridge, MA: National Bureau of Economic Research.

Burbio. 2021. "Burbio's K-12 School Opening Tracker." https://cai.burbio.com/school-opening-tracker/.

CDC (Centers for Disease Control and Prevention). 2021. "Risk for COVID-19 Infection, Hospitalization, and Death by Race/Ethnicity." CDC, September 9, 2021. https://www.cdc.gov/coronavirus/2019-ncov/covid-data/investigations-discovery/hospitalization-death-by-race-ethnicity.html.

Chang, Connie. 2020. "Remote School as the Gateway Drug to Social Media." *New York Times*, December 10, 2020. https://www.nytimes.com/2020/12/10/well/family/children-social-media.html?searchResultPosition=7.

Clifford, Stephanie. 2020. "Schools Clamored for Seesaw's App: That Was Good News, and Bad News." *New York Times*, October 25, 2020. https://www.nytimes.com/2020/10/25/technology/seesaw-school-app.html?searchResultPosition=1.

Cohen, Julie. 2019. *Between Truth and Power: The Legal Foundations of Informational Capitalism*. Oxford: Oxford University Press.

Collins, Chuck. 2021. "Updates: Billionaire Wealth, U.S. Job Losses and Pandemic Profiteers." Inequality, August 23. https://inequality.org/great-divide/updates-billionaire-pandemic/.

Cray, Kate. 2020. "How Do You Find a Home for a Foster Child at a Time Like This?" *Atlantic*, October 11, 2020.

FBI (Federal Bureau of Investigation). 2018. "Education Technologies: Data Collection and Unsecured Systems Could Pose Risks to Students." Public Service Announcement, I-091318-PSA, September 13, 2018. https://www.ic3.gov/Media/Y2018/PSA180913.

Foroohar, Rana. 2020. "Big Tech's Viral Boom Could Be Its Undoing." *Financial Times*, May 17, 2020.

Fourcade, Marion. 2021. "Ordinal Citizenship." *British Journal of Sociology* 72 (2): 154–73. https://doi.org/10.1111/1468-4446.12839.

Fourcade, Marion, and Kieran Healy. 2017. "Seeing Like a Market." *Socio-Economic Review* 15 (1): 9–29. https://doi.org/10.1093/ser/mww033.

Fourcade, Marion, and Daniel N. Kluttz. 2020. "A Maussian Bargain: Accumulation by Gift in Digital Capitalism." *Big Data and Society* 7 (1). https://doi.org/10.1177/2053951719897092.

Goldstein, Dana, and Alicia Parlapiano. 2021. "The Kindergarten Exodus." *New York Times*, August 7, 2021. https://www.nytimes.com/2021/08/07/us/covid-kindergarten-enrollment.html?searchResultPosition=1.

Goldstein, Dana, and Eliza Shapiro. 2020. "Teachers are Wary of Returning to Class, and Online Instruction Too." *New York Times*, July 29, 2020. https://www.nytimes.com/2020/07/29/us/teacher-union-school-reopening-coronavirus.html?searchResultPosition=1.

Harwell, Drew. 2020. "Mass School Closures in the Wake of the Coronavirus are Driving a New Wave of Student Surveillance." *Washington Post*, April 1, 2020. https://www.washingtonpost.com/technology/2020/04/01/online-proctoring-college-exams-coronavirus/.

Heaven, Will D. 2021. "Hundreds of AI Tools Have Been Built to Catch COVID. None of Them Helped." *MIT Technology Review*, July 30, 2021. https://www.technologyreview.com/2021/07/30/1030329/machine-learning-ai-failed-covid-hospital-diagnosis-pandemic/.

Herold, Benjamin. 2021. "'No Going Back' From Remote and Hybrid Learning, Districts Say." *Education Week*, January 7, 2021. https://www.edweek.org/technology/no-going-back-from-remote-and-hybrid-learning-districts-say/2021/01.

Horwitz, Josh. 2020. "Alibaba Extends its Reach in China as Coronavirus Outbreak Opens Doors." *Reuters*, May 28, 2020. https://www.reuters.com/article/us-health-coronavirus-alibaba-analysis/alibaba-extends-its-reach-in-china-as-coronavirus-outbreak-opens-doors-idUSKBN2340TG.

Isaac, Mike. 2020. "The Economy is Reeling: The Tech Giants Spy Opportunity." *New York Times*, June 13, 2020. https://www.nytimes.com/2020/06/13/technology/facebook-amazon-apple-google-microsoft-tech-pandemic-opportunity.html.

Kahn, Lina. 2019. "The End of Antitrust History Revisited." *Harvard Law Review* 133 (5): 1655–82.

Klein, Naomi. 2020. "Screen New Deal." *Intercept*, May 8, 2020. https://theintercept.com/2020/05/08/andrew-cuomo-eric-schmidt-coronavirus-tech-shock-doctrine/.

Koenig, Rebecca. 2021. "Online Tutoring in China Was Booming. Then Came a Dramatic Shift in Regulations." EdSurge, July 26, 2021. https://www.edsurge.com/news/2021-07-26-online-tutoring-in-china-was-booming-then-came-a-dramatic-shift-in-regulations.

Leyshon, Andrew, and Nigel Thrift. 2007. "The Capitalization of Almost Everything: The Future of Finance and Capitalism." *Theory, Culture and Society* 24 (7–8): 97–115. https://doi.org/10.1177/0263276407084699.

Lossin, R. H., and Andy Battle. 2020. "Higher Education in the Age of Coronavirus: Resisting Distance Learning." *Boston Review*, April 30, 2020.

Lupton, Deborah, and Ben Williamson. 2017. "The Datafied Child: The Dataveillance of Children and Implications for their Rights." *New Media and Society* 19 (5): 780–94. https://doi.org/10.1177/1461444816686328.

Mbembe, Achille. 2021. "The Universal Right to Breathe." *Critical Inquiry* 47 (2): S58–S62. https://doi.org/10.1086/711437.

Meckler, Laura. 2021. "Nearly Half of Schools Are Open Full-Time, Survey Finds." *Washington Post*, March 24, 2021. https://www.washingtonpost.com/education/schools-reopen-data/2021/03/23/a7d10b42-8bed-11eb-9423-04079921c915_story.html.

Morozov, Evgeny. 2015. "Socialize the Data Centres!" *New Left Review*, no. 91.

Nadella, Satya. 2020. "Crisis Requires Co-ordinated Digital Response." *Financial Times*, April 30, 2020. https://www.ft.com/content/b645d2f8-89f9-11ea-a109-483c62d17528.

Nierenberg, Amelia, and Kate Taylor. 2021. "Chicago Families Debate School Reopening." *New York Times*, February 3, 2021. https://www.nytimes.com/2021/02/03/us/chicago-school-reopening.html.

Pardes, Arielle. 2020. "Silicon Valley Rethinks the (Home) Office." *Wired*, May 15, 2020.

Perrotta, Carlo, Kalervo N. Gulson, Ben Williamson, and Kevin Witzenberger. 2021. "Automation, APIs and the Distributed Labour of Platform Pedagogies in Google Classroom." *Critical Studies in Education* 62 (1): 97–113. https://doi.org/10.1080/17508487.2020.1855597.

Philippon, Thomas. 2019. *The Great Reversal: How America Gave Up on Free Markets*. Cambridge, MA: Belknap Press.

Przeworski, Adam. 2020. "COVID-19 Reveals the Fragility of Our Values." *Global* (blog), Graduate Institute Geneva, June 16, 2020. https://theglobal.blog/2020/06/16/covid-19-reveals-the-fragility-of-our-values/.

Rosenberg, Eli. 2021. "Albertsons is Laying Off Employees and Replacing Them with Gig Workers, as App Platforms Rise." *Washington Post*, January 6, 2021. https://www.washingtonpost.com/business/2021/01/06/vons-albertsons-doordash-prop-22-layoffs/.

Saad, Lydia, and Ben Wigert. 2021. "Remote Work Persisting and Trending Permanent." Gallup, October 13, 2021. https://news.gallup.com/poll/355907/remote-work-persisting-trending-permanent.aspx.

Schleifer, Theodore. 2020. "Google's Former CEO Hopes the Coronavirus Makes People More 'Grateful' for Big Tech." *Vox*, April 14, 2020. https://www.vox.com/recode/2020/4/14/21221141/coronavirus-eric-schmidt-google-big-tech-grateful.

Schwartz, Heather L., David Grant, Melissa K. Diliberti, Gerald P. Hunter, and Claude M. Setodji. 2020. *Remote Learning Is Here to Stay: Results from the First American School District Panel Survey*. Santa Monica: Rand Corporation. https://www.rand.org/pubs/research_reports/RRA956-1.html.

Shapiro, Eliza, Erica L. Green, and Juliana Kim. 2021. "Missing in School Reopening Plans: Black Families' Trust." *New York Times*, February 1, 2021. https://www.nytimes.com/2021/02/01/us/politics/school-reopening-black-families.html.

Singer, Natasha. 2017. "How Google Took Over the Classroom." *New York Times*, May 13, 2017. https://www.nytimes.com/2017/05/13/technology/google-education-chromebooks-schools.html.

Soltani, Ashkan, Ryan Calo, and Carl Bergstrom. 2020. "Contact-Tracing Apps are Not a Solution to the COVID-19 Crisis." Brookings Techstream (blog), April 27, 2020. https://www.brookings.edu/techstream/inaccurate-and-insecure-why-contact-tracing-apps-could-be-a-disaster/.

SSRC (Social Science Research Council). 2021. *Surveillance and the 'New Normal' of COVID-19: Public Health, Data, and Justice*. New York: Social Science Research Council. https://covid19research.ssrc.org/public-health-surveillance-and-human-rights-network/report/.

Stiglitz, Joseph E. 2019. "Market Concentration is Threatening the US economy." *Project Syndicate*, March 11, 2019. https://www.project-syndicate.org/commentary/united-states-economy-rising-market-power-by-joseph-e-stiglitz-2019-03.

Taylor, Kate. 2021. "13,000 School Districts, 13,000 Approaches to Teaching During COVID." *New York Times*, January 21, 2021. https://www.nytimes.com/2021/01/21/us/schools-coronavirus.html.

Taylor, Keeanga-Yamahtta. 2021. "What's at Stake in the Fight over Reopening Schools." *New Yorker*, February 9, 2021. https://www.newyorker.com/news/our-columnists/whats-at-stake-in-the-fight-over-reopening-schools.

Teräs, Marko, Juha Suoranta, Hanna Teräs, and Mark Curcher. 2020. "Post-COVID-19 Education and Education Technology 'Solutionism': A Seller's Market." *Postdigital Science and Education*, no. 2: 863–78. https://doi.org/10.1007/s42438-020-00164-x.

USC Dornsife (University of Southern California Dornsife). 2020. "Understanding Coronavirus in America Study." https://uasdata.usc.edu/index.php.

Wall Street Journal. 2021. "How Big Tech Got Even Bigger." *Wall Street Journal*, February 6, 2021. https://www.wsj.com/articles/how-big-tech-got-even-bigger-11612587632.

Williamson, Ben. 2017. "Who Owns Educational Theory? Big Data, Algorithms and the Expert Power of Education Data Science." *E-Learning and Digital Media* 14 (3): 105–22. https://doi.org/10.1177/2042753017731238.

Williamson, Ben. 2020a. "New Financial Actors and Valuation Platforms in Education Technology Markets." Code Acts in Education (blog), December 15, 2020. https://codeactsineducation.wordpress.com/2020/12/15/new-financial-platforms-education/.

Williamson, Ben. 2020b. "Edtech Index Investing." Code Acts in Education (blog), September 15, 2020. https://codeactsineducation.wordpress.com/2020/09/15/edtech-index-investing/.

World Bank, and CCAF (Centre for Alternative Finance). 2020. *The Global COVID-19 FinTech Regulatory Rapid Assessment Study*. World Bank Group and the University of Cambridge.

Zuckerberg, Mark. 2020. "How Data Can Aid the Fight Against COVID-19." *Washington Post,* April 20, 2020. https://www.washingtonpost.com/opinions/2020/04/20/how-data-can-aid-fight-against-covid-19/.

CHAPTER 18

"CBDCs Mean Evolution, not Revolution"

Central Bank Digital Currencies in the Time of COVID

Horacio Ortiz

"COVID-19 will be remembered by economic historians as the event that pushed CBDC development into top gear" — a prediction expressed at a web seminar organized by the London School of Economics in June 2020 on the topic of central bank digital currencies (CBDCs) (Hall 2020; see also Cœuré 2020a). Their speaker, Benoît Cœuré, a former member of the Executive Board of the European Central Bank, is now head of the Innovation Hub at the Bank of International Settlements (BIS), in charge of coordinating and advancing research on CBDCs for the sixty-three central banks that control the organization. The assertion sounds almost absurd, if only because CBDCs are currently a marginal project for most central banks, but we must consider that the declaration of a "crisis" is often an occasion to define what should be normal (Roitman 2014). Cœuré's statement, then, is part of the way in which central banks' official discourses propose to imagine CBDCs and the future of money, making such discourses co-constitutive with particular definitions of COVID. These imaginaries are the object that this chapter examines.

The term "central bank digital currencies" refers to some means of payment based on digital technologies, issued by a central bank and used in individual everyday transactions recorded at that central bank. The People's Bank of China (PBoC) launched pilot programs in 2020, and the European Central Bank (ECB) plans to do so in 2021. Cœuré, in his assertion, was referring to regular surveys conducted by the BIS: in January 2021, 84 percent of the sixty-five central banks surveyed were conducting research or pilot programs on CBDCs, up from a third four years earlier (Boar and Wehrli 2021: 5). Part of this rise started before the pandemic, in reaction to Libra, Facebook's digital currency project. But the pandemic added a different dimension to CBDCs. They now became part of discussions surrounding the role of central banks, governments, and money in the production and transformation of social hierarchies, as the lives of billions of people around the world came to be affected by new forms of death, panic, lockdowns, and transformations in global interdependences.

In this chapter I do not start with an a priori definition of what money or CBDCs are or should be. Instead, I follow a pragmatist approach that looks at the multiple ways in which money is defined in actual practice (Dodd 2014; Guyer 2004; Hart and Ortiz 2014; Maurer 2017). To do so, I propose to analyze how money is imagined in the documents about CBDCs published by four institutions: the world's three most influential central banks — the ECB, the PBoC, and the Federal Reserve (the Fed) of the United States (US) — and, finally, the BIS.[1] Central banks play different roles depending on their national jurisdictions and their positions in global hierarchies. In particular, they conduct monetary policy, supervise and coordinate the banking system, and guarantee the production of bills and coins. Since the 1990s, they have tended to assume a monetarist stance, according to which they do not take active part in fiscal policy (Polillo and Guillén 2005). Yet, studying the reactions to

---

1. These documents have different formats and statuses. Some are official documents published in the name of the banks, others are speeches by members of the institutions. But I consider them together as they are all published on these institutions' websites. The PBoC has not published official documents on CBDCs since the beginning of the pandemic. I use the articles published by Fan Yifei, deputy governor of the PBoC (Fan Y. 2020), and Zhou Xiaochuan, the still-influential governor of the institution between 2002 and 2018 but who qualified that he was not speaking on its behalf (Zhou 2021). These documents agree on the main problematizations of CBDCs, although not on everything of course, and I will explore some of their differences below. For simplicity's sake, I will not quote each document for each assertion.

the financial upheavals of 2008 in the US and the United Kingdom, Paul Langley has shown that the supposed monetarist consensus is actually combined with Keynesianism. Monetary policy is also partly ad hoc, based on the instruments at hand, and informed by imaginaries regarding the emotions and habits of money users that do not fit clearly with any economic theory (Langley 2015). In these roles, central banks are fundamental in the production of global hierarchies. The fact that the Fed, the ECB, and the PBoC can be considered today the world's three most powerful central banks is directly related to the history of colonial expansion, the World Wars, the Cold War, and the rise of manufacturing in China in their aftermath. Although it remains out of the scope of this chapter to address all these historical processes, I show how the hierarchies that these processes have created are intimately connected to the ways in which central banks imagine CBDCs, whose design and possibilities are understood as ways of potentially redrawing global power relations.

The quote in the title of this chapter, which places "evolution" in contrast with "revolution" — also taken from Cœuré (2020b) — expresses a political and temporal tension that has become prominent during the pandemic. In the face of COVID, CBDCs are the site of conflicting calls either for the restoration of past dynamics or else for the production of new social hierarchies. In this chapter, I discuss three issues around which these conflicts are shaped and play out: the definition of money, the political responsibility of distribution, and the definition of monetary sovereignty.

The "Nature" of Money

The idea that CBDCs are an "evolution" is part of a functionalist definition of money, formalized for centuries in liberal philosophies, that defines money as a technical means determined by the needs of exchange. In this frame, the social hierarchies that result from exchange are conceived as not depending on money itself. An alternative to functionalism emphasizes the constitutive role of political authorities in the stabilization of money as a shared social standard. CBDCs, as a technological product of public authorities, are situated at the intersection of these two views on money. Marion Fourcade (2011) has shown how money practices have shaped divergent definitions of nature in conflicts around the determination of indemnities after oil spills. If we turn to the present situation with COVID, it is a certain definition of the nature of money that co-constitutes CBDCs and the pandemic together as part of a historical continuity. By foregrounding this naturalized view of money in the face of a natural disaster like the pandemic, the documents analyzed here attempt to neutralize some of the potential political meaning of CBDCs.

The main way in which these documents problematize CBDCs in relation to COVID is as a technological transformation of the otherwise unchanged roles of money as medium of exchange, unit of account, and store of value. COVID is thus presented as exogenous to money and society, creating new conditions for transactions — an "accelerator" of the already ongoing rise in the use of digital payments that, as in other crises, has also been accompanied by a rise in cash hoarding (Bank of Canada et al. 2020: 2; ECB 2020: 7). This is attributed partly to the fear of virus transmission through the handling of bills and coins, the increased use of e-commerce, and the digitization of social interactions — payments being one type. According to these documents, COVID is simply one moment that does not challenge the historical continuity of the roles of money.

In this view, the inevitability of CBDCs is due to their technological features, which allow for the expansion of transactions. They should be adopted because they can be used offline, via phone apps or cards charged with money, and they can increase transactions by integrating people into monetary exchanges who do not otherwise have bank accounts (Boakye-Adjei 2020). Also, since CBDCs are written in code, they could be designed to integrate features like positive or negative interest, as well as contractual clauses between parties that would be activated by the monetary units themselves — so-called "smart contracts" (Wong and Maniff 2020: 5; Zhou 2021). Payments would then benefit from the creativity of the private sector of the digital economy, as would society at large. This assignment of a natural character to CBDCs echoes the idea that payment methods are part of an ecosystem: "A balance would need to be struck between encouraging diversity and competition within the ecosystem, while maintaining sufficient regulatory standards of private service providers" (Bank of Canada et al. 2020: 13; see also Brainard 2020a: 3; ECB 2020: 7; Fan Y. 2020). In line with liberal theory, the sole role attributed to money in the face of the pandemic is to ensure the continuity of private transactions (Théret 2019).

Of the largest central banks, the PBoC was the first to roll out pilot CBDC projects among its population. Between April 2020 and March

2021, CBDCs have been distributed in pilot programs in four cities: Beijing, Shenzhen, Suzhou, and Chengdu. These programs consisted of giving out, through a lottery, amounts of RMB 200 that recipients could spend over one week using a dedicated app in select shops within the cities or online through the e-commerce platform Jingdong. In declarations to the press, authorities considered the project a success, given that participation in the lottery was much bigger than the amounts distributed and most ticket winners spent the money. Since then, some banks have offered their individual clients the ability to use the CBDC, which is increasingly being accepted in retail shops. The PBoC deputy governor's declarations regarding the historical place of CBDCs are in line with those published by the BIS, the ECB, and the Fed: "At every historical period, the development of productive forces induces new demands, and technological iteration has led money transformations from material goods, metals, paper and the like to electronic and digital forms, in order to increase money's circulation rate and consumers' welfare" (Fan Y. 2020; see also Lagarde 2020).

Yet, Cœuré placed evolution in contrast with revolution because CBDCs might give powers to public authorities that go well beyond this definition of money. A current critique of liberal approaches of money is that they tend to minimize the importance of public authorities in the definition of money as a shared social standard. The documents analyzed here acknowledge this aspect of money, assigning a foundational role to public authorities: "We should safeguard the role of sovereign money, a public good that central banks have been managing for centuries in the public interest and that should be available to all citizens to satisfy their need for safety" (Panetta 2020a: 2). The documents offer a reminder that central banks guarantee bank deposits in the case of bankruptcy and maintain the stability of the means of payment on which most transactions depend. Central banks' universal rejection of Facebook's attempt to launch Libra can be explained partly along these lines. This currency was projected to be used within the social network, composed of over 2.5 billion accounts across the world. A bankruptcy of Facebook could have left Libra holders with nothing because these deposits could not have been guaranteed. CBDCs, on the other hand, would be a "direct liability" on the central bank, which cannot go bankrupt on its own currency (Bank of Canada et al. 2020: 4).

The power of central banks over individual transactions could be much higher with CBDCs. All transactions would be totally traceable by central banks and could only be made anonymous by design. Central banks, like other banks, would indeed have to guarantee total traceability in order to comply with regulations designed to prevent tax evasion, money laundering, and criminal transactions like the financing of terrorism (Bank of Canada et al. 2020: 6; ECB 2020: 27; Fan Y. 2020; Zhou 2021). This fits the liberal frame by denying undue privilege to those violating the law. At the same time, it forces central banks to address issues of increased digitization that were dramatized by the pandemic. CBDCs thus connect directly with the varied imaginaries of digital surveillance, either as a danger for privacy or as the legitimate guarantee of fairness invoked in banking regulation. The ECB and the BIS explore explicitly all the technical features of CBDC design that can be deployed in order to limit these powers (ECB 2020; Bank of Canada et al. 2020).

The documents consider how the technological possibilities of CBDCs can extend the uses of money as well as the power of central banks. They also explore the digital design features that would be necessary to keep CBDCs an "evolution" as opposed to provoking a "revolution." It is thus by explicit technological design that the documents hope to maintain what they presuppose is a natural "ecosystem" to which both money and COVID belong. Thus naturalized, inequalities predating the pandemic can be considered the legitimate result of individual "transactions." This naturalization of the liberal definition of money, produced in tension with the avowed constitutive role of central authorities and technological design, is all the more unstable in that it occurs within the context of a debate about the potential distributive role of CBDCs.

Distribution

A central concern in the documents is the way in which CBDCs, due to their technical features and their backing by central banks, could radically transform the distribution of money in society. This has taken on new meanings with the pandemic and the programs of cash transfers deployed worldwide by governments with different ideologies and administrative systems. At stake are the relative roles of the financial industry and the state in the distribution of money.

In the jurisdictions addressed in this chapter, banks serve as the major contributors to monetary creation through the issuance of loans that are deposited into bank accounts. Monetary transactions, in turn, occur mainly digitally through these accounts. Depending on the jurisdiction, regulation restricts the money creation process by obliging banks to hold reserves in central banks, or to hold some minimum amount of their own capital as reserves, etc. This money is considered private because it is held in institutions that can default on their liabilities, even in cases in which they are state-owned (Bank of Canada et al. 2020: 4). Of course this arrangement is the product of a complex history, but the documents unsurprisingly reproduce the regulatory justifications for it, assuming that money creation and the distribution of credit should be concentrated in the financial industry given its technical expertise.

In March 2020, during negotiations in the US congress over a pandemic relief bill, a draft of the law proposed that money transfers be made through a "digital dollar" (Brett 2020), wording that would be abandoned a few days later. According to Robert Hockett, one of the economists behind the initiative, CBDCs can not only make transactions safer and faster, they can also allow the Fed and the treasury to transfer cash directly to those who need it, bypassing the "baroque system of bank middlemen who we hope will pass cheap credit to consumers. Instead we just drop the helicopter money into our digital wallets" (Hockett 2020: 36). Besides, if the Fed and the treasury recorded all transactions, they would have much better information to develop monetary and fiscal policies. Moreover, given that they would not be using this information for profit, they would also be more efficient than banks at creating money. Banks would thus lose their present role in money creation and would only be able to operate as intermediaries between supply and demand of money, much like current mutual funds. The BIS documents indeed remark that in so-called "emerging markets," CBDCs are viewed as ways to implement poverty reduction programs by directly transferring money to those who are unbanked but have cellphones or smartphones, while in richer regions the focus is on the efficiency of payments systems (Boar and Wehrli 2021: 3).

The documents produced by the central banks analyzed here systematically reject the possibility that central banks could lose their supposed "independence" from the treasury and take any direct role in the creation of money or the distribution of credit. They problematize such a loss of independence not only as a project to be rejected, but also as an unintended consequence of CBDCs that must be reined in — people could prefer to hold their money in CBDCs backed by central banks instead of in bank deposits that can be totally or partially lost if a bank defaults. In the case of a "digital bank run" (Balz 2020: 3), banks could lose all or a relevant fraction of their deposits, losing their ability to provide credit. The documents explain that if central banks end up holding these deposits, they could either lend to banks so that they keep lending in turn, or else take over the role of banks altogether and issue loans to companies and individuals directly (Peebles 2021).

The documents all consider such a scenario as a real possibility that must be avoided absolutely. The BIS survey shows that most CBDC projects propose a two-tiered system, where transactions are recorded at the central bank while banks and other payment service providers hold the CBDCs. These institutions would process all payments and retain control over the distribution of credit. In order to avoid digital bank runs, CBDCs could be designed with a maximum cap on the amount held in each account and with limitations on the kind of transactions for which they can be used. Some proponents consider that they could also pay lower interest rates than bank deposits, although they remark that this may not actually render banks more attractive, given the general low-rate environment (Bank of Canada et al. 2020; Mersch 2020).

The project of the PBoC is designed along these lines with a two-tier structure. Its name "Digital Payments/Electronic Currency," according to Zhou, implies that CBDCs may not necessarily be issued by the central bank. There could be multiple forms of money issued by different institutions, and the role of the central bank could just be to centralize information and guarantee interoperability. In China, mobile payments have expanded rapidly since the mid-2010s, and nowadays more than 800 million people use the digital payment apps of Alibaba (Alipay) and Tencent (Wechat Pay) in everyday transactions. Based on this payment data, these companies developed financial services in banking and insurance. Without being regulated as banks, they extended loans to small to medium-sized enterprises and consumers that were poorly served by banks. At the end of 2020, the government issued new regulations limiting these activities and giving more space to banks, the overwhelming majority of which are state-owned. But these two companies remain central to the state-backed projects of fostering gross domestic product (GDP) growth through innovation in the digital sector and extending the use of digital technologies in everyday life. These companies have developed in great part with the support of governments at the central, provincial, and local levels (Wang 2020). They are officially privately owned, but many of their top management are members of the Communist Party. In this context, CBDCs are presented as a new form of digital payment, one that would enrich the "ecosystem" and operate through banks and companies like Alibaba and Tencent without challenging their current roles in the creation of money and the distribution of credit.

Fan Yifei and Zhou Xiaochuan do not mention COVID in their discussion of the distributive possibilities of CBDCs. This is probably in part because GDP growth in China was 2.3 percent for 2020 against around 6 percent in previous years, and the circulation of the virus in the country had practically been halted since March 2020. The distributive potential of CBDC is only mentioned in one of the articles published in the *People's Daily* as part of the official debate regarding CBDCs (Fan Z. 2020). This remains in stark contrast with the role Hockett gave CBDCs in the proposed draft to the US Congress. In these two directions, CBDCs appear as a site where continuity and radical change are problematized in relation to the disruptions, or lack thereof, brought by the pandemic. The different positions of governments and central banks in relation to the pandemic and within the global hierarchy of currencies and wealth distribution, are constitutive of imaginations about the future of money in the form of CBDCs. In turn, the pandemic itself is either problematized as a social event that demands a radical rethinking of society, or as an external shock that can be absorbed by the natural evolution of the ecosystem, even if it is a nature that can only be obtained by digital design. The next section analyzes how this tension between "evolution" and "revolution" also concerns the way money is co-constituted with notions of state sovereignty.

Sovereignty

Simmel ([1900] 1978) put forward the idea that society is constituted as a series of monetary interdependences, as each user of money depends on other users for money to be accepted. This insight is useful in exploring the way that CBDCs help central banks problematize hierarchies within and between monetary spaces. In doing so, central banks imagine societies and state sovereignty produced by digital technologies as the result of the relationship between COVID and money.

When the documents consider that CBDCs could replace private money because of their apparent safety given their state backing, they assert the foundational role of state sovereignty for the stability of the social hierarchies produced by the financial industry. But because they fear total state control of the monetary space, they also recommend a CBDC design that would make such a scenario impossible. This, in turn, problematizes the relations between different currencies as power relations.

While the documents propose to protect the role of the financial industry in the creation of money, they take an opposite view regarding currencies produced by non-state actors. Currencies based on distributed ledger technologies, like Bitcoin, are not considered a major issue because they cannot become means of payment for large populations, since they consume too much energy for too small a number of transactions. On the contrary, the documents hold that the main spark for the acceleration of CBDC projects was Facebook's attempt to launch Libra in 2019 (Bank of Canada et al. 2020: 12–13; Brainard 2020a: 2; ECB 2020: 11–12). Besides its potential instability, the documents consider that national currencies deemed fragile could be displaced by Libra and other "stable coins" (i.e., coins produced by non-state actors and pegged to national currencies or other assets) (Brainard 2020b: 10; ECB 2020: 11–12; Fan Y. 2020; Zhou 2021). The documents thus present the acceleration of CBDC projects as a means of preventing the threat posed by currencies like Libra — CBDCs are, in other words, a way to occupy the space of digital payments with money controlled by central banks, so that this space may not be occupied by others (Bank of Canada et al. 2020: 12–13).

Expansive monetary and fiscal policies have different global effects depending on a country's place in the hierarchy of currencies. In particular, US policies tend to affect the rest of the world, as part of the money issued within the US is used elsewhere, sometimes displacing other national currencies. The dominant position of the US dollar depends on particular institutional arrangements that would have to be replicated, or that could be redrawn, with the development of CBDCs. In the documents analyzed here, the relationship between different states is then problematized as a hierarchy between national CBDCs. CBDCs of different countries could be exchanged between devices, such as smartphones, challenging the control of foreign exchange by banks. This could produce new geographies of monetary circulation beyond state borders. The documents are particularly concerned that people could drop national currencies deemed fragile for CBDCs backed by powerful states, or what they call "digital dollarization" (Bank of Canada et al. 2020: 8; Zhou 2021). The documents explain that, in order not to challenge current hierarchies of national currencies, or to do so only marginally, CBDCs should be designed so that only residents, tourists, and other visitors could use them. Digital design and legal cooperation should prevent CBDC circulation among devices or users not registered in the system controlled by the central banks (ECB 2020: 29; Zhou 2021).

The Fed, ECB, and PBoC offer differing views on the role of CBDCs in the global competition among national currencies, reflecting their own relative positions. The ECB and the PBoC hold that CBDCs would offer a chance to reinforce the role of their currency in global transactions while claiming that they do not seek hegemony and want to respect other national spaces (ECB 2020: 11–12; Fan Y. 2020; Panetta 2020b; Zhou 2021). Both Fan and Zhou assert that one of the aims of the PBoC's CBDC project is to prevent the threat of non-state currencies like Libra. Subsequently, Zhou (2021) considers that, just like dollarization, "renminbization" (人民币化) must be avoided as CBDC use extends to cross-border transactions. At the end of 2020 and the beginning of 2021, the PBoC entered into an agreement with the Society for Worldwide Interbank Financial Telecommunication, which provides the SWIFT functionality, to explore the possibility of using the CBDC in international payments, and also signed agreements with Thailand, Hong Kong, and the United Arab Emirates to explore cross-border use. Already in August 2020, Lael Brainard (2020a: 2), a member of the Fed's Board of Governors, responded to the possibility of these developments saying that "China has moved ahead rapidly on its version of a CBDC. ... Given the dollar's important role, it is essential that the Federal Reserve remain on the frontier of research and policy development regarding CBDCs."

In the time of COVID, expansive monetary and fiscal policies address social hierarchies within national monetary spaces and play out within a global hierarchy of currencies. The design of CBDCs could either transform or maintain these two types of hierarchies. They could redraw the inequalities that result from the supposedly natural role of money in individual transactions, and they could lead to new displacements or replacements between currencies. The documents thus problematize monetary sovereignty in the face of COVID as part of power relations that, depending on the digital design of CBDCs, could lead to monetary *status quo*, evolution, revolution, or war.

Conclusion

CBDCs are an occasion for central banks to assert particular definitions of money and digitization, the role of CBDCs in the constitution of monetary hierarchies, and the role of central banks themselves. With COVID, CBDCs have become part of conflicts between those pursuing continuity on the one hand and those pursuing radical change on the other. In turn, COVID is problematized as part of the history and political possibilities of money and digitization.

Central banks assert the primacy of money as a tool for individual transactions, of the financial industry in the distribution of credit, and of state sovereignty in global monetary relations. At the same time, they oppose these positions to the possibility that money might be used to transform social hierarchies through the direct intervention of public authorities, something they perceive as latent in the technological features of CBDCs and that has become an explicit concern with COVID. The assertion of state sovereignty can, in turn, be problematized as part of a competition among the most powerful central banks, hierarchically ordered in the global landscape, that must be redrawn with CBDC design.

The most powerful central banks seek to assert continuity based on a naturalized view of money's history, while the multifarious "natures" of COVID play out in the conflicting possibilities offered by CBDCs. In this process, these institutions co-constitute the pandemic and the future of money, in a tension they wish they could resolve, conjuring "evolution" against "revolution."

Acknowledgements

This chapter has benefited from the incisive work of the editors of the volume, Didier Fassin and Marion Fourcade, as well as the thorough reading of Isabelle Guérin, Fleur Johns, Benjamin Lemoine, Ma Xue, Susana Narotzky, Federico Neiburg, Bruno Théret, and Alden Young. I had the chance to explore many ideas that inspired this chapter during my time as a Member of the Institute for Advance Study, Princeton, in 2019–20, a position funded by the Florence Gould Foundation Fund. All errors are, of course, mine.

References

Balz, Burkhard. 2020. "Digital Currencies, Global Currencies." Speech presented at the China Europe Finance Summit — A Hybrid Conference on Sino-European Capital Markets, October 20, 2020. https://www.bis.org/review/r201020g.htm.

Bank of Canada, European Central Bank, Bank of Japan, Sveriges Riksbank, Swiss National Bank, Bank of England, Board of Governors Federal Reserve System, and Bank of International Settlements. 2020. *Central Bank Digital Currencies: Foundational Principles and Core Features.* Report No 1. Basel: Bank of International Settlements. https://www.bis.org/publ/othp33.htm.

Boakye-Adjei, Nana Y. 2020. "COVID-19: Boon and Bane for Digital Payments and Financial Inclusion." Financial Stability Institute, FSI Briefs, no. 9, July 24, 2020. https://www.bis.org/fsi/fsibriefs9.htm.

Boar, Codruta, and Andreas Wehrli. 2021. "Ready, Steady, Go? — Results of the Third BIS Survey on Central Bank Digital Currency." Bank for International Settlements, BIS Papers, no. 114. https://www.bis.org/publ/bppdf/bispap114.htm.

Brainard, Lael. 2020a. "An Update on Digital Currencies." Speech made to the Federal Reserve Board and Federal Reserve Bank of San Francisco's Innovation Office Hours, San Francisco, August 13, 2020. https://www.federalreserve.gov/newsevents/speech/Brainard20200813a.htm.

Brainard, Lael. 2020b. "The Digitalization of Payments and Currency: Some Issues for Consideration." Remarks by Lael Brainard, Member of the Board of Governors of the Federal Reserve System at the Symposium on the Future of Payments, Stanford Graduate School of Business, Stanford, California, February 5, 2020. https://www.federalreserve.gov/newsevents/speech/brainard20200205a.htm.

Brett, Jason. 2020. Coronavirus Stimulus Offered by House Financial Services Committee Creates New Digital Dollar. *Forbes*, March 24, 2020. https://www.forbes.com/sites/jasonbrett/2020/03/23/new-coronavi/.

Cœuré, Benoit. 2020a. "Digital Currencies and Stable Coins as Crisis Management Tools." Web seminar lecture, Center for Economic Policy Research, London School of Economics, June 11, 2020. https://youtu.be/QGMHGI9xev4.

Cœuré, Benoit. 2020b. "CBDCs Mean Evolution, Not Revolution." Op-ed for CoinDesk, October 20, 2020. https://www.bis.org/speeches/sp201021a.htm.

Dodd, Nigel. 2014. *The Social Life of Money*. Princeton: Princeton University Press.

ECB (European Central Bank). 2020. *Report on the Digital Euro*. October 2020. https://www.ECB.europa.eu/euro/html/digitaleuro-report.en.html.

Fan, Yifei (范一飞). 2020. "关于数字人民币M0定位的政策含义分析" (Analysis of the policy implications of the position of the digital renminbi in M0). 中国金融新闻网 (China Financial News), September 15, 2020. https://www.financialnews.com.cn/pl/zj/202009/t20200915_200890.html.

Fan, Zhiyong (范志勇). 2020. "何谓数字货币？它为什么如此重要？" (What is called digital currency? Why is it so important?). 人民网 (People's Daily Online), August 26, 2020. http://blockchain.people.com.cn/n1/2020/0826/c417685-31837438.html.

Fourcade, Marion. 2011. "Cents and Sensibility: Economic Valuation and the Nature of "Nature"." *American Journal of Sociology* 116 (6): 1721–77. https://doi.org/10.1086/659640.

Guyer, Jane. 2004. *Marginal Gains: Monetary Transactions in Atlantic Africa*. Chicago: University of Chicago Press.

Hall, Ian. 2020. "Central Bank Digital Currency Developments Hit 'Top Gear' Amid Coronavirus." *Global Government Forum*, June 18, 2020. https://www.globalgovernmentforum.com/central-bank-digital-currency-developments-hit-top-gear-amid-coronavirus/.

Hart, Keith, and Horacio Ortiz. 2014. "The Anthropology of Money and Finance: Between Ethnography and World History." *Annual Review of Anthropology*, no. 43: 465–82.

Hockett, R. 2020. "The Democratic Digital Dollar: A 'Treasury Direct' Option." Just Money, "Money in the Time of Coronavirus," Special Edition Roundtable, March 25, 2020, 36–40. https://justmoney.org/a-special-edition-roundtable-1/.

Lagarde, Christine. 2020. "The Future of Money — Innovating While Retaining Trust." European Central Bank, November 30, 2020. https://www.ECB.europa.eu/press/inter/date/2020/html/ECB.in201130~ce64cb35a3.en.html.

Langley, Paul. 2015. *Liquidity Lost: The Governance of the Financial Crisis*. Oxford: Oxford University Press.

Maurer, Bill. 2017. "Money as Token and Money as Record in Distributed Accounts." In *Distributed Agency*, edited by N. J. Enfield and Paul Kockelman, 109–16. Oxford: Oxford University Press.

Mersch, Yves. 2020. "An ECB Digital Currency — a Flight of Fancy?" Speech, Consensus 2020 virtual conference, European Central Bank, May 11, 2020. https://www.ECB.europa.eu/press/key/date/2020/html/ECB.sp200511~01209cb324.en.html.

Panetta, Fabio. 2020a. "From the Payments Revolution to the Reinvention of Money." Speech, Deutsche Bundesbank conference on the "Future of Payments in Europe," November 27, 2020. https://www.ECB.europa.eu/press/key/date/2020/html/ECB.sp201127~a781c4e0fc.en.html.

Panetta, Fabio. 2020b. "Unleashing the Euro's Untapped Potential at Global Level." Remarks at Meeting with Members of the European Parliament, July 7, 2020. https://www.ECB.europa.eu/press/key/date/2020/html/ECB.sp200707~3eebd4e721.en.html.

Peebles, Gustav. 2021. "Banking on Digital Money: Swedish Cashlessness and the Fraying Currency Tether." *Cultural Anthropology* 36 (1): 1–24. https://doi.org/10.14506/ca36.1.01.

Polillo, Simone, and Mauro F. Guillén. 2005. "Globalization Pressures and the State: The Worldwide Spread of Central Bank Independence." *American Journal of Sociology* 110 (6): 1764–1802. https://doi.org/10.1086/428685.

Roitman, Janet. 2014. *Anti-Crisis*. Durham: Duke University Press.

Simmel, Georg. [1900] 1978. *The Philosophy of Money*. New York: Routledge.

Théret, Bruno. 2019. "Bonjour la finance, au revoir la monnaie! Pourquoi la fin annoncée du cash peut être vue comme une performation de la doctrine monétaire qui sous-tend la théorie financière de l'efficience des marchés." *Revue de l'Euro*, no. 54: 1–22.

Wang, Jing. 2020. "The Party Must Strengthen Its Leadership in Finance!": Digital Technologies and Financial Governance in China's Fintech Development. *The China Quarterly* First View: 1–20. https://doi.org/10.1017/S0305741020000879.

Wong, Paul, and Jesse L. Maniff. 2020. "Comparing Means of Payment: What Role for a Central Bank Digital Currency?" FEDS Notes, August 13, 2020. Washington, DC: Board of Governors of the Federal Reserve System, https://doi.org/10.17016/2380-7172.2739.

Zhou, Xiaochuan (周小川). 2021. "数字时代的中国支付体系现代化-DC/EP与数字人民币" (The modernization of the Chinese payment system in the era of digitalization — DC/EP and the digital renminbi). 链得得 (Chain DD), February 16, 2021. https://www.chaindd.com/3498726.html.

CHAPTER 19

Modeling Pandemic

Fleur Johns

"We need new models" has been a regular refrain amid the COVID pandemic. New models of public-private partnership for vaccine delivery; new models of disease spread and mortality characteristics; new models of aged care; new economic models — all these and more have been called for of late. In these calls, the term "model" might mean different things yet is nonetheless a recurrent point of reference. It encapsulates a set of intersecting knowledge practices now ubiquitously understood as essential for navigating the complexities of contemporary life. Its recurrence also speaks to recognized limits of these knowledge practices. The cry "we need new models" laments uncertainty, fear, and suffering and expresses an aspiration that these may be surmounted through human ingenuity, computationally enhanced, together with a *sotto voce* disquiet as to whether this is possible. What the "model" signifies in these calls is a world of which people may yet be mindful modelers.

As these calls illustrate, modeling has been central to prevailing experiences of, and debates surrounding, the COVID pandemic. Indeed, the pandemic may be said to exist as a model, or a composite of models, in many people's perception. Consider, for example, the situation of lay people logging onto the Johns Hopkins University COVID dashboard — at one point reported to be receiving a billion hits per day. To do so is to grasp the scale and properties of the pandemic by recourse to mathematical models, albeit relatively simple ones. By working backwards from one other genre of pandemic-related modeling output — social distancing policies — and examining how modeling shaped such policies, this chapter probes how certain types of models, and their instantiation in law, policy, and official guidance, have promoted particular understandings of social life. It elucidates the characteristics of the world to which modeling-for-social-distancing in a pandemic has testified, and the awkwardness of their fit with some people's worlds more than others. In so doing, this chapter explores something of these models' centers and peripheries, foregrounds and backgrounds, hierarchies and priorities, preoccupations and blind spots. What this chapter illuminates beyond this specific case are the different vectors along which practices of ordering move. Modeling may be as significant a regulatory activity as treaty-making or the adoption of legislation. Yet it tends to enter such processes obliquely as a matter of practice, and thereby to bypass most prospects for democratic debate. Models that so move assign differing capacities to live a perceptible and appreciable life and to structure debate over what is worth discerning, what gets considered, and how, in times of COVID. Models structure, in other words, the sensory economy (Johns 2017); they do so in ways that have implications for the many economies traversed in this book. These are the stakes of pandemic modeling on which this chapter dwells.

Models are not, however, monstrous. The aim of this chapter is not to try to expose modeling as some malevolent or suspicious force in economy and society in times of COVID. The goal is likewise not to argue about contending models' relative merits nor advocate for particular models' improvement in one way or another. Rather, this chapter draws attention to how significant a force of economic and social ordering modeling has been in this global pandemic. It aims to show how a broad of range of people and institutions have stakes in the preference of one modeling technique over another, and in the choices, distinctions, links, and hierarchies invariably embedded within models. It seeks to demonstrate, as a consequence, how worthy of attention, informed critique, and cross-referencing against other knowledge forms such influential models are. Modeling is an invaluable practice of social and economic ordering and analysis; it ought not be an indubitable one.

Models and Modeling

To embark on the study just outlined requires something to be said about modeling as a genre of knowledge practice and about what the term "model" may imply in the context of pandemic-related knowledge production. This entails generalization across a number of distinct professional practices, each of which merits, and has attracted, dedicated investigation. These include scientific modeling, mathematical modeling, financial and economic modeling, and social modeling.

Across these different areas of work, the word "model" denotes a representation of, or proxy for, some target about which knowledge is sought, whether that target be actual or ideal (Portides 2013). A model describes a structure or puts forward an archetype or set of archetypes (OED 2021). A model is also an analogue in the sense that it typically posits relations of similarity and difference to some worldly phenomena, or to a theoretical description of some worldly phenomena. Models' analogical status does, however, vary in degree. Some models are designed to be positive analogues of the "real world." An example would be models used in species distribution modeling, to try to predict the distribution of an extant species over space and time. Others are "working pictures" developed for instrumental purposes and then dispensed with — at most, only ever formally analogous to something in the world (Hesse 2017, 1966). One example of the latter would be English chemist John Dalton's early nineteenth-century modeling of the atom on a hard, wooden ball, similar to one used in billiards. The idea that the model necessarily represents something other than itself may also be strained. Some models produce data in their own right about their own rendering of nonexistent phenomena (as when Daisyworld computer simulation models may produce data about planetary scenarios such as life never having existed on Earth) (Huneman and Lemoine 2014). The broad genre of knowledge practice with which this chapter is concerned is that involved in making, analyzing, disseminating, predicting with, and otherwise being informed by models.

Within this expansive category of knowledge practice, scientific modeling is a distinct and influential strain. Many have noted the centrality of modeling to science. Models in science may be material (physical, such as a scale model of the DNA molecule) or formal (such as a wave equation) (Hesse 2017). Put another way, scientific models may be *in vivo*, *in vitro*, or *in silico* (Huneman and Lemoine 2014). They may take the form of particular organisms standing in for other species or taxa for purposes of investigating certain biological processes or testing pharmacological interventions. The *Drosophila* genus of fruit flies used by geneticists is an example. They may be comprised of laboratory reproductions of particular biochemical processes. One example is a model of osmotic shock (sudden change in salt concentration in surrounding solution) in yeast or *Escherichia coli* cells induced for biochemical analysis. Or they may take the form of computer simulations, such as cellular automata and other agent-based models, representing the behavior of complex systems over time.[1]

A distinguishing characteristic of scientific models — as distinct from scientific "laws" — is their contingency, partiality, and amenability to pluralism and iterative adjustment. As Joachim Schummer (2014: S98) has observed, "different models for the same field of application can peacefully coexist and usefully complement each other, because they might employ different approximations. ... Both laws and models are comparable tools for explanations and predictions, but laws assume exclusive explanatory power while models can explain only those aspects [that] they have been built" to explain. Although laws may approximate and vary in scope, a law proposed in science is typically designed to cover a broader class, and to issue more enduring precepts, than a scientific model.

Mathematical modeling often intersects with scientific modeling. Computer simulations, for instance, may be regarded as instances of both. Nonetheless, mathematicians' usage of the term "model" diverges somewhat from its typical usage in science. As noted above, mathematical modeling sometimes entails description of a "real world" or ideal

---

1. The term "agent-based models" refers to computer models that stage recurrent, competitive interactions among elements representing autonomous decision-making entities called agents. Within the ambit of the model, they allow for an individual agent's behavior to depend upon the state of its neighborhood and its interactions with other individual agents and require data on these interactions (Bonabeau 2002). Although some agent-based modeling employs differential equations, it is often distinguished from equation-based modeling (Parunak et al. 1998). The latter entails the construction of models comprised of equations expressing relationships among certain classes of observable or attributable characteristics, and the evaluation of these equations, and the change in the characteristics that they produce, over time. Agent-based models create something of a virtual world populated by individual archetypes, whereas equation-based models assemble and work with quantifiable categories.

system using mathematical concepts and language. Yet mathematicians also use the term model to denote a structured realization or representation of data (comprised of variables, equations, and assumptions or boundary conditions) in which all elements of a particular theory are satisfied (Suppes 1960). Some mathematical models may also represent results from the testing of ad hoc hypotheses without necessarily expressing a fundamental theory in full; the liquid drop theory of nuclear structure does not, for example, explain all nuclear phenomena (Portides 2011, 2013). Data scientists' use of the term "model" is more akin to the latter: the term refers to a standardized, reproducible set of procedures that may be deployed predictively against data, often derived from the processing of training data by a learning algorithm.

Financial and economic modeling is that branch of the practice concerned with creating textual and mathematical representations of markets and economic processes. An economic model is a "story with a specified structure" that comprises "an accepted way of representing the [complex] economic world in a simpler way so that [economists] can think about its features" (Gibbard and Varian 1978: 666; Morgan 2001: 380; see also Morgan 2012). Modeling in this mode is used to guide investment decision-making, product pricing, and risk assessment, among other practices. In these contexts, the concern of modeling is not generally with faithful reproduction of the world. Rather, the aim of modeling is the approximation of certain economic or financial phenomena, by recourse to stated assumptions, from the manipulation and analysis of which certain insights and predictions may be drawn. A "good" model, according to prevailing expectations in much of this field, is economically plausible (albeit inexactly so), analytically tractable, and useful for market purposes. That a model's assumptions may be unverified or somewhat unrealistic does not generally consign that model to uselessness. In this mode, modeling has been fundamental to the burgeoning of financial economics, and associated trading activities, since the mid-twentieth century (MacKenzie 2006).

Social modeling, in contrast, is a far less professionalized practice than any of the foregoing. To describe and compare social models is to subscribe to the idea that path dependency, institutional design, and other factors yield certain distinctive patterns or "models" of social, political, and economic organization, the merits and demerits of which may be compared. Modeling in this mode has been a feature of law and policy making wherever the transfer, replication, or scaling up of particular governance institutions have been at issue — all matters central to imperialism and colonialism. One can, for example, find numerous scattered references to government in one colony offering a "model" for another in the correspondence of officials charged with colonial rule (e.g., Lord William Bentinck 1831, quoted in Leonard 2020: 397n125).

Social modeling grew in prevalence and influence over the second half of the twentieth century, building on the historical-comparative sociology of Max Weber and his use of ideal types (Weber 2019). Since then, Europe, East Asia, particular countries, or other portions of the world have come to be "seen as containers of specific and separate national and regional cases of economic and social performance, cases that are defined through comparison and demarcation from each other in terms of similarities and differences" (Stråth 2007: 336). Entanglements and obscurities tend to be de-emphasized so that relatively clear-cut models of society may be described and compared. A model, in this context, is a preformed, unitary example used as a basis for evaluation and experiment. The "model" in this setting is more analogous to a scientific animal model than to a computer simulation. Nonetheless, the activity of modeling at issue (namely, description and comparison) stands quite apart from the technical practices of scientific, mathematical, or economic modeling, as noted above. This and all the other modes of modeling described above have been brought to bear, in combination, upon the COVID pandemic.

Modeling COVID

SARS-CoV-2, the novel coronavirus that causes COVID-19 and the associated pandemic, have both been the focus of extensive scientific and mathematical modeling, through computer simulation especially (Jewell et al. 2020; Adam 2020). Models employed have included SIR or SEIR models, epidemiological models that compute the number of people theoretically infected, or projected to be infected, with a contagious illness in a given population over time by assigning numbers of people to various compartments: susceptible, exposed, infectious, and removed (that is, immune or deceased). Propagation and diffusion of SARS-CoV-2 have also been analyzed using genetic evolution models, representing incidence of mutation and mutation rates across time and space. Similarly, interactome models of SARS-CoV-2 in humans have been used to study how viral-host interactions affecting proteins and other molecules within cells may regulate associated pathogenesis.

Certain numbers derived from scientific and mathematical modeling have loomed especially large in popular consciousness and governmental communication about this pandemic, two examples being the basic reproduction number (R_0) and effective reproduction number (R).[2] Likewise, particular instances of modeling appear to have been particularly influential in policy making and public debate concerning this pandemic, especially when linked to numerical targets (Rhodes and Lancaster 2020).[3] The impact of the modeling work of mathematical epidemiologist Neil Ferguson and his team at Imperial College London is a noteworthy example. Projections from their models reportedly prompted policy changes by the government of the United Kingdom (Adam 2020).

Financial and economic modeling of the actual and projected impacts of COVID has likewise been widespread. OECD economists have, for instance, modeled base-case, best-case, and downside scenarios of the pandemic's economic effects using the NiGEM Model, a quarterly econometric model based on real economic data from forty-six countries (twenty-eight from Europe, including the United Kingdom, eleven from Asia and Australasia, six from the Americas, and one from Africa) and some nineteen regions maintained by the National Institute of Economic and Social Research in Britain (Boone 2020). These modelers' focus has been on extraordinary disruptions produced by the pandemic — interruptions in supply, declines in demand, and loss of confidence — rather than preexisting, structural features of the economy bearing upon COVID outcomes, such as inequality, urbanization, or the distribution of access to health care. In this account, the pandemic's economic repercussions have been cast as "fallout" and the emergence of the SARS-CoV-2 virus characterized as a "hit" and a "shock," as though analyzing a military attack, industrial accident, or natural disaster (Boone 2020). We return to these story-telling dimensions of modeling practice below.

Social modeling of a less technical kind has also been apparent in analyses of the COVID pandemic. Comparisons among national policy responses to the pandemic have proliferated (e.g., Greer et al. 2021).

---

2. With respect to any one disease, the R_0 and R numbers express, respectively, the average number of secondary infections produced by a case of infection in a population without immunity and the average number of people to whom one infected person is actually passing the virus at a given time.
3. On model-projection-target links in health governance more broadly, see Rhodes and Lancaster (2021).

In scholarly, clinical, and public discussion of the pandemic, certain national archetypes of COVID policy response have more commonly been popularized and compared than others. Those advancing particular policy recommendations have frequently done so with reference to one or other national model — the "Singapore model," for example (e.g., Wei 2020). The "Swedish model"— a "relaxed strategy" premised on the build-up of herd immunity within a national population — has been a particular target of scrutiny and debate (e.g., Ramachandran 2020).

In these various settings, COVID modeling has been a mode of argument as well as an analytical practice. To model is to give shape, to craft, or to fashion. Models assemble certain elements and entities and "offer them to experience already linked together" (Foucault 2001: 389). When models feature humans, or human proxies, they confer upon those figures certain characteristics, functions, needs, and desires, and strip away other properties. Modeling entails determining precisely what will suffice to approximate that which is modeled, or otherwise inform decision-making on that subject matter. In so doing, modeling involves carving out cores (or determining what is essential) and dispensing with inessential aspects of phenomena represented. As the discussion below will show, these norms and priorities often travel and persist via models and in policies in which they come to be embedded.

Models of the COVID pandemic have proliferated along with the profusion of relevant scholarly literature. Even so, as noted above, a relatively small subset of the models advanced in this scholarly work have found expression in policy statements, official recommendations, and legal norms designed to counter the pandemic, limit its spread, and mitigate its adverse effects. The next section focuses on one genre of law and policy output related to COVID that is underpinned, in large part, by modeling: social distancing requirements.

Social Distancing as a Modeling Output

Some commentators have asserted that social distancing recommendations pronounced in the face of the COVID pandemic "are based on studies of respiratory droplets carried out in the 1930s" (Prather et al. 2020). The provenance of these policies is, however, difficult to establish with such precision; their evidence base is more cumulative and collage-like than this suggests (Qureshi et al. 2020). Nonetheless, it is certainly the case that modeling of the dispersal of droplets, and of associated disease transmission, underpins the policies adopted around the world to try to ensure that people keep their distance from one another. Diseases like COVID, that partially manifest in respiratory symptoms, are known to be passed on through airborne transmission of virus-containing droplets emitted during breathing, speaking, coughing, and sneezing. Prior decades' modeling of the emission, movement, and settling of these droplets makes up a key part of the knowledge base on which social distancing policies are founded. These encompass policies effecting school closure, workplace, and enterprise closure or circumscribed operation, case isolation, and a range of other measures designed to reduce interpersonal contact. For purposes of this discussion, let us focus on recommendations to maintain a minimum amount of physical distance among people's bodies.

From the early days of the COVID pandemic, the World Health Organization (WHO) advised people to keep at least one meter or about three feet away from others. China, Egypt, France, India, Liberia, Norway, Singapore, Thailand, and other nations issued similar recommendations, as did Denmark (after reducing the minimum recommended distance from two meters to one in May 2020). The Centers for Disease Control and Prevention (CDC) in the United States recommended that people maintain a distance of at least six feet (or 1.8 meters) between themselves and others. Meanwhile, Australia, Bolivia, Germany, Italy, the Netherlands, Serbia, Spain, South Africa, and other nations indicated that 1.5 meters is the minimum distance from others that people should maintain. The United Kingdom initially recommended people keep at least two meters or approximately 6.5 feet away from others but dropped this to "one meter plus" as of early July 2020, while recommending adoption of other measures to prevent viral transmission. Botswana, Canada, and Vietnam advised people to stay at least two meters apart. South Korea suggested likewise, while accepting one meter as a minimum distance in certain environments.

As well as being the subject of health advice and other "soft" governance measures, these minimum social distances have been rendered enforceable in a range of ways backed by the coercive power of the state. Legislation and regulations requiring the closure of schools and certain businesses, stipulating the conditions under which schools and businesses may open, and prohibiting gatherings of certain sizes: these are illustrative of the hardening of social distancing requirements around the world. In many jurisdictions, those who congregate or operate in breach of these may be subject to heavy fines or even jail terms. All states in Australia, for example, have introduced penalties for individuals and businesses conducting themselves in breach of social distancing requirements. In the State of New South Wales in Australia, orders made under the state's Public Health Act enable individuals to be fined up to AUD 11,000 (nearly USD 8,000) initially (and more for continuing to breach the rules), or sentenced to six months in jail, for violating such restrictions. In India, jail terms of up to two years may be imposed, alongside fines, upon those who refuse to comply with public health directions issued under the Disaster Management Act. In Singapore, regulations promulgated under the Infectious Diseases Act have made breaches of social distancing measures punishable by fines (up to SGD 10,000 or nearly USD 7,500) or imprisonment of up to six months, or both. In Denmark, violations of restrictions imposed under the Danish Epidemics Act are punishable by fines (up to DKK 40,000 or nearly USD 6,500 per instance, increased for repeat offences) or jail terms of up to six months. Across the United States, noncompliance with regulations and executive orders mandating social distancing may attract civil or criminal penalties, including (potentially) orders to suspend business operations, license revocations, misdemeanor arrests, fines, or imprisonment (typically for terms up to 30 days, but in some jurisdictions — Indiana, for example — up to 180 days).

The rationales offered by the WHO when communicating these distancing requirements to the public made implicitly clear their foundation on the modeling of muco-salivary respiratory droplets' exhalation and airborne movement. When explaining why people must stay at least one meter apart, the WHO website stated that "when someone coughs, sneezes, or speaks they spray small liquid droplets from their nose or mouth which may contain virus. If you are too close, you can breathe in the droplets, including the COVID virus if the person has the disease." Within months of such guidelines being issued to deal with the COVID pandemic, however, researchers attacked the soundness of their evidence base and questioned the correspondence between distancing recommendations and insights derived from scientific modeling. As noted above, prevailing social distancing rules have been broadly founded on assumptions that the SARS-CoV-2 virus is primarily transmitted via respiratory droplets, larger versions of which had been shown to settle fairly quickly after emission under the force of gravity. Research making use of technology capable of detecting extremely small (submicron) aerosols suggested, however, that airborne transmission could occur via a continuum of droplet sizes embedded in clouds of exhaled air. Smaller aerosolized droplets have been shown capable of remaining airborne for many hours and travelling distances far greater than the one or two meters specified for social distancing, with environmental factors such as ventilation bearing significantly on viral transfer. In short, evidence supportive of physical distancing of between one and two meters has been shown to be sparse or outdated (Bahl et al. 2020; Prather et al. 2020; Qureshi et al. 2020). If social distancing requirements were founded on models of airborne rather than droplet transmission, the distances mandated could well have been much greater, or regulatory requirements might have focused more on ventilation conditions and masking than on physical proximity, for example. It was not until the end of April 2021, however, that the WHO updated the Q&A page of its website to acknowledge that SARS-CoV-2 could spread in poorly ventilated indoor settings regardless of physical distancing because "aerosols remain suspended in the air or travel farther than 1 metre" (Chamary 2021).

The particular models by which social distancing measures have been and should be informed may be a matter of debate, yet these regulations remain an output of modeling, nonetheless. What seems apparent in the convergence of national policies around a relatively limited range of options for mandating social distancing — all in the one-to-two-meter range — is the cumulative impact of model-borne thinking and practice across several fields. Scientific modeling underpinned the initial identification of a risk of viral transfer via muco-salivary droplets, and the prospect of its mitigation through human bodies' physical distancing. Economic modeling encouraged governments and international organizations to focus on policy arrangements that seem analytically tractable, and useful or "saleable" for current market purposes, even if the assumptions on which they are based may be questionable. Social modeling supported the idea that collective social conduct is best organized, grasped, and evaluated by recourse to a preexisting array of patterns or archetypes, assigned to national containers. It fostered a tendency to take something off the shelf, as it were, rather than approach social analysis and policy making *ab initio* or at larger or smaller scales (planetary, regional, or city- or community-scale, for instance). In all these ways, social distancing policies are artefacts of a modeled world.

Modeled Worlds

What, then, are the characteristics of the modeled worlds to which social distancing policies testify? Much of the scholarly commentary on the epistemology of models from outside the natural sciences and mathematics fields has revolved around their potential to mislead. Of particular concern has been models' propensity to generate an illusion of truth, integrity, and predictive capacity even while exhibiting any number of weaknesses, including poor or biased input data; empirically incorrect assumptions; highly sensitive estimates; thin historical analysis with inattention to prior model-based outcomes; lack of transparency; and want of consultation with domain experts (Ellison 2020; Ioannidis, Cripps, and Tanner 2020). In relation to the COVID pandemic specifically, some have claimed that efforts to forecast its trajectory and impact on the basis of modeling have "largely failed" despite "involving many excellent modelers, best intentions, and highly sophisticated tools" (Ioannidis, Cripps, and Tanner 2020: 4).

In this chapter, the relative truth value of different models is not of immediate concern. Instead, the focus is on the social and economic ordering work that they do. Whether or not COVID modeling has succeeded or failed in particular instances, and regardless of the strength or weakness of particular models, models are nonetheless offering up particular renderings of the pandemic and the world it has afflicted. Models are artefacts with politics; they champion certain arrangements of relation, power, and authority over others (Winner 1980). In this light, let us identify some recurrent features of models representing the COVID pandemic and of the world that they offer to experience.

First, these models are prosocial insofar as they tend to incline modeled units toward one another and highlight reciprocal impacts among them (harmful as well as beneficial ones). Ideals of absolute autonomy or libertarian freedom are not readily secured by modeling because models are by nature about interactions and interdependencies. A modeled COVID pandemic is a systemic phenomenon within which boundaries at all scales — biological, territorial, and political — are permeable. Those who envision themselves as isolates — people such as the "solitary nonemployed persons" who effect "hikikomori," or complete social withdrawal, as described in the Japanese labor economist Yuji Genda's work (2019) — find no place for their self-understanding in a modeled world. It would be a mistake, however, to equate models' prosociality with evenhandedness or disinterest. In their prosocial dimensions, models tend to put forward an impression of inclusiveness that belies their selective slicing and differential weighting. Models' partiality may be methodologically justified, but it cannot be wished away. The sociality of models is a classified and ranked condition of unavoidable connectedness.

Second, the modeled world of the COVID pandemic is taken, for the most part, to be governable — and governable in a partitionable mode. Borders may be closed. Bodies may be rearranged in space and time, contained within categories (nations and genders, for instance), and disciplined to adhere to those arrangements. Modeled worlds are amenable to varying degrees of human mastery (depending on their stochastic dimensions and error rates), but most tend to have humans at both their centers and their helms. The systems that they represent — the worlds that models make — are largely anthropocentric, even though the precipitant for their creation may have been viral zoonosis (as in the case of SARS-CoV-2). At the same time, both models and public communications referencing models tend to presume broad familiarity with modeling practices among their audiences. This is despite the fact of "pervasive misperception of models" having been well documented, including among the literate and otherwise privileged (e.g., Wagner et al. 2010).

This presumed governability of the world that models make is conditional upon evoking and then screening out sites and modes of relative ungovernability, and those for whom modeled messaging may make little sense. This is among pandemic models' "infra-legal" effects (Johns 2013). Those people for whom the modeled governance measures (such as social distancing measures) are unlikely to be effective — say, for slum-dwellers living under conditions not amenable to social distancing, persons with a disability requiring intimate care, or those whose work demands intimacy without a health-care rationale (such as sex workers) — may only register in the unexplained negative spaces of a model: perhaps as a percentage of the population presumed noncompliant, or as an error rate. This is true, too, of people who tend to be represented poorly or scantly in models for other reasons, such as those about whom there is a paucity of epidemiological data.[4] Those negative spaces may be read to invite governmental intervention, or they could be interpreted as too intractable, unruly, or insignificant to be worthy of attention. Either way, those upon whom prevailing governance techniques are more likely to have clear purchase, and those to

---

4. Diane Korngiebel and her colleagues (2015: 1744) observe that certain populations, such as indigenous peoples, are poorly represented in epidemiological data sets for a range of reasons that may include "culturally discordant survey content," "ineffective data collection methods," and "ethnic and racial misclassification."

whom model-based communications speak most easily — they are first in line as objects of analysis and care when modeling a pandemic. Models of the COVID pandemic produce and presume "ungovernability," as health care long has (Al-Dewachi 2017). They do so by orienting themselves around those who are presumed governable by virtue of being amenable to partition.

Third and finally, modeled worlds of the COVID pandemic are event oriented. It was noted above how models of the economic effects of the pandemic have tended to cast the emergence of the SARS-CoV-2 virus as a "shock." This is understandable, notwithstanding the many settings in which a zoonotic pandemic of this kind had been anticipated and projected. Nonetheless, it has implications for how reactions to the virus are framed. When the pandemic is modeled as a singular event, it is not cast as the culmination of known historical processes, such as deforestation and habitat destruction (often highlighted as causal factors in zoonosis), or the underfunding or paucity of public health care (again, a recognized factor in COVID outcomes). This tends to encourage reactions framed as counter-events: successive reactions of a *staccato*, finite nature.

Most commonly, the effects of the SARS-CoV-2 virus are modeled over a definite, relatively short time span. Models are generally not crafted to account for long-term factors contributing to the virus's emergence in humans, nor as if this virus were likely to become endemic. This is in part because of the "disappointingly short horizon of predictability for epidemic models" (Wong et al. 2020). This has the effect of bringing legal and policy measures introduced in the face of the pandemic neatly under the umbrella of emergency, prompting recourse to extraordinary powers designed for disaster and relatively unfettered by "normal" accountability processes. It also delinks the social welfare measures that have been introduced in many jurisdictions to deal with the pandemic from the routine infrastructure of state support. As a consequence, shortfalls and vulnerabilities illuminated afresh by the pandemic may be more likely to be addressed with piecemeal, short-term measures rather than dealt with in enduring ways. When we model the COVID pandemic as an event, it becomes harder to understand it as something to which many routine human practices have contributed — such as, say, changes in macroeconomic policies affecting deforestation in low- and middle-income countries (Angelsen and Kaimowitz 1999). This suggests little occasion to revisit the past or to try to reorient those preexisting routines.

Conclusion

The world that we have come to know over the course of the COVID pandemic is, in many respects, a modeled world — shaped by scientific, mathematical, economic, and social models and their intersection. This is a world of unavoidable interdependence. It is a world amenable to human governance premised on partition and apportionment, seemingly without too much agony or ambivalence. It is a world comprehensible and addressable in terms of relatively discrete, recent events. It is, as consequence of these features, a world of priorities and blind spots. That which may be well modeled in these terms tends to occupy the foreground of public perception and debate. Those phenomena and human experiences poorly aligned with a world so framed — the disconnected, the hybrid, the persistent, the nonhuman, the unstudied, and so on — become harder to register and accommodate amid first order concerns. As noted above, "we need new models" has been a regular refrain amid the COVID pandemic. This has often been well justified. Yet perhaps, alongside new models, we need to make more room for cross-referencing these against unmodeled knowledge about the COVID pandemic as well, including forms of knowledge most strongly associated with the humanities, social sciences, and creative arts (narrative knowledge, for instance). In these and other ways, scholarly, policy, and community decision-making concerning the pandemic must remain alive to the politics of modeling. It is a politics in which we all now have a stake.

Acknowledgements

The author acknowledges the support of the Institute for Advanced Study (IAS), Princeton, during the writing of this chapter. Thanks are due also to the editors of this volume and to all those in the School of Social Sciences at the IAS during the year 2019–20 for their collegiality and insights, and to Caroline Compton and Wayne Wobcke for comments on prior versions of this chapter. Versions of this chapter were presented at the 24th Biennial Conference of the Association of Asian Social Science Research Councils in 2021 and at the 2021 Annual Meeting of the Society for the Social Studies of Science (4S); it benefited from the generous feedback of audiences and co-panelists at both events.

References

Adam, David. 2020. "Special Report: The Simulations Driving the World's Response to COVID-19: How Epidemiologists Rushed to Model the Coronavirus Pandemic." *Nature* 580 (7803): 316–18. https://doi.org/10.1038/d41586-020-01003-6.

Al-Dewachi, Omar. 2017. *Ungovernable Life: Mandatory Medicine and Statecraft in Iraq*. Stanford: Stanford University Press.

Angelsen, Arild, and David Kaimowitz, 1999. "Rethinking the Causes of Deforestation: Lessons from Economic Models." *World Bank Research Observer* 14 (1): 73–98. https://doi.org/10.1093/wbro/14.1.73.

Bahl, Prateek, Con Doolan, Charitha de Silva, Abrar A. Chughtai, Lydia Bourouiba, and C. Raina MacIntyre. 2020. "Airborne or Droplet Precautions for Health Workers Treating Coronavirus Disease 2019?" *Journal of Infectious Diseases*. https://doi.org/10.1093/infdis/jiaa189.

Bonabeau, Eric. 2002. "Agent-Based Modeling: Methods and Techniques for Simulating Human Systems." *Proceedings of the National Academy of Sciences* 99 (suppl. 3): 7280–87. https://doi.org/10.1073/pnas.082080899.

Boone, Laurence. 2020. "Tackling the Fallout from COVID-19." In *Economics in the Time of COVID-19*, edited by Richard E. Baldwin and Beatrice Weder di Mauro, 37–44. London: CEPR Press.

Chamary, J. V. 2021. "WHO Finally Admits Coronavirus Is Airborne: It's Too Late." *Forbes*, May 4, 2021. https://www.forbes.com/sites/jvchamary/2021/05/04/who-coronavirus-airborne/?sh=129da7334472.

Ellison. Geroge T. H. 2020. "COVID-19 and the Epistemology of Epidemiological Models at the Dawn of AI." *Annals of Human Biology* 47 (6): 506–13. https://doi.org/10.1080/03014460.2020.1839132.

Foucault, Michel. 2001. *The Order of Things*. London: Routledge.

Genda, Yuji. 2019. *Solitary Non-Employed Persons: Empirical Research on Hikikomori in Japan*. Singapore: Springer.

Gibbard, Allan, and Hal R. Varian. 1978. "Economic Models." *Journal of Philosophy* 75 (11): 664–77. https://doi.org/10.5840/jphil1978751111.

Greer, Scott L., Elizabeth J. King, Elize Massard da Fonseca, and André Peralta-Santos, eds. 2021. *Coronavirus Politics: The Comparative Politics and Policy of COVID-19*. Ann Arbor: University of Michigan Press.

Hesse, Mary. 1966. *Models and Analogies in Science*. Notre Dame: University of Notre Dame Press.

Hesse, Mary. 2017. "Models and Analogies." In *A Companion to the Philosophy of Science*, edited by W. H. Newton-Smith, 299–307. Malden: Blackwell.

Huneman, Philippe, and Maël Lemoine. 2014. "Introduction: The Plurality of Modeling." *History and Philosophy of the Life Sciences* 36 (1): 5–15. https://doi.org/10.1007/s40656-014-0002-5.

Ioannidis, John P. A., Sally Cripps, and Martin A. Tanner. 2020. "Forecasting for COVID-19 Has Failed." *International Journal of Forecasting*. https://doi.org/10.1016/j.ijforecast.2020.08.004.

Jewell, Nicholas P., Joseph A. Lewnard, and Britta L. Jewell. 2020. "Predictive Mathematical Models of the COVID-19 Pandemic: Underlying Principles and Value of Projections." *JAMA* 323 (19): 1893–94. https://doi.org/10.1001/jama.2020.6585.

Johns, Fleur. 2013. *Non-Legality in International Law: Unruly Law*. Cambridge: Cambridge University Press.

Johns, Fleur. 2017. "Data, Detection, and the Redistribution of the Sensible in International Law." *American Journal of International Law* 111 (1): 57–103. https://doi.org/10.1017/ajil.2016.4.

Korngiebel, Diane M., Maile Taualii, Ralph Forquera, Raymond Harris, and Dedra Buchwald. 2015. "Addressing the Challenges of Research with Small Populations." *American Journal of Public Health* 105 (9): 1744–47. https://doi.org/10.2105/AJPH.2015.302783.

Leonard, Zak. 2020. "Law of Nations Theory and the Native Sovereignty Debates in Colonial India." *Law and History Review* 38 (2): 373–407. https://doi.org/10.1017/S0738248019000415.

MacKenzie, Donald. 2006. *An Engine, not a Camera: How Financial Models Shape Markets*. Cambridge, MA: MIT Press.

Morgan, Mary S. 2001. "Models, Stories and the Economic World." *Journal of Economic Methodology* 8 (3): 361–84. https://doi.org/10.1080/13501780110078972.

Morgan, Mary S. 2012. *The World in the Model: How Economists Work and Think*. Cambridge: Cambridge University Press.

OED. 2021. "Model, n. and adj." *Oxford English Dictionary Online*, Oxford University Press. Updated September 2021. http://www.oed.com/view/Entry/120577.

Parunak, H. Van Dyke, Robert Savit, and Rick L. Riolo. 1998. "Agent-Based Modeling vs. Equation-Based Modeling: A Case Study and Users' Guide." In *Multi-Agent Systems and Agent-Based Simulation: First*

International Workshop, MABS '98, Paris, France, July 4–6, 1998: Proceedings, edited by Jaime S. Sichman, Rosaria Conte, and Nigel Gilbert, 10–25. Berlin: Springer.

Portides, Demetris. 2011 "Seeking Representations of Phenomena: Phenomenological Models." *Studies in History and Philosophy of Science* 42 (2): 334–41. https://doi.org/10.1016/j.shpsa.2010.11.041.

Portides, Demetris. 2013. "Models." *The Routledge Companion to Philosophy of Science*, edited by Martin Curd and Stathis Psillos, 429–39. London: Routledge.

Prather, Kimberly A., Chia C. Wang, and Robert T. Schooley. 2020. "Reducing Transmission of SARS-CoV-2." *Science* 368 (6498): 1422–24. https://doi.org/10.1126/science.abc6197.

Qureshi, Zeshan, Nicholas Jones, Robert Temple, Jessica P. J. Larwood, Trisha Greenhalgh, and Lydia Bourouiba. 2020. "What Is the Evidence to Support the 2-Metre Social Distancing Rule to Reduce COVID-19 Transmission?" Centre for Evidence-Based Medicine, 22 June, 2020.

Ramachandran, Raja. 2020. "COVID-19 — a Very Visible Pandemic." *Lancet* 396 (10248): e13–e14. https://doi.org/10.1016/S0140-6736(20)31673-1.

Rhodes, Tim, and Kari Lancaster. 2020. "Mathematical Models as Public Troubles in COVID-19 Infection Control: Following the Numbers." *Health Sociology Review* 29 (2): 177–94. https://doi.org/10.1080/14461242.2020.1764376.

Rhodes, Tim, and Kari Lancaster. 2021. "Excitable models: Projections, Targets, and the Making of Futures without Disease." *Sociology of Health and Illness* 43 (4): 859–80. https://doi.org/10.1111/1467-9566.13263.

Schummer, Joachim. 2014. "The Preference of Models over Laws of Nature in Chemistry." *European Review* 22 (S1): S87–S101. https://doi.org/10.1017/S1062798713000781.

Stråth, Bo. 2007. "Social Models? A Critical View on a Concept from a Historical and European Perspective." *European Review* 15 (3): 335–52. https://doi.org/10.1017/S1062798707000348.

Suppes, Patrick. 1960. "A Comparison of the Meaning and Uses of Models in Mathematics and the Empirical Sciences." *Synthese* 12 (2/3): 287–301. https://doi.org/10.1007/BF00485107.

Wagner, Wendy, Elizabeth Fisher, and Pasky Pascual. 2010. "Misunderstanding Models in Environmental and Public Health Regulation." *New York University Environmental Law Journal* 18 (2): 293–356.

Weber, Max. 2019. *Economy and Society: A New Translation*. Translated by Keith Tribe. Cambridge, MA: Harvard University Press.

Wei, Shang-Jin. 2020. "Ten Keys to Beating Back COVID-19 and the Associated Economic Pandemic." In *Mitigating the COVID Economic Crisis: Act Fast and Do Whatever It Takes*, edited by Richard Baldwin and Beatrice Weder di Mauro, 71–76. London: CEPR Press.

Winner, Langdon. 1980. "Do Artifacts Have Politics?" *Daedalus* 109 (1): 121–36.

Wong, George N., Zachary J. Weiner, Alexei V. Tkachenko, Ahmed Elbanna, Sergei Maslov, and Nigel Goldenfield. 2020. "Modeling COVID-19 Dynamics in Illinois under Nonpharmaceutical Interventions." *Physical Review X*, no. 10. https://doi.org/10.1103/PhysRevX.10.041033.

CHAPTER 20

The Pandemic Economy of Face Masks

From Critical Shortage to Fashion Accessory and Political Statement

Virág Molnár

On April 15, 2020, New York Governor Andrew Cuomo issued an order requiring the wearing of face masks in public settings where social distancing was not possible, including public transportation, crowded sidewalks, or grocery stores. I barely managed to secure a face mask to be able to comply with this new rule as a New York City resident. I literally had to arrange an in-person pick-up with the owner of a small sustainable fashion boutique in Brooklyn who happened to live in my neighborhood and whose small local factory started producing cloth masks. I had ordered the face mask from her online store more than two weeks earlier because at that point she was the only retailer who offered a speedy delivery. She failed to follow through on her promise and kept on postponing the shipping date until I started bombarding her with desperate emails. I did not have a sewing kit to whip up a mask from an old T-shirt, nor rubber bands to hold in place the origami folds of the no-sew version that was popularized by the Surgeon General of the United States (US) in a widely circulating how-to video.

I mournfully remembered the moment in February when I had last caught a glimpse of a box of surgical masks in my local Rite Aid drugstore. At the time I congratulated myself for resisting the urge to buy a box, as the expert advice reverberated in my head that surgical face masks were for health-care workers and for those already sick or caring for the sick. It was not until June 2020 that surgical face masks would resurface in drugstores. Even then customers had to ask for it at the register and the roughly fivefold price increase for a box of fifty masks did make one feel like one was getting some illicit ware from under the counter. Later I could not stop scolding myself for being so naïve and for completely shedding the hoarding instincts I grew up with in a socialist shortage economy. When socialist authorities began to insist that you do not need something and there would not be any shortage of it anyways, that's when it was time to dart to the store and start panic buying on an epic scale. Unlearning these reflexes after 1989 took me a long time, and here I was now, in the epicenter of the pandemic, paying the price for my successful capitalist reeducation by being left without toilet paper, hand sanitizer, and face masks. My sluggish and inept response was emblematic of denizens of affluent Western societies where critical shortages of consumer goods, hoarding, price gouging, bartering, and black markets are experienced as exotic and quickly passing moments, not as staples of everyday routines.

Face masks, however, went on to become a political symbol of the pandemic, not simply because the critical shortage of personal protective equipment (PPE) aggravated the spread of the virus. Critical shortage — in itself the result of political failures — was combined with shifting and contradictory guidelines from experts, as well as reluctant and ad hoc enforcement, which together created the conditions for the political instrumentalization of this utilitarian object. And while there was widespread consternation that a humble item like a face mask could become so politically divisive, it is important to remember that face coverings in public have always been politicized, especially in Western liberal democracies, which created an important backdrop to the political trajectory of face masks.

In mapping the pandemic economy of face masks, I draw on Arjun Appadurai's notion of "things-in-motion" to capture how face masks as material objects have shifted through different uses, meanings, and value regimes (Appadurai 1986; Foster 2006). I rely on this concept primarily as a method of tracking the rapidly evolving modalities and infrastructures of face mask circulation in the context of a global public health crisis.

The Politics of Face Coverings in the Public Sphere

Long before the coronavirus mask wars erupted in the US or the *Querdenker* (lateral thinkers) in Berlin stormed the German Reichstag in August 2020, face coverings were highly contested in the public sphere of liberal democracies.[1] The politicization, and increasing criminalization, of face coverings in public life over the past two decades can be traced back to two main sources. The first involved the introduction of so-called "burqa bans" that aimed to regulate Muslim women primarily, though not exclusively, in European societies. The second was linked to the emergence of new forms of radical political activism in the wake of anti-globalization and anti-corporate protests, which made face masks integral to their tactical repertoire.

France and Belgium were the first two countries that introduced nationwide general bans on face veils in 2010 and 2011, respectively.[2] But other European countries, including the Netherlands, Austria, Italy, Norway, and Spain have followed suit in recent years while Germany and Denmark have been planning to advance similar measures. While these laws are commonly referred to as "burqa bans" or "niqab bans," they are carefully phrased as general prohibitions that do not target specific populations but universally abrogate the right to cover the face, usually enumerating a set of often clumsy and inconsistent exceptions.[3] The neutral formulation is meant to conceal the underlying discriminatory intent of such legislation. These niqab bans have received extensive

---

1. The public sphere is used here as a descriptive category to denote the central arena for societal communication (Wessler and Freudenthaler 2018).
2. It is interesting to note, however, that contemporary prohibitions on face veils and hijabs originated in the Arab and Muslim worlds in the context of modernization, Westernization, and nationalism. Turkey was in fact the first country to pass a modern veil ban in 1923 (Winet 2012: 237).
3. The French law, for instance, exempted the wearing of surgical masks for the promotion of good health in the aftermath of the 2002–4 severe acute respiratory syndrome (SARS) epidemic. Face coverings are also allowed in sports practices, festivals, artistic or traditional events, and for professional reasons (for a comprehensive list, see Table 1 in Akou 2021).

media attention and enjoyed widespread popular support, even though the number of women who actually wear Islamic face veils in Europe is extremely small (Brems, Vrielink, and Chaib 2013; Gohir 2015).[4] The debates about veil bans are also based on assumptions about Muslim women's motives for wearing face veils rather than their actual reasons and experiences (Gohir 2015; Odeh 1993). In addition to comprehensive national bans, there are widespread prohibitions enacted by local laws or institutions such as schools. Some bans are thus limited to particular contexts, including public schools, municipal offices, libraries, and public markets, but do not apply to public streets and all public spaces (Winet 2012). These bans normally carry fines, ranging from EUR 100 to 300, or impose other penalties for wearing face veils in non-sanctioned places. The justification for Islamic face-veil bans has revolved around various arguments: pointing to the security risk it represents, because of the inability to establish the wearer's identity, to its infringing on gender equality and perpetuating patriarchy, and its undermining of the idea of "living together" (*le vivre ensemble*) by creating a fundamental unease in the majority population for conflicting with basic norms of reciprocity and transparency in a democratic society (Akou 2021; Brems 2014; Brems, Vrielink, and Chaib 2013; Winet 2012).

Interestingly, anti-mask laws in the US show curious parallels with niqab bans. They make up a body of local laws — there is no federal legislation on this issue — and thus vary considerably across US jurisdictions. But most of them emerged historically between the 1920s and 1950s to assist law enforcement against various incarnations of the Ku Klux Klan (Winet 2012; Southern Poverty Law Center 1999). The anti-mask laws can be divided into criminal and general laws. The former requires some explicit intent to commit crime independent of the face covering, while the latter is based on broad prohibitions against people wearing face coverings to conceal their identity.[5] It is these general anti-mask laws that resemble niqab bans, in part because they both originally stem from domestic security and terrorism concerns. The Ku Klux Klan has repeatedly tried to challenge anti-mask laws, arguing that the Klan

---

4. In three European countries — Belgium, France, and the Netherlands — that have significant Muslim populations, the number of women who are reported to wear face veils is below 0.5 percent of the Muslim population (Brems, Vrielink, and Chaib 2013: 70).
5. The general anti-mask laws also normally itemize a range of uses that are not seen as harmful and are therefore exempted.

mask is a symbolic expression that should be protected under the First Amendment,[6] but has thus far failed to overturn them (Winet 2012).[7]

Masks and other face coverings have also been deemed controversial in the public sphere in relation to a new generation of political protests. The alter-globalization movement — or global justice movement — increasingly embraced masks as a tactical tool in the aftermath of violent protests in cities such as Seattle (1999) or Genoa (2001), drawing attention to expanding surveillance and police aggression in public spaces (Beer 2018; Ruiz 2013). It was, however, the Zapatista uprising in 1994 against the enactment of the North American Free Trade Agreement that represented a symbolic turning point with respect to the use of masks. Zapatistas clad themselves in black balaclavas to preserve their anonymity and escape state persecution, while simultaneously pairing them with colorful indigenous clothing and symbols. This blending of symbols ensured that the mask stops being "simply a means of evading state surveillance and becomes instead an expression of indigenous resistance" (Ruiz 2013: 267). The Zapatistas have thus shifted the cultural understanding of masks, increasing their legitimacy in political protest movements.

The presence of masks in political demonstrations has expanded into a wide range of distinct uses. At one end of the spectrum, protesters from the militant anarchist Black Block routinely mask their faces as part of their intentionally threatening attire, which also includes black pants, jumpers, and combat boots, designed to project archetypal images of rebellion. And because Black Block is more of a transnational tactic than an organization, its protest style and outfit serve to signal group identity rather than just conceal the identity of the wearers (Holston 2014; Juris 2008; Ruiz 2013). Occupy Wall Street protests popularized more theatrical uses by embracing the Guy Fawkes masks that were pioneered by the hacktivist group Anonymous and were lifted from the graphic novel *V for Vendetta* (Beer 2018; Riisgaard and Thomassen 2016). The

---

6. While we tend to think about the typical Ku Klux Klan attire as a hood, not a mask, it has fallen under the anti-mask laws, which have also been applied more recently against protesters from the Occupy Movement and Anonymous (wearing Guy Fawkes masks).
7. At the same time, the constitutional rights of students who wore masks while protesting the Shah in the Iranian revolution in the 1970s were upheld, suggesting that masks became the symbol of opposition and were thus protected as symbolic speech.

other end of the spectrum includes groups like Pink & Silver that embrace a carnivalesque approach to masks. Pink & Silver anti-globalization activists are mostly, though not exclusively, women "who attend demonstrations dressed in tutus, sparkly tights, butterfly wings, sequined masks, and feather boas" (Ruiz 2013: 270). Their tactical repertoire, often described as "tactical frivolity," combines the wild masks and outlandish outfits with "playful mockery, ritualized inversion, gender bending, drumming, dance" (Juris 2008: 77). Masked protesters have become so commonplace that when *Time* magazine in 2011 named "The Protester" as Person of the Year, the cover portrayed the graphic image of a generic masked protester designed by street artist Shepard Fairey.

Masks in these protests do not simply serve to conceal the identities, and protect the anonymity, of protesters, but also to accentuate the collective over the individual (Ruiz 2013; Spiegel 2015). Another important function of the mask in these anti-globalization, anti-capitalist, and antiauthoritarian movements is to expose how increasing surveillance has eroded the public sphere and uncovered its tainted power dynamics. For instance, nearly ubiquitous mask wearing among Hong Kong democracy protesters in 2019–20 was chiefly provoked by the alarming extent of urban surveillance employed against participants, leading often to their aggressive prosecution. This in turn led the Hong Kong government in 2019 to invoke colonial-era emergency powers and introduce an anti-mask law that banned face masks at protests.[8] Violence and property damage were generally blamed by the government on protesters wearing masks and dressed in black outfits.

Most importantly, face-veil bans, anti-mask laws, and shifting mask use in political protests should remind us that face coverings in public have long been highly politicized and closely associated with freedom of expression.

The Breakdown of Global Supply Chains and Scramble for Face Masks

In many ways, no other object better encapsulates the pandemic than the face mask. It is a seemingly humble product that has been elevated into a fetishized commodity in every corner of the world (Subramanian 2020). The unprecedented global scramble for this item, which is matched in

---

8. The law was largely upheld by a Hong Kong court in April 2020 after a constitutionality challenge.

ferocity only by the spread of the virus itself, has painfully demonstrated that efficient free markets remain illusory. The pandemic upended global supply chains, and governments — which have increasingly and recklessly put their faith in the seamless operation of global markets — frantically deployed every imaginable means of securing masks for their citizens.

The worldwide critical shortage of masks can be traced to two main reasons. On the one hand, over the past two decades the manufacturing of PPE, particularly face masks, has been gradually outsourced to China. Before the pandemic, about 50 percent of all the masks were produced there, a figure that shot up to as high as 85 percent with the onset of the crisis (Subramanian 2020). The global division of labor broke down, not so much because the manufacturing of masks was complicated or capital intensive but because of an acute shortage of the special nonwoven polypropylene material, commonly known as "meltblown," that acts as filter in N95 masks. The meltblown industry is built on stable, long-term demand, and it takes months to install new assembly lines or significantly expand the manufacturing capacity of an existing plant. The actual know-how of face-mask manufacturing is also spread across multiple countries, which prevented a rapid local response to the paucity of masks (Block 2020). Moreover, in February 2020 the Chinese government began blocking the export of meltblown from China and buying up all masks that were manufactured in its territory, including masks produced by foreign-owned plants like 3M or the British company JSP Safety. Overseas Chinese companies were also asked to purchase and ship back available masks to China (Subramanian 2020). The Chinese diaspora also mobilized itself as so-called *daigou* shoppers,[9] buying up masks abroad and reselling them in China (Dougherty 2020). It was only in mid-March 2020 that China started relaxing rules regarding exports of meltblown and masks. This is when the flow of face masks reversed, and China began directing them toward Western countries in dire need of protective equipment. Despite this, the market continued to fail, and China often used mask shipments to strategically engage in so-called "mask diplomacy" with foreign governments, rather than trying to meet the most urgent demand.[10]

---

9. *Daigou* is a form of surrogate shopping, a gig-economy practice in which members of the Chinese diaspora buy anything (mostly luxury goods) that can be resold at a profit in China.

10. A curious explanation for the breakdown of supply chains for medical equipment was entertained by Richard Thaler, a doyen of behavioral

On the other hand, the governments in Europe and that of the USA had to reckon with depleted national stockpiles, facing a severe lack of essential supplies and protective gear. National stockpiles had been increasingly neglected since the end of the Cold War, with the exception of a few nations such as Finland, which now benefited from being "prepper" countries (Anderson and Libell 2020). France's stockpile of masks, for example, had diminished from 1.7 billion, following the H1N1 pandemic of 2009, to 150 million, at the outset of the COVID pandemic (Onishi and Méheut 2020), as a result of waning concern and dwindling funds.[11] Replenishing stockpiles was not seen as a political priority in the absence of an acute crisis, leading to reduced funding after 2010 (Torbati and Arnsdorff 2020). In March 2020, the US stockpile contained only about 1 percent of the projected national need (Manjoo 2020a). Meanwhile, health-care systems had been restructured around "just in time" deliveries, with hospitals only stocking supplies sufficient for a couple of days, convinced that their needs could be promptly fulfilled on the free market.[12] At the same time, the US government, while also grappling with the problem of meagre stockpiles, was reluctant to activate emergency tools like the Defense Production Act to procure vital supplies and equipment. This Korean War-era law gives the government the power to compel companies to prioritize the government's order over those of other clients, to control the distribution of a company's products, or to issue loans to expand a vendor's capacity. It can also be used to crack down on hoarding and price gouging. But even though the Defense Production Act has been invoked hundreds of thousands of times a year,

---

economics. He argued that "fairness norms" were responsible for the market failure: essential supplies were provided through long-term deals between hospitals and wholesalers and the latter felt that it was not fair to raise prices during the crisis. This is why hospitals (and governments) turned to questionable suppliers (Thaler 2020).

11. The French minister of health constituted a huge stockpile in preparation for the H1N1 pandemic, which never materialized. The policy and especially its cost was sharply criticized afterwards. The French government also destroyed large quantities of stockpiled masks at the beginning of the pandemic, on account that they were "expired."

12. In Sweden, for instance, the privatization of the state pharmaceutical monopoly in 2009 also contributed to the depletion of national stockpiles. Until then the government maintained medicine supplies for times of crisis, but following the privatization no other agency took over this responsibility (Anderson and Libell 2020).

primarily for military purposes but also for disaster relief and recovery efforts, the US government has been hesitant to deploy it for nonmilitary matters, even during the coronavirus pandemic. President Trump, for his part, went as far as likening the invocation of the Defense Production Act to the nationalization of businesses in Venezuela (Kanno-Youngs and Swanson 2020).

As a result of these processes, national governments entered into a Hobbesian struggle to scoop up the world's mask reserves by any means and at any cost. Stories have abounded of how government agents were brandishing their geopolitical power on the tarmacs of various airports in support of this end. French officials, for instance, were outbid by surprise American buyers on the runway of a Shanghai airport, who snatched a cargo container of masks that was slated to be flown out to France (Subramanian 2020). In another case, a shipment of respirator masks by US manufacturer 3M was allegedly intercepted in Thailand and diverted to the US, never reaching its original destination of Berlin, an incident that the German interior minister called an act of "modern piracy" (Chazan, Politi, and Mallet 2020). The US government also blocked the export of American-made 3M masks to Canada and tried to force 3M to send about 10 million N95 respirator masks produced in its Singapore hub for distribution in Asian markets to the US instead. In Europe, a French export ban prevented the Gothenburg-based medical device company Mölnlycke Health Care from sending masks and rubber gloves to desperate hospitals in Italy and Spain from its central storage center in Lyon, France. It was only after bitter diplomatic wrangling that France relented on its export restrictions and allowed the masks to leave the French warehouse (Anderson and Libell 2020). Besides reports of deals getting upended at the last minute, either because other countries offered higher prices or government agencies stepped in to seize the goods, there were also countless accounts of outlandish security measures that both sellers and buyers had to undertake to protect their purchases.[13]

But national governments were not the only players in the haywire market for masks. Just as there was no coordination among member states of the European Union, there was no centralized federal effort in the US either, leaving individual state governments to fend for themselves and forcing them to resort to the assistance of often-dubious entrepreneurs.

---

13. These included disguising transportation vehicles as food service delivery trucks or hiring security details outfitted with rifles and clad in camo and bulletproof vests (Seelye et al. 2020; Subramanian 2020).

The conditions again were eerily reminiscent of the turbulent market transition in postsocialist countries in the 1990s, now simply referred to in Eastern Europe as the era of "wild capitalism."

Several media outlets celebrated the can-do spirit and grassroots ingenuity of "ordinary citizens" who stepped into the shoes of failing governments to source protective equipment for at-risk health-care workers. On April 17, 2020, National Public Radio's *Planet Money* program broadcast the reassuring tale of "The Mask Mover" about the owner of a local moving business who helped the state of Illinois procure 1.5 million masks from China. The suspenseful story involved a small business owner of a local moving company, with zero experience in transporting PPE, adroitly mobilizing his contacts while persuading the assistant state comptroller to break every conceivable state procurement rule. He got her to shut down the entire payment processing system of the state to issue a USD 3.5 million emergency check for him as prepayment for the masks, which she then drove to a roadside McDonald's restaurant and handed to him in person. Similarly, the *New Yorker* waxed lyrical about groups of volunteers from diverse professional backgrounds (teachers, lawyers, a fashion publicist, a tech ethnographer, a data specialist, and the recently unemployed) who established groups like Last Mile PPE and its New York focused sub-group #NYCPPE (Russell 2020). These volunteers set up networks to help move odd shipments of masks and other PPE to individual New York health-care workers, such as a consignment of thousands of masks that a Boston-based management consultant got her hands on through a friend in Shanghai.

But for all the heartwarming stories depicting the outsized efforts of ordinary citizens, there were other sordid stories of hoarding and price gouging (see Figure 4). In May, prosecutors charged a used-car dealer in New Jersey who teamed up with Macedonia's former minister of foreign investment to pose as an authorized 3M dealer and offer to sell New York City 7 million masks at a more than 400 percent markup from their list price (Rashbaum 2020). The same day a former Madison Avenue drugstore owner was also charged for selling thousands of N95 masks out of the trunk of his car to doctors and funeral directors at a 50 percent markup, noting that "this stuff is like gold right now." Even Bethenny Frankel, a long-time cast member of the "Real Housewives of New York City," who was recruited by the governor's office of New York to find masks, found herself embroiled in a hoax when she decided to track down an offer for 500 million masks she received in an email (Nicas 2020). The dramatic surge of the virus pushed both New York City and

Figure 4: Flyer on a lamppost advertising professional grade PPE, Greenwich Village, New York. (Source: Photograph by Virág Molnár.)

New York state administrators to enter into quick deals and pay upfront for PPE that was, in the end, never delivered, defective, substandard, or no longer needed. At the end of 2020, New York state was trying to recover, or get at least partial refunds on, one-third of the USD 1.1 billion it spent on emergency medical supplies and equipment during the spring.

Embracing the Mask as an Everyday Fashion Accessory

One clear sign that the coronavirus was here to stay for the long haul was the face mask becoming a fashion accessory, a staple of everyday wear (see Figure 5). The catastrophically short supply of mass-produced masks, in tandem with fears that people would buy up medical grade masks desperately needed for health-care workers, greatly complicated how the public was to approach face masks. Shifting expert advice — most importantly the Centers for Disease Control and Prevention (CDC) making a U-turn on face masks and suggesting in early April that even cloth masks could provide some protection and were advisable

Figure 5: Signs asking for mask wearing on entrance door of Thai restaurant in Cobble Hill, Brooklyn. (Source: Photograph by Virág Molnár.)

to wear — catapulted face masks into one of the hottest wardrobe must-haves of the season.

Fashion's involvement in the face mask race began with some haute couture fashion brands, such as Burberry, Louis Vuitton, and Prada, switching their production lines to making masks for health-care workers. This was followed by a surging army of DIYers who started sewing masks for family, friends, and frontline workers, oftentimes ending up selling the surplus on the online crafts marketplace Etsy (see Figure 6). Print and social media were overflowing with meticulous how-to patterns and videos for making face masks. And many people, facing a paucity of store-bought options, responded to expanding local mask requirements by simply repurposing ordinary pieces of clothing: scarfs, bandanas, and even bras and other intimates (see Figure 7). While fashion permanently changed into loungewear as the world went into lockdown, fashion magazines still tried to stay relevant by featuring models in face masks as well as mask-wearing essential health-care workers on their covers, with the Portuguese Vogue being one of the early trendsetters.

But increasingly, pivoting toward face masks became a lifeline for many clothing manufacturers. Small local fashion labels were at the forefront of this shift as they often operated local production facilities and employed a smaller number of sewers and cutters, making the retooling

Figure 6: Local fashion boutique on Atlantic Avenue, Brooklyn, selling its masks on Etsy. (Source: Photograph by Virág Molnár.)

Figure 7: Local fashion boutique donating income from masks to charity, Cobble Hill, Brooklyn. (Source: Photograph by Virág Molnár.)

Pandemic Exposures: Economy and Society in the Time of Coronavirus

of production easier than for larger businesses. Diversifying into face masks also allowed firms to qualify as essential business and thus remain open. Many of these smaller brands also offered either a "buy one, give one" model or were donating a portion of each purchase to frontline workers or a COVID-related charity. Face masks, moreover, provided an opportunity to absorb the copious amounts of scrap material generated by the fashion industry, as well as the extra fabric that companies were unable to use given low consumer demand for clothes. In New York City, for instance, laundry services were among the first businesses to offer face masks for sale, utilizing the scrap materials they accumulate through their alteration services (see Figure 8). Interestingly, even street vendors who normally sell fake designer handbags and umbrellas on the sidewalks of New York City quickly changed their product line into face masks, shortly thereafter adding Black Lives Matter-themed apparel (including face masks with protest messages) (see Figure 9).

Face masks, however, have swiftly grown into a lucrative business option even for mainstream brands (see Figure 10), with some analysts beginning to raise fears about a potential market bubble. The Italian luxury

Figure 8: Cleaner in the West Village selling face masks, New York. (Source: Photograph by Virág Molnár.)

The Pandemic Economy of Face Masks

Figure 9: Street vendor's stand at Borough Hall, downtown Brooklyn, selling Black Lives Matter-themed masks. (Source: Photograph by Virág Molnár.)

fashion label Off-White's EUR 80 arrow face mask was the world's hottest men's fashion product in the first quarter of 2020, according to the fashion industry's Lyst Index.[14] In August, Burberry became the first luxury brand to launch an entire mask "collection" available in the company's signature plaid pattern for USD 120. Face masks today pretty much mirror any typical accessory category: products range from the USD 1 bargain version to extravagant, unique creations, like the diamond-studded face mask that was commissioned by a US-based Chinese businessman from an Israeli jeweler for USD 1.5 million, or French designer Anne-Sophie Cochevelou's custom-made pieces adorned with Barbie heads and Pokémon toys. The French designer's stance is that

---

14. To find the world's hottest product, the Lyst index filters more than six million items by volume of social media mentions, searches, page views, interactions, and sales across thousands of online stores. Colors are grouped for styles, and global demand per volume of available stock is taken into account.

Figure 10: Luxury lingerie brand selling a "care mask" in its flagship SoHo store. (Source: Photograph by Virág Molnár.)

disposable surgical masks can make people anxious. She aims, therefore, to inspire everyone to get creative and playful with their masks, suggesting how turning face masks into relatable fashion items may actually offer a kind of everyday coping strategy with the pandemic.

Other struggling fashion brands were hoping to introduce face masks as an entry-level product that would draw in and/or retain customers. In the case of US apparel giant Gap Inc., which was already on the verge of extinction before the pandemic, launching face masks across all its brands provided a life-saving boost. Masks became a key driver in Gap's surge in online sales and became its bestselling item, contributing USD 130 million dollars to its overall sales in the second quarter of 2020 (Bluestein 2020). Major sportswear companies like Adidas added logoed face masks to its collection, while NBA teams in the US and soccer clubs in Europe introduced face masks with their team logos. The website

MaskClub.com offers a monthly subscription service with licensed designs from Sesame Street, Sanrio, and Nickelodeon. Ads for face masks now follow us everywhere in our online searches. According to some forecasts, by 2021 the US market for face masks could amount to USD 6 billion. On Etsy, masks are now the top-selling product and, as of the second quarter of 2020, about 29 million face masks were sold through the site (Bluestein 2020). And cities like New York have installed face-mask vending machines in busy subway stops (see Figure 11).

Figure 11: PPE vending machine at the Barclays Center subway stop, Brooklyn. (Source: Photograph by Virág Molnár.)

And of course, politicians and celebrities have played their part in driving up (or down) the popularity of face masks. At the MTV Video Music Awards in September 2020, for instance, Lady Gaga paraded a set of eccentric masks, prompting a palpable spike in online searches for "bold" and "colorful" mask styles (Elan 2020). Actors sported lavish and artful masks at the Venice Film Festival in September 2020, the first such event held in person since the onset of the pandemic. Kim Kardashian provoked controversy when she joined the ranks of designers in capitalizing on face masks, adding a full line to her five-skin-tone shapewear label. Her launch was followed by a social media backlash criticizing the mismatch of color tones between the masks and a black model featured in the label's Instagram ads (Ferrier 2020). As for politicians, the president of Slovakia, Zuzana Čaputová, was the first to wear a mask that was carefully styled with her outfit. In the US, Nancy Pelosi, the Speaker of the House, raised face-mask wearing fashion consciousness to new heights (Friedman 2020), while Scottish Prime Minister Nicola Sturgeon used her tartan face mask to make a Scottish identity statement and raise money for the charity Shelter Scotland.

But the relationship between politics and face masks did not stop at the accessorizing of politicians. Instead, face masks increasingly became a symbol of deeper divisions, providing a new prop in the intensifying culture wars — a topic I explore in the next section. Simultaneously, there has also been a significant increase in face masks being used as a canvas for political messaging.[15] Naomi Osaka, for instance, wore different masks each bearing the name of black victims of police brutality at the US Open. Her politically charged masks became one of the precedents prompting bans of Black Lives Matter clothing in several professional sports (Elan 2020b).

Mask Wars

Behavioral economists suggest that if one wants to successfully create a new norm — like that of mask wearing — communication is of the utmost importance. The norm itself should be unambiguous and the answer to whether one is abiding by it or not should be a clear yes or no. Vague norms tend not to work.[16] The messenger advancing the new norm also matters and should be someone the community respects and can relate to emotionally.

---

15. For instance, Michigan state senator Dale Zorn had to apologize for a wearing a homemade face mask that closely resembled a Confederate flag (García 2020).
16. Erez Yoeli, behavioral economist, interviewed on *Planet Money*, National Public Radio, August 7, 2020.

Messaging about face masks during the pandemic has failed to meet any of these criteria. At first people were advised by local and international public health agencies not to wear masks at all. Then only N95 masks were declared to provide sufficient protection against the virus, but, given the global shortages, they were supposed to be saved for front-line health-care workers. And then, in a sharp turnaround, even cloth masks became endorsed in many places as an effective public health measure. These inconsistencies eroded trust in expert advice and undermined the possibility of a broad mandate for mask wearing, turning this simple and affordable protective tool into a contentious political object. In several European countries, deep-seated cultural resistance to face coverings also contributed to the ambivalence toward mask requirements.[17] Tellingly, when Austria imposed mask wearing in drugstores, supermarkets, and on public transportation, Chancellor Sebastian Kurz noted that this would require a "big adjustment" because "masks are alien to our culture" (Onishi and Méheut 2020).

Whereas some countries — Austria, the Czech Republic, and Slovakia among them — ended up quickly introducing broad nationwide mask mandates, other countries followed a more hodgepodge approach. In the US, in particular, the response has been extremely fragmented and fraught with political tension from the beginning. This came despite economic forecasts by Goldman Sachs that a national mask mandate could have slashed infections and saved the US economy from experiencing a 5 percent decline in its GDP (Franck 2020). As there was no federally coordinated effort to procure PPE, there were also no clear federal guidelines on face masks. Mask requirements were introduced at the state, county, and municipal levels (see Figure 12) but authorities could contradict each other regarding them. Texas governor Greg Abbott, for instance, initially banned local governments from requiring face coverings in the state, only to completely reverse this decision in July. Similarly, Georgia governor Brian Kemp voided mask mandates across the state and sued the city of Atlanta to prevent it from enforcing its mask requirement.[18]

---

17. European reluctance is often contrasted with the broad acceptance of mask wearing as a social protective measure in Asian societies, considered first and foremost a legacy of the SARS pandemic in 2003 but also frequently used against air pollution (especially in China).
18. Kemp, too, walked back from banning local authorities to introduce mask mandates and eventually decided to drop the suit against Atlanta.

Figure 12: Public service announcement of the obligation to wear a mask at the Canal Street subway station in New York City. (Source: Photograph by Virág Molnár.)

President Trump, who could have offered clear guidance on masks to the country, instead became a model of inconsistency and evasion. When the CDC changed its position on masks and began recommending them, he reluctantly took notice but also immediately distanced himself, noting that "wearing a face mask as I greet presidents, prime ministers, dictators, kings, queens — I don't know ... somehow I don't see it for myself." The *New York Times* published detailed infographics that tracked Trump's zigzagging positions with respect to masks, which helped to turn masks into a flashpoint in the culture wars and a symbol of government overreach (Manjoo 2020b). As a result of these developments, "masks have become this politicized symbol, a way to signal in-group identity. Instead of debating the health or the science, for some, it's become a debate over individual rights ... people who resist masks the most cite personal freedom as their reason," said host Mary Childs on *Planet Money* on August 7, 2020.

Enforcement itself was patchy and contradictory, even in areas like New York City where mask mandates were introduced early on and without much controversy. In the beginning, enforcement provoked criticism for disproportionately targeting minorities, especially black people. Then during the summer as the Black Lives Matter protests grew in scale and intensity, new challenges to the implementation of social distancing and mask wearing rules would arise (see Figure 13).

Figure 13: Street art in Gowanus, Brooklyn, of Black Lives Matter protestor wearing a Covid mask. (Source: Photograph by Virág Molnár.)

Commercial establishments also faced difficulties in enforcing mask wearing requirements (see Figures 14 and 15). Shouting matches, temper tantrums, physical altercations, and even occasional shootings over wearing or not wearing face masks became quotidian scenes across retail environments. Airlines have also been inconsistent in enforcing their own rules regarding mask wearing and social distancing, for want of the unifying federal guidelines that would have granted them authority. Clear and transparent emergency procedures, developed in consultation with government agencies, unions, and other stakeholders, were enacted in response to previous emergencies like 9/11. In the case of COVID, however, no such coordination has taken place, and airlines have been left to their own devices. Their inconsistency is thus predictable — the

Pandemic Exposures: Economy and Society in the Time of Coronavirus

Figure 14: "No mask, no pizza" sign at a pizzeria in Brooklyn. (Source: Photograph by Virág Molnár.)

Figure 15: Sign on entrance door to a coffee shop in SoHo requesting patrons to wear masks. (Source: Photograph by Virág Molnár.)

airlines cannot, after all, expect flight attendants to be the main agents of enforcement.

The perception that mask requirements are a form of government tyranny is not, for that matter, new to the coronavirus pandemic. San Francisco's decision to introduce a mask ordinance in late 1918, as deaths started soaring in the second wave of the Spanish Flu, led to the creation of the Anti-Mask League, codifying the status of face masks as a political symbol (Dolan 2020). Today, however, attitudes toward mask wearing do not simply reflect the partisan divide. Anti-maskers are also aligned with well-organized anti-vaxxer groups, signaling that mask resistance is part of a broader and more worrisome anti-scientific stance.

In a notable episode in New York City's fight against the second wave of COVID in mid-October 2020, the city decided to introduce targeted lockdown measures in neighborhoods that had the highest uptick in the number of infections, including some Orthodox Jewish neighborhoods in Brooklyn. In response, hundreds of members of Brooklyn's Hasidic Jewish community stormed the streets of Borough Park, protesting the new coronavirus restrictions, setting fires along 13th Avenue, and tossing surgical face masks into the flames.

The run-up to the US presidential elections in November 2020 further intensified the political symbolism of face masks. The attendees of Trump rallies eschewed masks and donned hats with the logo "MAGA," standing for Trump's slogan "Make America Great Again," instead. The right-wing extremists who stormed the US Capitol in January 2021 overwhelmingly wore no masks, which not only distinguished them from the radical-left Antifa protesters keen on face coverings, but also facilitated the identification of rioters. And in a sharp turn, the transition of power to the new administration was punctuated by the fact that the very first executive order signed by President Biden included a mask mandate on federal property. Similarly, the executive orders signed the following day as part of a new national strategy against the pandemic extended mask wearing to airports, airplanes, trains, and all forms of public transportation (Biden 2021). The new president also introduced a hundred-day mask challenge to Americans, giving masks a prominent place in marking the beginning of the post-Trump era.

Conclusion

On the one hand, a year into the pandemic masks have been embraced by many as something of a panacea — short of an effective vaccine — despite the initial contradictory messaging. On the other hand, refusing to wear a face mask is the most visible individual expression of virus skepticism and resistance to lockdown measures. Face masks have thus become the unlikely totem of the COVID pandemic — the material object that connects so many of the different contexts in which the pandemic is experienced: the private and the public, the home and health care, global economic supply chains and political institutions. They are the "things-in-motion" (Appadurai 1986) that weave together various layers of the lived experience of lockdowns and the restricted lifeworlds of pandemic times. Moreover, their presence has suddenly become ubiquitous against the backdrop of the growing politicization of face coverings in the public sphere, especially in Western liberal democracies, which foreshadowed the political instrumentalization of this quotidian object. The fraught procurement of face masks and other PPE also carries an important warning for the vaccine rollout: supply chain hiccups quickly translate into political tensions, erode trust, and pit states against each other in a time when global cooperation is most desperately needed.

References

Akou, Heather M. 2021. "The Politics of Covering the Face: From the 'Burqa Ban' to the Facekini." *Fashion Theory* 25 (1): 5–30. https://doi.org/10.1080/1362704X.2018.1546491.

Anderson, Christina, and Henrik P. Libell. 2020. "Always Stockpiling for World War III, Finland Doesn't Need to Hunt for Masks: Foreign Desk." *New York Times*, April 6, 2020. https://www.nytimes.com/2020/04/05/world/europe/coronavirus-finland-masks.html.

Appadurai, Arjun. 1986. *The Social Life of Things: Commodities in Cultural Perspective*. Cambridge: Cambridge University Press.

Beer, Andreas. 2018. "Just(ice) Smiling? Masks and Masking in the Occupy-Wall Street Protests." *European Journal of American Studies* 13 (4). https://doi.org/10.4000/ejas.13982.

Biden, Joseph. 2021. *National Strategy for the COVID-19 Response and Pandemic Preparedness*. January 21, 2021. Washington, DC: White House.

Block, Fred. 2020. "I, Face Mask: A Reconsideration of the Classic Essay, 'I, Pencil'." Public Seminar, May 27, 2020. https://publicseminar.org/essays/i-face-mask/.

Bluestein, Adam. 2020. "The End of the Booming Mask Economy is Near." Marker, September 24, 2020. https://marker.medium.com/the-end-of-the-booming-mask-economy-is-near-1c53b47a9402.

Brems, Eva, ed. 2014. *The Experiences of Face Veil Wearers in Europe and the Law*. Cambridge: Cambridge University Press.

Brems, Eva, Jogchum Vrielink, and Saïla Ouald Chaib. 2013. "Uncovering French and Belgian Face Covering Bans." *Journal of Law, Religion and State* 2 (1): 69–99. https://doi.org/10.1163/22124810-00201004.

Chazan, Guy, James Politi, and Victor Mallet 2020. "US Swoop Sees 3M Masks Allgedly Diverted from Berlin." *Financial Times*, April 4, 2020. https://www.ft.com/content/03e45e35-ab09-4892-899d-a86d-b08a935c.

Dolan, Brian. 2020. "Unmasking History: Who Was Behind the Anti-Mask League Protests during the 1918 Influenza Epidemic in San Francisco?" *Perspectives in Medical Humanities* 5 (19). https://doi.org/10.34947/M7QP4M.

Dougherty, Michael B. 2020. "What the Masks Mean: On Seeing Face to Face." *National Review* 72 (11): 18.

Elan, Priya. 2020. "Face Masks Pick Perilous Path from Health Protector to Fashion Accessory." *Guardian*, September 10, 2020. https://www.theguardian.com/fashion/2020/sep/10/face-mask-fashion-accessory-coronavirus.

Ferrier, Morwena. 2020. "Kim Kardashian West's Face Masks Provoke Controversy." *Guardian*, May 20, 2020. https://www.theguardian.com/fashion/2020/may/20/kim-kardashian-wests-face-masks-provoke-controversy.

Foster, Robert J. 2006. "Tracking Globalization: Commodities and Value in Motion." In *Handbook of Material Culture*, edited by Christopher Tilley, Webb Keane, Susanne Küchler, Mike Rowlands and Patricia Spyer, 285–303. London: Sage.

Franck, Thomas. 2020. "Goldman Sachs Says a National Mask Mandate Could Slash Infections and Save Economy from a 5% Hit." *CNBC*, June 30, 2020. https://www.cnbc.com/2020/06/30/goldman-sachs-says-a-national-mask-mandate-could-slash-infections-and-save-economy-from-a-5percent-hit.html.

Friedman, Vanessa. 2020. "The Many Masks of Nancy Pelosi." *New York Times*, May 21, 2020. https://www.nytimes.com/2020/05/20/fashion/nancy-pelosi-face-masks.html.

García, Sandra E. 2020. "Michigan Senator Apologizes for Mask That Looked Like Confederate Flag." *New York Times*, April 26, 2020. https://www.nytimes.com/2020/04/26/us/dale-zorn-face-mask.html.

Gohir, Shaista. 2015. "The Veil Ban in Europe: Gender Equality or Gender Islamophobia?" *Georgetown Journal of International Affairs* 16 (1): 24–33.

Holston, James. 2014. "'Come to the Street!': Urban Protest, Brazil 2013." *Anthropological Quarterly* 87 (3): 887–900. https://doi.org/10.1353/anq.2014.0047.

Juris, Jeffrey S. 2008. "Performing Politics: Image, Embodiment, and Affective Solidarity During Anti-Corporate Globalization Protests." *Ethnography* 9 (1): 61–97. https://doi.org/10.1177/1466138108088949.

Kanno-Youngs, Zolan, and Ana Swanson. 2020. "Wartime Law Has Been Used Routinely by Trump." *New York Times*, April 1, 2020. https://www.nytimes.com/2020/03/31/us/politics/coronavirus-defense-production-act.html.

Manjoo, Farhad. 2020a. "How the World's Richest Country Ran out of a 75-Cent Face Mask." *New York Times*, March 26, 2020. https://www.nytimes.com/2020/03/25/opinion/coronavirus-face-mask.html.

Manjoo, Farhad. 2020b. "Trump Can Still Make a Difference on Masks." *New York Times*, September 30, 2020. https://www.nytimes.com/2020/09/30/opinion/sunday/coronavirus-masks.html.

Nicas, Jack. 2020. "Bethenny Frankel's Dark Journey to Find Medical Masks." *New York Times*, May 21, 2020. https://www.nytimes.com/2020/05/21/technology/bethenny-frankel-medical-masks-coronavirus.html.

Odeh, Lama A. 1993. "Post-Colonial Feminism and the Veil: Thinking the Difference." *Feminist Review* 43 (1): 26–37. https://doi.org/10.1057/fr.1993.2.

Onishi, Norimitsu, and Constant Méheut. 2020. "Wearing Masks, Common in Asia, Rises in the West." *New York Times*, April 10, 2020.

Rashbaum, William K. 2020. "Used Car Salesman Charged in $45 Million Scheme to Sell N95 Masks." *New York Times*, May 28, 2020.

Riisgaard, Lone, and Bjørn Thomassen. 2016. "Powers of the Mask: Political Subjectivation and Rites of Participation in Local-Global Protest." *Theory, Culture and Society* 33 (6): 75–98. https://doi.org/10.1177/0263276416651685.

Ruiz, Pollyanna. 2013. "Revealing Power: Masked Protest and the Blank Figure." *Cultural Politics* 9 (3): 263–79.

Russell, Anna. 2020. "The Underground Efforts to Get Masks to Doctors." *New Yorker*, May 7, 2020.

Seelye, Katharine Q., Andrew Jacobs, Jo Becker, and Tim Arango. 2020. "Shortages Fuel Chaotic, Darwinian Competition for Medical Gear." *New York Times*, April 21, 2020.

Southern Poverty Law Center. 1999. "Unmasking the Klan." *Intelligence Report*, September 15, 1999.

Spiegel, Jennifer B. 2015. "Masked Protest in the Age of Austerity: State Violence, Anonymous Bodies, and Resistance 'in the Red.'" *Critical Inquiry* 41 (4): 786–810. https://doi.org/10.1086/681786.

Subramanian, Samanth. 2020. "How the Face Mask Became the World's Most Coveted Commodity." *Guardian*, April 28, 2020. https://www.theguardian.com/world/2020/apr/28/face-masks-coveted-commodity-coronavirus-pandemic.

Thaler, Richard. 2020. "When the Law of Supply and Demand Isn't Fair." *New York Times*, May 24, 2020. https://www.nytimes.com/2020/05/20/business/supply-and-demand-isnt-fair.html.

Torbati, Yeganeh, and Isaac Arnsdorff. 2020. "How Tea Party Budget Battles Left the National Emergency Medical Stockpiles Unprepared for Coronavirus." *ProPublica*, April 3, 2020.

Wessler, Hartmut, and Rainer Freudenthaler. 2018. "Public Sphere." *Oxford Bibliographies: Communication*. Oxford: Oxford University Press. https://doi.org/10.1093/obo/9780199756841-0030.

Winet, Evan D. 2012. "Face-Veil Bans and Anti-Mask Laws: State Interests and the Right to Cover the Face." *Hastings International and Comparative Law Review* 35 (1): 217–51.

CHAPTER 21

COVID and the Death Drive of Toxic Individualism

Ed Cohen

Toxic individualism dies hard. However, it might die fast. Since the beginning of the COVID pandemic in the spring of 2020, a movement to resist the myriad public health directives asking Americans to wear masks to reduce the spread of SARS-CoV-2 has erupted in the United States (US) — as well as in some countries in Europe and South America. Declaring that mask wearing represents an intolerable infringement on their individual liberties, the mask refuseniks have combined forces with those swayed by ex-President Donald Trump's disinformation campaign about his loss in the 2020 presidential election. Indeed, the two seem largely part of the same hyper-individualist political momentum. One of the most graphic demonstrations of this concurrence occurred on January 6, 2021, when hordes of unmasked, mostly white men rampaged through the US Capitol building in an abortive attempt to disrupt the finalization of Joseph Biden's electoral victory.[1] Happily flaunting their faces to a multitude of cell-phone cameras — often their own, which they used to live-stream the melee to others — the Trumpian insurgents not only failed to trump Biden's certification as the 46th president of the US, but their maskless visages rendered them easy targets for subsequent

---

1. For footage of these maskless marauders, see Luke Mogelson (2021).

arrest by federal police forces. One might have thought that even if they rejected masks on public health grounds, they might have donned them to avoid self-incrimination, but apparently not.

To my mind, a noteworthy poster boy for this self-sabotaging tendency — if not the death drive — among these representatives of America's toxic white male individualism might be a thirty-year-old Texas man who died in July 2020, after attending a "COVID party." Believing that the COVID pandemic was a media fabrication, a presumptively healthy man decided to attend an event at which he knew that another man who had been diagnosed as having COVID would be present. It is not clear what the logic behind this move could have been. Even if he had attended the party, interacted with the person who presented with COVID, and had not subsequently tested positive for the SARS-CoV-2 virus or contracted the disease, it would not have proved anything about whether or not the disease actually occurs, or whether it is transmissible. One of the great mysteries of modern medicine remains why there exists a variability of infection in the event of exposure to all known pathogens — none of which, no matter how contagious, is 100 percent communicable. In the case of SARS-CoV-2, this variability appears quite acute, as does the variation in symptoms among those who are infected. Hence, it is entirely possible to be exposed to the virus and not become infected for reasons that remain unclear. However, that is not what happened. Instead, this man, who deliberately exposed himself to the virus, became infected, got severely ill, and died. Sadly, his last words before being ventilated were reported to be, "I think I made a mistake," which raises the question: Why would someone put his life at risk in an illogical attempt to confirm that a well-documented pandemic is a hoax? What would lead someone to believe that the potential for a lethal SARS-CoV-2 infection not only does not exist, but that reports of its existence represent deceptive fabrications that require personal experiments to falsify? Clearly, there are deep psychic underpinnings to COVID denialism and the hostility and antagonism to mask wearing that coincides with it. While I have not done the extensive clinical research that would be needed to bear this out, I would nevertheless like to offer a psycho-political hypothesis: such reactive responses to public health protocols for COVID might manifest symptoms of the death drive of toxic individualism.

Consider the possibility that, despite (or perhaps even because of) decades of neoliberal admonishments that have exhorted us to consider ourselves as the entrepreneurs of ourselves, the quasi-natural status of "the individual" as the privileged political and economic atom of American identity might be coming unglued. Certainly, on the face of it, the COVID pandemic demonstrates that individualism as such is biologically counterfactual. Any epidemic would do as much. After all that is what makes an epidemic an epidemic. It demonstrates that as living organisms we coexist both with other humans and with other beings of different scales — say from bats to pangolins to viruses — some of which can affect us deleteriously. Contagious literally means "touching together." Thus, contagions show us that we are always already in contact with one another, and these connections constitute the conditions of possibility for an epidemic in the first place. We are never actually "independent" biologically speaking, since at the very least we all depend on the same planet to survive (Margulis and Sagan 1997).[2] (In Latin *pendo* means, among other things, to hang, so "dependent" indicates we are all hanging from the same tree of life.) Moreover, independence is not a biological concept, it is a political one, as is the notion of the biological individual per se: "In the early modern period, mirroring the appearance of the independent citizen, the notion of the autonomous individual agent framed a biology that was organized around the study of particulate, interacting, living entities" (Gilbert, Sapp, and Tauber 2012: 326).

Modern individualism, on the other hand, supposes that we are naturally discrete beings, owners of our own bodies and their labor, as John Locke famously proposed, and that our self-relations precede and supersede our relations with others. Hence, in the event of an epidemic, let alone a pandemic, there arises a tension between the dominant American political, economic, and psychological self-understandings and the biological conditions of our going-on-living-together. So, why does this come as such a shock to some people? And moreover, why does being asked to become even marginally aware of it seem to provoke such virulent denials and reactions? My theory is that the anger and animosity that we currently witness in the US — from ex-President Trump and from many of his supporters — in response to the seemingly sensible public health recommendation to wear a mask in order to protect others

---

2. Leaning on Lynn Margulis' rewriting of evolution from a symbiotic-bacterial perspective, Margulis and Dorion Sagan (1997: 94) repeatedly underscore the improper use of the metaphors "individual" and "independence" in biology and zoology: "Two other myths of zoology, that animals are independent beings and that an animal body is an individual organism, have also been supplemented."

from infection disclose that our ways of thinking about infectious diseases incorporate these contradictory assumptions about individualism as if they represented "natural facts." As a result, they both reveal and conceal the limits of individualism as a "way of life" (as in "the American way of life").

Let us reflect on why this might be the case. Etymologically, "epidemic" comes from two Greek roots: *epi-*, which means on, over, against, and *demos*, which means the people. So epidemic means something like a disease that comes "upon the people," meaning that at the most basic level epidemics as such affect collectives and not (just) individuals. But *demos* itself derives from the name given to divisions of the Athenian polis instituted in the sixth century BCE that superseded earlier forms of political organization through familial tribes and blood relations, replacing them with political groupings based on habitation (Vernant 1982). Thus, the "demic" in epidemic evokes a "geopolitical" way of organizing the collectivity (the polis) that superimposes politically defined spatial partitions on biological reproduction and kinship. Hence, the demos, the people, is always already what we might think of as a "biopolitical" formation (although not necessarily in a strictly Foucauldian sense). In order for something to appear as an epidemic, then, it has to have already had economic, political, and legal implications, because it has risen to the level of being a problem for the "life" of the demos. However, in the wake of immunity's biologization and medicalization, which developed in the context of nineteenth-century epidemics (especially cholera), we have come to think of infectious disease as something that takes place within individuals, within the boundaries of our skin envelope.[3] As a consequence, the political, economic, and legal effects that constitute an epidemic are now imagined as localized aggregations of biochemical events that occur within an individual body and are ramified across a large number of individual bodies. Epidemics therefore appear to us not as intrinsically collective phenomena that afflict "the people," but as coalescences of a multiplicity of individual phenomena that confront a "population."

At the heart of this (mis)understanding lies the immunity-as-host-defense model used to construe how multicellular organisms respond to the presence of pathogens, a model that only arose at the end of the

---

3. As Michel Foucault (1996: 277) once remarked: "It wasn't self-evident that the causes of illness were to be sought through the examination of individual bodies."

nineteenth century following a number of critical transformations in biological thought.[4] The first among these was Claude Bernard's introduction of a new concept, *milieu intérieur*, in the 1860s, which George Canguilhem ([1968] 1994: 131) described as not just fomenting a "historical rupture which inaugurates modern medicine" but also as constituting "a declaration of war on Hippocratic medicine." Bernard's was an explicitly individualist innovation — individualist in a political sense since he was a deeply conservative thinker who successfully cultivated the patronage of the Emperor Louis Napoleon to bankroll his lab. Naturalizing this political and economic premise, Bernard proposed that although an organism necessarily lives in a *milieu extérieur*, its essential domain is the *milieu intérieur* — which he declared the "real theater" of life. In Bernard's thinking, life "really" takes place within a well-defined envelope, whether cell-wall or epidermis, and tends "inward."[5] In other words, he explicitly bracketed the organism's vital context in order to constitute it as a quasi-closed system for the purposes of "scientific" experimentation in a laboratory (since open-systems resist biochemical and biophysical reduction). However, in so doing, and in order to do so, Bernard also "derealized" the *milieu extérieur* as henceforth irrelevant to the theater of life that provided the focus for reductionist bioscience. As a corollary to this epistemological and experimental reframing, he proposed — even before the germ theory of disease became credible, and long before vaccines and antibiotics were introduced — that a medicine should aspire to become actively interventionist by producing "arms" and "weapons" that could repel any encroachments on our inner dominion. First formulated almost one hundred and fifty years ago, Bernard's interiorizing theoretical orientation continues to underwrite all laboratory-based bioscience, as well as most contemporary biomedicine.

The germ theory of disease itself followed from Bernard's innovative insights. When the first bacteriologists (especially Louis Pasteur and Robert Koch) began isolating and visualizing microorganisms, they quickly correlated these microbes with pathogenesis in multicellular organisms. Unfortunately, both Pasteur and Koch had trained as chemists and not as biologists or zoologists, so their versions of germ theory

---

4. The following is based on the extended analysis in my book (Cohen 2009).
5. The use of the orientations "in" and "out" with respect to a living being that necessarily lives within a milieu, and thereby parses the milieu into "intérieur" and "extérieur," introduces some significant philosophical questions taken up by Gilbert Simondon (2021).

tended to imagine infected organisms as analogs of the culture mediums in which they grew their microbes — which made sense if you thought that the organism could be considered a closed system as Bernard taught them. Indeed, Pasteur's first explanation for why his attenuated chicken cholera bacteria effectively preempted infection by the bacteria's more virulent forms depended upon a "depletion theory" that literalized Bernard's notion: Pasteur considered the organism as a *de facto* culture medium that contained only a fixed amount of nutrients, as would have been the case with a flask, so that when he introduced attenuated microbes into an experimental organism, they would gobble up all the resources they needed to survive without causing disease; hence, when a more virulent form of the microbe was later introduced, there were not enough nutrients left for it to flourish, and therefore it would not induce pathology. While on the face of it this might have seemed plausible given the dominance of Bernard's paradigm of the organism as a closed system, germ theory as such unfortunately had a much more critical weakness: if microbes could be pathogenic and they were ubiquitous, why were we not all sick all the time? Or why were we even still alive at all?

A Russian zoologist, Elie Metchnikoff, provided an answer: because organisms responded to the presence of microbes in the *milieu intérieur* as if they had been "attacked." Recruiting an image imported from journalistic and political discourses about the cholera epidemics, which regularly beset Europe throughout the nineteenth century and which were popularly construed as colonial blowback or "attacks from the East," Metchnikoff shifted the locus of "attack" from the nation to the organism. And then he reasoned, if organisms are attacked, they would obviously need to "defend" themselves. He paradoxically named this defensive capacity "immunity," a legal term he appropriated from the diplomatic proceedings of the 1866 International Sanitary Conference convened by European nations in the wake of the recurrent cholera epidemics.[6] This was a fortuitous choice of metaphors since "immunity"

---

6. Now often credited as providing the prototype for the World Health Organization, seven International Sanitary Conferences were convened between 1832 and 1893 in response to the persistence of cholera epidemics. The conferences were legal, medical, diplomatic, and military convocations that attempted to negotiate the rules for enforcing quarantines and cordons sanitaires among them. Different nations had radically different vulnerabilities and different interests. Thus, Great Britain with its colonial and trade interests in India and at the furthest removed from South Asia

has served as an essential juridico-political instrument in the West since the Roman Empire. In fact, immunity represents a paradoxical juridico-political mechanism that underwrites the fiction that the law is universal by creating legal exceptions to it, so that in cases of immunity, not obeying the law becomes a way to obey it. As a result, immunity enables the political contingencies that inevitably arise within any social formation to circumvent the law while still maintaining its claims to universality.[7]

Metchnikoff's appropriation of immunity in order to describe his concept of host defense entirely transformed the theory and practice of modern medicine to the point where immunity now constitutes one of

---

(the presumed origin of the contagion) wanted weaker enforcements that limited interference with its interests, while the countries surrounding the Mediterranean (Turkey, Greece, Italy, France, and Spain) had few trade interests and their closer proximity render them more vulnerable to contagion. At the 1866 conference in Constantinople, the parties worked out an agreement whereby Britain would be "immune" from certain restrictions imposed by the conference because its location and its superior sanitation system made it more "immune" from the disease. This conflation of the juridico-political meanings of "immunity" with a new albeit very vague biological valence (places were immune, not people) provided Metchnikoff with a metaphor, which he then elided with another metaphor "defense." This elision was paradoxical since, in juridico-political terms, if you are immune, you do not have to defend yourself, and if you have to defend yourself, you are not immune. In Ed Cohen (2009), I argue that it is this paradoxicality intrinsic to the concept that makes it so useful to bioscience, but also inscribes its limits, especially with regard to the five persistent aporia of immune discourse: cancers, autoimmunity, commensals, pregnancy, and host-versus-graft disease.

7. Immunity was invented by the Roman empire in part as an instrument for establishing its hegemony. The Romans would expand their territories though military conquest, but it was often too costly for them to maintain a military presence in conquered territories in order to assure their allegiance to Rome. Instead, they created a legal ruse. They designated these domains as *civitates liberae et immunes*, free and immune cites, and conferred Roman citizenship upon the male denizens, while exempting them from the essential obligations of Roman citizenship: taxes and military service. Subsequently, throughout early modern European history, immunity served as the main instrument for negotiating the relative spheres of power between monarchs and the Roman Church. Church properties were designated as immune from monarchial power. This is why churches still pay no taxes and why it is possible to claim asylum in a church.

its shibboleths (i.e., if you do not think in terms of immunity, you are not practicing "real" medicine, as acupuncture, homeopathy, and Ayurveda demonstrate). Indeed, immunity-as-defense not only legitimated germ theory as if it were a "natural law" and provided a more credible explanation for why vaccines worked, but it also made medicine "modern" in a political and historical sense. By postulating that infectious diseases correspond to military incursions that require organisms to initiate defensive maneuvers, immunity-as-defense naturalized the modern political and economic disposition that C. B. Macpherson (1962) named "possessive individualism." Indeed, it seemed to biologically legitimate the philosophical precept that because your body is your property, you have a right to defend it, which was after all Thomas Hobbes' first premise of juridico-political personhood in the *Leviathan*. However, until Metchnikoff invented the immunity-as-host-defense, immunity had never had, nor could have had, a biological or medical significance, since it contradicted prevailing natural historical and medical theories grounded in Hippocratic environmentalism. Metchnikoff's immunity-as-defense rectified this incompatibility and thereby fully naturalized possessive individualism, not only in political and economic, but also biological and medical terms. Moreover, Metchnikoff's immunity-as-defense model, which he explicitly formulated on the basis of cholera's so-called "comma bacillus" (which Koch proclaimed the "cause" of cholera) transposed the tropes of attack and defense from the level of the nation *to the interior of the individual body*.

Unfortunately, using this model to scale up the effects of contagious diseases that we recognize as epidemics or pandemics from the individual to the population level does not require us to consider that such diseases only arise and proliferate because biologically, politically, and economically speaking we are always already deeply connected. The phylogenic history of infectious diseases is the history of collective human habitations, especially insofar as fixed agrarian settlements brought together species (e.g., humans, cattle, sheep, chickens, and pigs) that would never have "naturally" coexisted on their own, thereby creating the conditions within which zoonotic diseases could emerge (McNeill 1976). Moreover, ontogenically speaking, there is no individual without a collective, no "I" without a "we," as Emile Benveniste demonstrated (just as there is no baby without an adult, as Donald Winnicott reminded us). Thus, in the current conjuncture, the unequal distribution of mortality and morbidity rates for COVID only makes sense when we shift our focus from the individual to the collective. For, we cannot account for the radically disproportionate number of infections and deaths in the US among Black, Indigenous, and People of Color communities, as well as among the elderly, especially those living in care facilities, by considering only what happens in the *milieu intérieur*. Even if we frame our consideration in terms of the prevalence of "comorbidities" (diabetes, asthma, heart disease, etc.) among these groups, it begs the question of why these "comorbidities" appear so regularly among these particular groups, yet less frequently among cohorts that are younger, whiter, and more affluent.

No doubt the consequences of socioeconomic as well as racial and ethnic disparities manifest in individuals as biochemical events, altering vulnerabilities at the cellular and molecular levels. However, focusing on this level alone, as the source or the site of "the problem" that the COVID pandemic represents, fails to address the basic fact that while it may appear as if the disease primarily affects individual organisms — although it does so in very different ways for completely unknown reasons — these bodies always coexist with other organisms of different scales as their condition of going-on-living. Hence, while living organisms may localize the effects of viral contagion as transformations in cellular and biochemical processes — living organisms are after all transformations of matter and energy localized in time and space — this perspective cannot account for the variability of effects that can be mapped onto racial, ethnic, class, and age differentials with great regularity. Obviously, this does not mean that medical efforts to devise more effective treatments for those who manifest symptoms of SARS-CoV-2 infections are not important. Certainly, they are. Yet even these efforts need to recognize that in the absence of specific antiviral treatments, the "successes" of such treatments are limited to supporting the organism in its process of going-on-living long enough for its innate capacity to heal to reestablish a more functional norm — if it can. Moreover, we need to acknowledge that access to such resources by "individuals" depends on the political, economic, technological, environmental, and infrastructural contexts that they live within, and which vary widely according to geographical, racial, class, and other differences.

Unfortunately, our investments in the dominant biomedical ideology frequently cause us to misrepresent the facts on the ground. Despite the intensive international bioscientific exploration of SARS-CoV-2, which has yielded incredibly detailed insights about the biomolecular and biophysical properties of the novel coronavirus, there is a fundamental mismatch between the experimental and public health discourses about COVID. In part this incompatibility results from the way public health was recast at the end of the nineteenth century in the wake of the bacteriological-immunological revolution, and especially in relation to cholera. Before Koch isolated the comma bacillus and declared it to be the "cause" of cholera (rather than, say, the political and economic conditions that allowed the water supply to carry these bacteria to those who drank from and bathed in it), public health had an explicitly environmentalist ethos. For example, Koch's archrival Max von Pettenkofer, whom Koch dethroned as the chief public health officer of the German Empire (in fact Germany's public health authority is now named the Robert Koch Institute), did not subscribe to the germ theory of disease but instead held to an explicitly political and environmentalist perspective that foregrounded the vital entanglements among individuals: "Each individual derives advantage, not only from his own health, but just as much, and sometimes even more, from the health of other people, from his fellow men. ... A community, a city, performs not only an act of humanity when it makes provisions for the healing of illness and for improving the citizens' health, but at the same time it creates and invests a capital that yields dividends" (von Pettenkofer 1941: 487–88). Needless to say, this biological, political, ethical, and economic orientation, which foregrounded "community" rather than "immunity" and which, as a result, not only recognized but indeed valued the inextricable interaction among vulnerable individuals, has gotten lost in our current conjuncture (Cohen 2008).

In order elucidate exactly what is entailed by this loss, let us return to the persistent hostility and aggression that circulate around the public health recommendations to wear masks in conditions in which transmission of the airborne SARS-CoV-2 could occur. Now do not get me wrong. I hate wearing masks as much as the next person. As a very myopic person who always has to wear thick glasses, the steaming up that masks produce takes on an almost allegorical significance in this historical moment: I am always seeing through a (foggy) glass, darkly. Yet, no matter how annoying mask wearing can be, the aggressive affective and political responses to it manifestly exceed the material annoyance produced by actually wearing a mask. Indeed, it is not the mask's inconvenience that constitutes the primary objection to mask wearing; rather the dominant objection rejects the mask as an infringement on individual liberty and freedom. Now my gut response to this is: if wearing a mask is such an affront to your freedom that you have to reject it out of hand despite its well-documented efficacy in circumventing the transmission of SARS-CoV-2, then you must have a very tenuous sense of your freedom to begin with. Obviously, there are all kinds of required constraints that Americans comply with, which are much more costly or restrictive than mask wearing: taxes and seat belts, for example. Yet by and large people do comply with these requirements despite a small-but-vocal libertarian, anti-tax niche. (I do not know of a comparable anti-seat-belt movement.) So perhaps the excess hostility and animosity evoked by the seemingly less onerous request to wear masks *in order to prevent one from possibly infecting others* arises because such mask wearing implicitly requires recognizing that "being an individual" is not a biological fact but rather a tenuous political, economic, and psychological belief.

A basic misinterpretation about mask wearing makes this clear: many people who refuse to wear masks do not seem to comprehend that wearing a mask is not intended to protect the wearer from infection but to protect others from being infected by the wearer. To take just one egregious example, in the aftermath of a super-spreader event at the White House for the swearing-in ceremony of new conservative Supreme Court justice Amy Coney Barrett, ex-President Trump's attorney Rudy Giuliani remarked on national television that he never wore a mask and had not gotten sick, thus proving that mask wearing was unnecessary — demonstrating, too, his complete incapacity to take in what mask wearing means. (In any event, Giuliani did contract COVID, though perhaps not on this occasion.) As repulsive as I find Giuliani, he is not an entirely stupid person, so we can probably explain his rank misrecognition according to Jacques Derrida's (1978: 279) famous formulation: "Coherence in contradiction expresses the force of a desire." Giuliani simply could not apprehend that mask wearing is intended to protect others from him, not him from others, because he did not want to take in the reality that his individualist self-relation is always already contingent on his relation to others. In other words, in the face of COVID's biological falsification of the founding premise of toxic individualism, he desires it not to be so.

The 45th president of the US, Donald Trump, remained even more enthralled to this same individualist desire. Trump's response to his own SARS-Cov-2 infection and subsequent diagnosis with COVID remains exemplary in this regard. Famously eschewing mask wearing and encouraging those around him to emulate his disdain for the efficacy of masks to disrupt viral transmission — both those around him in the White House, as well as the thousands of maskless people who attended his presidential campaign rallies — Trump not surprisingly became infected.

At this point, Trump's personal physician, a military doctor, immediately intervened and mobilized all available pharmaceutical weapons against the virus, including unproven and unapproved plasma antibodies and monoclonal antibodies — which Trump then proudly proclaimed to have entirely cured him in record time, abetted by his allegedly superior genes. (After he left office, it became public that Trump's illness was much more life-threatening than revealed to the public at the time.) Now, why would Trump both accept and endorse the intervention of scientifically unproven experimental treatments that would be injected directly into his body while at the same time refusing the scientifically validated use of masks in order to preempt infections? Why would he advocate all sorts of acceptable and unacceptable protocols (including vaccines, hydroxychloroquine, bleach, or — astoundingly — light) that must be introduced into the *milieu intérieur* while reviling the use of masks which are simply worn to cover the mouth and nose without even encroaching on the bodily envelope? Perhaps because the latter demonstrates that bodies do not end at the epidermis and therefore cannot be fully contained as property, while the former absolutely conforms to this very proprietary presumption. The image of Trump arriving back at the White House by helicopter from Walter Reed Army Hospital and triumphantly whipping off his mask achieved an allegorical significance. Despite his brush with a serious infectious disease that materially proved the fallacy of his biological individuality, the Commander-in-Chief of the US Armed Forces bravely waved his mask for all to see in order to publicly deny the very thing that, as a living organism, he had just proven: that American individualism is biologically counterfactual. Coherence in contradiction expresses the force of a desire.

In the wake of Trump's loss in the 2020 presidential election, his false claims to have won by a landslide mobilized his unmasked minions to egregious outpourings of aggression. Culminating in the mission undertaken by thousands of maskless marauders to storm the US Capitol building to prevent Congress from contradicting Trump's lies (yet more coherence in the face of contradiction), these shock troops of white male ethno-nationalism gleefully paraded their exposed faces for all to see. This confluence of behaviors underscores the ways that toxic individualism has taken its contradictions to new heights as the expression of a pathological desire, almost as if double dipping on the death drive of toxic individualism. In light of this death-defying conjunction, it seems important to notice the gradual emergence of a countervailing political *though not medical* discourse that seeks to address such toxicity: healing.

Throughout pandemic, it has seemed to me a remarkable form of oversight that the notion of healing has been almost entirely absent from any discussion of COVID. This omission is especially puzzling since insofar as anyone has recovered from the symptoms of a SARS-CoV-2 infection, they have done so because of their intrinsic capacity to heal.

While modern medical personnel have been rightly applauded for their heroic lifesaving and life-supporting efforts on behalf of those who have been most acutely afflicted by the effects of viral infection, their actions have been entirely in the service of extending life long enough for the organism to heal itself. As of this moment, there are no proven effective treatments that can directly address, let alone mitigate or "cure," COVID.[8] Instead, there are a multitude of supportive measures that can try to forestall death for long enough that those infected will heal — if they do. How this happens, no one really knows because, in the wake of the emergence of bacteriology, virology, and immunology in the early twentieth century, the notion of healing, which had underwritten medical practice for over two thousand years, precipitously dropped out of modern medical discourse. So it seems interesting to notice that at precisely the moment when the conjunctive forces of toxic individualism converged at the US Capitol Building, the very person that they sought to preempt from becoming president had affirmed healing as a political possibility. In his first speech after being declared the winner of the 2020 presidential election, President-elect Joseph Biden proclaimed: "It's time for America to unite. And to heal." While I am not sure what Biden had in mind with his statement, it seems at the very least that it expressed a desire to mitigate the death drive that toxic individualism has been unleashing on the nation at large, since healing represents the possibility of holding the death drive at bay — at least for a while. Thus, although healing no longer occupies a pride-of-place in modern medicine, insofar as medicine instead depends on immunity's individualist presumptions, it may be the case that in the context of the COVID pandemic the reemergence of healing within political discourse might represent the return of the repressed that in this case could disrupt a death drive that seeks to pull all of us down along with it. Here's hoping …

---

8. In November 2020 the US Food and Drug Administration passed an emergency use authorization for a monoclonal antibody therapy, bamlanivimab, for people with mild to moderate cases of COVID who are at risk of progressing to more severe forms of the disease due to age or comorbidities.

References

Canguilhem, Georges. (1968) 1994. *Études d'histoire et de philosophie des sciences concernant les vivants et la vie*. Paris: Vrin.

Cohen, Ed. 2008. "Immune Communities, Common Immunities." *Social Text* 26 (1): 95–114. https://doi.org/10.1215/01642472-2007-021.

Cohen, Ed. 2009. *A Body Worth Defending: Immunity, Biopolitics and the Apotheosis of the Modern Body*. Durham: Duke University Press.

Derrida, Jacques. 1978. "Structure, Sign and Play in the Discourse of the Human Sciences." Chap. 10 in *Writing and Difference*, translated by Alan Bass. Chicago: University of Chicago Press.

Foucault, Michel. 1996. "Impossible Prison." In *Foucault Live*, edited by Sylvère Lotrangier, translated by Lysa Hochroth and John Johnston. New York: Semiotext(e).

Gilbert, Scott F., Jann Sapp, and Alfred I. Tauber. 2012. "A Symbiotic View of Life: We Have Never Been Individuals." *Quarterly Review of Biology* 87 (4): 325–41. https://doi.org/10.1086/668166.

Guardian. 2020. "30-Year-Old Dies after Attending 'COVID Party' in Texas." July 12, 2020. https://www.theguardian.com/world/2020/jul/13/30-year-old-dies-covid-party-texas.

Macpherson, C. B. 1962. *The Political Theory of Possessive Individualism: Hobbes to Locke*. Oxford: Clarendon Press.

Margulis, Lynn, and Dorion Sagan. 1997. *Slanted Truths. Essays on Gaia, Symbiosis, and Evolution*. New York: Copernicus.

McNeill, William. 1976. *Plagues and Peoples*. New York: Anchor Press.

Mogelson, Luke. 2021. "A Reporter's Footage from Inside the Capitol Siege." *New Yorker*, January 17, 2021. https://www.newyorker.com/news/video-dept/a-reporters-footage-from-inside-the-capitol-siege.

Simondon, Gilbert. 2021. *Individuation in Light of Notions of Form and Information*. Minneapolis: University of Minnesota Press.

Vernant, Jean-Pierre. 1982. *The Origins of Greek Thought*. Ithaca, NY: Cornell University Press.

Von Pettenkofer, Max. 1941. "The Value of Health to a City: Two Lectures, Delivered in 1873." Translated by Henry Sigerist. *Bulletin of the History of Medicine* 10 (4): 593–613.

Index

A

accountability, 38, 55, 145, 356
activists, 5, 131, 214, 218–20, 227–28, 240, 248, 258, 277
Afghanistan, 4, 161
Africa, 5, 10, 40–41, 143–45, 149, 151, 161, 302, 306, 391; Sub-Saharan, 2, 144, 254, 323
African Americans, 98, 165, 211, 215–17, 351
ageism, 13, 185, 195, 199
agencies, international, 146, 329–31
agenda: international, 115; national, 193; political, 287
agriculture, 213, 247, 250, 253, 255, 257, 260, 271, 280–81; abandoned, 281; commercial, 281, 290; labor-intensive, 281; subsistence, 276, 281
aid, 146, 148, 155, 211–12, 215, 218, 298, 304, 330, 332, 338; financial, 68–69; humanitarian, 302, 304, 312; international, 330; mutual, 13, 209–25, 276, 287
airports, international, 302
Alibaba, 356
anthropocentric, 397
antibodies, 66; monoclonal, 444
anxiety, 24, 33, 123, 284
Arendt, Hannah, 164
Argentina, 42, 45
assets, 71, 76, 90, 110, 112–13, 284–85, 360, 362, 378; financial, 111; large-scale, 111; movable, 50; nationalizing, 45; targeted, 114
austerity, 28–29, 41, 46, 51, 59–60, 431
Australia, 155, 393–94
Austria, 407, 423
authoritarianism, 109, 125–27, 130, 133–37, 155, 205–6
authorities: central, 132, 374; Chinese, 127–29; local, 132, 254, 423; medical, 203; political, 140, 350, 371; public, 62, 196, 351, 371, 373, 380; scientific, 177; socialist, 406

autonomy, 108, 187, 206, 213, 217–20

B

balance, state-market, 21, 29, 32
banks, 42, 73, 90–91, 94–95, 98–99, 111–12, 121, 356, 370, 373–76, 378; central, 11–12, 15, 28, 88, 105–8, 110–14, 116–18, 131, 369–71, 373–80; large, 111; private, 15, 113; traditional, 91
bans, 112, 231, 277, 407–8, 422
al-Bashir, Omar (President), 141
Belgium, 131, 193, 407–8
benefits: accessing government, 328; compensatory, 65; expected economic, 185; grocery, 62; individual, 64; job, 347; shrinking, 170; social, 156, 262; state unemployment, 64; temporary, 69; universal health care, 255
Berlin Wall, 27, 32, 123
Biden, Joseph (President), 70, 74–76, 427–28, 433, 445
biochemical events, 436, 441
biomedicine, contemporary, 437
biopolitics, 2, 162, 206, 446
Black lives Matter, 4
Black Panther Party, 213, 224
bombs, 160, 301; cluster, 296
Botswana, 393
Brazil, 11, 61, 63–65, 67–71, 75, 80, 124, 169, 322, 328–29, 332
Burke, Edmund, 30, 33
Burkina Faso, 143
Bush, George W. (President), 161
businesses: big, 27; brick-and-mortar, 347; essential, 418; imperiled, 84; mafia, 277; small, 11, 63, 84, 88–89, 95, 99, 102, 181, 285, 332; vulnerable, 84
business owners, 83, 89, 91, 94, 194; black, 83, 91

C

Canada, 216, 271, 332, 372–76, 378, 381, 393, 413
Canguilhem, Georges, 164, 172, 437, 446
capitalism, ix, 78, 106–7, 119, 172, 187, 189, 212, 218, 220, 223; digital, 356, 363; financial, 11; racial, 210
carceral systems, 230, 240–41
care: elder, 72, 113, 196, 198, 220; medical, 231, 237, 239, 308
care facilities, 203, 441; long-term, 72
CARES (Coronavirus: Aid, Relief, and Economic Security Act), 63, 87
cases, COVID; first, 305–6, 331; isolated, 196; local, 132; new, 142, 144; regional, 390; reported, 308, 318; suspected, 167, 297
cash, 63, 69, 75–76, 112, 219, 281, 284–85, 287, 289, 329, 336
cash transfers, 77, 277, 282, 374
casualties, 160–61, 172
CBDCs (central bank digital currencies), 15, 369–81
Central Africa, 5
central banks: independent, 109–10, 114; largest, 372; role of, 370, 379
century: mid-twentieth, 106, 389; seventeenth, 157, 234; sixteenth, 26; twenty-first, 361

charity, ix, 5, 210, 216–17, 219–20, 225, 237, 283, 417
charter schools, 350
children, 62, 164–65, 178–79, 199–200, 202–3, 282–83, 286, 301, 304, 325, 327, 349–51, 356–57, 359; minority, 351; starving Yemeni, 304; teenaged, 311; young, 288, 359
Chile, 109, 171, 322, 328
China, 23, 123–24, 126–27, 130, 155, 158, 356, 361, 364, 376–77, 379, 411, 414
choice, 10, 12, 111, 121, 179–80, 186–87, 217–18, 279, 286, 352, 361; forced, 177; fortuitous, 438; ideological, 47; shared, 77; tragic, 159, 172
cholera, 14, 295, 297, 300–302, 308, 310, 313, 318, 436, 440, 442
claims: false, 444; prevalent, 29; social, 47
class, 7, 16, 120, 134, 194, 209, 243, 358, 363, 388, 441; capitalist, 106; middle, 199; upper, 165, 277
colonialism, 4, 212, 390
color: borrowers of, 86, 90–91; communities of, 83, 90, 100, 239, 351; people of, 84, 351
communities: early Christian, 219; financial, 46, 49; grassroots, 148; low-income, 312; marginalized, 234; needy, 219; poor, 68; racialized, 216; rural, 90; underbanked, 90; vulnerable, 209
comorbidities, 157, 441, 445
compassion, 219–20, 277

competition, 97, 210, 260, 347, 372, 380; global, 379; unfair, 260
conditions: biological, 435; critical, 308; deplorable, 280; exploitative labor, 249; inhumane, 309; overcrowded, 255; social, 15; structural, 276, 290, 297; unhygienic, 234; ventilation, 395
confinement, 7, 12, 51, 165, 199–202, 205–6, 248, 276, 298
consequences: crucial, 76; dramatic, 287; indirect, 169; long-term, 3, 6, 12, 17, 93; major social, 12; measurable, 182; tragic, 159
conservatism, 205; social, 177
conspiracy, 16, 137, 163, 309
contagion, 2, 135, 235, 243, 254, 257, 263, 346, 349, 435, 439
contracts: agricultural worker program, 252; bond, 42; fraudulent, 256; free labor, 251; illegal, 258; incomplete, 48
control: congressional, 87; deliberate, 27; increased, 126; strict, 13
corpses, 237, 302
countries: advanced, 25; ageist, 198; authoritarian, 126; creditor, 42; debtor, 41–42; democratic, 124, 131; emerging, 37, 51; high-income, 37, 72; low-income, 44; market, 42; middle-income, 37, 53, 398; non-EU, 256, 260; poor, 40, 329; poorest, 40; postsocialist, 414; socialist, 123
COVAX (COVID-19 Vaccines Global Access), 17
COVID, 4–12, 17–18, 59–61, 63–65, 67–69, 71–73, 123–25,

128–29, 149, 193–95, 231–34, 261–64, 296–98, 305–9, 371–72, 379–80, 391–93, 433–35, 439–43, 445
CPIC (Center for Permanent Information on the Coronavirus), 330
credit, 47, 54, 80, 87, 89, 113, 120, 279, 283, 290, 375–76, 380; automated, 356; cheap, 375; new tax, 87
crimes, 157, 229–30, 242, 408
crisis, 22–25, 28–29, 38–39, 41, 43–45, 73–75, 134, 143–45, 150, 202–3, 221, 275–78, 280–82, 284–85, 297–301, 311–13, 315–17, 319, 324–25, 333–34; acute, 412; climate, 75, 115, 298; endemic, 321, 333; existential, 299; medical, 209; overcrowding, 229; permanent, 277; political, 120, 140, 330; prolonged, 311; refugee, 298; structural, 61, 260; uncontrollable, 38; worst humanitarian, 297, 300
culture wars, 422, 424
Cuomo, Andrew (Governor), 181, 357
currencies, 27, 45, 51, 148, 373, 377–79, 381; digital, 15, 380–82; global hierarchy of, 377, 379; invisible, 358; national, 322, 378–79
cybersecurity, 347
Czech Republic, 229, 423

D

Darwinism, 180

death rate, 129, 165–66, 193, 318, 351
deaths, 3–5, 72–73, 124, 127–28, 131–32, 142, 144–45, 155–56, 159–61, 164, 167, 171–72, 180, 185–86, 278–80, 296–97, 311–12, 323–24, 326, 329–30; malaria, 5; quick, 296–97, 311–12; slow, 14, 296–97, 311
debt, 11, 40–45, 49, 52, 56, 66, 69–71, 75, 236, 238, 275, 278–79, 281–88, 290; erase, 284; honoring, 66; household, 68, 75–77; mounting, 74; national, 158; public, 28, 41, 156; renegotiating, 68, 70; student loan, 70; unpaid, 290
democracy, ix, 51, 55, 106–7, 110, 118–19, 121, 124–25, 137–38, 223, 360; global, 125; humane, 135; liberal, 407
democratic regimes, 12, 125, 133
Denmark, 393–94, 407
deprivation, 67, 75, 144, 166, 240, 279
diabetes, 187, 201, 239, 441
dictatorship, 12, 130, 137, 150, 424
digitization, 372, 374, 379-81, 383
digital: surveillance, 4, 357, 374; technologies, 75, 355, 369, 376–77
discourse, 29, 160, 369, 446; general, 25; masculine, 202
discrimination, 11, 77, 86, 98, 102, 196, 198, 262, 296, 334; caste, 287; legal, 239; racial, 86, 259
disease, 2–3, 124, 127, 179, 195, 198, 227–29, 232–40, 328–30, 332–34, 391, 393–94, 434, 436, 438–41; cardiovascular, 169;

communicable, 299; contagious, 228, 232, 234, 236, 239–40, 440; germ theory of, 437, 442; heart, 239, 441; rare, 185, 187; unfamiliar, 310; zoonotic, 39, 440

disinformation, 3, 309

distance, physical, 8, 249, 287, 327, 393, 395

distance learning, 350, 353

doctors, 12, 127, 130, 132–33, 136, 157, 183, 188, 300, 308–9, 313

Dominican Republic, 322, 326, 328, 330, 334

droplets: muco-salivary, 395; virus-containing, 393

E

earthquake, 211, 301, 324, 330–31, 335, 338

East Asia, 2, 4, 16, 109, 223, 390

Eastern Europe, 119, 223, 254, 414

ECB (European Central Bank), 52, 108, 112, 118, 121, 158, 369–74, 378–79, 381–82

economic models, 15, 389, 400

economic policy, 22–23, 25, 27–28, 30, 33–34, 46, 84, 117

economy: advanced, 25, 106; brick-and-mortar, 355; capitalist, 106-7, 210; criminal, 277; digital, 355, 372; global, 33, 39, 107, 322; humane, 276; local, 257, 276, 288; market, 28, 76, 121; mixed, 107, 110; moral, 13, 157, 175; non-farm, 280; planned, 28, 38; political, 29–30, 33, 55, 106, 120, 157, 207, 362; rural, 290; salaried, 143; traditional, 157; urban, 286, 289

ecosystem, 39, 372, 374, 376–77

education: children's, 361; hybrid, 353; mass, 351; political, 221; private, 286; public, 352; remote, 193

effects: cascading, 76; distancing, 188; global, 334, 378; legal, 436; lock-in, 9; social, 37–38

Egypt, 56, 300, 393

EIDL (Economic Injury Disaster Loans), 88

eldercide, 73

e-learning, 361, 366

employees: fired, 93; full-time, 346; long-term, 347; lower income, 95

employers, 65, 94, 250–52, 254–56, 258–59, 280, 283–84, 288

employment, 63, 78, 97, 165, 254, 277, 280, 283; formal, 279; informal, 252; male, 289; off-farm, 276; urban, 283

epidemic, 3, 6, 156, 162, 166, 292, 297–98, 300, 302, 305–7, 310–11, 435–36, 440; nineteenth-century, 436

equality, political, 108

Erdoğan, Recep Tayyip (President), 193

ethics, 91–92, 121, 189, 220–21, 324

Ethiopia, 41, 302, 305–6, 309

Europe, 118–19, 130, 133, 144, 248–49, 261, 263–64, 298, 300, 390–91, 412–13, 429–30, 433

exploitation: capitalist, 206, 279; gendered, 249; humiliating, 280; racial, 72

F

failures: government's, 203; political, 406; systemic market, 61
families, 62–63, 66–67, 87, 127–28, 164, 194–95, 198–200, 280–83, 285–86, 289–90, 295–96, 311, 325–26, 328–29, 350–51; beneficiary, 68; low-income, 170, 350; nonwhite, 351; poor, 63, 212; strong, 199; vulnerable, 303; wealthy, 351
farmers, 98, 147, 252, 254, 256–60, 262–64, 281, 285, 290, 331, 338; individual, 251; larger, 281, 290; large-scale, 291; mobilizations of, 248, 260; small, 252, 260, 279, 281; supported, 257
Fauci, Anthony (MD, NIAID Director), 134
FBI (Federal Bureau of Investigation), 213, 358, 363
fear, 123–24, 126, 130, 132, 134–35, 163, 166, 178, 241, 243, 308, 316, 331–32, 415, 418
Federal Reserve, 12, 87, 92, 112–13, 115, 370, 379
fevers, 193, 234, 238, 242, 305–6
finance: global, 51, 118; personal, 181; private, 43, 111; public, 38, 43
financial sector, 69, 77, 112, 181
food, 69, 75, 231–32, 235, 237, 239–40, 281–83, 285–89, 297, 302–3, 323, 326, 335
food banks, 62, 211, 215
Foucault, Michel, 162, 240, 436
foundations, 12, 108, 214–15, 218, 352, 394; analytical, 5; charitable, 215; democratic, 9; intellectual, 28; philanthropic, 352
France, 71–73, 143, 150, 155–60, 162, 165–68, 170, 172, 329, 332, 402, 407–8, 413
freedom, 33, 48, 125, 139, 141–42, 146–47, 156, 221, 238, 250, 442–43; libertarian, 396; personal, 424; suppress, 163
funds: bail, 216; corporate, 92; current mutual, 375; pension, 73, 200; stimulus, 211

G

GAFA (Google, Apple, Facebook, and Amazon), 356
gender, 16, 134, 147, 179, 251–52, 262, 271, 347, 408, 410, 430
genocides, 161, 309
Georgia, 238, 243–44
Germany, 124, 131, 155–58, 249, 305, 393, 407
gerocide, 180, 189, 192
Giuliani, Rudy (Mayor), 443
Global North, 17, 149, 171, 312
Global South, 10, 17, 37, 42, 52, 79, 171, 210, 212, 224
gloves, 249, 413
goods: basic, 146, 322; consumer, 406; selling, 286
governments: authoritarian, 124, 126, 128, 205; central, 282; civilian, 141–42; effective, 25; elected, 108, 125; far-right, 64; federal, 63–64, 70, 86, 91, 349; nationalist, 14; new socialist, 255; pragmatic, 28; recognized, 299, 306; socialist, 260

groups: disadvantaged, 169; minoritized, 186; philanthropic, 215; private equity, 72; racial, 169; secessionist, 305; social, 157; watchdog, 92; white non-profit, 216

growth, economic, 65, 68, 185, 278–79, 290

H

Haiti, 5, 15, 231, 301, 322–26, 328–38, 340–41

Hamdok, Abdalla (Prime Minister), 139

health, 3; ill, 232, 239, 241; mental, 231, 309, 345; nutritional, 231; psychological, 309

health insurance, 25, 94, 156; private, 60; universal, 24

health services, 174, 195, 232, 234

hierarchies: agrarian caste, 280; implicit, 14; moral, 12

Hippocratic environmentalism, 440

HIV, 15, 162, 211, 234

Hobbes, Thomas, 440

Hong Kong, 379

hospitals, 127, 132, 157, 159, 211–12, 295, 301, 303, 308, 316, 412; private, 50; public, 157, 301; temporary, 130

hotels, 83, 89, 93–94, 181, 307

hotspots, 248, 255

housing, 69, 77, 118, 248, 254, 259, 262, 278, 286; decent, 259; prices, 348; regular, 263

Houthi-controlled territories, 303, 307, 309

humanitarian assistance, 297–99, 302, 312

human rights, 161, 252, 265, 271, 357

Human Rights Watch, 133, 137, 242, 315

Hungary, 4, 12, 123–24, 126, 128–30, 133, 137

hunger, 3, 277, 282, 295, 297, 299, 311, 325, 327, 335

hygiene, 201, 307, 313, 330–31

I

ideologies, 11, 29, 214, 374

IIF (Institute for International Finance), 43, 52, 55

illnesses, 127, 131, 166, 249, 254, 300, 307, 326, 329, 436, 442; contagious, 390; mental, 6; respiratory, 308; untreated, 311

IMF (International Monetary Fund), 38, 40–42, 46, 51–52, 54–55, 109, 111, 119, 146

immobility, 8, 15, 261, 279, 326, 331

immunity: herd, 298, 392; weak, 196

incarceration, 13, 167, 214, 228, 232–34, 236, 242–43; mass, 228–29, 232, 241

income, 2, 11, 17, 62, 67–69, 76, 204, 212, 257, 262, 283–84; annual, 64, 239; disposable household, 69; family's, 323; hard-earned, 251; insufficient real, 283; minimum, 59; regular, 204; replacement, 66; supplemental, 282

India, 13–14, 17, 210, 212–13, 217, 279–80, 284, 292–93, 393–94, 438
Indigenous, 86, 211, 409, 441
individualism, 26, 435–36
industries, 7, 83, 345, 360; brick kiln, 287; concentrated delivery service, 348; pharmaceutical, 147; retail, 71
inequalities, 13, 15, 23–24, 74, 77, 165, 169–70, 204, 207, 220, 334, 360, 363; cruel, 123; educational, 352; extreme, 114; growing, 4, 24, 170; social status, 7; structural, 298; unaddressed, 68
inequities, 86, 91, 95, 112; centuries-old, 334
infantilization, 200, 202–3
infrastructures, 76, 108, 111, 198, 248, 359, 407; basic, 250; damaged, 303; digital, 346, 360; physical, 9, 76, 348; transport, 303
injustices, 5, 171, 227–28; pandemic-related racial, 216
institutions: correctional, 164, 166; democratic, 50, 126; formal care, 195, 199; intransigent, 232; long-term care, 73; medical, 189; modern carceral, 240; nonmarket, 110; private, 109, 111, 198; public, 9, 361
intelligence, artificial, 355
intensive care units, 157, 159, 164, 188, 195
interest rate, lower, 376; monthly, 285; short-term, 114;
interventions, 2, 17, 31, 48, 61, 64, 110, 115, 187, 322, 444;

biopolitical, 4; constraining, 13; crucial, 218; direct public, 47; exceptional, 2; governmental, 397; international, 15; political, 48, 264
investors: financial, 357; passive, 360; private, 42, 49–51
Iran, 230
Iraq, 161, 400
isolation, 3, 6, 13, 62, 167, 231, 261
Israel, 148, 150

J

Japan, 111, 381, 400
justice, 149, 166–68, 217, 219, 238, 244, 258, 334, 366; criminal, 214, 227; economic, 12, 214, 360; social, 76

K

Kenya, 43, 143, 148
Keynes, John Maynard, 26–28, 30, 33–34, 106, 118, 184, 191, 371
kinship, 251, 276, 287, 289, 327, 341, 436

L

labor, 27, 30, 72, 77, 96, 198, 248, 250, 252, 260–61, 263–65; agricultural, 248, 250, 252, 256–57; competitive, 47; female, 250–51; informal, 251; migrant, 14, 212, 248, 250, 256–57, 259, 262–63, 277; seasonal, 219; skilled, 71; undeclared, 256
laissez-faire, 26, 31, 34, 184

Latin America, 2, 10, 28, 79, 119, 125, 223, 231
laws: anti-mask, 408; antitrust, 355; domestic, 42, 51; federal, 358; local, 408; municipal, 45; state data privacy, 358; strictest, 359
leaders, 12, 124–25, 131–33, 346; authoritarian, 124, 126, 134; democratic, 124, 134; female, 124
legislation, 31, 42, 92, 129, 261, 386, 393, 407
lenders, 45, 87–88, 90–91, 94–95, 113, 284
liberalism, 107–8, 121
libertarianism, 163, 177, 188
liberties, 1, 12, 163, 166–67, 171, 201, 240; individual, 158, 433, 442; natural, 31
Libya, 4
life: biological, 168, 171, 278; economic, 26; everyday, 6, 14, 201, 210, 212, 376; normal, 8, 163, 286; physical, 12, 163; political, 140, 149; public, 142, 203, 357, 407; quality of, 158, 170, 198; recognition of, 156, 162, 165; sanctity of, 161; social, 12, 39, 164, 386, 428; value of, 162, 171
loans, 62–63, 65, 69–70, 84–85, 87–96, 158, 285, 289, 327, 374; extended, 376; federal, 93; mortgage, 69; new, 70; subsidized, 277
lockdown, 21, 23, 127–28, 143, 145–49, 156, 193, 196, 200–206, 275–78, 280–81, 283–84, 286–88, 290, 292; complete, 155, 203; enforced, 200; first, 178, 275, 278; global, 209; mass, 83; nationwide, 306; strict, 256
Locke, John, 435
logics: austere utilitarian, 177; equilibrium, 184; mathematical, 186; protectionist, 198; social, 83–84

M

Macron, Emmanuel (President), 71, 158
marginalization, 6, 16, 107, 142, 147, 194, 348
Markazi camp for refugees, 296, 310
markets: asset, 112; black, 406; bond, 37; emerging, 37, 53, 375; financial, 28, 60, 97, 101, 108, 114; global, 99, 158, 411; job, 325; public, 408; rural, 89; seller's, 357, 366
Marxism, 106, 117, 220, 225
masks, ix–x, 3, 8, 16–17, 203, 206, 211, 249, 256, 405–7, 409–31, 433–35, 442–44; eccentric, 421; making, 416; protective, 158, 177; sequined, 410; use of, 409, 444; wearing, 330, 410, 430, 442
Mattis, James (US Secretary of Defense), 304
measures: austerity, 39, 158, 255; draconian, 65, 167; extreme, 159, 167; masking, 187; regulatory, 114; sanitary, 259; short-term, 398; social welfare, 398; temporary, 76

media, 126, 133, 135, 201, 203, 252, 258, 261, 263, 297, 304, 330, 332
medical discourse, 194, 444; modern, 445; popular, 198
medications, 203, 232; antianxiety, 286
meltblown industry, 411
Middle East, 2, 5
migrants, 3–4, 12, 14, 249–50, 252–55, 257–58, 265, 276–77, 280, 325, 328; circular, 279; domestic, 14; Ethiopian, 300, 302, 310; male, 250; stranded, 252; sub-Saharan, 259; surviving, 309; temporary, 258
migration, 280, 315, 325, 328–29, 338, 341, 348
military, 139, 160, 298, 303, 314, 439
Mill, John Stuart, 30
minimum wage: current, 65; real, 74; stipulated, 258
minorities, 170, 217, 285, 425; ethnic, 68, 125, 312; ethnoracial, 3, 12, 167; racial, 216
misinformation, 195, 309
mobility, 194, 198, 200, 202, 205, 249, 251, 254–56, 321, 323–24, 326, 333, 336; elderly's, 203; resignifying, 322; social, 286, 290
modeling, 385–87, 389–96, 398–99, 401; agent-based, 388, 400–401; economic, 387, 389–91, 395; equation-based, 388, 401; mathematical, 387–88, 390–91; scientific, 387–88, 394–95; social ordering, 386
models: business, 42, 72, 111, 358; epidemiological, 390, 400; equation-based, 388; growth-based, 86; mathematical, 386, 389, 402; national, 392; referencing, 397; social, 389, 399, 402
Mohammed VI (King), 230
Moïse, Jovenel (President), 322, 338
money, 94, 96, 102, 233, 237, 257, 259, 285, 287, 292, 323–28, 332, 370–83; creation of, 375–76, 378; definition of, 371, 373; distribution of, 374; future of, 369, 377, 380, 382
Mongolia, 43
Morocco, 230, 241, 250–51
mortality, acute respiratory infection, 5
MSF (Médecins Sans Frontières), 301, 308, 316, 339
Muslims, 14, 212, 217, 277, 300, 304, 309

N

NAACP (National Association for the Advancement of Colored People), 215–16
neighborhoods, 143, 211–12, 217, 282, 285, 295, 388, 405, 427; disadvantaged, 156; low-income, 88, 352; poor urban, 212
neoliberal, 13, 16, 46, 60, 108, 115, 118–19, 170, 434
Netanyahu, Benjamin (Prime Minister), 4
Netherlands, 393, 407–8
New Mexico, 358
New South Wales, 394
New Zealand, 124

NGOs, 210, 212, 215, 217–21, 252, 254, 261, 263, 285, 329–30; large, 257; local, 254
Nigeria, 143
nonprofits, 63, 214–16, 218
North America, 215, 238
Norway, 393, 407
nursing homes, 7, 72–73, 78–79, 157, 159, 164, 172, 181, 195

O

Obama, Barack (President), 188
Occupy Wall Street, 409
online platforms, 210, 347, 352
Orbán, Viktor (Prime Minister), 126, 129–30, 137
organizations: civil, 132; economic, 389; humanitarian, 308; nongovernmental, 210, 252, 329; private, 52; social, 9; white philanthropic, 215
outbreaks, 127–28, 181, 228, 230–31, 234–35, 295–96, 300–302, 305, 307, 318, 328; extreme, 229; first, 38; initial, 128; potential, 230; undetected, 306; worst, 134

P

Pakistan, 43
Panama, 323
patients: hospitalized, 3; infected, 308; profitable, 73; younger, 186
PBoC (People's Bank of China), 106, 116, 370–72, 376, 379
peace: fragile, 146; public, 32
Peru, 329, 332

philanthropy, 213, 215–16, 219, 224
Pink & Silver, 410
Pitt, William (Prime Minister), 30
plagues, 123, 135–36, 200, 235, 240, 446; fourteenth-century, 155
platform, 355, 357; small local media, 258; video meeting, 357
police, 8, 45, 128, 131–32, 280–81, 289
policies, 12–13, 21–23, 41–42, 84–85, 87, 89, 145, 158–60, 163, 194, 231, 241, 386, 391–93, 399–400; austerity, 28, 60, 66; biopolitical, 194; educational, 349; fiscal, 28, 54–55, 105, 108, 110, 370, 375, 378; food security, 63; government's pandemic, 203; industrial, 107; macroeconomic, 398; neoliberal, 3, 158, 194; neoliberal welfare, 195; open border, 128; restrictive, 358; social distancing, 386, 393, 395; social welfare, 60; unpopular, 146
politicians, 11, 76, 131, 159, 201, 248, 421–22; civilian, 145; conservative, 85; senior, 195
politics: authoritarian, 123, 200; global, 135; inequitable, 205; liberal, 33; polarized, 182
Pompeo, Michael (Secretary of State), 304
poverty: acute, 59; extreme, 67–68, 171, 217, 252, 265, 321; perpetuating, 238; skyrocketing, 68
power: autocratic, 129, 135; coercive, 393; emergency, 3, 129, 410; geopolitical, 413; monarchial, 439

PPE (personal protective equipment), 132–33, 212, 306, 406, 411, 414–15, 428
PPP (Paycheck Protection Program), 63, 78, 88–91, 93–96, 98–103
practices: economic, 219; gendered, 199; gig-economy, 411; medical, 445; racist, 91; social, 14
prices, 111, 116, 156, 158, 256, 260, 268, 303, 310, 406, 412–13
prisoner release, 229, 231
prisoners: diseased, 235; female, 234; low-income, 232; male, 234
prisons, 3, 7–8, 12–13, 131, 143, 165–68, 174, 227–44, 357, 394; crowded, 238; federal, 167; filthy, 235; long-term, 166; short-term, 165
privacy, 24, 92, 167, 352, 357–58, 360, 374
privilege, 205; epistemic, 15; undue, 374
production: distributed, 23; global, 3; industrial, 23; reframed data, 359; strawberry, 249
profit, 72, 236, 347, 350, 360, 375, 411; corporate, 181, 184
programs: biological warfare, 309; federal, 62; grant, 93; housing, 86; housing insurance, 86; innovation, 135; lending, 86–87; minimum-income, 75; rural employment, 282; universal basic income, 76
propaganda, 132, 160
properties, 92, 238, 326, 386, 392, 440, 444; biophysical, 441; church, 439; federal, 427; private, 219
protests, 132, 139–41, 147, 156, 231, 257, 334, 409–10; anti-corporate, 407; global, 4; massive, 147; violent, 409; weeklong, 132
Puerto Rico, 211, 224
punishment, 13, 17, 59, 62–63, 65–66, 68, 84–85, 87–92, 94–96, 200–201, 212–14, 240–41, 373–74; divine, 200; non-corporal, 240

Q

quarantine, 185, 200, 204–6, 233, 249, 254, 328

R

race, 16, 179, 228, 252
recession, 1, 37, 102, 156, 185, 329
refugees, 126, 296, 299–301, 304, 309, 311, 313, 318
regimes: autocratic, 129, 131; mass carceral, 233; tax, 47
regulations, 72, 147, 194–95, 364, 374, 393–95; banking, 374; environmental, 249; financial, 50, 110; zoning, 188
relatives, 92, 159, 287–89, 309, 328
rents, 62, 88–89, 95, 200, 253, 348
repercussions, 5; economic, 391; financial, 148; major, 156; pandemic's, 115; social, 169; socioeconomic, 171
repression, 16, 171, 213
resilience, 6, 186, 280, 310

resistance: deep-seated cultural, 423; indigenous, 409; the NGO-ization of, 224; political, 214, 218, 221; romanticize, 289; social, 360
resources, 15, 61, 63, 75, 214, 217–19, 221, 330, 333, 438, 441; financial, 262; inadequate, 3; medical, 157; scarce, 285, 333
restaurants, 155, 158, 181, 185, 196, 279, 288, 306, 345, 348
restrictions, 143–45, 156, 163, 193, 196, 198, 256, 259, 262, 323, 325, 394; border, 310; import, 303; strict, 322; temporary, 8; visa, 299
revolution, 9, 29–30, 54, 117–18, 222–23, 369, 371, 373–75, 377, 379–81, 383
rice, 281, 283, 325
Riyadh Agreement, 305–6
Roosevelt, Franklin D. (President), 113
Rousseff, Dilma (President), 65
RSF (Rapid Support Forces), 142, 148
Russia, 129, 227

S

sacrifices: demanded, 185; language of, 179, 182; real, 44
safety net, 52, 170; social, 6, 25
Sanders, Bernie (Senator), 70
sanitation, 164, 253–54, 259, 301
SARS (severe acute respiratory syndrome), 297, 317, 407, 423
Saudi Arabia, 148, 299–300, 304–6, 309

SBA (Small Business Administration), 84–86, 88–92, 95–96, 101
scarcity, 30, 195, 289
schools: elementary, 358; evangelical, 351; public, 361, 408; traditional, 349; virtual, 350, 352
sectors, 71, 73, 111–12, 116, 247, 251, 256–57, 345, 347, 354, 359; agricultural, 247, 252; private, 40, 43–44, 52, 87, 372
senior citizens, 178, 194, 196, 199
shock, 22, 38–39, 391, 398, 435; external, 377; osmotic, 388
smallpox, 234, 236, 240
social divisions, veiled, 6
social media, 127, 132, 139, 141, 194, 196, 308, 310, 356, 362, 416, 419
social networks, 8, 194, 322, 328, 330, 332, 355, 373
Somalia, 4
South Africa, 162, 292, 393
South America, 328–29, 332, 433
South Asia, 292, 438
South India, 275, 293
South Korea, 124, 155, 213, 393
South Pacific, 2
sovereignty, 47, 50–51, 56, 160, 162, 337, 339, 377
Spain, 129, 132, 247–53, 255–57, 259–61, 263–67, 269, 271, 273, 407, 413
Spanish Flu, 123, 155, 427
starvation, 184, 295–97, 300, 302, 304–5
stigmatization, 3, 14, 16, 87, 206, 234, 310
students, 313, 350, 352, 357–59, 361–63, 409

Sturgeon, Nicola (Prime Minister), 422
Sudan, 5, 12, 139–40, 142–46, 148–51, 301, 308
suicides, 167, 169, 174, 184, 277, 288, 297
supplies, medical, 132, 415
supply chains, 7, 23–24, 83, 249, 346, 410–11
support: international, 132, 299; legal, 94; popular, 408; public, 141, 229, 353; strategic, 288
supremacy, 86, 277
surveillance, 9, 24, 163, 213–14, 353, 358, 366, 409–10
systems: administrative, 374; biometric credit-score, 284; communication, 123; judicial, 166; medical, 308; payment processing, 414; rationing, 189; social security, 67, 255; weak immune, 196

T

Taiwan, 124
Tamil Nadu, 275, 278–79, 292
taxes, 43, 69, 72, 131, 439, 443
tax revenues, 65, 258; collapsing, 37
teachers, 349–50, 352–54, 357–59, 361, 363, 414
technocracy, ix, 106–9, 117
technologies: advanced, 123, 126; educational, 359; financial, 49, 91; new, 6, 15, 126
Thailand, 213, 379, 393, 413
transactions: contactless, 9; criminal, 374; cross-border, 379; financial, 52; global, 379; private, 372; small, 327
transformations, 9; economic, 10; imagined, 11
triage, medical, 182
Trump, Donald (President), 3, 7, 46, 91, 124–26, 131, 133, 135, 138, 300, 304, 424, 430, 435, 443–44
tuberculosis, 234, 239
Turkey, 12–13, 123–24, 126, 128–29, 131–32, 137, 193, 195, 198–99, 204–7, 407

U

UK (United Kingdom), 11, 25, 61–62, 65, 68–71, 80, 111, 129, 131–32, 391, 393
unemployment, 3, 27, 67, 83, 89, 156, 169, 187, 209, 347; high, 169; increased, 66; low, 68; massive, 256; rates, 45, 63, 68, 99, 211; skyrocketing, 250
United Arab Emirates, 143, 305, 379
United Nations, 161–62, 297, 318, 322

V

vaccinations, 310, 312, 334
vaccines, 2, 7–8, 16, 149, 168, 177, 186, 307–8, 437, 440, 444
values: materialistic, 181; monetary, 60, 327; social, 112; supreme, 162, 171
Vietnam, 393
violence, 120, 141, 165, 167, 173, 184, 210, 212–14, 228, 259, 335; critique of, 136, 172; domestic, 214; racial, 216; sexual,

229; slow, 297, 317; structural, 165
virtual world, 2, 388
virus, 4–7, 13–15, 39, 124, 127–31, 134–38, 230–31, 233, 261–62, 308–10, 314–15, 323–24, 328, 334, 398, 434

W

wages, 63, 65–66, 71, 74, 80, 248, 255, 257–58, 280, 282, 286
war, 14, 131, 171–72, 174, 242, 289, 296, 299–301, 304, 307, 313; civil, 15, 140, 145, 151, 305; Persian Gulf, 161, 173; Second World, 24–25, 52, 107, 115
water, 140, 235, 247, 253–55, 257, 259, 297, 303
wave, 60, 90, 186, 190, 300, 307, 310, 323, 345, 350; first, 25, 142, 144–45, 256–57, 259, 301, 307, 309, 329; second, 7, 25, 67–68, 145, 212, 248, 256, 261–62, 307, 310, 427
wealth, 27, 45, 108, 131, 134, 182; collective, 347; white, 101, 215
welfare, 26, 45, 66, 69, 75–76, 81, 86, 261, 373; benefits, 60, 74–75, 206; regimes, 60–61, 67, 73, 75; states, 24–25, 46–47, 121, 156, 170, 222–23

WHO (World Health Organization), 124, 127–29, 244, 296, 301, 307, 314–15, 319, 329, 331, 334, 341, 393–95
women, 199–202, 235, 237, 239, 251, 258, 276, 281–85, 289, 329, 335, 408, 410; high-caste, 285; landless, 281; poor, 64
work: child's, 358; community, 196; domestic, 72; legitimate, 133; precarious, 257; scholarly, 392; unpaid, 74
workers, 63–65, 67, 71, 74, 81, 93–95, 97, 158, 248–49, 251–58, 260–62, 264, 276–77, 287–88, 290; essential, 3, 73, 186, 220, 248, 256, 261; frontline, 128, 186, 416, 418; health-care, 186, 195
World Bank, 33, 40, 52, 55, 116, 146, 171, 325, 330, 341–42, 356

Y

Yemen, 5, 295–319; northern, 301, 307–8, 310; war in, 171, 313

Z

Zapatistas, 219, 222, 409